S·A
Special A

Volume 3

Story & Art by
Maki Minami

STORY

★At the tender age of 6, carpenter's daughter Hikari Hanazono suffered her first loss to the wealthy Kei Takishima in a wrestling match. Now the hardworking Hikari has followed Kei to the most elite school for the rich just to beat him! I call this story "Overthrow Takishima! Rise Above Perpetual Second Place!!" It's the story of Hikari's sweat, tears and passion, with a little bit of love thrown in!

★In the previous volume, Hikari brilliantly foiled Yahiro Saiga's plan to use her against Kei! But she is still haunted by three little words from Yahiro: "Kei loves you."

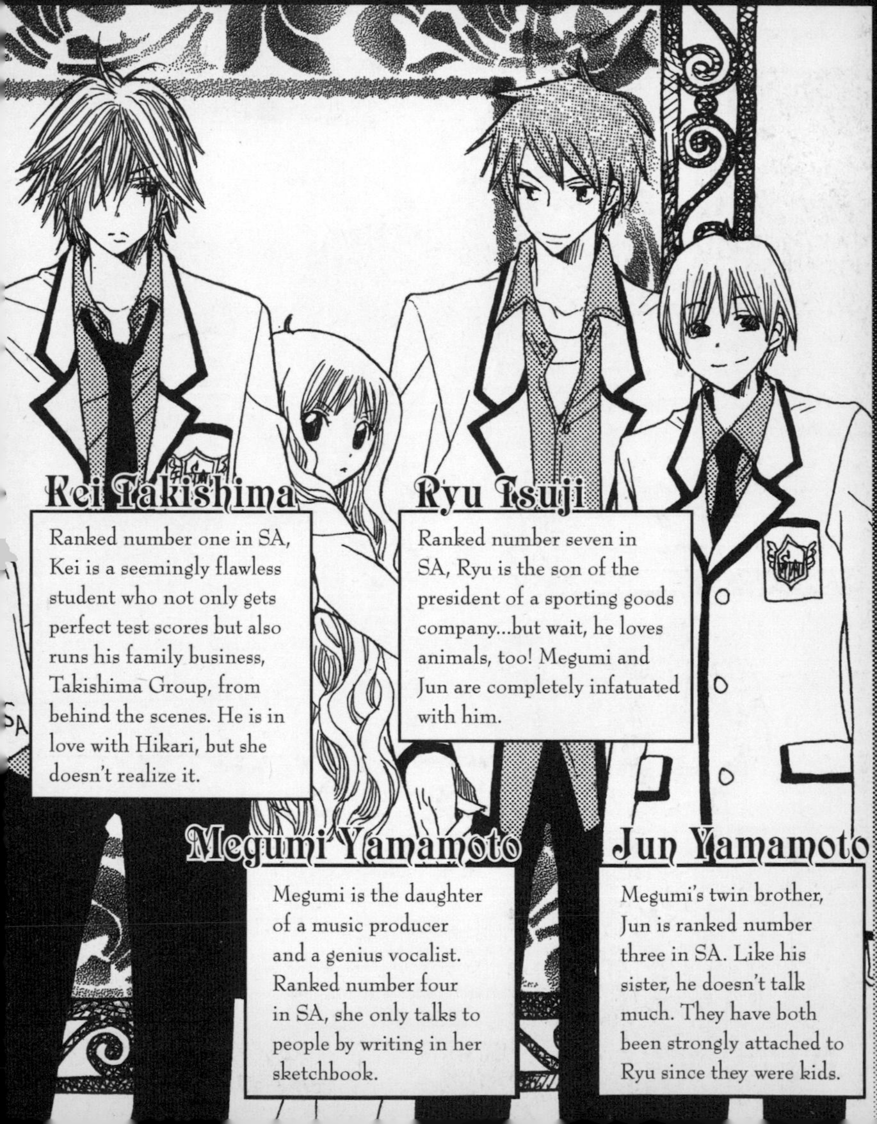

Kei Takishima

Ranked number one in SA, Kei is a seemingly flawless student who not only gets perfect test scores but also runs his family business, Takishima Group, from behind the scenes. He is in love with Hikari, but she doesn't realize it.

Ryu Tsuji

Ranked number seven in SA, Ryu is the son of the president of a sporting goods company...but wait, he loves animals, too! Megumi and Jun are completely infatuated with him.

Megumi Yamamoto

Megumi is the daughter of a music producer and a genius vocalist. Ranked number four in SA, she only talks to people by writing in her sketchbook.

Jun Yamamoto

Megumi's twin brother, Jun is ranked number three in SA. Like his sister, he doesn't talk much. They have both been strongly attached to Ryu since they were kids.

S·A CHARACTERS

What is “Special A”?

Hikari goes to an elite school called Hakusenkan High School. This school divides each grade level into groups A through F, according to the students’ test scores. Group A includes only the top seven students in each class. Then the top seven students from all grades’ A groups are put into a group called Special A, which is considered much higher than all others. Known as SA, they are “the elite among the elite.”

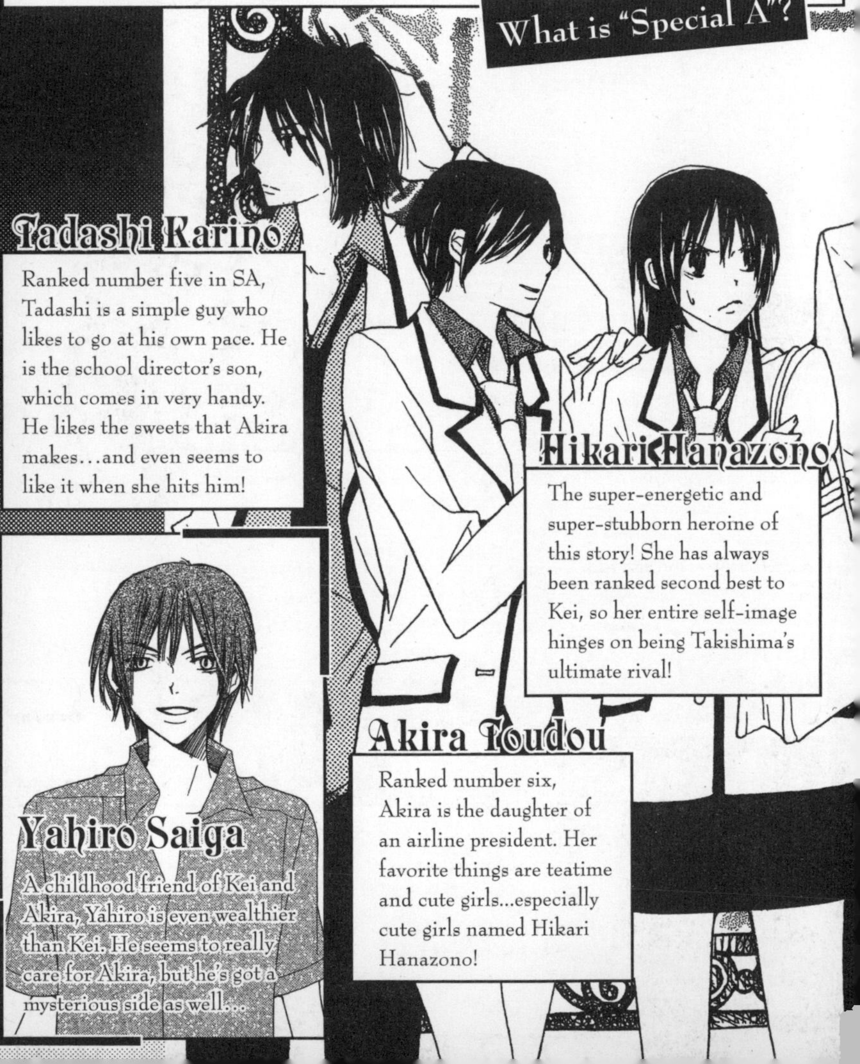

Tadashi Karino

Ranked number five in SA, Tadashi is a simple guy who likes to go at his own pace. He is the school director’s son, which comes in very handy. He likes the sweets that Akira makes...and even seems to like it when she hits him!

Hikari Hanazono

The super-energetic and super-stubborn heroine of this story! She has always been ranked second best to Kei, so her entire self-image hinges on being Takishima’s ultimate rival!

Akira Toudou

Ranked number six, Akira is the daughter of an airline president. Her favorite things are teatime and cute girls...especially cute girls named Hikari Hanazono!

Yahiro Saiga

A childhood friend of Kei and Akira, Yahiro is even wealthier than Kei. He seems to really care for Akira, but he’s got a mysterious side as well...

Contents

Right Where He Belongs

Chapter 11

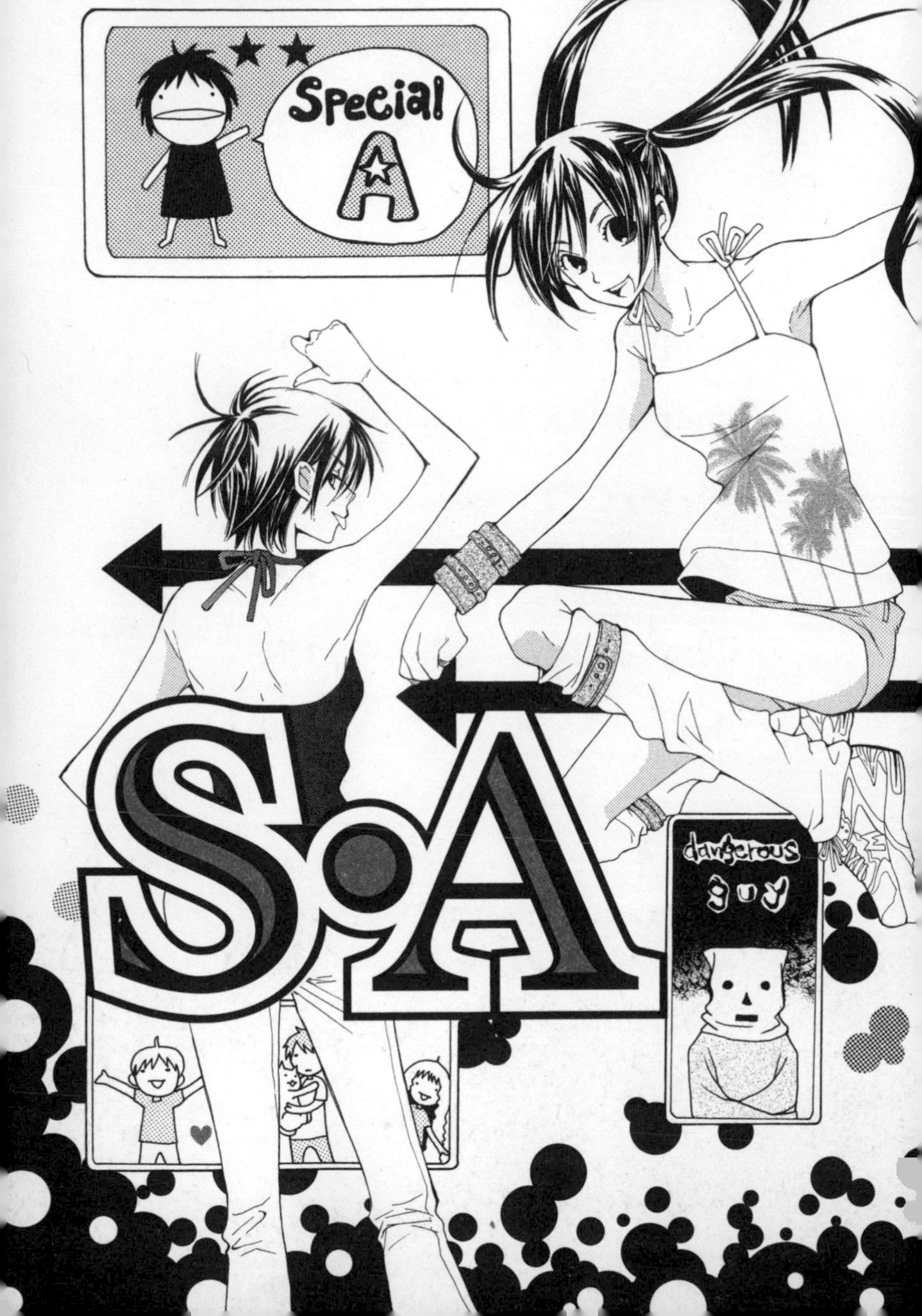
Special
A
S·A
dangerous
guy

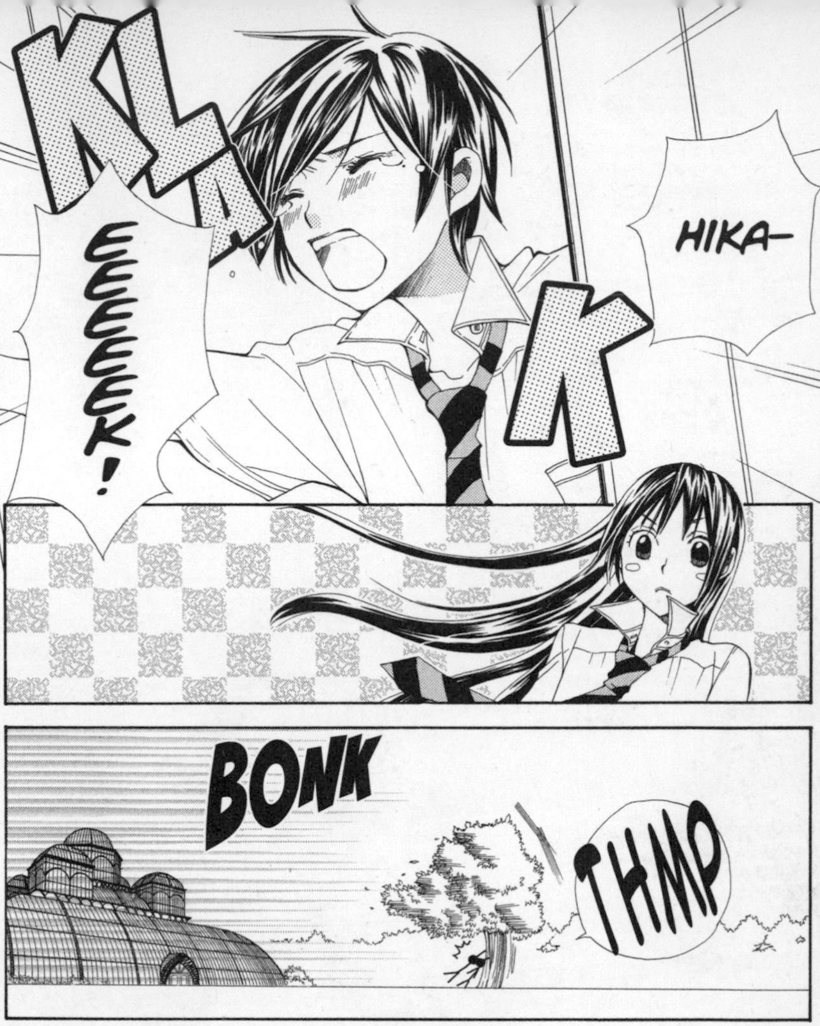
HIKA—
KLAKK
EEEEEK!
BONK
THMP

• PROFILE •

IN VOLUME TWO, I SAID I WOULD START WRITING CHARACTER PROFILES, AND THAT'S WHAT I'M GOING TO DO. WHAT? YOU DON'T REALLY NEED THEM? NOW, NOW, DON'T SAY THAT...PLEASE, JUST ONE! PLEASE!

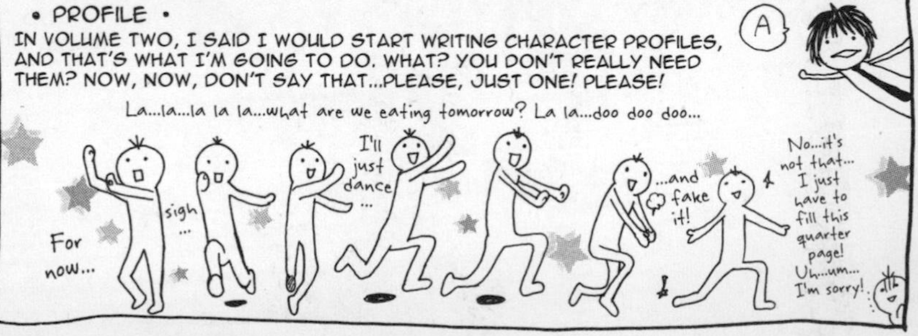
A
La...la...la la la...what are we eating tomorrow? La la...doo doo doo...
For now...
sigh...
I'll just dance...
...and fake it!
No...it's not that... I just have to fill this quarter page! Uh...um... I'm sorry!

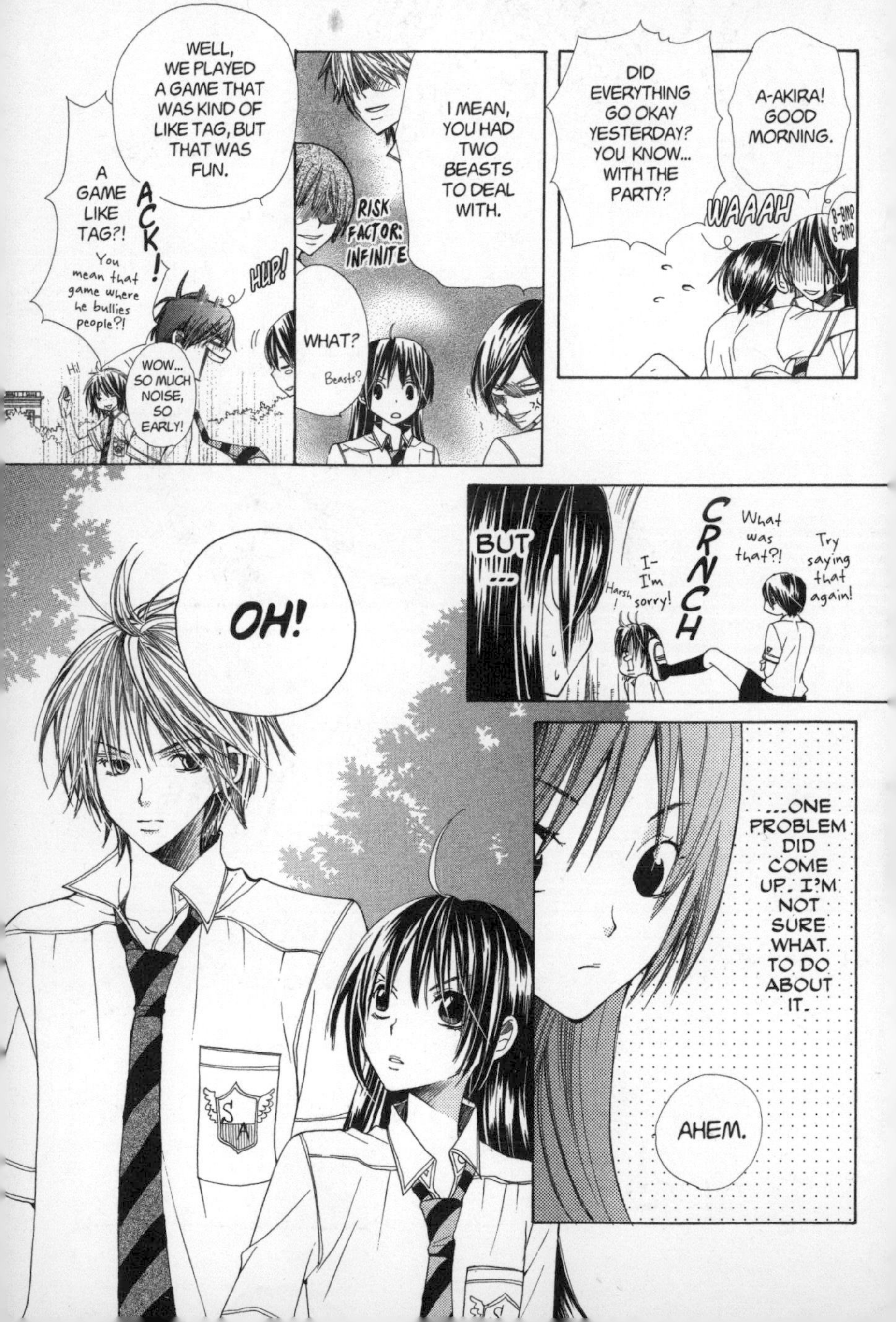
A-AKIRA! GOOD MORNING.
DID EVERYTHING GO OKAY YESTERDAY? YOU KNOW... WITH THE PARTY?
WAAAH
B-BMP B-BMP
I MEAN, YOU HAD TWO BEASTS TO DEAL WITH.
RISK FACTOR: INFINITE
WHAT?
Beasts?
WELL, WE PLAYED A GAME THAT WAS KIND OF LIKE TAG, BUT THAT WAS FUN.
A GAME LIKE TAG?!
ACK!
You mean that game where he bullies people?!
HUP!
WOW... SO MUCH NOISE, SO EARLY!
Hi!
Try saying that again!
What was that?!
CRNCH
I- I'm sorry!
Harsh!
BUT I...
...ONE PROBLEM DID COME UP. I'M NOT SURE WHAT TO DO ABOUT IT.
AHEM.
OH!

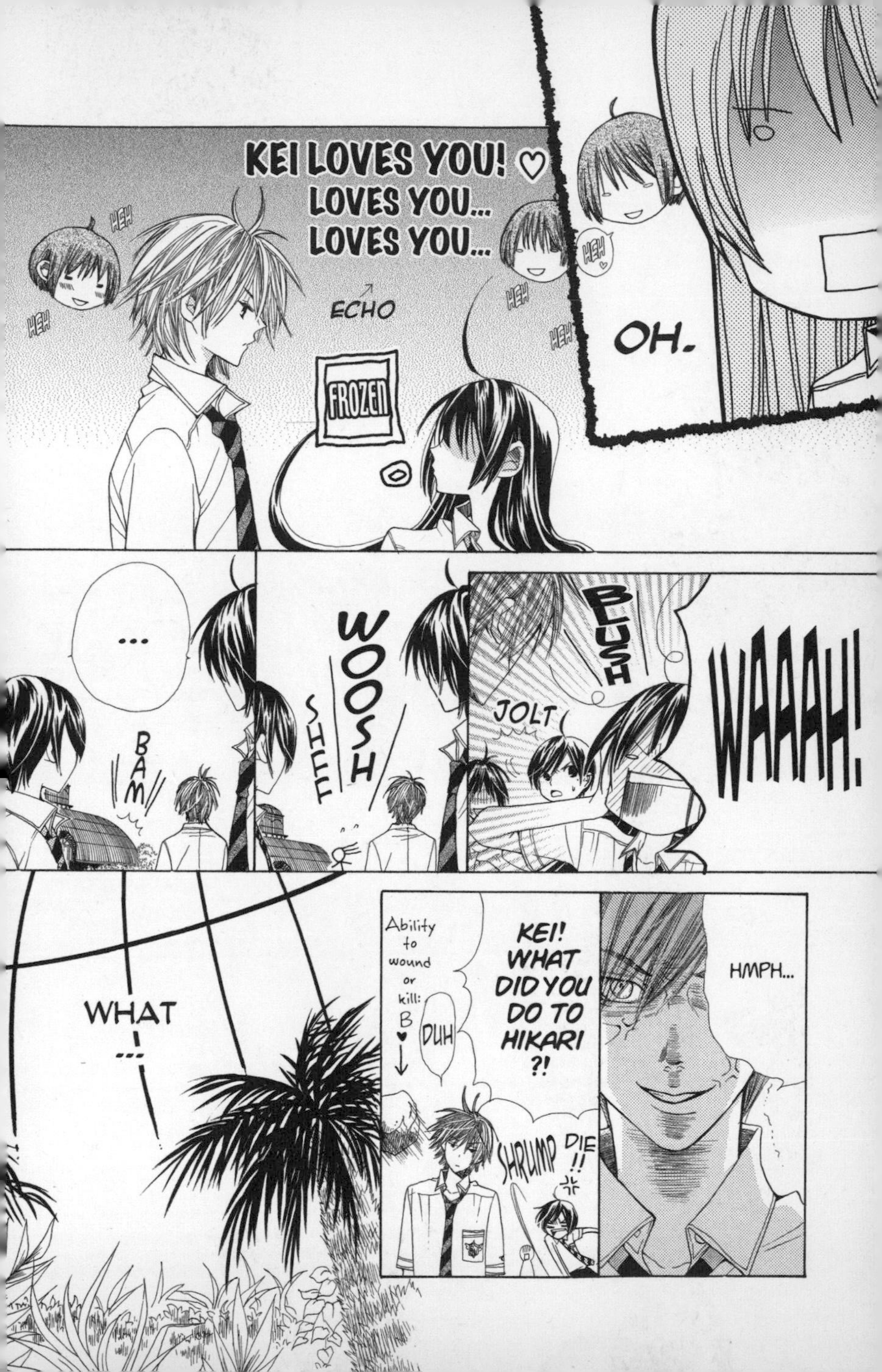
HEH
OH.
KEI LOVES YOU! ♡
LOVES YOU...
LOVES YOU...
ECHO
HEH
HEH
HEH
HEH
FROZEN
WAAAH!
BLUSH
JOLT
WOOSH
SHFF
...
BAM
HMPH...
KEI! WHAT DID YOU DO TO HIKARI?!
Ability to wound or kill: B
DUH
SHRUMP
DIE!!
WHAT---

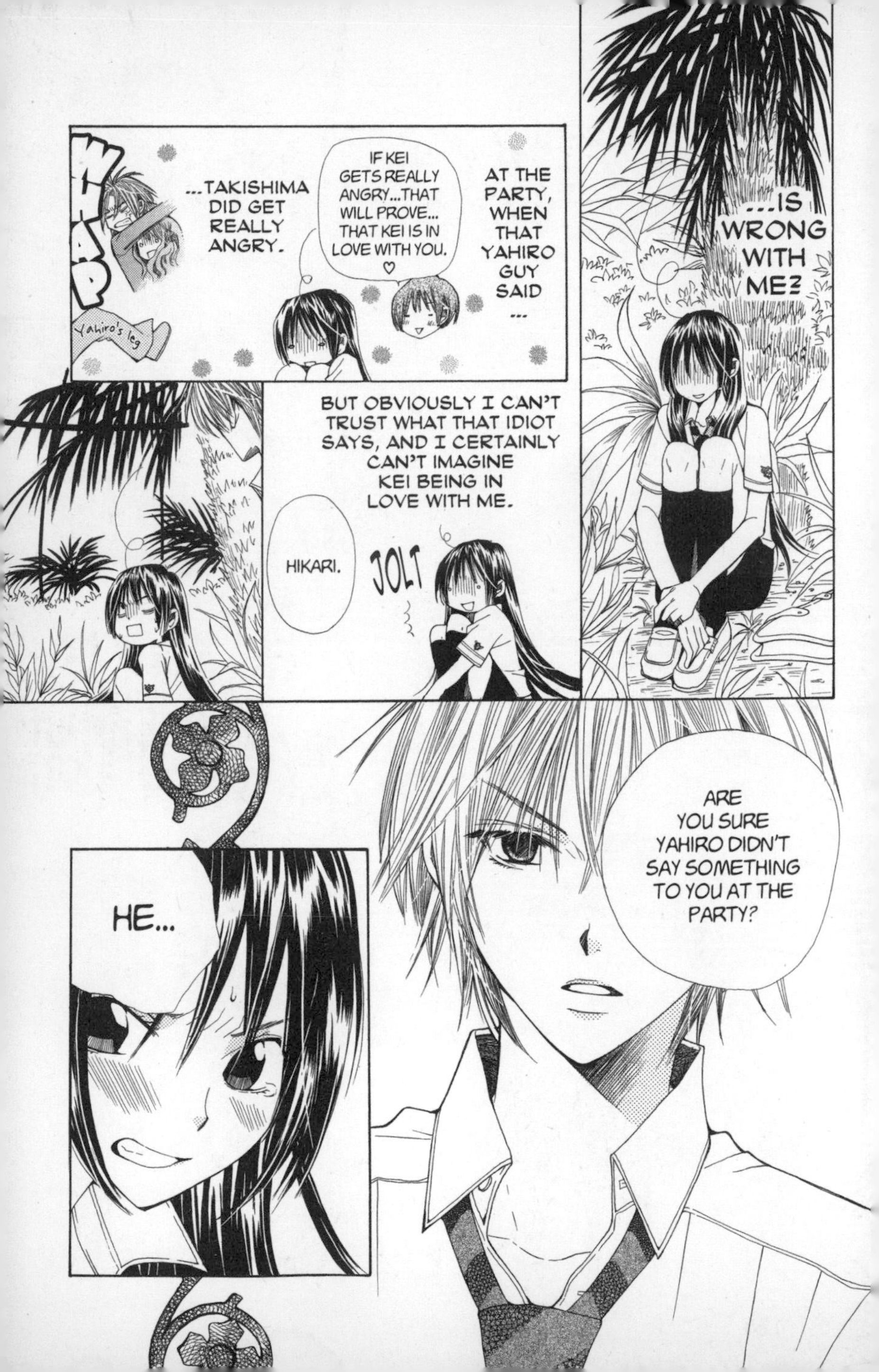
...IS WRONG WITH ME?
AT THE PARTY, WHEN THAT YAHIRO GUY SAID ...
IF KEI GETS REALLY ANGRY...THAT WILL PROVE... THAT KEI IS IN LOVE WITH YOU. ♡
...TAKISHIMA DID GET REALLY ANGRY.
WHAP
Yahiro's leg
BUT OBVIOUSLY I CAN'T TRUST WHAT THAT IDIOT SAYS, AND I CERTAINLY CAN'T IMAGINE KEI BEING IN LOVE WITH ME.
JOLT
HIKARI.
ARE YOU SURE YAHIRO DIDN'T SAY SOMETHING TO YOU AT THE PARTY?
HE...

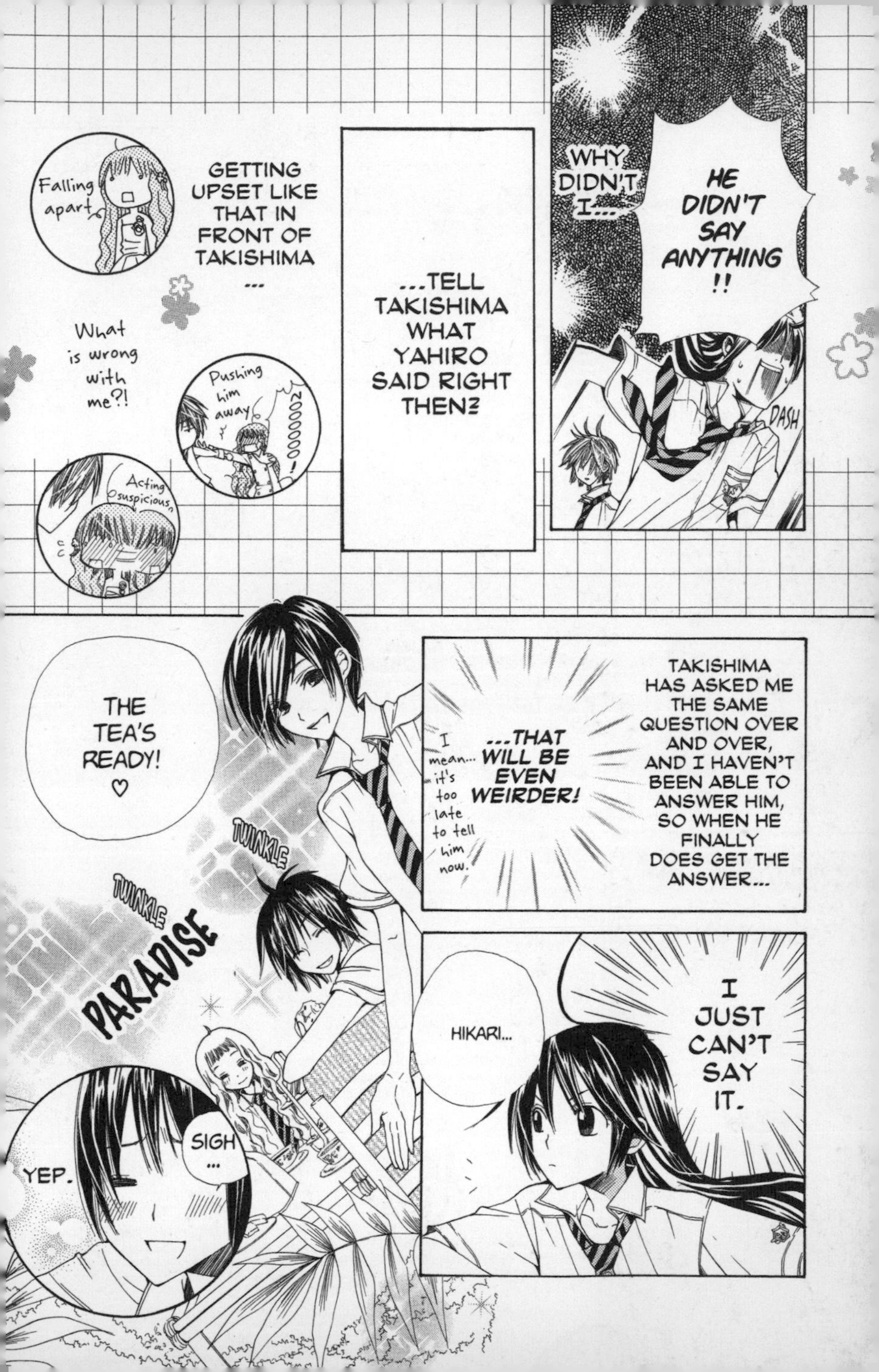
HE DIDN'T SAY ANYTHING!!
WHY DIDN'T I...
DASH
...TELL TAKISHIMA WHAT YAHIRO SAID RIGHT THEN?
GETTING UPSET LIKE THAT IN FRONT OF TAKISHIMA...
Falling apart
What is wrong with me?!
Pushing him away
NOOOOOO!
Acting suspicious
TAKISHIMA HAS ASKED ME THE SAME QUESTION OVER AND OVER, AND I HAVEN'T BEEN ABLE TO ANSWER HIM, SO WHEN HE FINALLY DOES GET THE ANSWER...
...THAT WILL BE EVEN WEIRDER!
I mean... it's too late to tell him now.
I JUST CAN'T SAY IT.
HIKARI...
THE TEA'S READY! ♡
TWINKLE
TWINKLE
PARADISE
SIGH...
YEP.

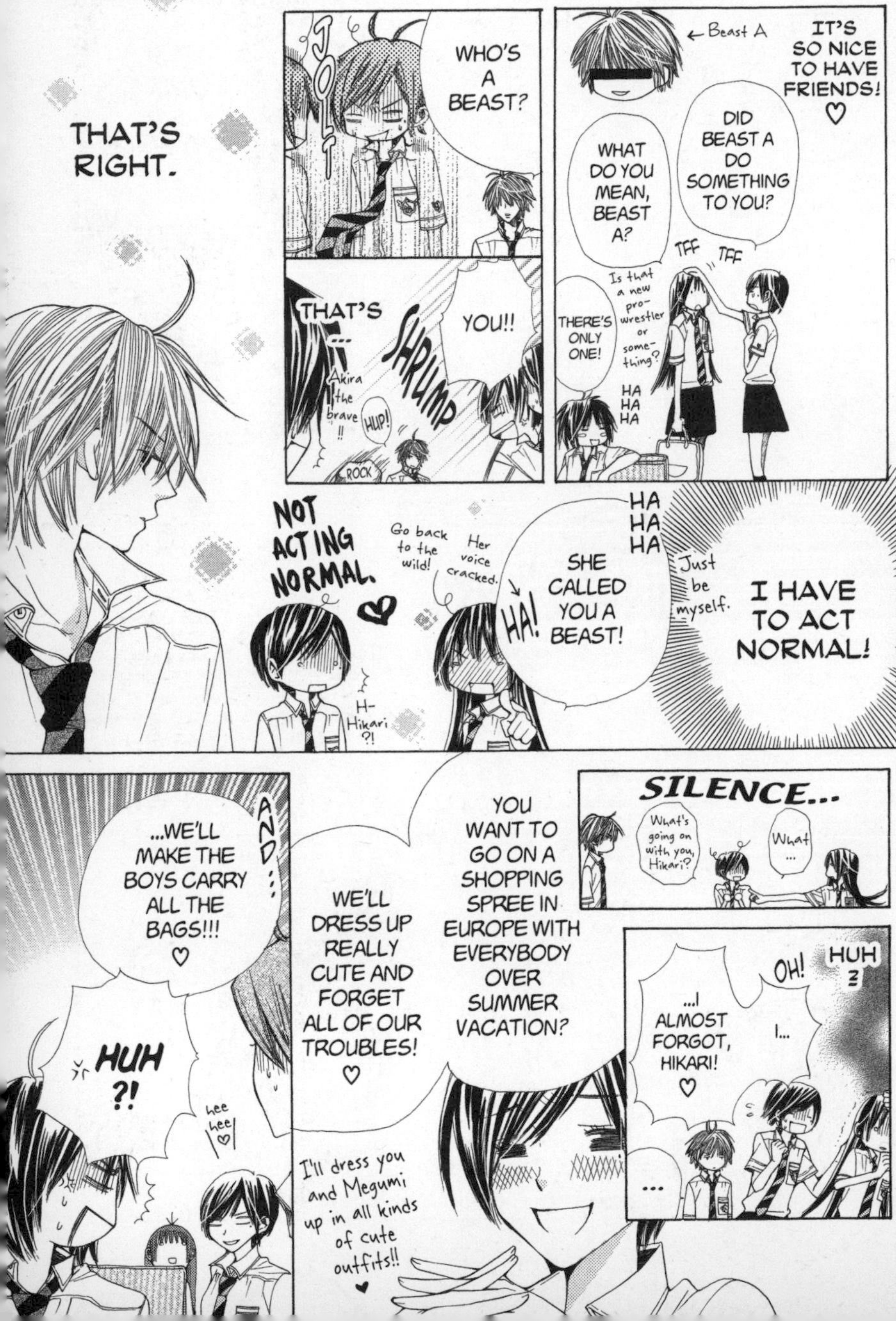
IT'S SO NICE TO HAVE FRIENDS! ♡
← Beast A
DID BEAST A DO SOMETHING TO YOU?
WHAT DO YOU MEAN, BEAST A?
TFF TFF
Is that a new pro-wrestler or some-thing?
THERE'S ONLY ONE!
HA HA HA
WHO'S A BEAST?
JOLT
YOU!!
THAT'S...
SHRUMP
Akira the brave!!
HUP!
ROCK
I HAVE TO ACT NORMAL!
Just be myself.
HA HA HA
SHE CALLED YOU A BEAST!
HA!
Her voice cracked.
Go back to the wild!
NOT ACTING NORMAL.
H-Hikari?!
THAT'S RIGHT.
SILENCE...
What...
What's going on with you, Hikari?
HUH
OH!
I...
...I ALMOST FORGOT, HIKARI! ♡
...
YOU WANT TO GO ON A SHOPPING SPREE IN EUROPE WITH EVERYBODY OVER SUMMER VACATION?
WE'LL DRESS UP REALLY CUTE AND FORGET ALL OF OUR TROUBLES! ♡
I'll dress you and Megumi up in all kinds of cute outfits!! ♥
AND...
...WE'LL MAKE THE BOYS CARRY ALL THE BAGS!!! ♡
HUH?!
hee hee ♡

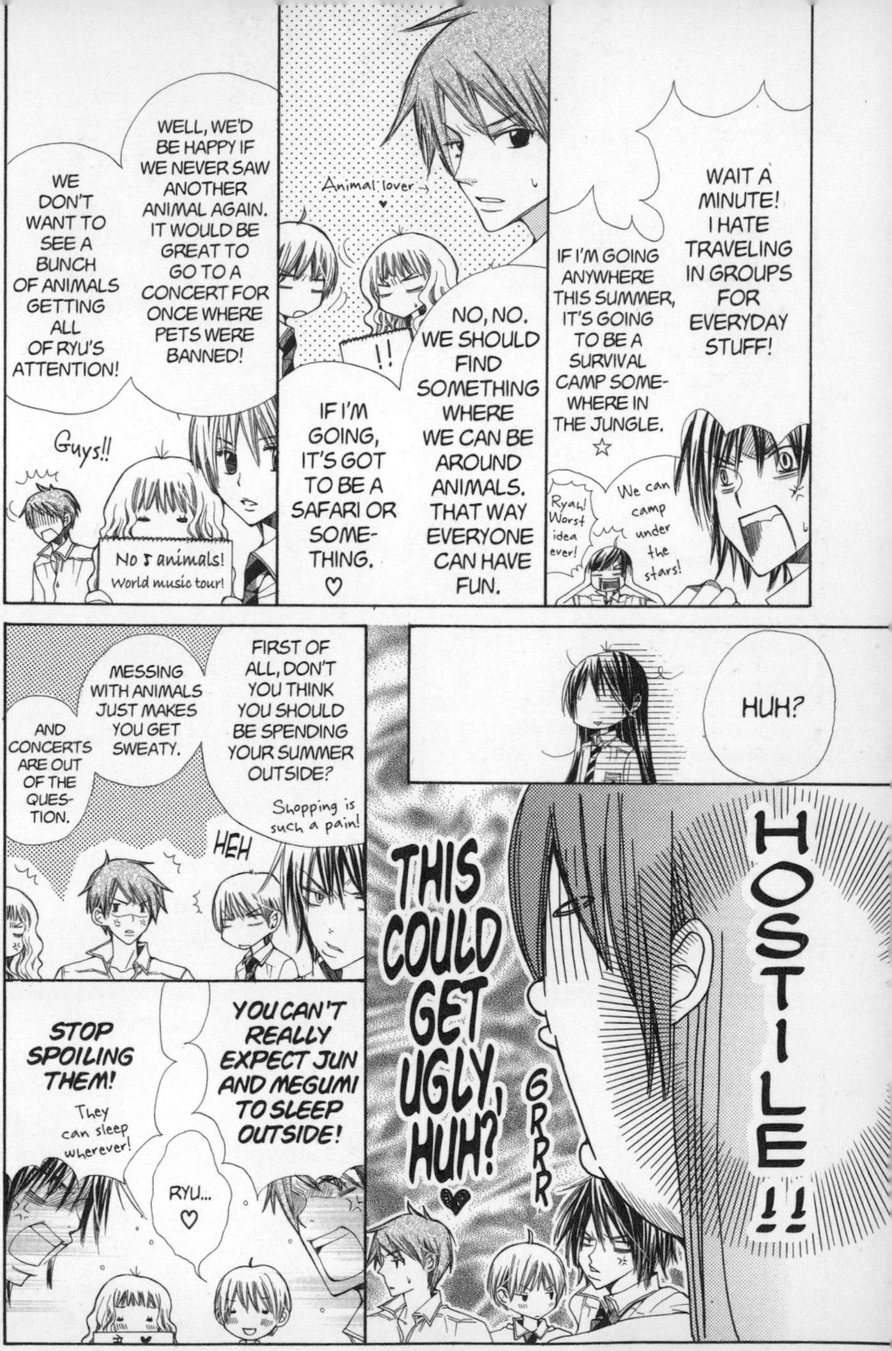
WAIT A MINUTE! I HATE TRAVELING IN GROUPS FOR EVERYDAY STUFF!
IF I'M GOING ANYWHERE THIS SUMMER, IT'S GOING TO BE A SURVIVAL CAMP SOME-WHERE IN THE JUNGLE. ☆
We can camp under the stars!
Ryah! Worst idea ever!
NO, NO. WE SHOULD FIND SOMETHING WHERE WE CAN BE AROUND ANIMALS. THAT WAY EVERYONE CAN HAVE FUN.
Animal lover →
!!
IF I'M GOING, IT'S GOT TO BE A SAFARI OR SOME-THING. ♡
WELL, WE'D BE HAPPY IF WE NEVER SAW ANOTHER ANIMAL AGAIN. IT WOULD BE GREAT TO GO TO A CONCERT FOR ONCE WHERE PETS WERE BANNED!
WE DON'T WANT TO SEE A BUNCH OF ANIMALS GETTING ALL OF RYU'S ATTENTION!
Guys!!
No ♪ animals! World music tour!
HUH?
HOSTILE!!
THIS COULD GET UGLY, HUH?
GRRR
FIRST OF ALL, DON'T YOU THINK YOU SHOULD BE SPENDING YOUR SUMMER OUTSIDE?
MESSING WITH ANIMALS JUST MAKES YOU GET SWEATY.
AND CONCERTS ARE OUT OF THE QUES-TION.
Shopping is such a pain!
HEH
YOU CAN'T REALLY EXPECT JUN AND MEGUMI TO SLEEP OUTSIDE!
RYU... ♡
STOP SPOILING THEM!
They can sleep wherever!

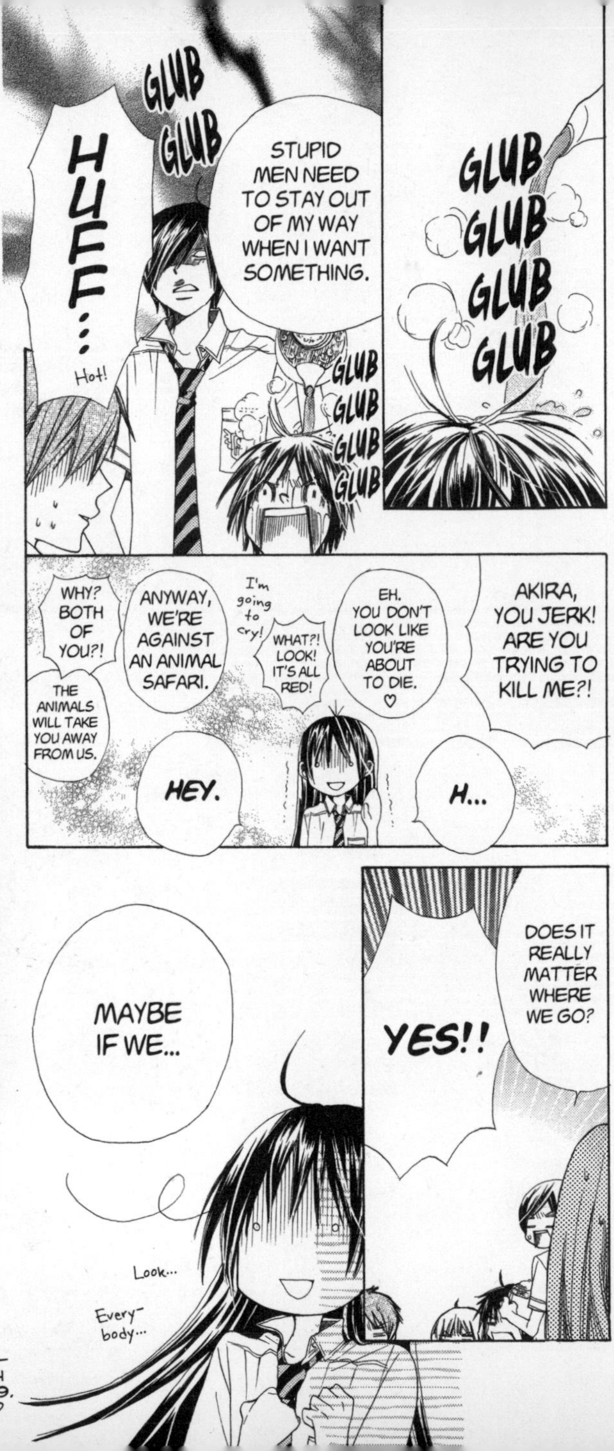
GLUB GLUB GLUB GLUB
GLUB GLUB
STUPID MEN NEED TO STAY OUT OF MY WAY WHEN I WANT SOMETHING.
HUFF...
Hot!
GLUB GLUB GLUB GLUB
AKIRA, YOU JERK! ARE YOU TRYING TO KILL ME?!
EH. YOU DON'T LOOK LIKE YOU'RE ABOUT TO DIE. ♡
WHAT?! LOOK! IT'S ALL RED!
I'm going to cry!
ANYWAY, WE'RE AGAINST AN ANIMAL SAFARI.
WHY? BOTH OF YOU?!
THE ANIMALS WILL TAKE YOU AWAY FROM US.
H...
HEY.
DOES IT REALLY MATTER WHERE WE GO?
YES!!
MAYBE IF WE...
Look...
Every-body...

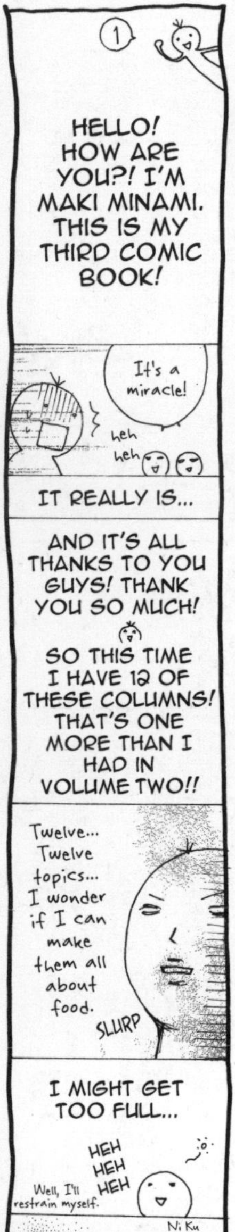
1
HELLO! HOW ARE YOU?! I'M MAKI MINAMI. THIS IS MY THIRD COMIC BOOK!
It's a miracle!
heh heh
IT REALLY IS...
AND IT'S ALL THANKS TO YOU GUYS! THANK YOU SO MUCH!
SO THIS TIME I HAVE 12 OF THESE COLUMNS! THAT'S ONE MORE THAN I HAD IN VOLUME TWO!!
Twelve... Twelve topics... I wonder if I can make them all about food.
SLURP
I MIGHT GET TOO FULL...
HEH HEH HEH
Well, I'll restrain myself.
Ni Ku 29

"NI KU" IS A PLAY ON WORDS— IN JAPANESE IT MEANS BOTH "MEAT" AND THE NUMBER 29. -ED

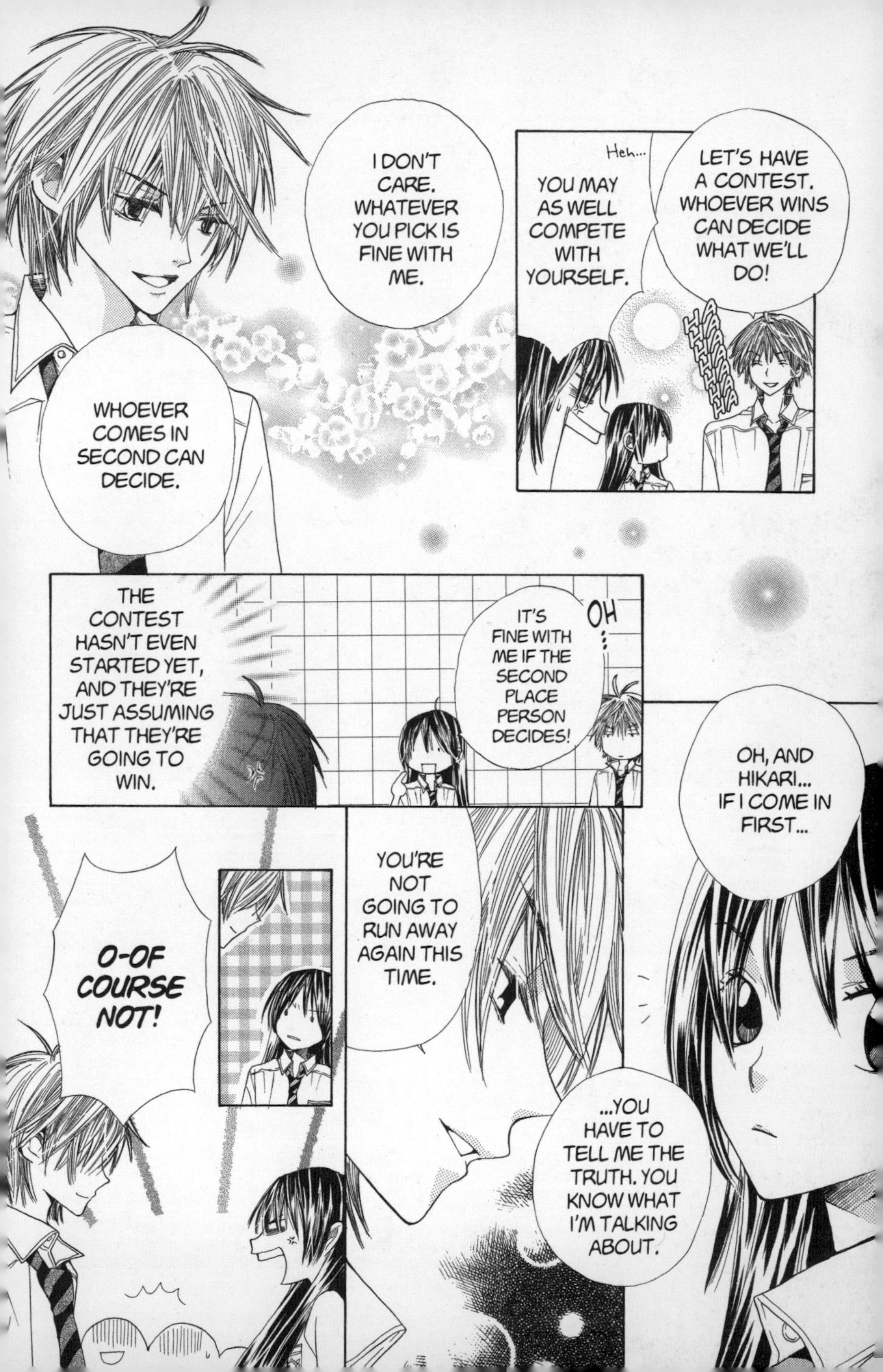
LET'S HAVE A CONTEST. WHOEVER WINS CAN DECIDE WHAT WE'LL DO!
Heh...
YOU MAY AS WELL COMPETE WITH YOURSELF.
I DON'T CARE. WHATEVER YOU PICK IS FINE WITH ME.
WHOEVER COMES IN SECOND CAN DECIDE.
OH...
IT'S FINE WITH ME IF THE SECOND PLACE PERSON DECIDES!
THE CONTEST HASN'T EVEN STARTED YET, AND THEY'RE JUST ASSUMING THAT THEY'RE GOING TO WIN.
OH, AND HIKARI... IF I COME IN FIRST...
...YOU HAVE TO TELL ME THE TRUTH. YOU KNOW WHAT I'M TALKING ABOUT.
YOU'RE NOT GOING TO RUN AWAY AGAIN THIS TIME.
O-OF COURSE NOT!

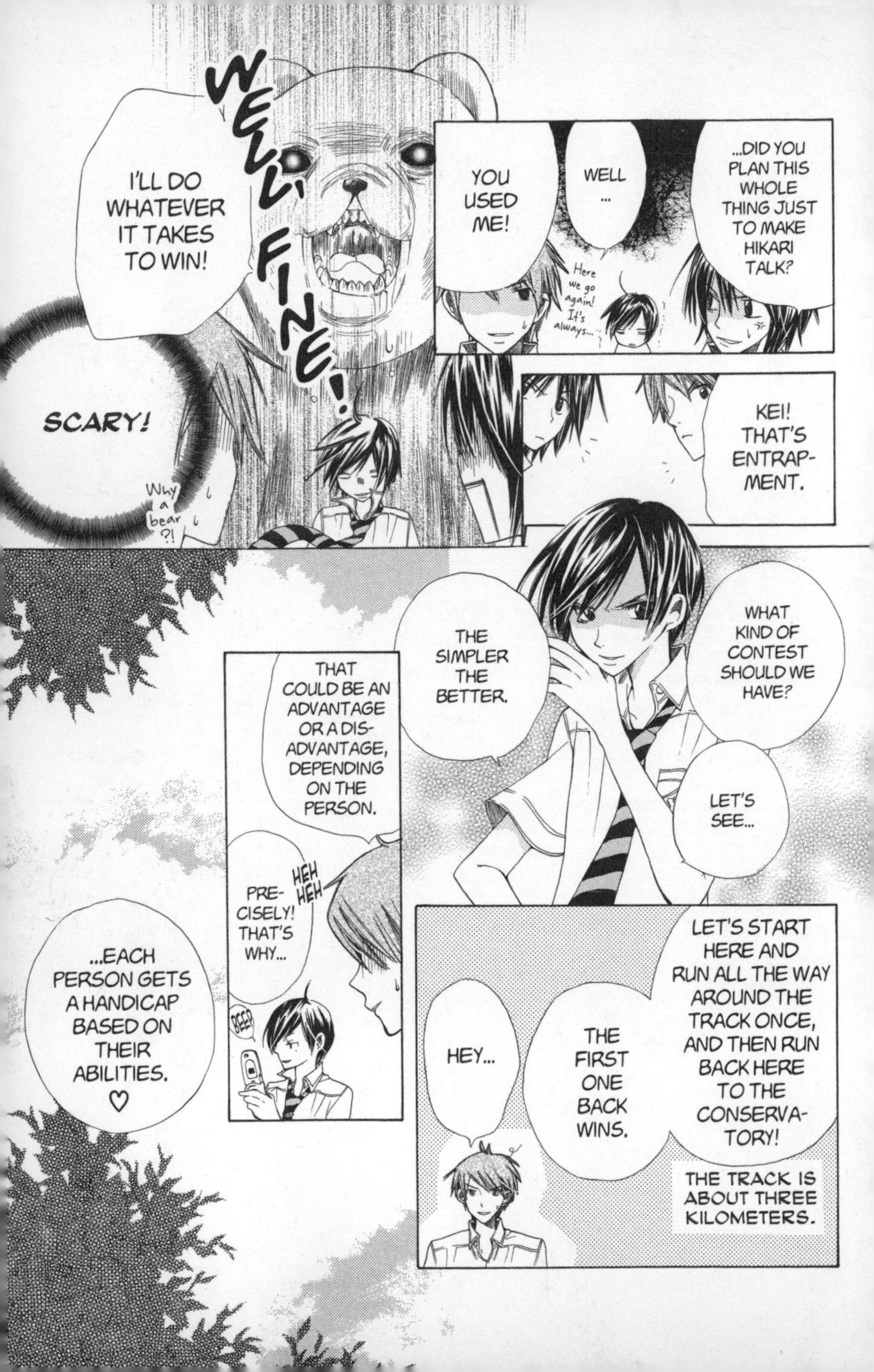
...DID YOU PLAN THIS WHOLE THING JUST TO MAKE HIKARI TALK?
WELL ...
YOU USED ME!
Here we go again! It's always...
KEI! THAT'S ENTRAP-MENT.
I'LL DO WHATEVER IT TAKES TO WIN!
WELL, FINE!
SCARY!
Why a bear ?!
WHAT KIND OF CONTEST SHOULD WE HAVE?
THE SIMPLER THE BETTER.
LET'S SEE...
THAT COULD BE AN ADVANTAGE OR A DIS-ADVANTAGE, DEPENDING ON THE PERSON.
HEH HEH
PRE-CISELY! THAT'S WHY...
BEEP
...EACH PERSON GETS A HANDICAP BASED ON THEIR ABILITIES. ♡
LET'S START HERE AND RUN ALL THE WAY AROUND THE TRACK ONCE, AND THEN RUN BACK HERE TO THE CONSERVA-TORY!
THE FIRST ONE BACK WINS.
HEY...
THE TRACK IS ABOUT THREE KILOMETERS.

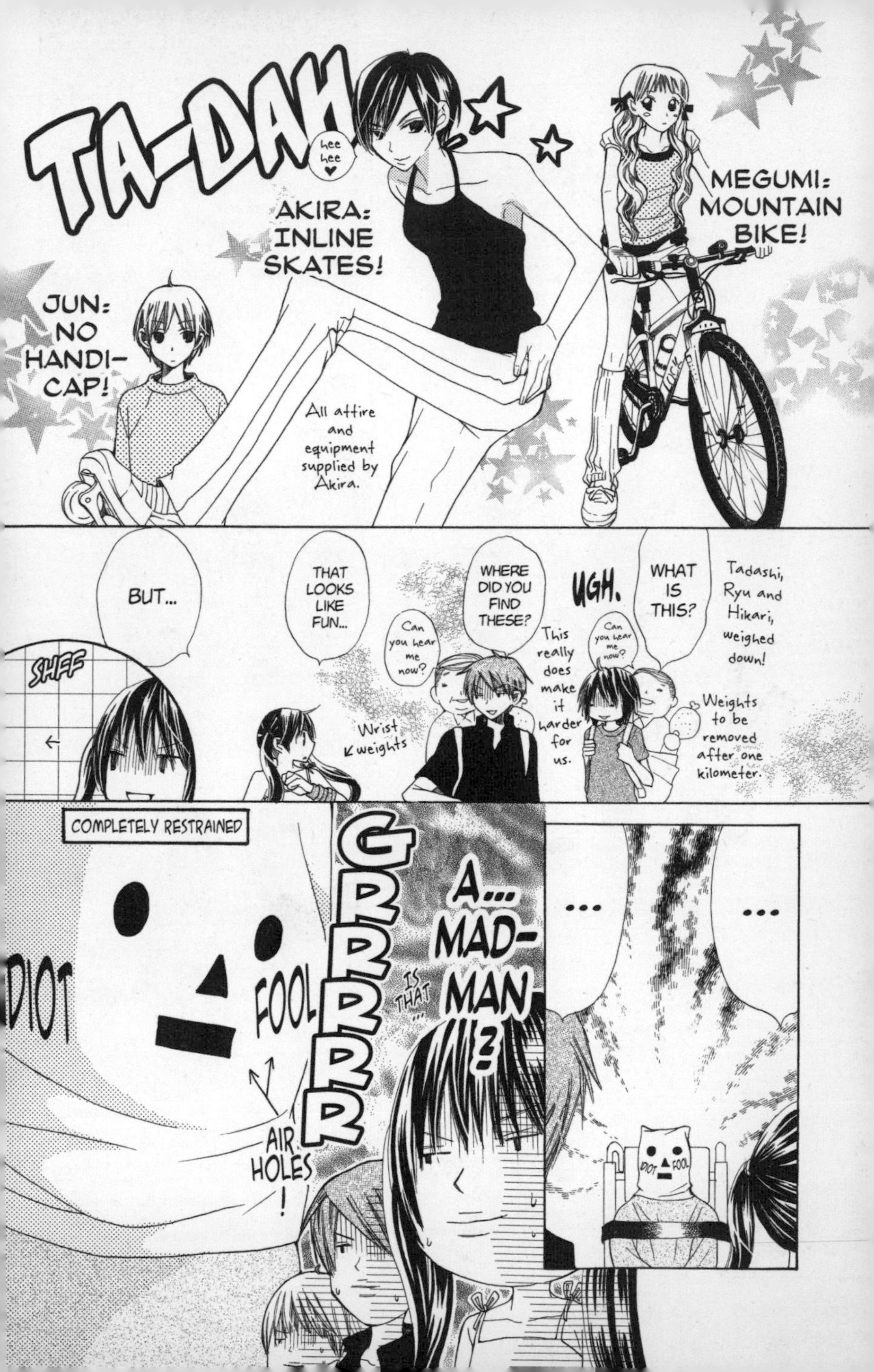
TA-DAH
hee hee ♥
MEGUMI: MOUNTAIN BIKE!
AKIRA: INLINE SKATES!
JUN: NO HANDI-CAP!
All attire and equipment supplied by Akira.
Tadashi, Ryu and Hikari, weighed down!
WHAT IS THIS?
Can you hear me now?
Weights to be removed after one kilometer.
UGH.
This really does make it harder for us.
WHERE DID YOU FIND THESE?
Can you hear me now?
THAT LOOKS LIKE FUN...
Wrist weights
BUT...
SHFF
...
...
DIOT FOOL
A... MAD-MAN?!
IS THAT...
GRRRRR
COMPLETELY RESTRAINED
FOOL
DIOT
AIR HOLES!

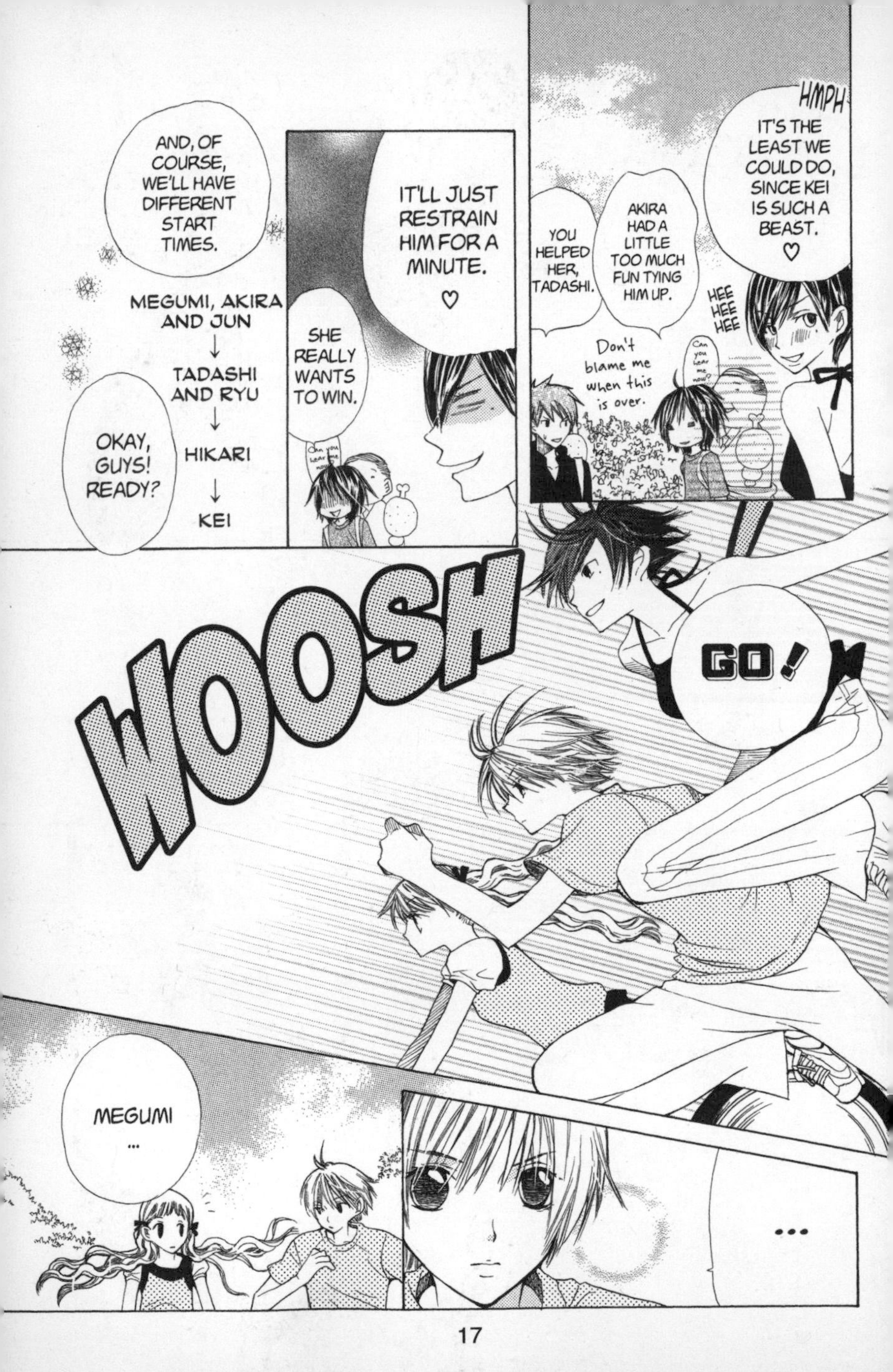
HMPH
IT'S THE LEAST WE COULD DO, SINCE KEI IS SUCH A BEAST. ♡
HEE HEE HEE
AKIRA HAD A LITTLE TOO MUCH FUN TYING HIM UP.
YOU HELPED HER, TADASHI.
Can you hear me now?
Don't blame me when this is over.
IT'LL JUST RESTRAIN HIM FOR A MINUTE. ♡
SHE REALLY WANTS TO WIN.
AND, OF COURSE, WE'LL HAVE DIFFERENT START TIMES.
MEGUMI, AKIRA AND JUN
↓
TADASHI AND RYU
↓
HIKARI
↓
KEI
OKAY, GUYS! READY?
GO!
WOOSH
...
MEGUMI ...

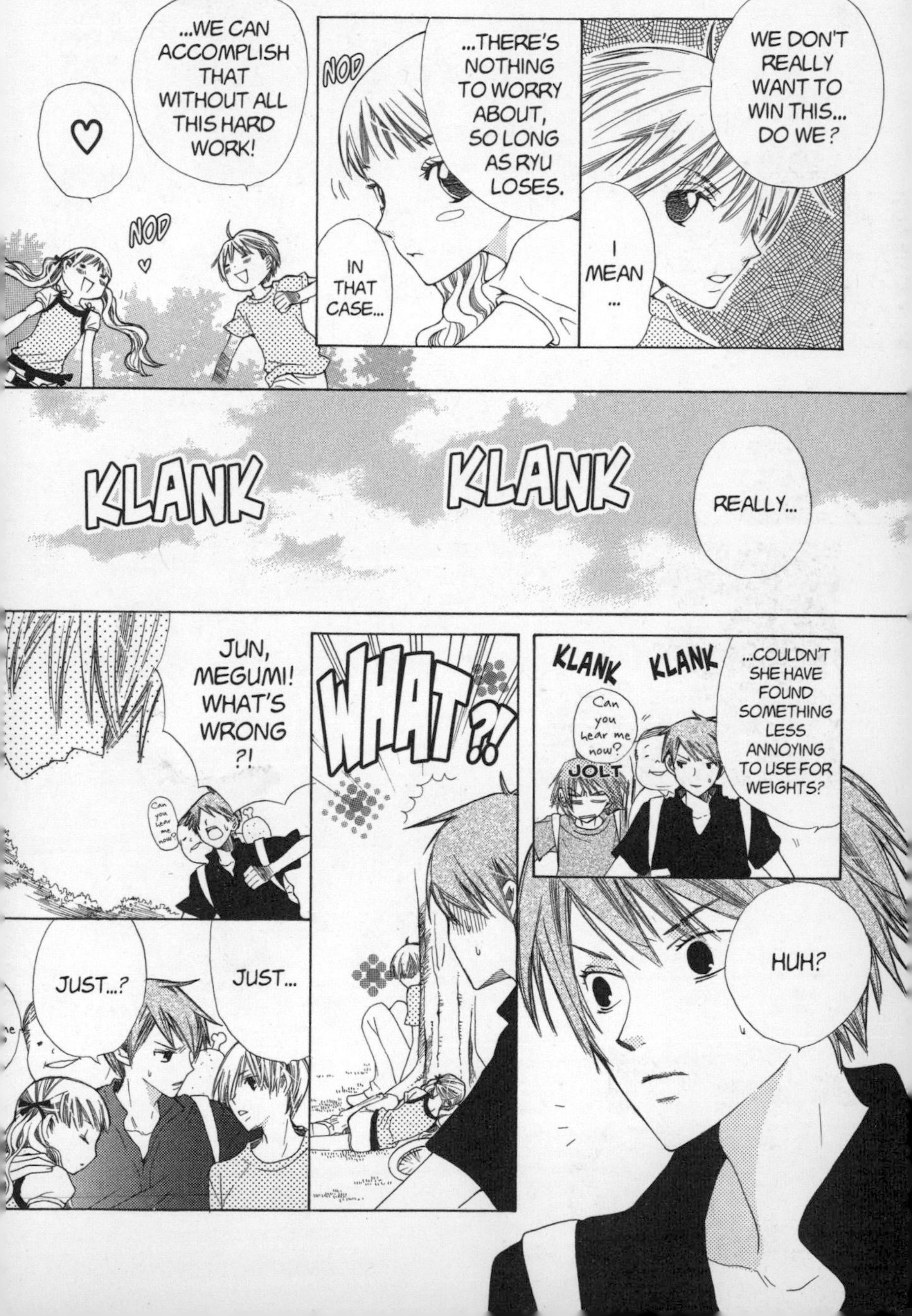
WE DON'T REALLY WANT TO WIN THIS... DO WE?
I MEAN ...
NOD
...THERE'S NOTHING TO WORRY ABOUT, SO LONG AS RYU LOSES.
IN THAT CASE...
...WE CAN ACCOMPLISH THAT WITHOUT ALL THIS HARD WORK!
♡
NOD ♡
REALLY...
KLANK
KLANK
KLANK
KLANK
...COULDN'T SHE HAVE FOUND SOMETHING LESS ANNOYING TO USE FOR WEIGHTS?
Can you hear me now?
JOLT
WHAT?!
JUN, MEGUMI! WHAT'S WRONG?!
Can you hear me now?
HUH?
JUST...
JUST...?

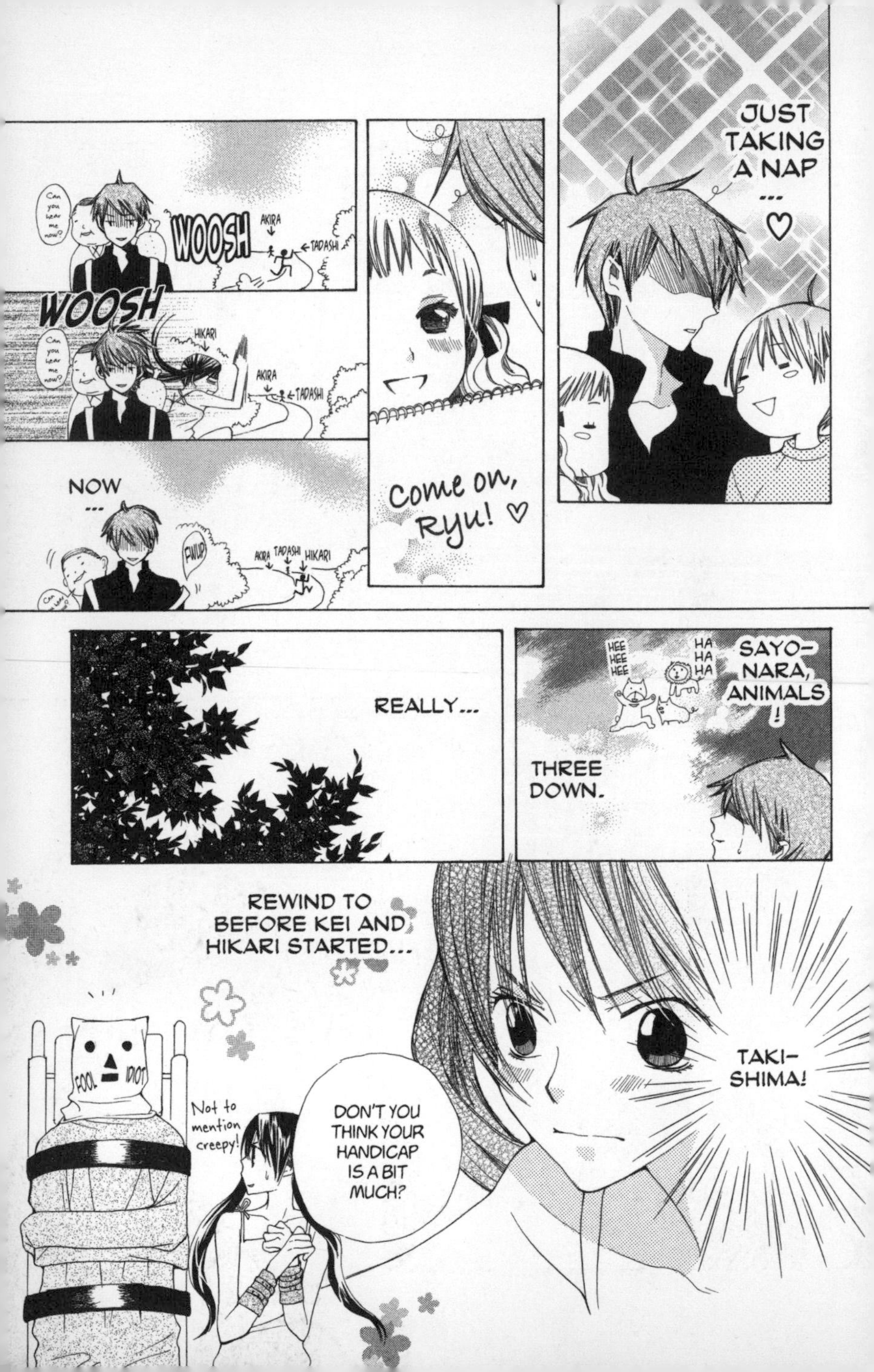
JUST TAKING A NAP ... ♡
Come on, Ryu! ♡
Can you hear me now?
WOOSH
AKIRA
TADASHI
WOOSH
Can you hear me now?
HIKARI
AKIRA
TADASHI
NOW ...
FWUP
AKIRA
TADASHI
HIKARI
SAYONARA, ANIMALS!
HA HA HA
HEE HEE HEE
THREE DOWN.
REALLY...
TAKI-SHIMA!
REWIND TO BEFORE KEI AND HIKARI STARTED...
DON'T YOU THINK YOUR HANDICAP IS A BIT MUCH?
Not to mention creepy!
FOOL
IDIOT

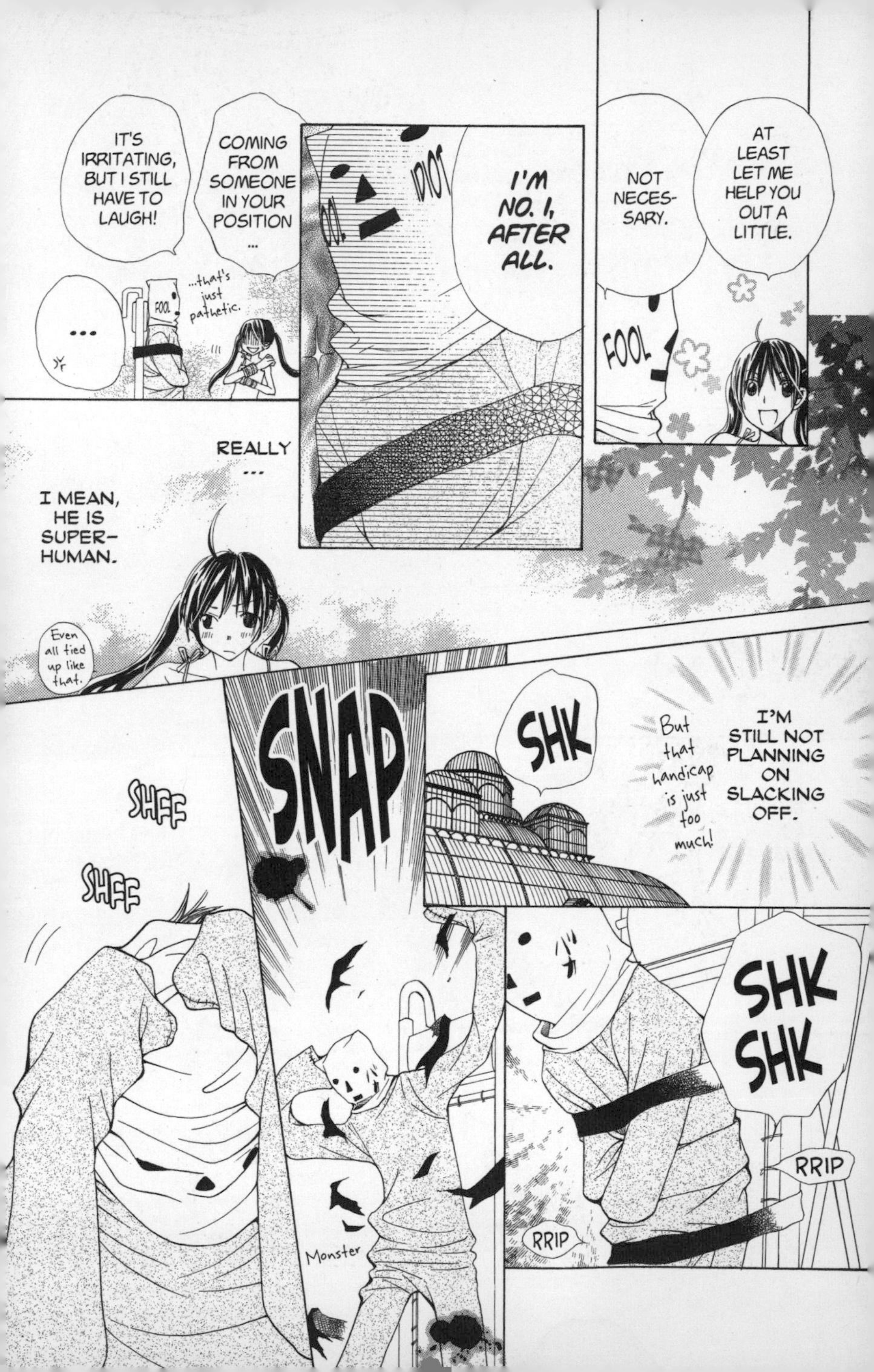
AT LEAST LET ME HELP YOU OUT A LITTLE.
NOT NECES-SARY.
FOOL
I'M NO. 1, AFTER ALL.
IDIOT
COMING FROM SOMEONE IN YOUR POSITION ...
IT'S IRRITATING, BUT I STILL HAVE TO LAUGH!
...that's just pathetic.
FOOL
...
REALLY ...
I MEAN, HE IS SUPER-HUMAN.
Even all tied up like that.
I'M STILL NOT PLANNING ON SLACKING OFF.
But that handicap is just too much!
SHK
SNAP
SHFF
SHFF
SHK SHK
RRIP
RRIP
Monster

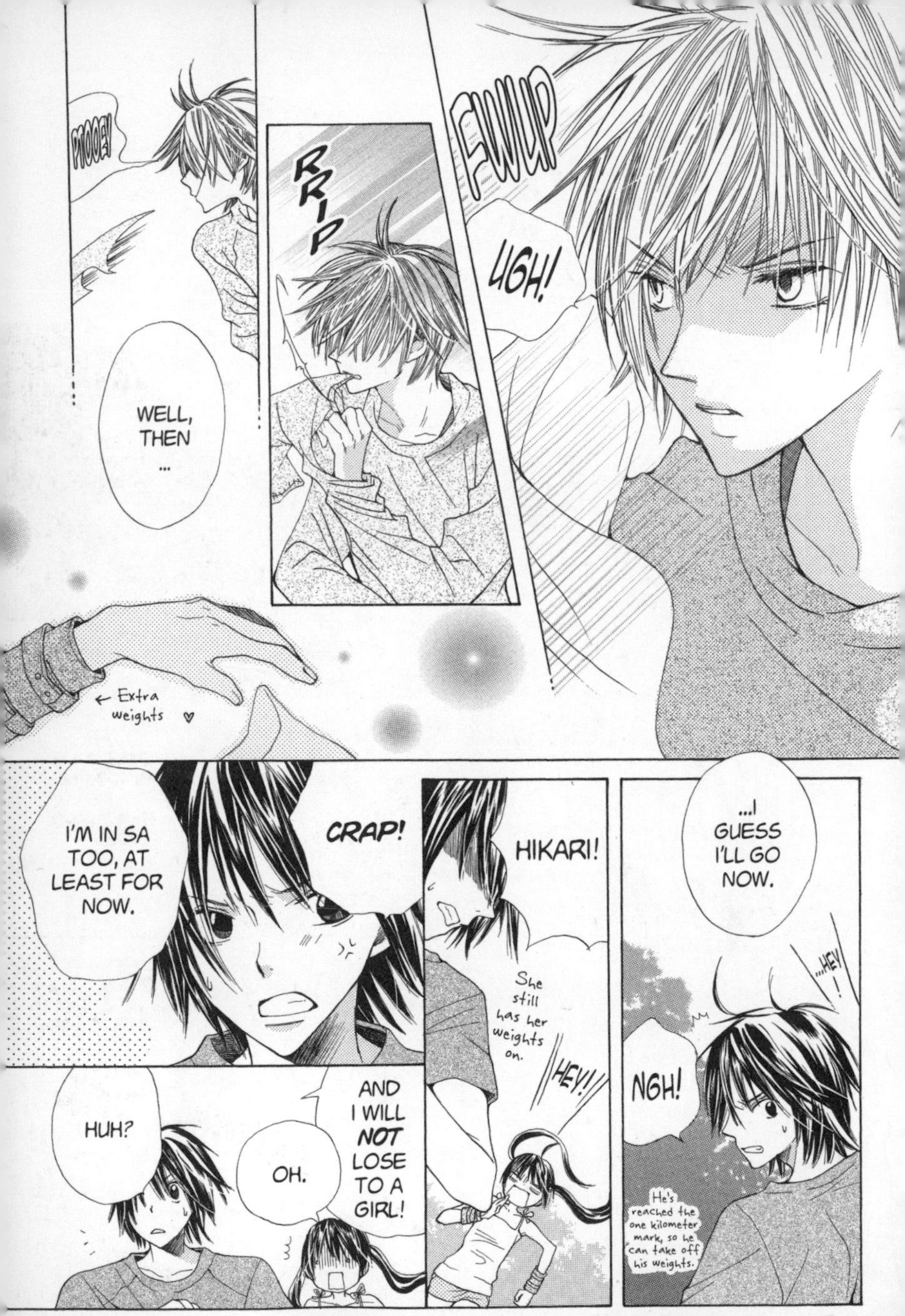
FWUP
UGH!
RRIP
PTOOEY
WELL, THEN ...
← Extra weights ♥
...I GUESS I'LL GO NOW.
...HEY!
NGH!
He's reached the one kilometer mark, so he can take off his weights.
HIKARI!
She still has her weights on.
HEY!!
I'M IN SA TOO, AT LEAST FOR NOW.
CRAP!
AND I WILL NOT LOSE TO A GIRL!
OH.
HUH?

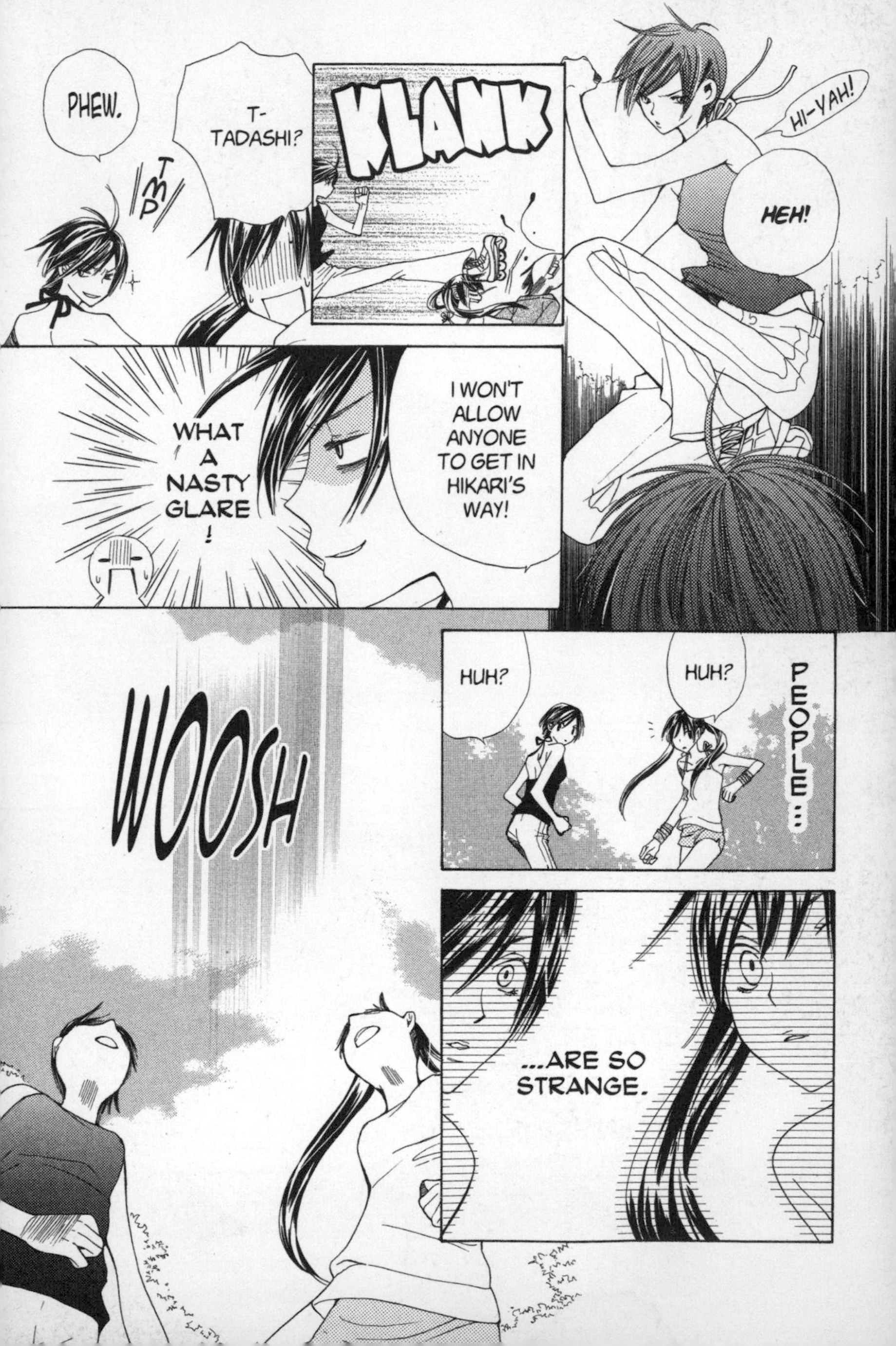
HI-YAH!
HEH!
KLANK
T-TADASHI?
TMP
PHEW.
I WON'T ALLOW ANYONE TO GET IN HIKARI'S WAY!
WHAT A NASTY GLARE!
PEOPLE...
HUH?
HUH?
...ARE SO STRANGE.
WOOSH

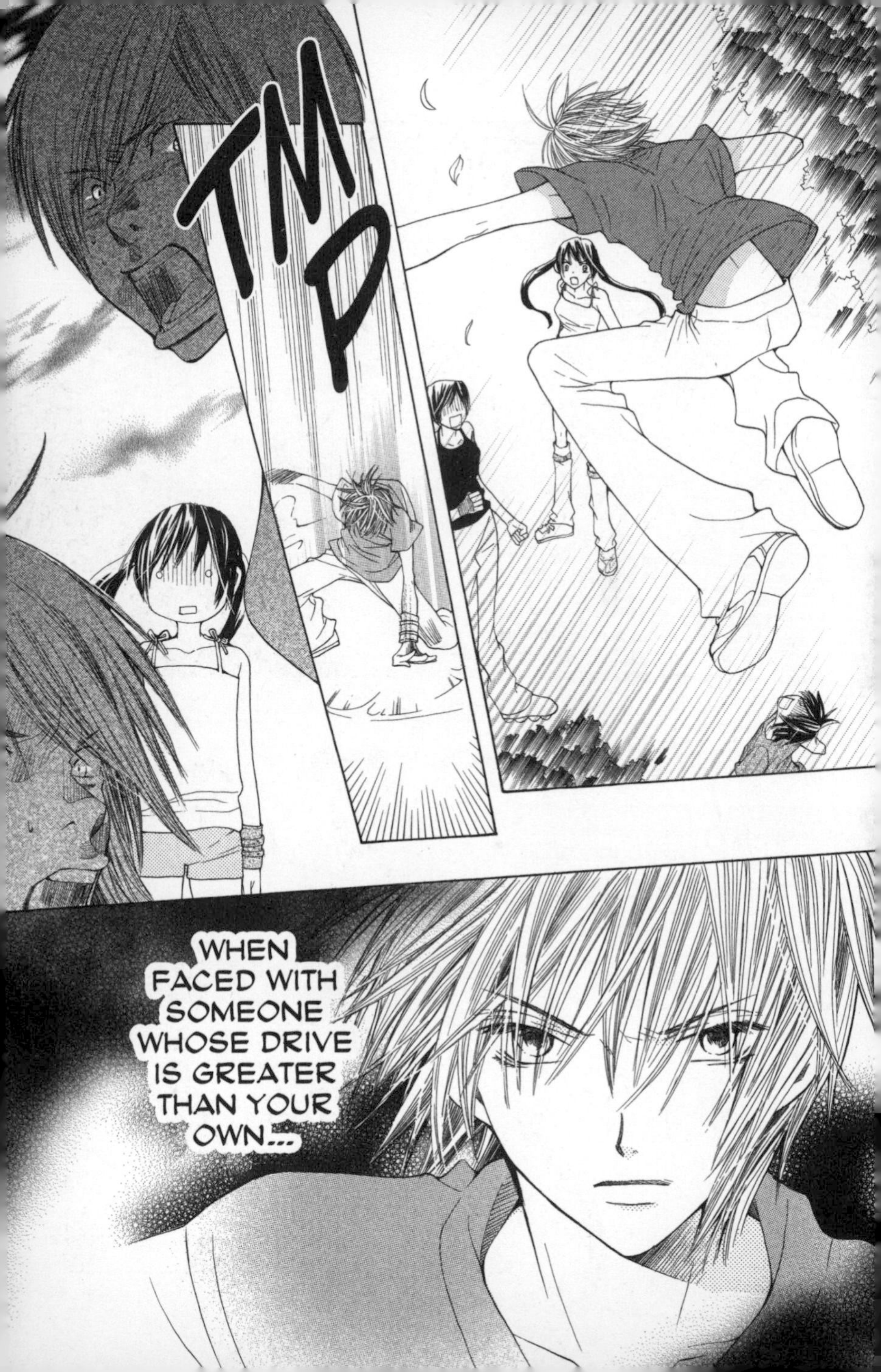
TMP
WHEN FACED WITH SOMEONE WHOSE DRIVE IS GREATER THAN YOUR OWN...

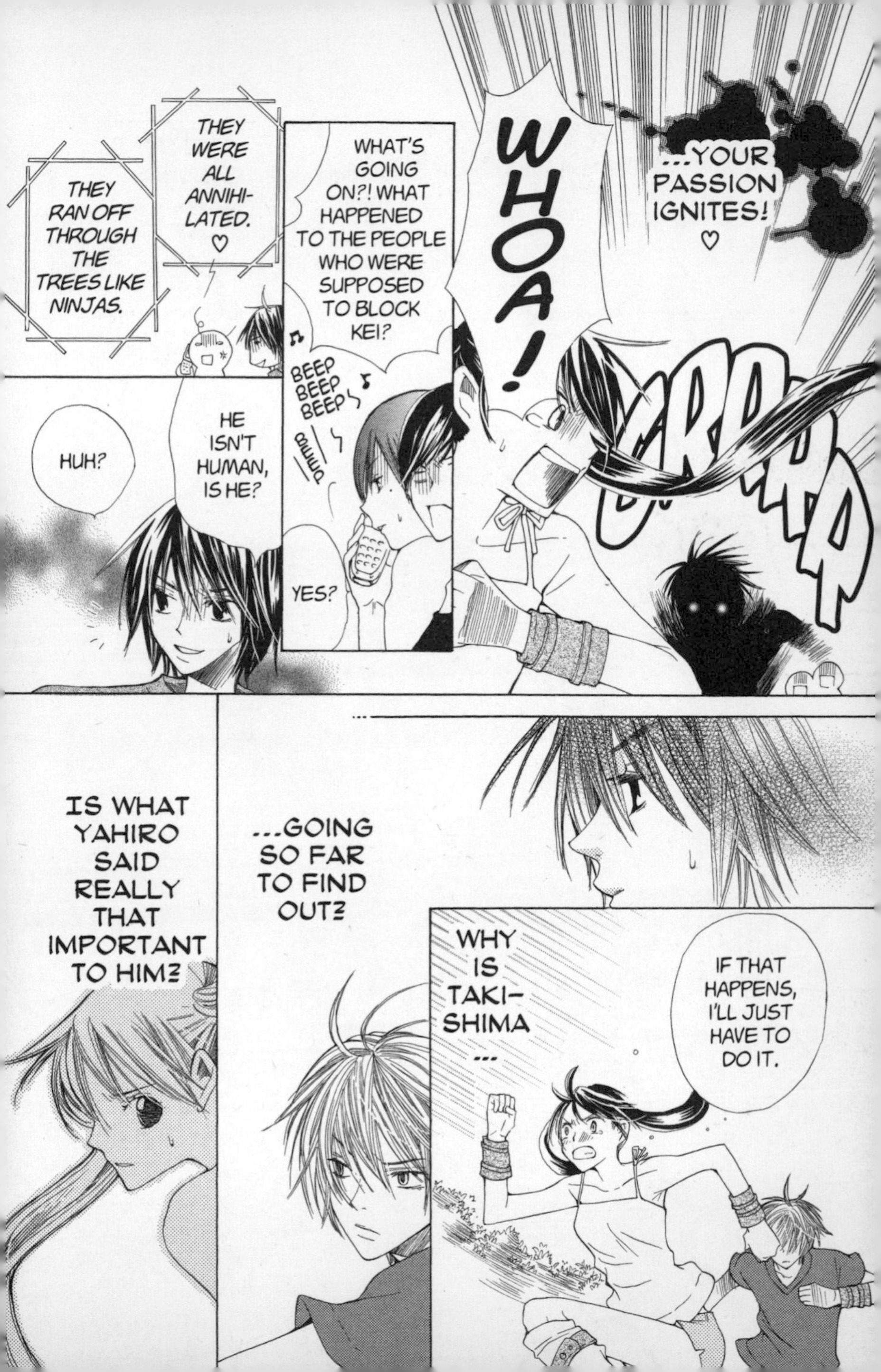
...YOUR PASSION IGNITES! ♡
WHOA!
WHAT'S GOING ON?! WHAT HAPPENED TO THE PEOPLE WHO WERE SUPPOSED TO BLOCK KEI?
BEEP BEEP BEEP
YES?
THEY WERE ALL ANNIHI-LATED. ♡
THEY RAN OFF THROUGH THE TREES LIKE NINJAS.
HE ISN'T HUMAN, IS HE?
HUH?
...
IF THAT HAPPENS, I'LL JUST HAVE TO DO IT.
WHY IS TAKI-SHIMA ...
...GOING SO FAR TO FIND OUT?
IS WHAT YAHIRO SAID REALLY THAT IMPORTANT TO HIM?

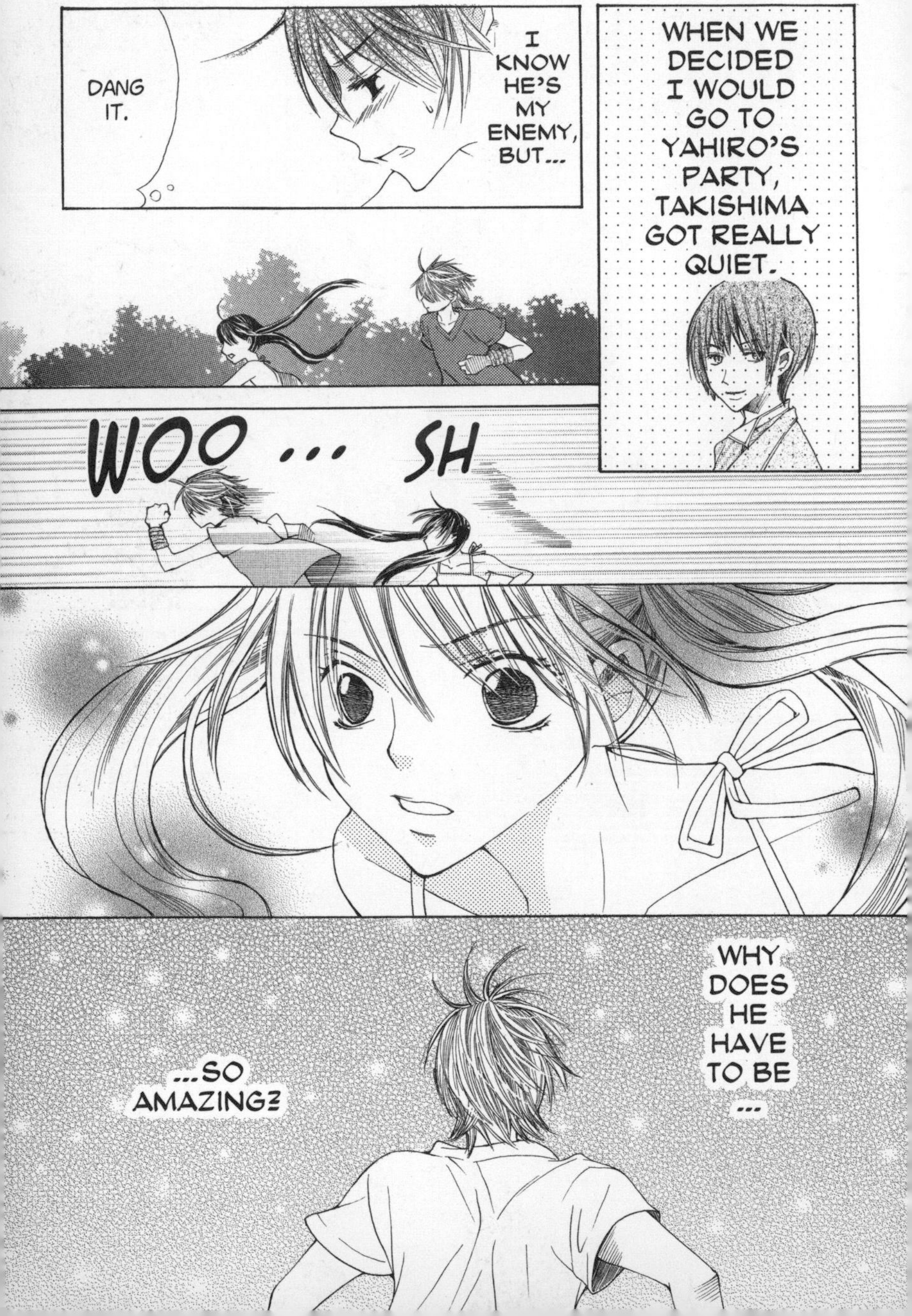
WHEN WE DECIDED I WOULD GO TO YAHIRO'S PARTY, TAKISHIMA GOT REALLY QUIET.
I KNOW HE'S MY ENEMY, BUT...
DANG IT.
WOO ... SH
WHY DOES HE HAVE TO BE ...
...SO AMAZING?

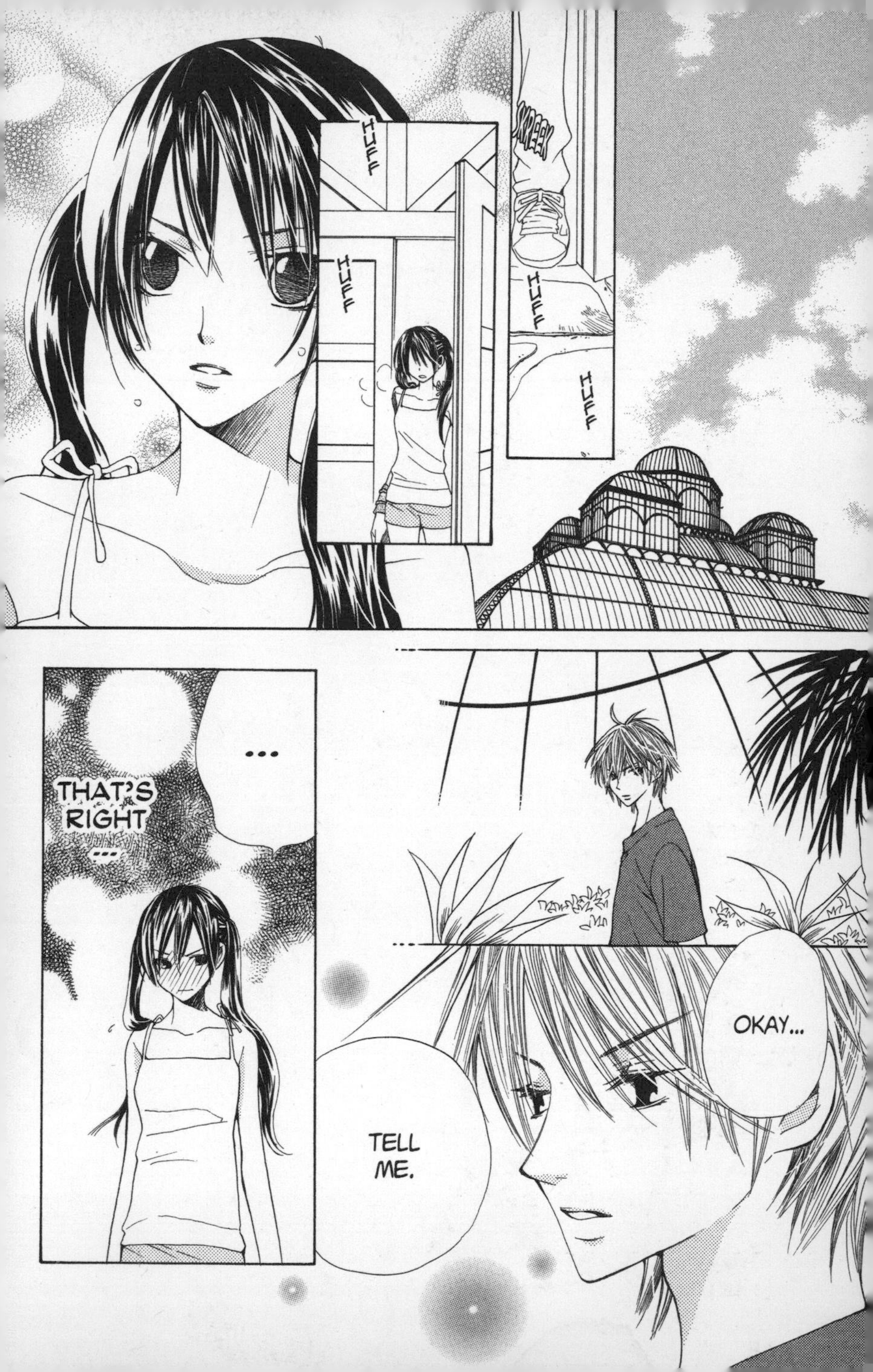
SKREEK
HUFF
HUFF
HUFF
HUFF
OKAY...
TELL ME.
...
THAT'S RIGHT ...

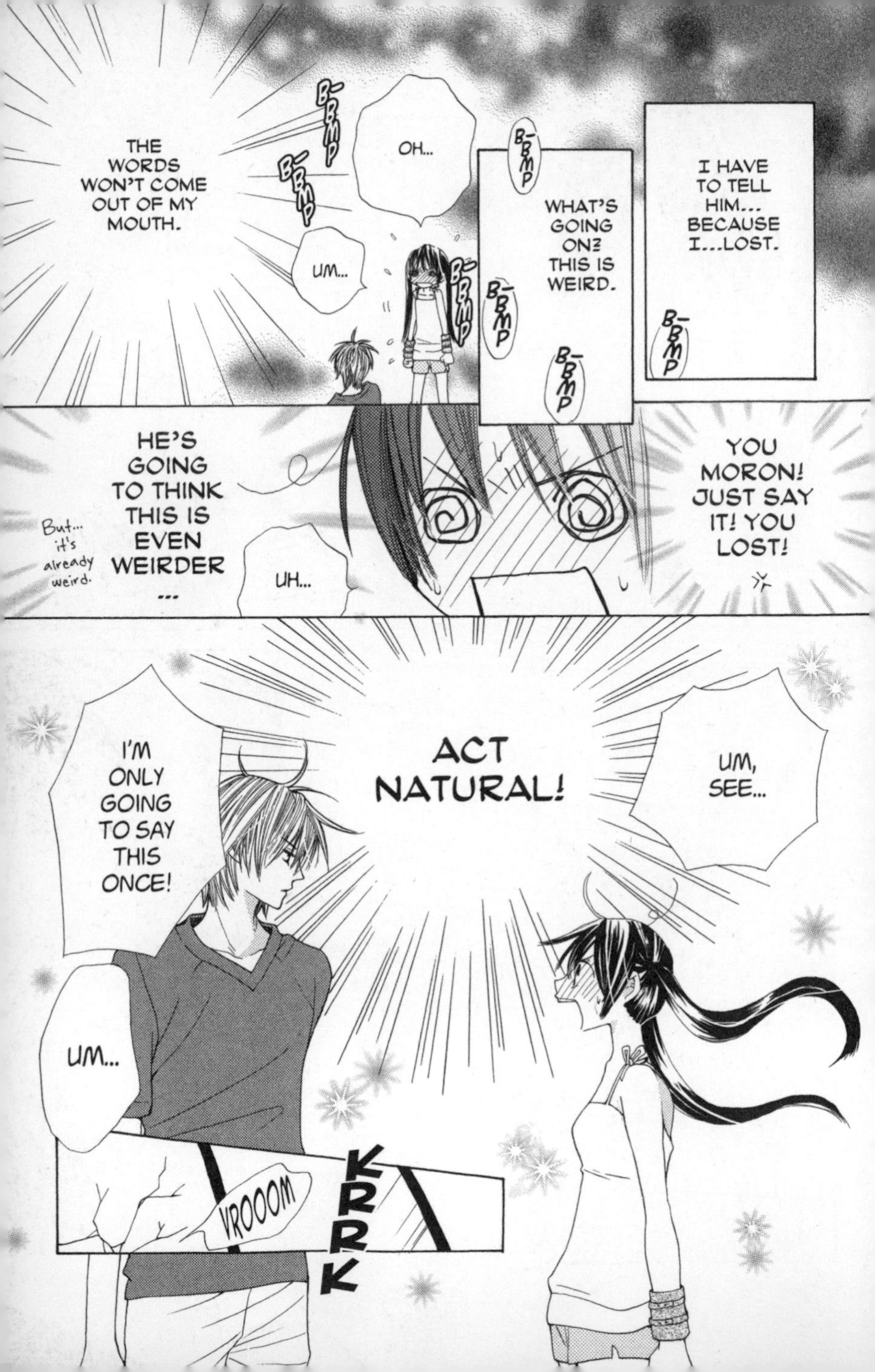
I HAVE TO TELL HIM... BECAUSE I...LOST.
B-BMP
WHAT'S GOING ON? THIS IS WEIRD.
B-BMP
B-BMP
B-BMP
OH...
B-BMP
B-BMP
THE WORDS WON'T COME OUT OF MY MOUTH.
UM...
B-BMP
YOU MORON! JUST SAY IT! YOU LOST!
UH...
HE'S GOING TO THINK THIS IS EVEN WEIRDER...
But... it's already weird.
UM, SEE...
ACT NATURAL!
I'M ONLY GOING TO SAY THIS ONCE!
UM...
KRRRK
VROOOM

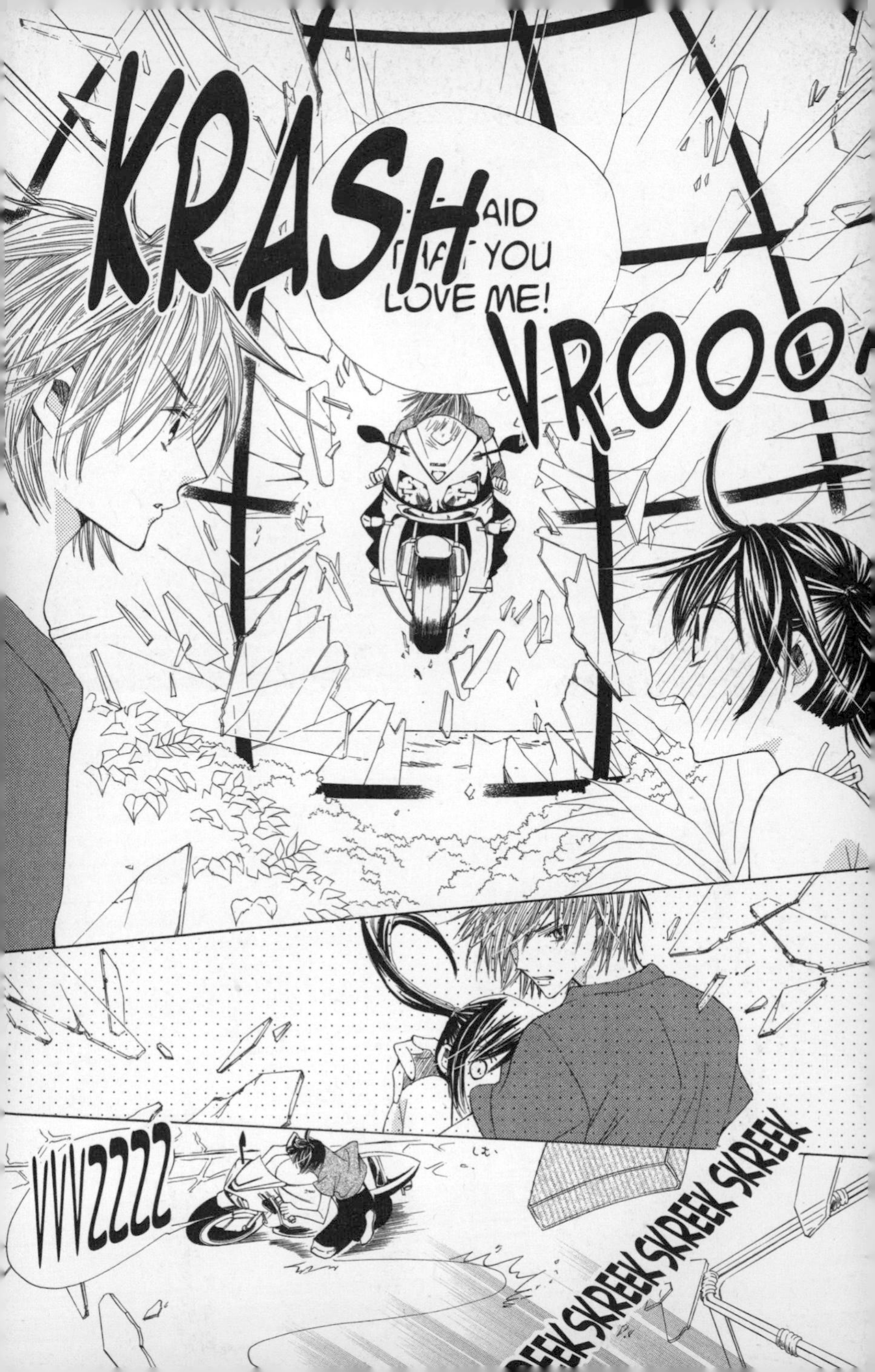
KRASH
AID THAT YOU LOVE ME!
VROOO
REEK SKREEK SKREEK SKREEK
VVVZZZZ

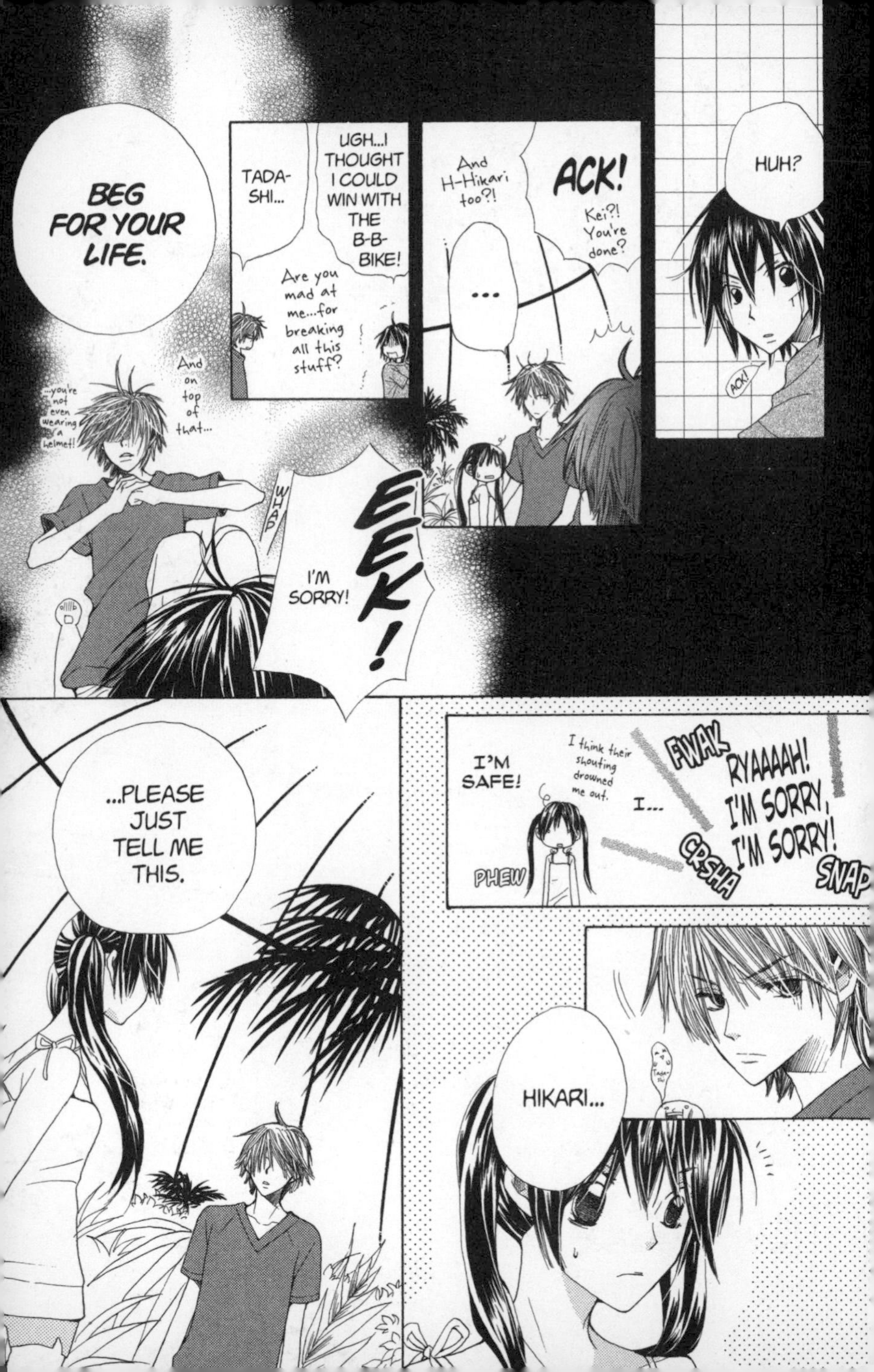
HUH?
ACK!
ACK!
Kei?! You're done?
And H-Hikari too?!
...
UGH...I THOUGHT I COULD WIN WITH THE B-B-BIKE!
TADA-SHI...
Are you mad at me...for breaking all this stuff?
BEG FOR YOUR LIFE.
And on top of that...
...you're not even wearing a helmet!
WHAP
EEEK!
I'M SORRY!
RYAAAAH! I'M SORRY, I'M SORRY!
SNAP
CRSHA
FWAK
I...
I think their shouting drowned me out.
I'M SAFE!
PHEW
HIKARI...
...PLEASE JUST TELL ME THIS.

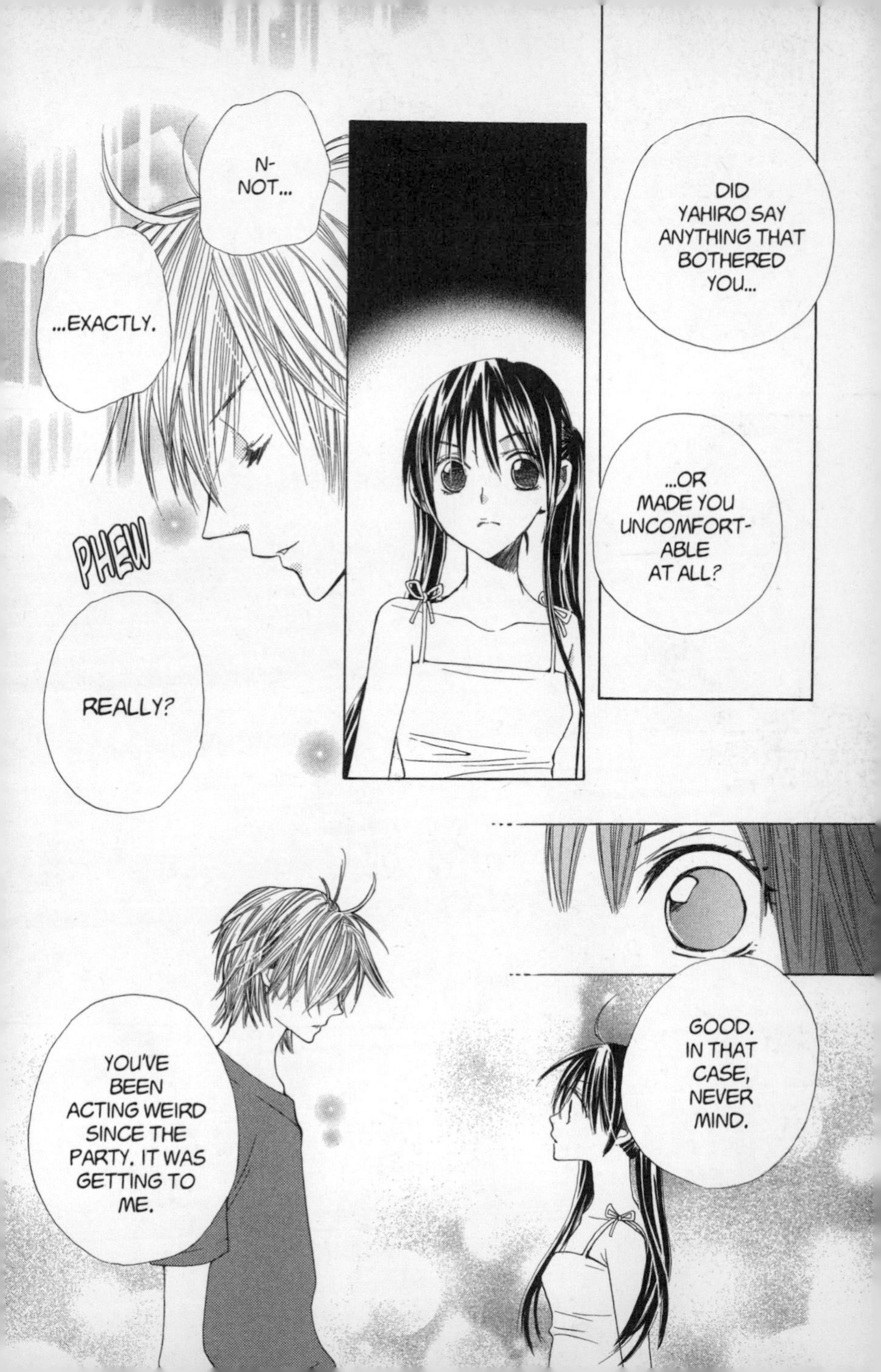
DID YAHIRO SAY ANYTHING THAT BOTHERED YOU...
...OR MADE YOU UNCOMFORT-ABLE AT ALL?
N-NOT...
...EXACTLY.
PHEW
REALLY?
GOOD. IN THAT CASE, NEVER MIND.
YOU'VE BEEN ACTING WEIRD SINCE THE PARTY. IT WAS GETTING TO ME.

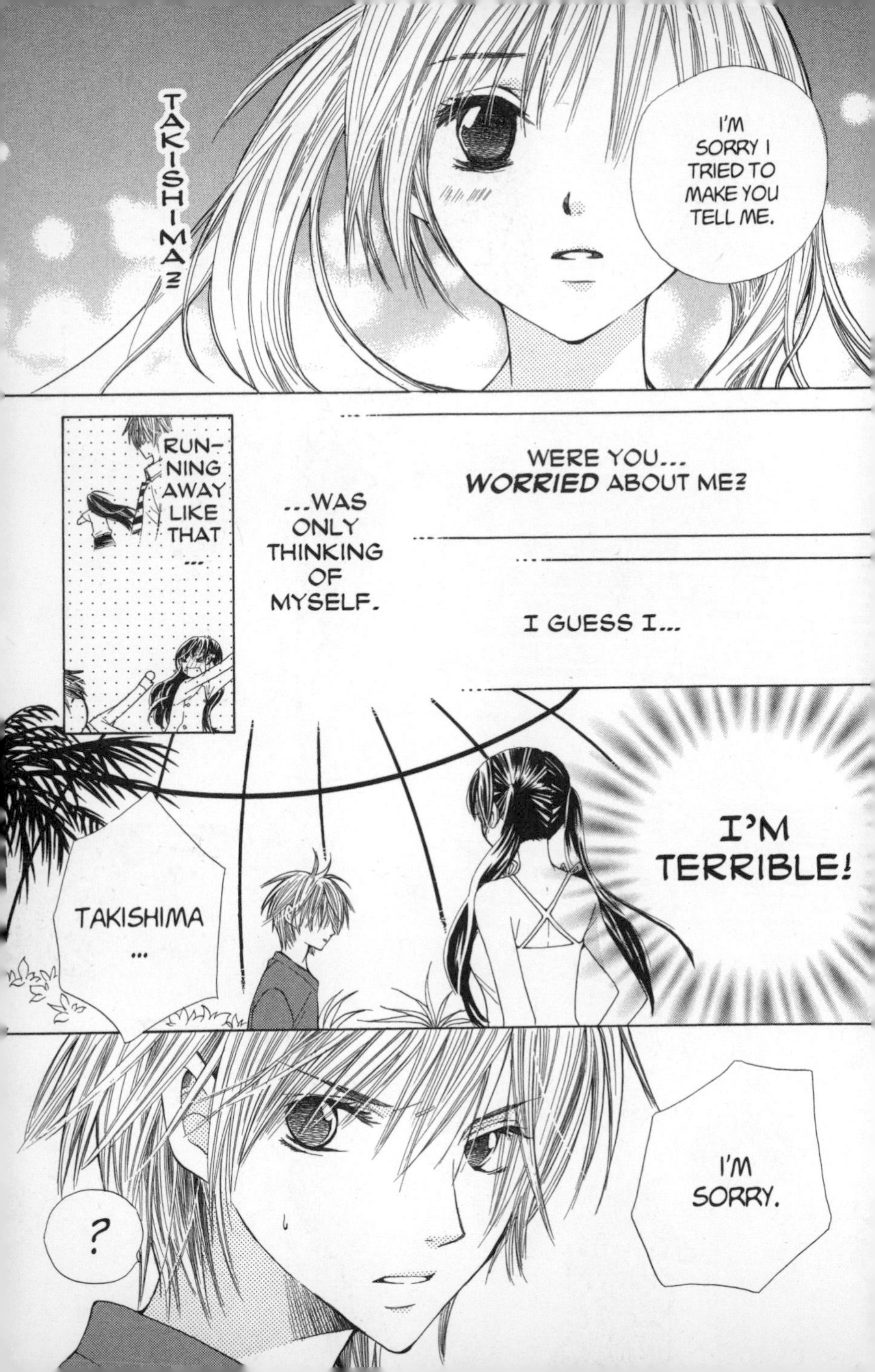
I'M SORRY I TRIED TO MAKE YOU TELL ME.
TAKISHIMA?
WERE YOU... *WORRIED* ABOUT ME?
I GUESS I...
...WAS ONLY THINKING OF MYSELF.
RUNNING AWAY LIKE THAT ...
I'M TERRIBLE!
TAKISHIMA ...
I'M SORRY.
?

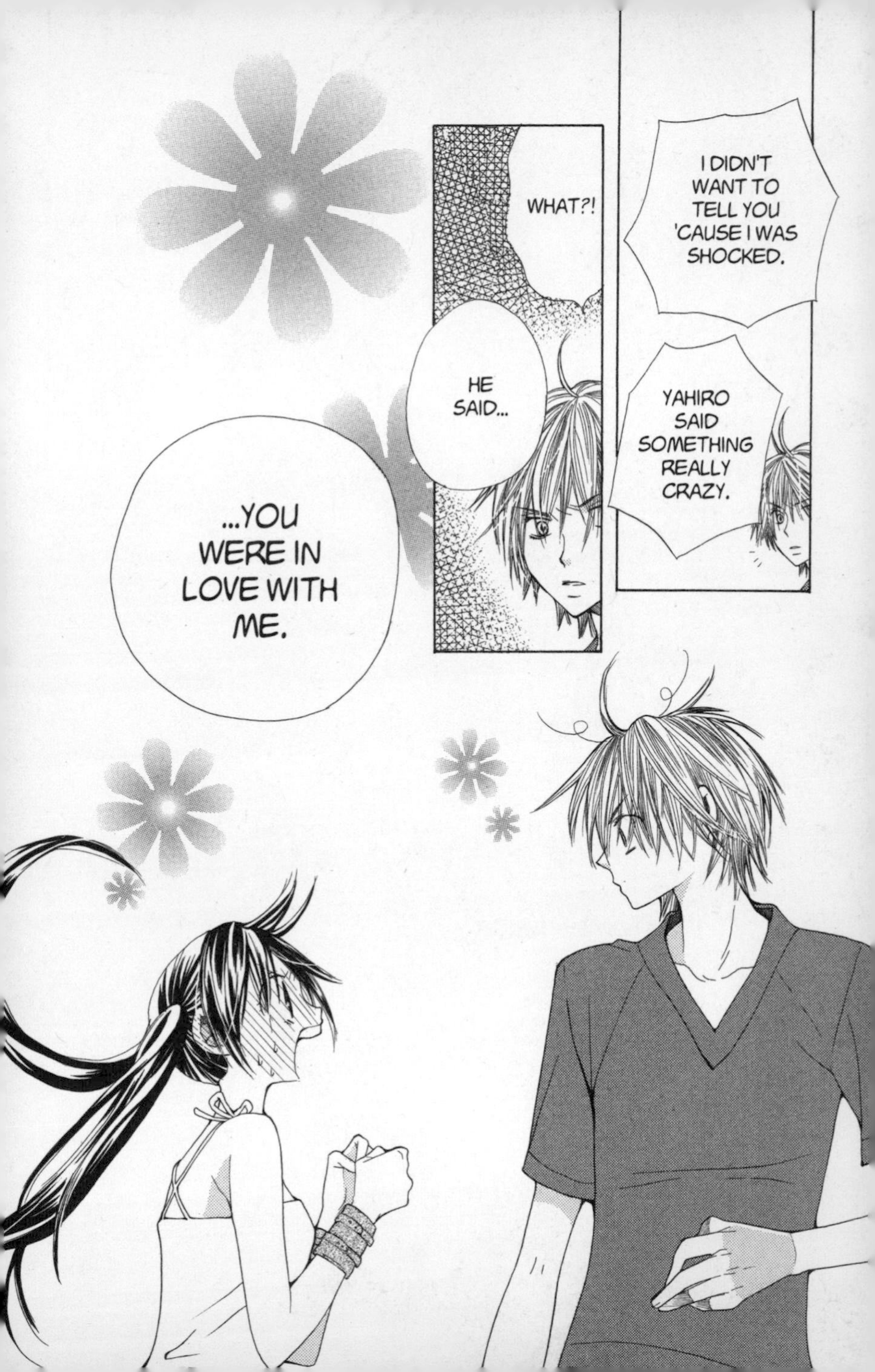
I DIDN'T WANT TO TELL YOU 'CAUSE I WAS SHOCKED.
YAHIRO SAID SOMETHING REALLY CRAZY.
WHAT?!
HE SAID...
...YOU WERE IN LOVE WITH ME.

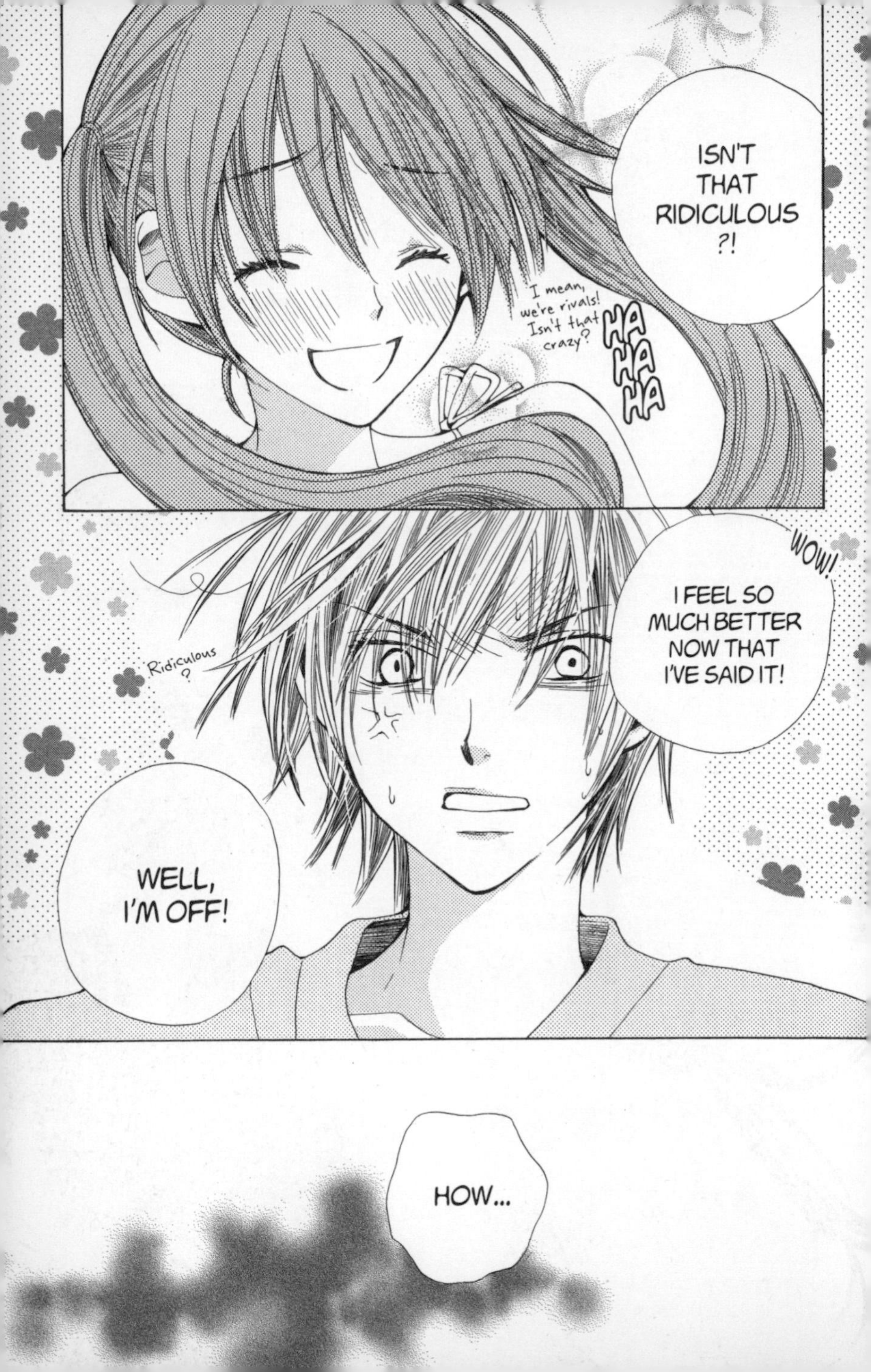
ISN'T THAT RIDICULOUS ?!
I mean, we're rivals! Isn't that crazy?
HA HA HA
WOW!
I FEEL SO MUCH BETTER NOW THAT I'VE SAID IT!
Ridiculous?
WELL, I'M OFF!
HOW...

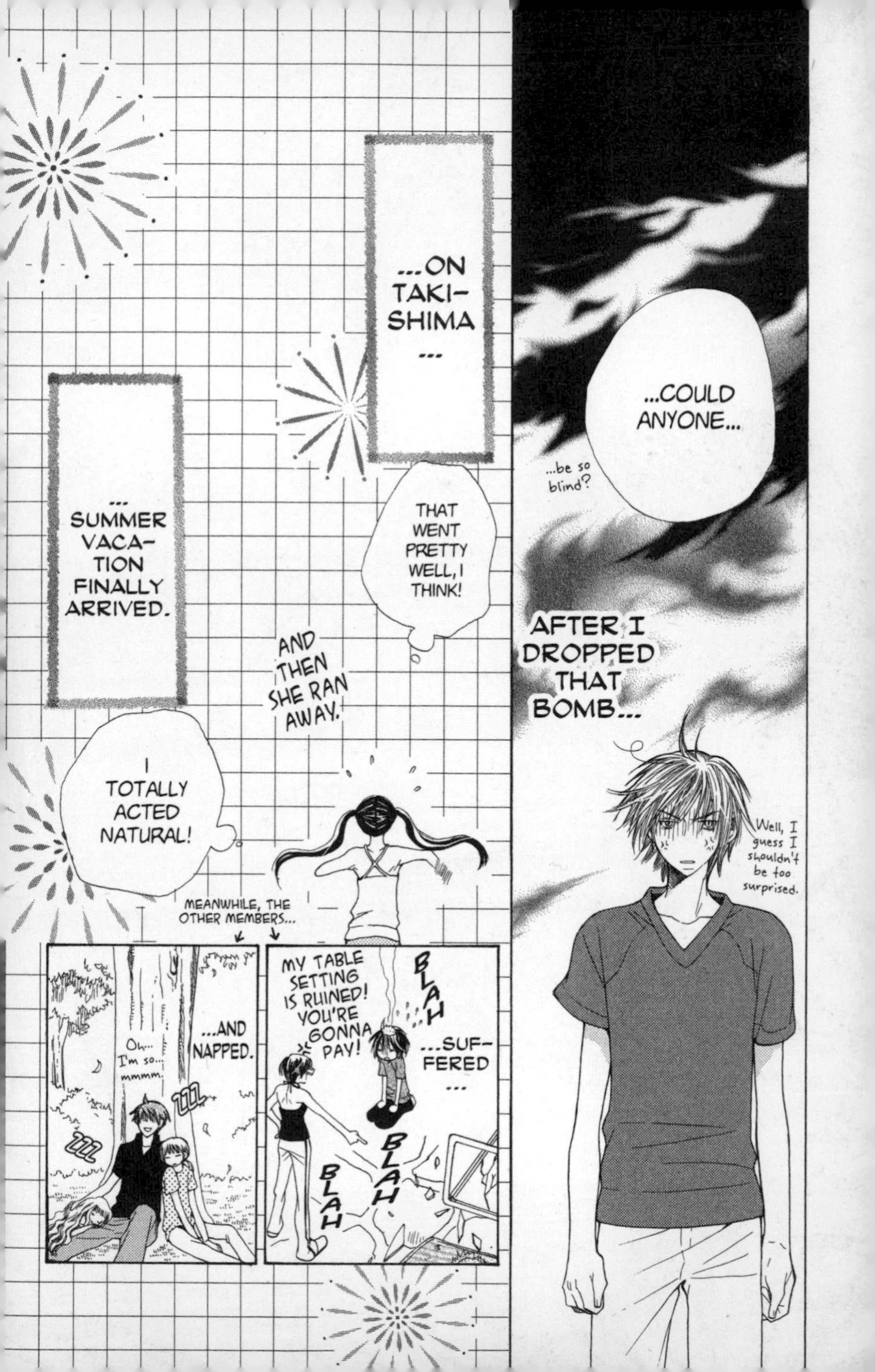
...COULD ANYONE...
...be so blind?
AFTER I DROPPED THAT BOMB...
Well, I guess I shouldn't be too surprised.
...ON TAKI-SHIMA...
... SUMMER VACA-TION FINALLY ARRIVED.
THAT WENT PRETTY WELL, I THINK!
AND THEN SHE RAN AWAY.
I TOTALLY ACTED NATURAL!
MEANWHILE, THE OTHER MEMBERS...
...SUF-FERED...
MY TABLE SETTING IS RUINED! YOU'RE GONNA PAY!
BLAH
BLAH
BLAH
...AND NAPPED.
Oh... I'm so... mmmm.
ZZZ
ZZZ

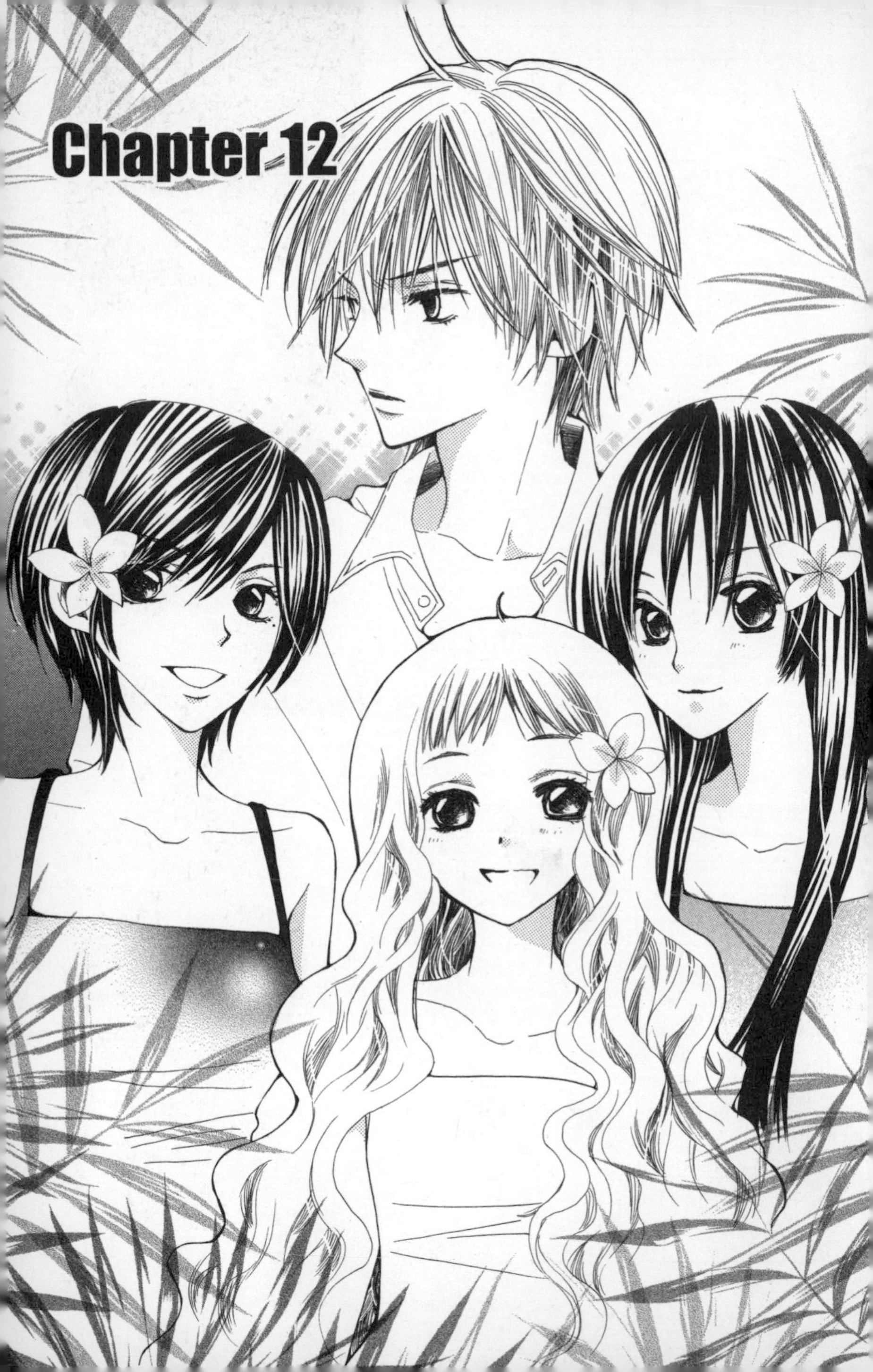
Chapter 12

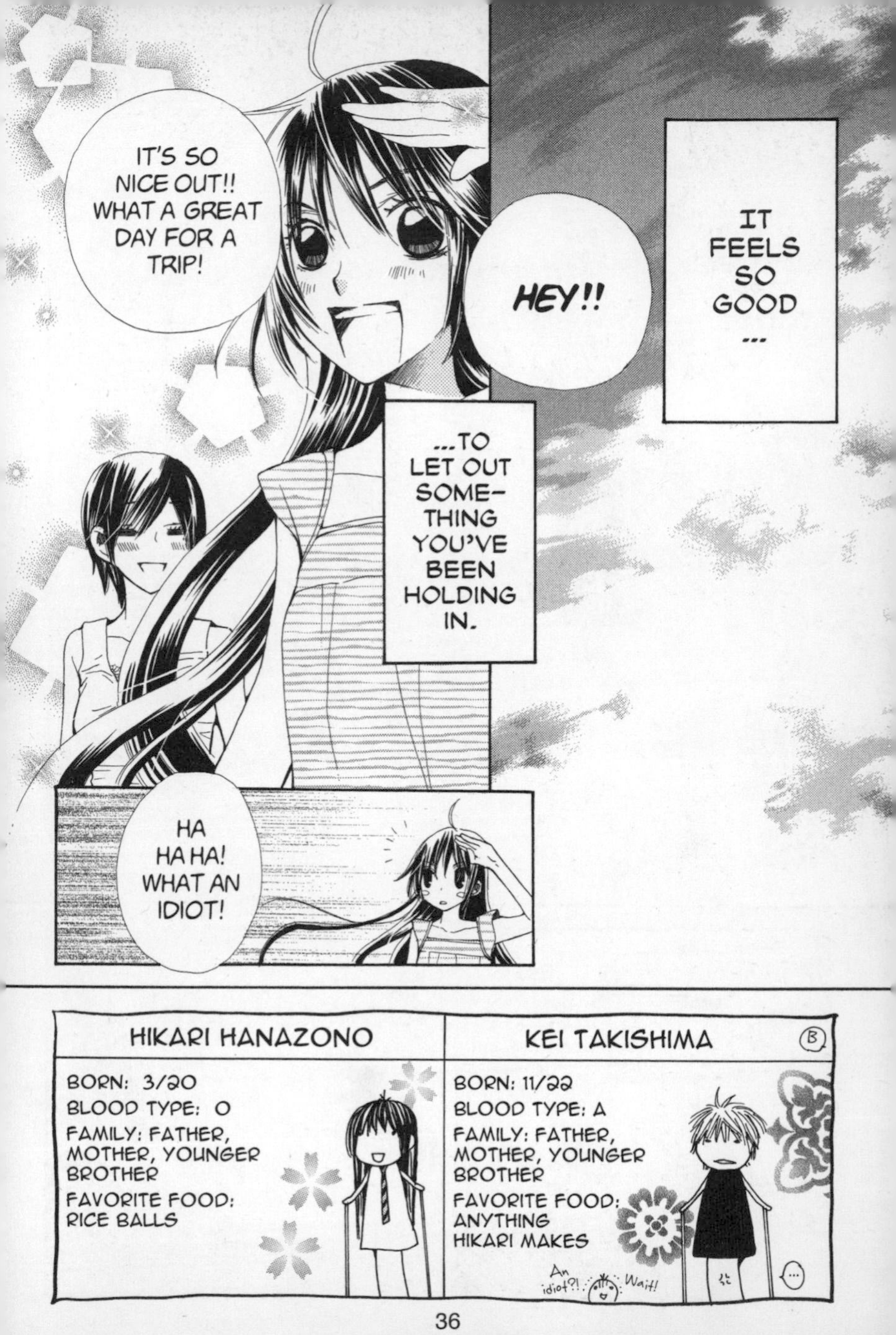
IT FEELS SO GOOD ...
...TO LET OUT SOMETHING YOU'VE BEEN HOLDING IN.
HEY!!
IT'S SO NICE OUT!! WHAT A GREAT DAY FOR A TRIP!
HA HA HA! WHAT AN IDIOT!

HIKARI HANAZONO	KEI TAKISHIMA (B)
BORN: 3/20	BORN: 11/22
BLOOD TYPE: O	BLOOD TYPE: A
FAMILY: FATHER, MOTHER, YOUNGER BROTHER	FAMILY: FATHER, MOTHER, YOUNGER BROTHER
FAVORITE FOOD: RICE BALLS	FAVORITE FOOD: ANYTHING HIKARI MAKES
	An idiot?! Wait! ...

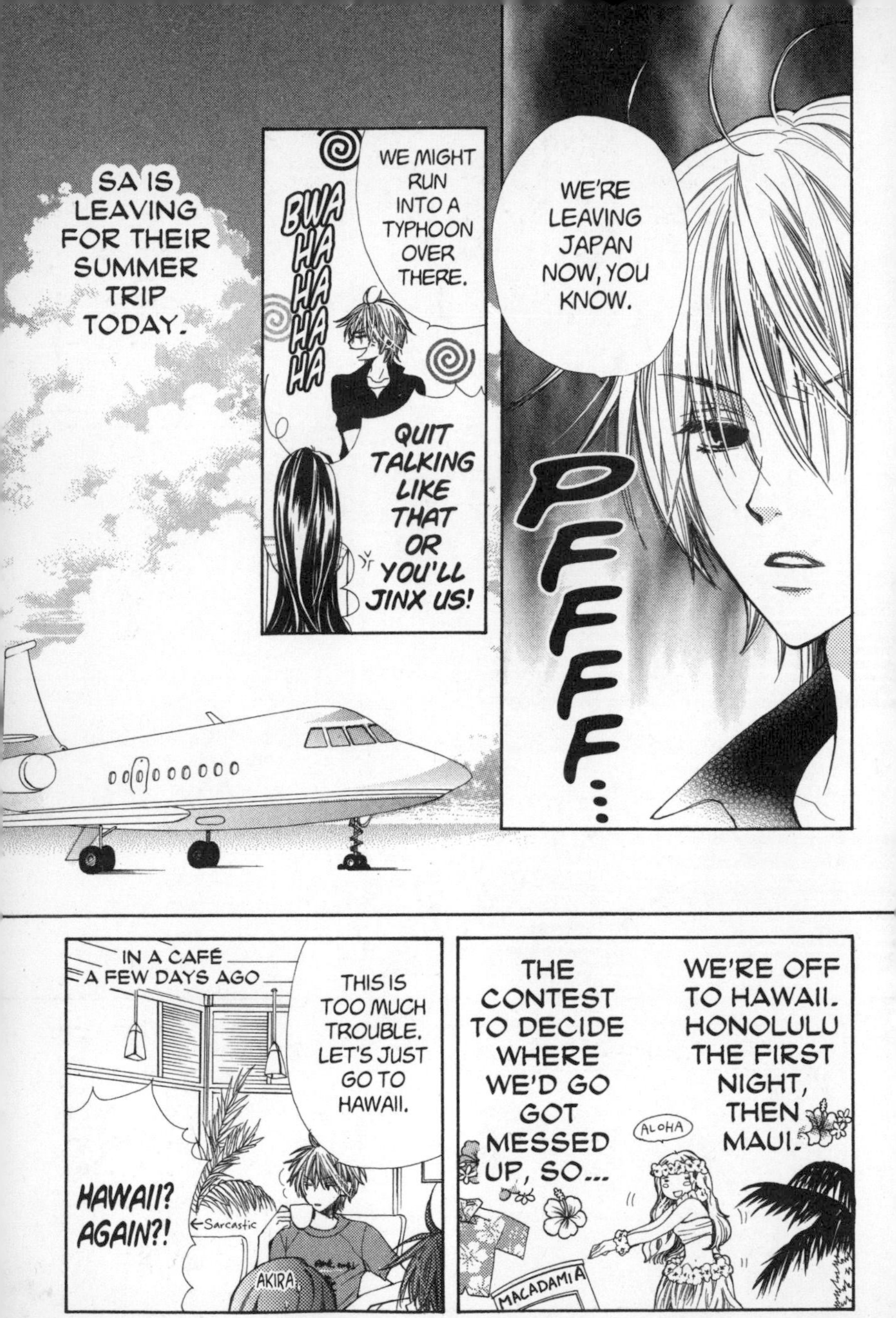
WE'RE LEAVING JAPAN NOW, YOU KNOW.
PFFFF...
WE MIGHT RUN INTO A TYPHOON OVER THERE.
BWA HA HA HA HA HA
QUIT TALKING LIKE THAT OR YOU'LL JINX US!
SA IS LEAVING FOR THEIR SUMMER TRIP TODAY.
WE'RE OFF TO HAWAII. HONOLULU THE FIRST NIGHT, THEN MAUI.
THE CONTEST TO DECIDE WHERE WE'D GO GOT MESSED UP, SO...
ALOHA
MACADAMIA
IN A CAFÉ A FEW DAYS AGO
THIS IS TOO MUCH TROUBLE. LET'S JUST GO TO HAWAII.
HAWAII? AGAIN?!
←Sarcastic
AKIRA

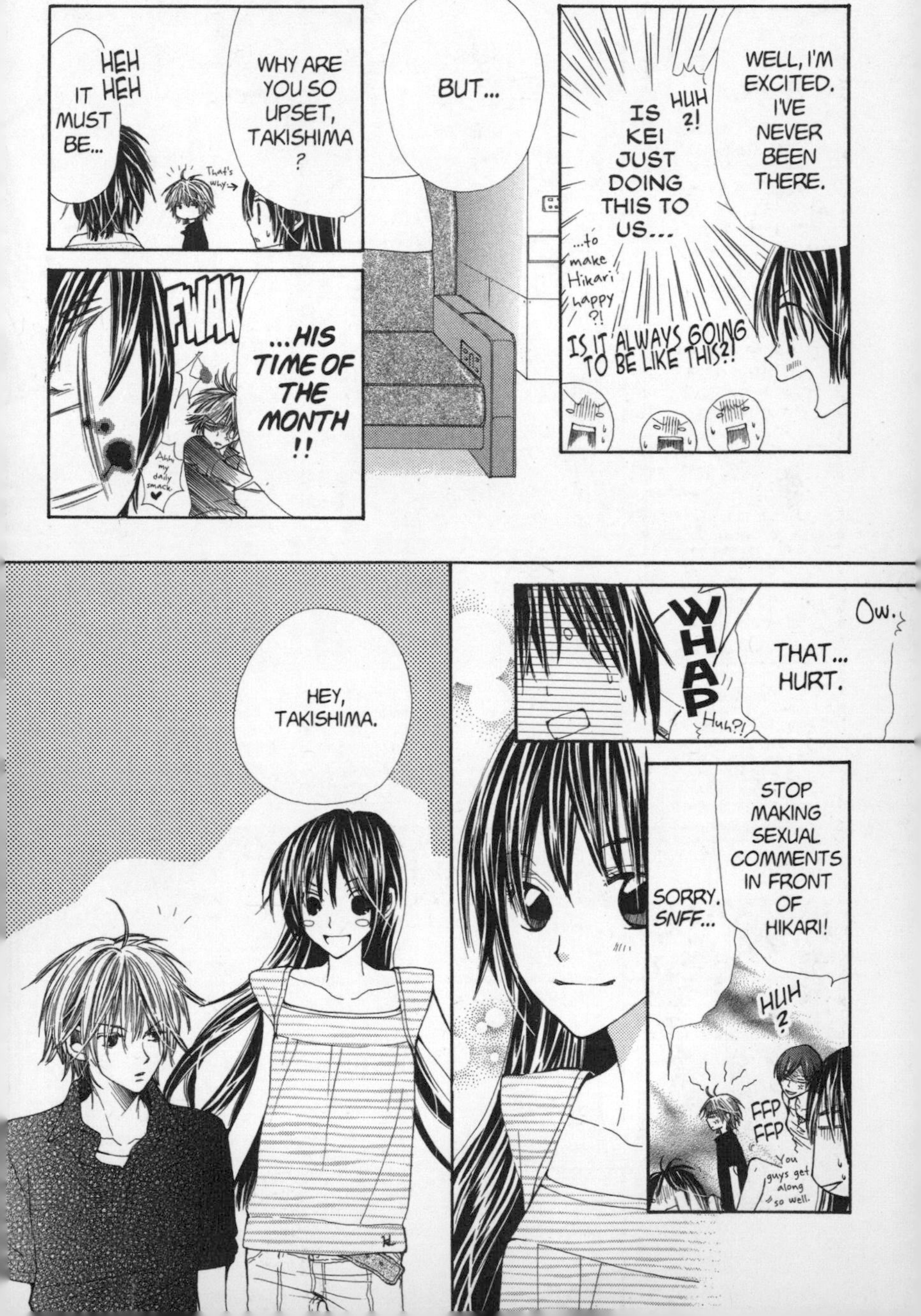
WELL, I'M EXCITED. I'VE NEVER BEEN THERE.
HUH ?!
IS KEI JUST DOING THIS TO US...
...to make Hikari happy ?!
IS IT ALWAYS GOING TO BE LIKE THIS?!
BUT...
WHY ARE YOU SO UPSET, TAKISHIMA ?
HEH HEH
IT MUST BE...
That's why.
FWAK
...HIS TIME OF THE MONTH !!
Ahh my daily smack ♥
Ow.
THAT... HURT.
WHAP
Huh?!
STOP MAKING SEXUAL COMMENTS IN FRONT OF HIKARI!
SORRY. SNFF...
HUH ?
FFP FFP
You guys get along so well.
HEY, TAKISHIMA.

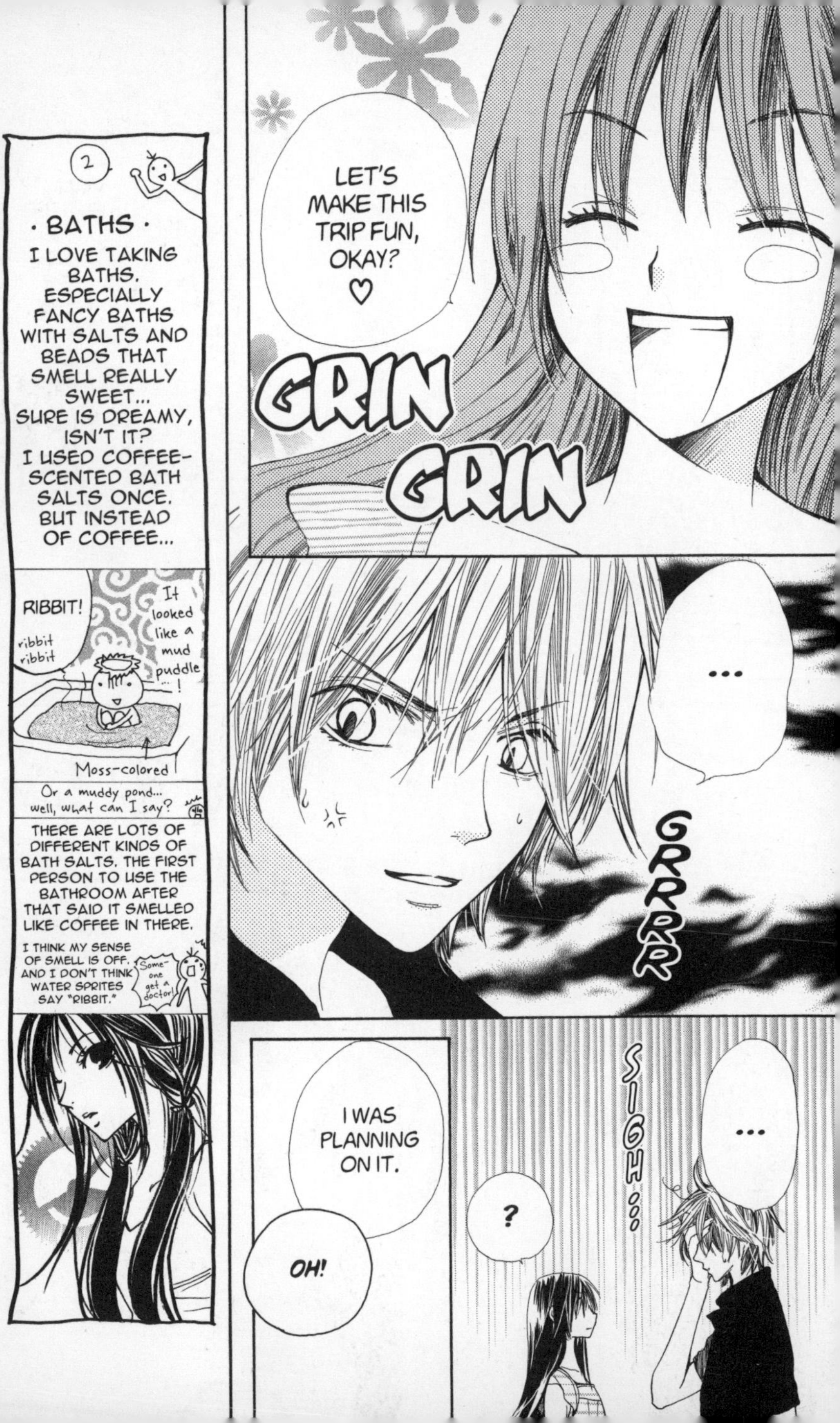
LET'S MAKE THIS TRIP FUN, OKAY? ♡
GRIN GRIN
...
GRRRR
SIGH...
...
?
I WAS PLANNING ON IT.
OH!
2
· BATHS ·
I LOVE TAKING BATHS. ESPECIALLY FANCY BATHS WITH SALTS AND BEADS THAT SMELL REALLY SWEET... SURE IS DREAMY, ISN'T IT? I USED COFFEE-SCENTED BATH SALTS ONCE. BUT INSTEAD OF COFFEE...
RIBBIT!
ribbit ribbit
It looked like a mud puddle...!
Moss-colored
Or a muddy pond... well, what can I say?
THERE ARE LOTS OF DIFFERENT KINDS OF BATH SALTS. THE FIRST PERSON TO USE THE BATHROOM AFTER THAT SAID IT SMELLED LIKE COFFEE IN THERE.
I THINK MY SENSE OF SMELL IS OFF. AND I DON'T THINK WATER SPRITES SAY "RIBBIT."
Someone get a doctor!

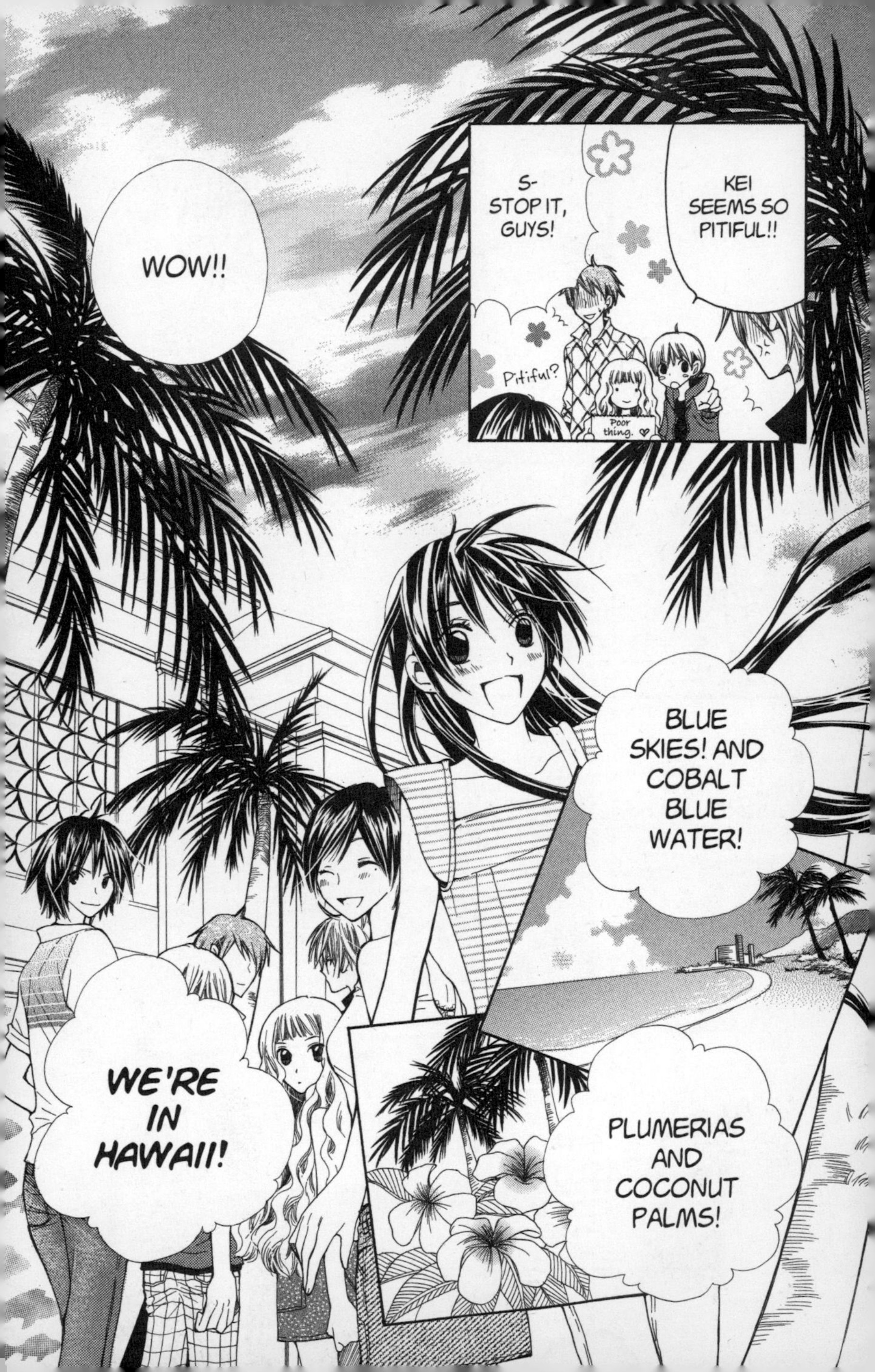
KEI SEEMS SO PITIFUL!!
S-STOP IT, GUYS!
Pitiful?
Poor thing.
WOW!!
BLUE SKIES! AND COBALT BLUE WATER!
PLUMERIAS AND COCONUT PALMS!
WE'RE IN HAWAII!

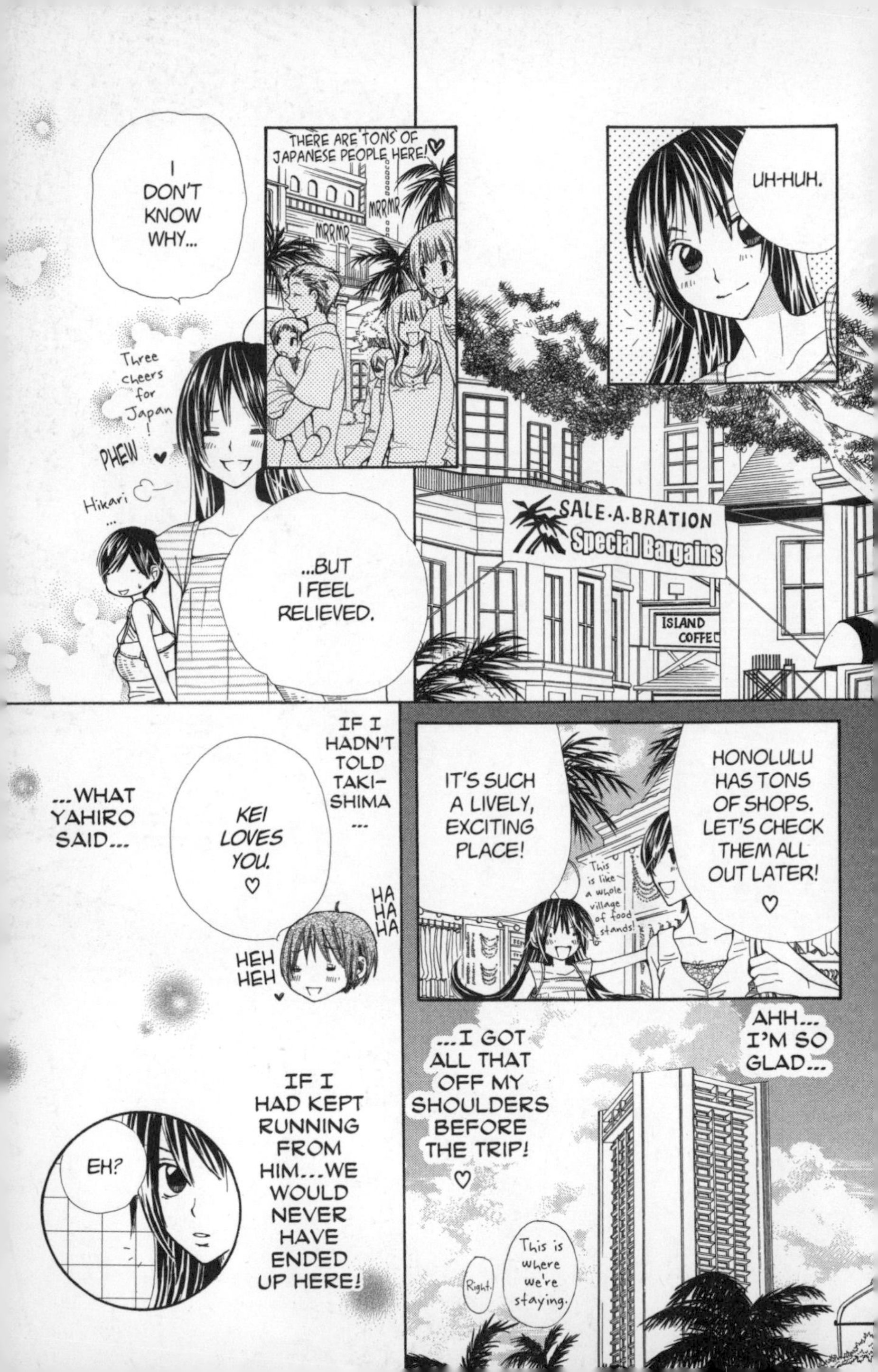
UH-HUH.
THERE ARE TONS OF JAPANESE PEOPLE HERE!
MRRMR
MRRMR
SALE-A-BRATION
Special Bargains
ISLAND COFFE
I DON'T KNOW WHY...
...BUT I FEEL RELIEVED.
Three cheers for Japan!
PHEW
Hikari...
HONOLULU HAS TONS OF SHOPS. LET'S CHECK THEM ALL OUT LATER!
IT'S SUCH A LIVELY, EXCITING PLACE!
This is like a whole village of food stands!
AHH... I'M SO GLAD...
...I GOT ALL THAT OFF MY SHOULDERS BEFORE THE TRIP!
This is where we're staying.
Right.
IF I HADN'T TOLD TAKI-SHIMA...
KEI LOVES YOU.
HA HA HA HA
HEH HEH
...WHAT YAHIRO SAID...
IF I HAD KEPT RUNNING FROM HIM...WE WOULD NEVER HAVE ENDED UP HERE!
EH?

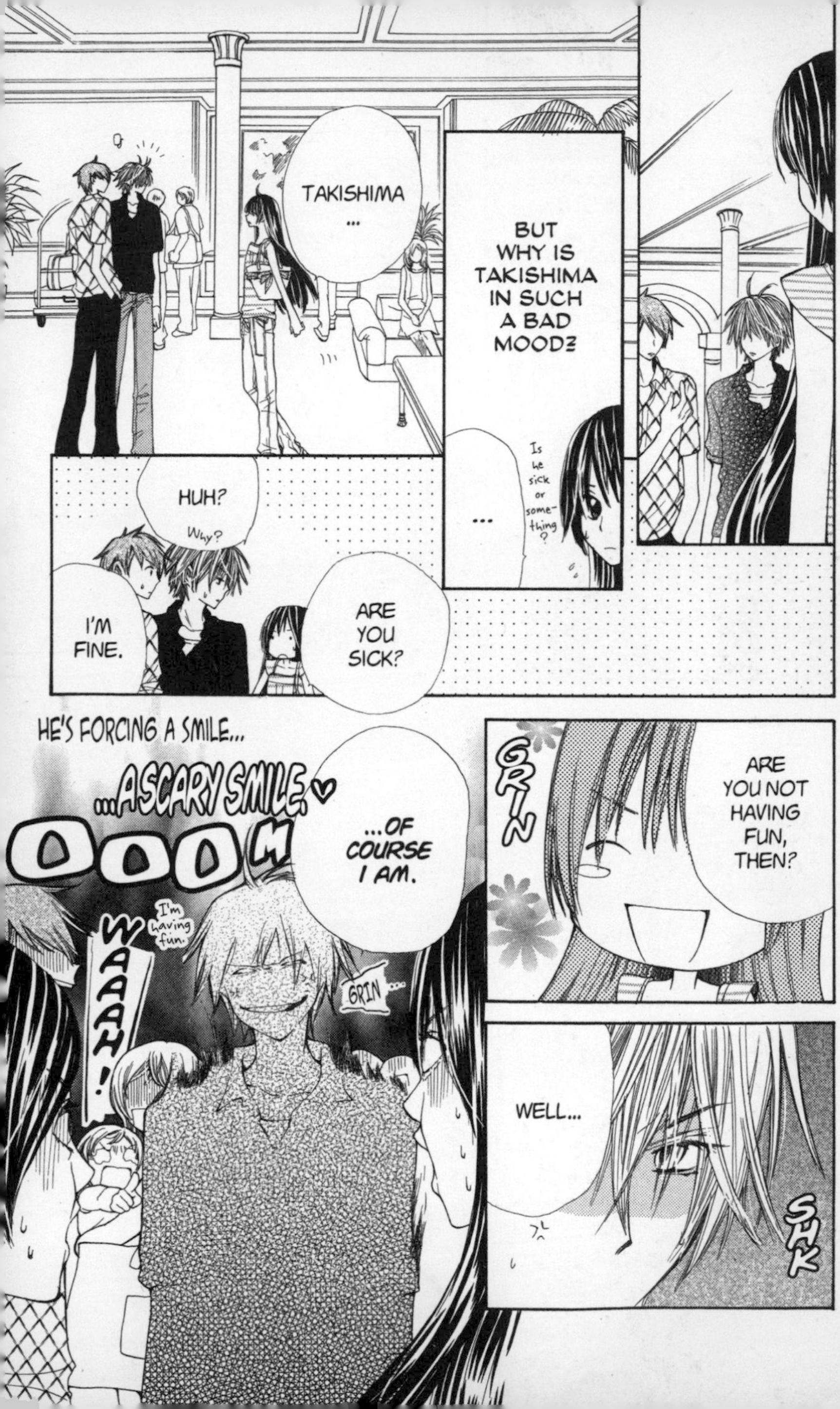
BUT WHY IS TAKISHIMA IN SUCH A BAD MOOD?
...
Is he sick or something?
TAKISHIMA ...
ARE YOU SICK?
HUH?
Why?
I'M FINE.
GRIN
ARE YOU NOT HAVING FUN, THEN?
WELL...
SHK
...OF COURSE I AM.
GRIN...
HE'S FORCING A SMILE...
...A SCARY SMILE.♥
OOOM
I'm having fun.
WAAAAH!

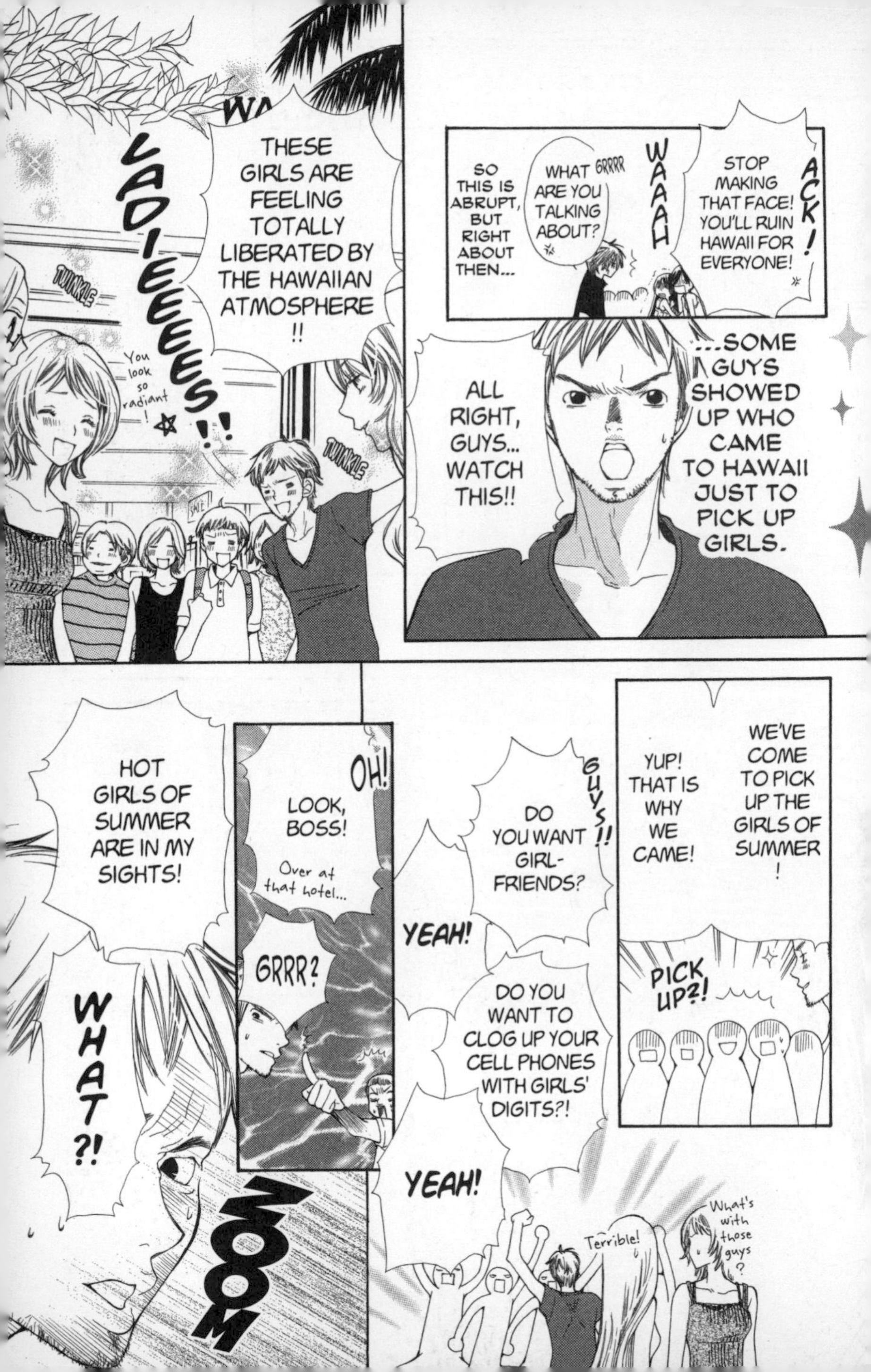
STOP MAKING THAT FACE! YOU'LL RUIN HAWAII FOR EVERYONE!
ACK!
WAAAH
WHAT ARE YOU TALKING ABOUT?
GRRRR
SO THIS IS ABRUPT, BUT RIGHT ABOUT THEN...
...SOME GUYS SHOWED UP WHO CAME TO HAWAII JUST TO PICK UP GIRLS.
ALL RIGHT, GUYS... WATCH THIS!!
WA
LADIEEEEES!!
THESE GIRLS ARE FEELING TOTALLY LIBERATED BY THE HAWAIIAN ATMOSPHERE!!
TWINKLE
TWINKLE
You look so radiant!
WE'VE COME TO PICK UP THE GIRLS OF SUMMER!
YUP! THAT IS WHY WE CAME!
PICK UP?!
GUYS!!
DO YOU WANT GIRL-FRIENDS?
YEAH!
DO YOU WANT TO CLOG UP YOUR CELL PHONES WITH GIRLS' DIGITS?!
YEAH!
What's with those guys?
Terrible!
OH!
LOOK, BOSS!
Over at that hotel...
GRRR?
HOT GIRLS OF SUMMER ARE IN MY SIGHTS!
WHAT?!
ZOOM

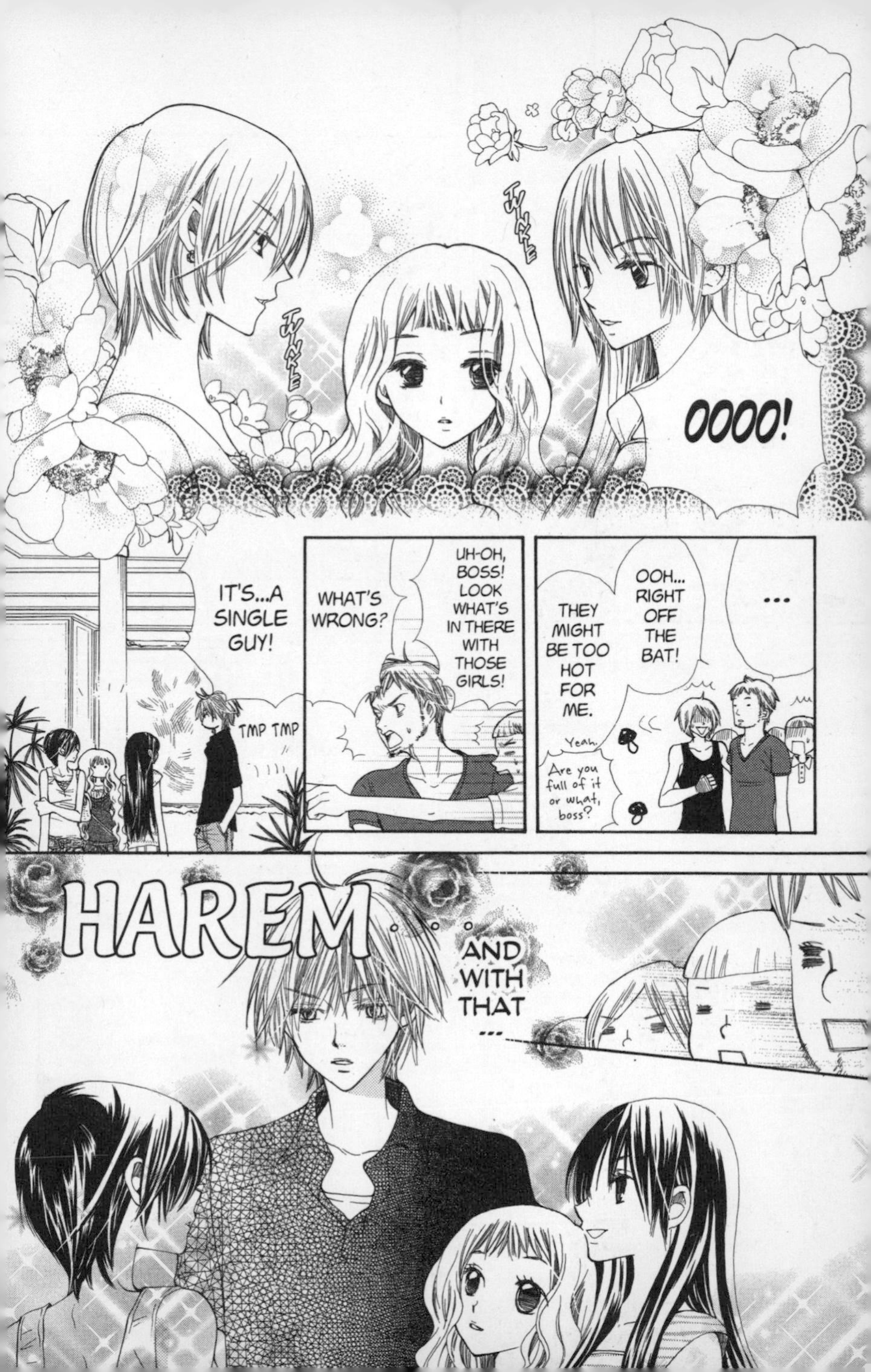
OOOO!
TWINKLE
TWINKLE
...
OOH... RIGHT OFF THE BAT!
THEY MIGHT BE TOO HOT FOR ME.
Yeah.
Are you full of it or what, boss?
UH-OH, BOSS! LOOK WHAT'S IN THERE WITH THOSE GIRLS!
WHAT'S WRONG?
IT'S...A SINGLE GUY!
TMP TMP
AND WITH THAT ...
HAREM...

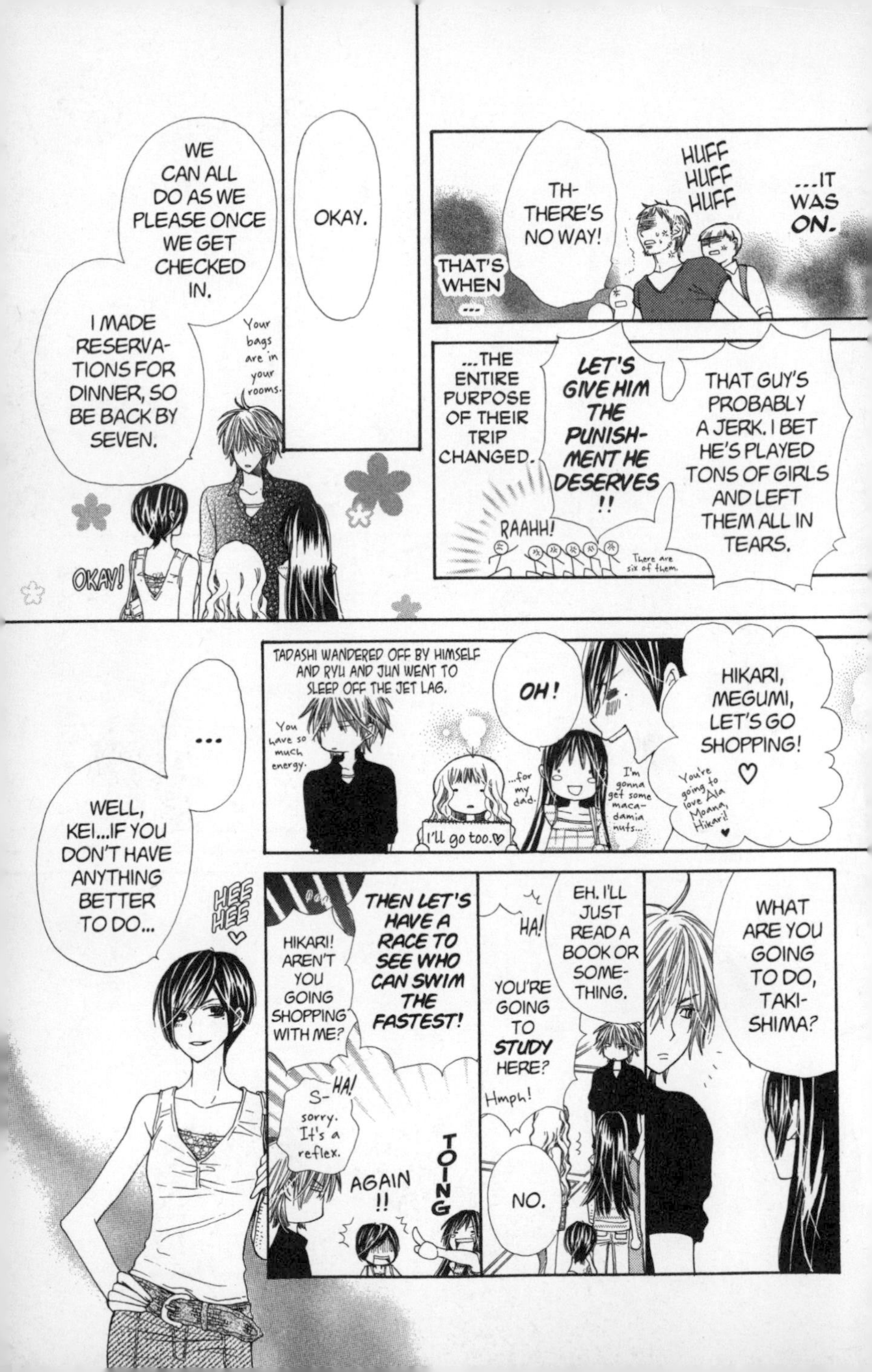
...IT WAS ON.
HUFF HUFF HUFF
TH- THERE'S NO WAY!
THAT'S WHEN ...
THAT GUY'S PROBABLY A JERK. I BET HE'S PLAYED TONS OF GIRLS AND LEFT THEM ALL IN TEARS.
LET'S GIVE HIM THE PUNISHMENT HE DESERVES !!
...THE ENTIRE PURPOSE OF THEIR TRIP CHANGED.
RAAHH!
There are six of them.
OKAY.
Your bags are in your rooms.
WE CAN ALL DO AS WE PLEASE ONCE WE GET CHECKED IN.
I MADE RESERVATIONS FOR DINNER, SO BE BACK BY SEVEN.
OKAY!
HIKARI, MEGUMI, LET'S GO SHOPPING! ♡
You're going to love Ala Moana, Hikari! ♥
OH!
I'm gonna get some macadamia nuts...
...for my dad.
I'll go too.♡
TADASHI WANDERED OFF BY HIMSELF AND RYU AND JUN WENT TO SLEEP OFF THE JET LAG.
You have so much energy.
WHAT ARE YOU GOING TO DO, TAKISHIMA?
EH. I'LL JUST READ A BOOK OR SOMETHING.
HA!
YOU'RE GOING TO STUDY HERE?
Hmph!
NO.
THEN LET'S HAVE A RACE TO SEE WHO CAN SWIM THE FASTEST!
HIKARI! AREN'T YOU GOING SHOPPING WITH ME?
HA!
S- sorry. It's a reflex.
TOING
AGAIN !!
...
WELL, KEI...IF YOU DON'T HAVE ANYTHING BETTER TO DO...
HEE HEE ♡

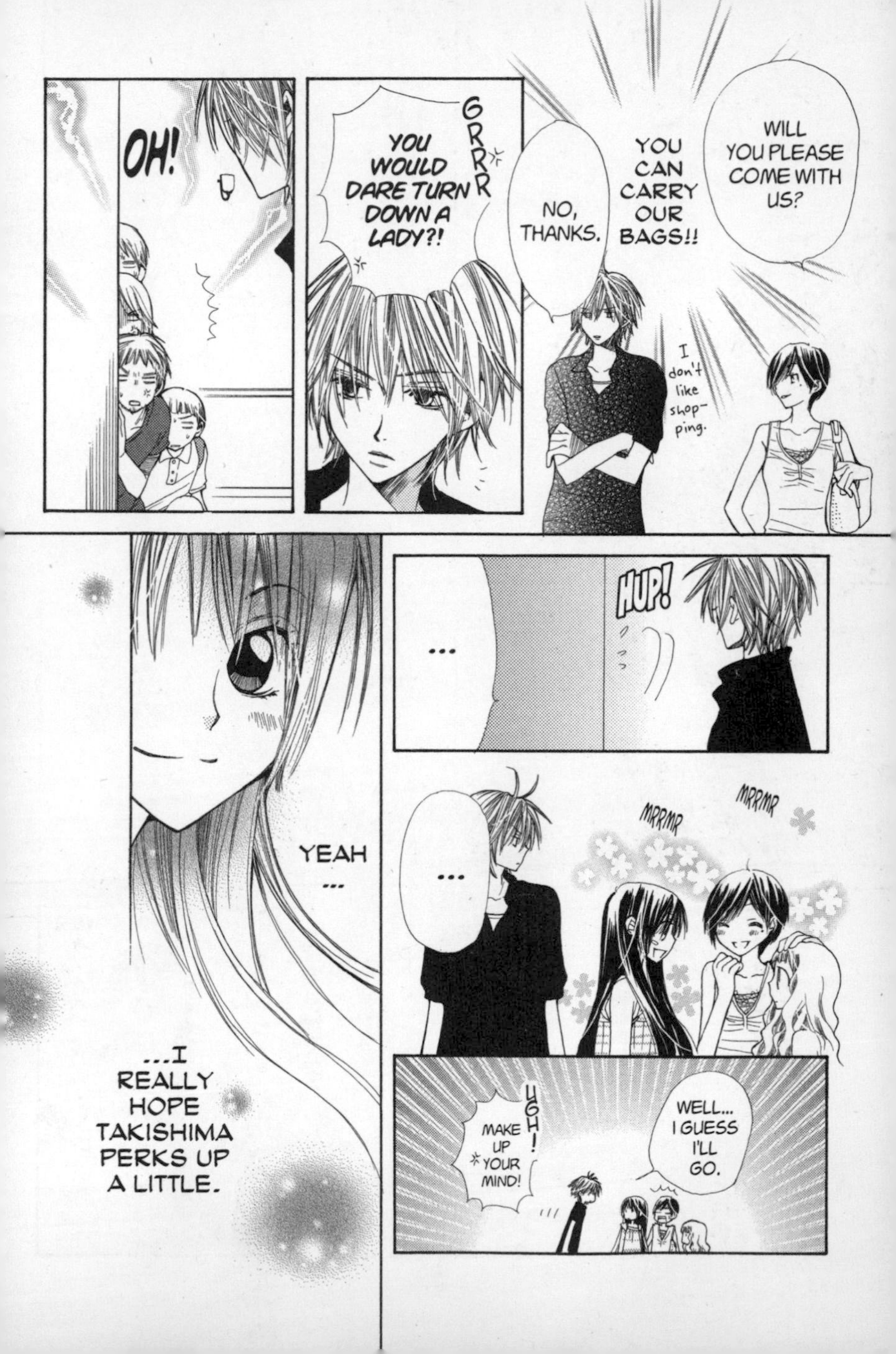
WILL YOU PLEASE COME WITH US?
YOU CAN CARRY OUR BAGS!!
NO, THANKS.
I don't like shopping.
GRRR
YOU WOULD DARE TURN DOWN A LADY?!
OH!
HUP!
...
MRRMR
MRRMR
...
WELL... I GUESS I'LL GO.
UGH!
MAKE UP YOUR MIND!
YEAH ...
...I REALLY HOPE TAKISHIMA PERKS UP A LITTLE.

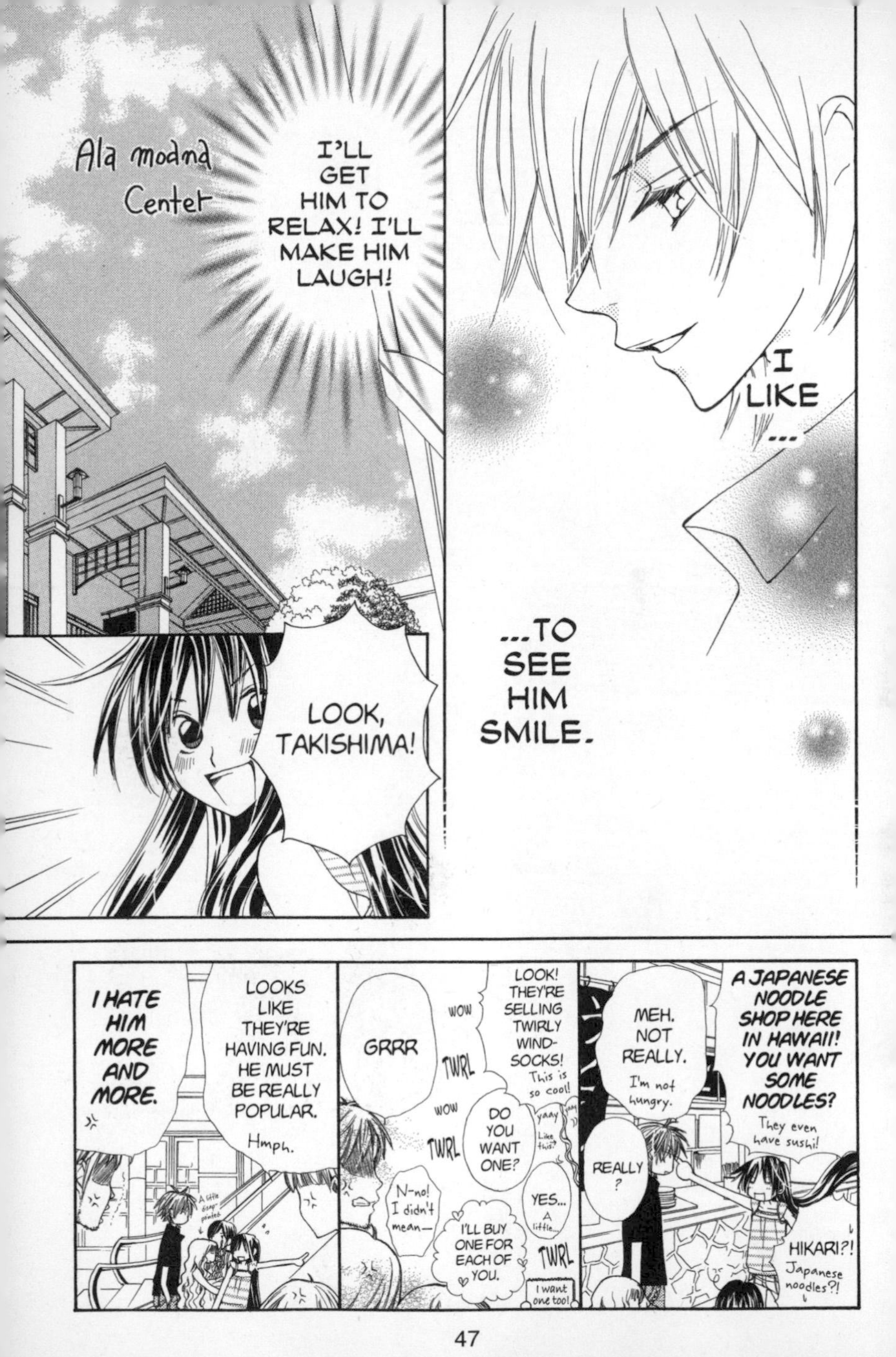
I LIKE...
...TO SEE HIM SMILE.
Ala moana Center
I'LL GET HIM TO RELAX! I'LL MAKE HIM LAUGH!
LOOK, TAKISHIMA!
A JAPANESE NOODLE SHOP HERE IN HAWAII! YOU WANT SOME NOODLES?
They even have sushi!
MEH. NOT REALLY.
I'm not hungry.
REALLY?
HIKARI?!
Japanese noodles?!
LOOK! THEY'RE SELLING TWIRLY WIND-SOCKS!
This is so cool!
yaaay
Like this?
WOW
TWRL
GRRR
WOW
TWRL
DO YOU WANT ONE?
YES... A little...
TWRL
I'LL BUY ONE FOR EACH OF YOU.
N-no! I didn't mean—
I want one too!
LOOKS LIKE THEY'RE HAVING FUN. HE MUST BE REALLY POPULAR.
Hmph.
I HATE HIM MORE AND MORE.
A little disap-pointed

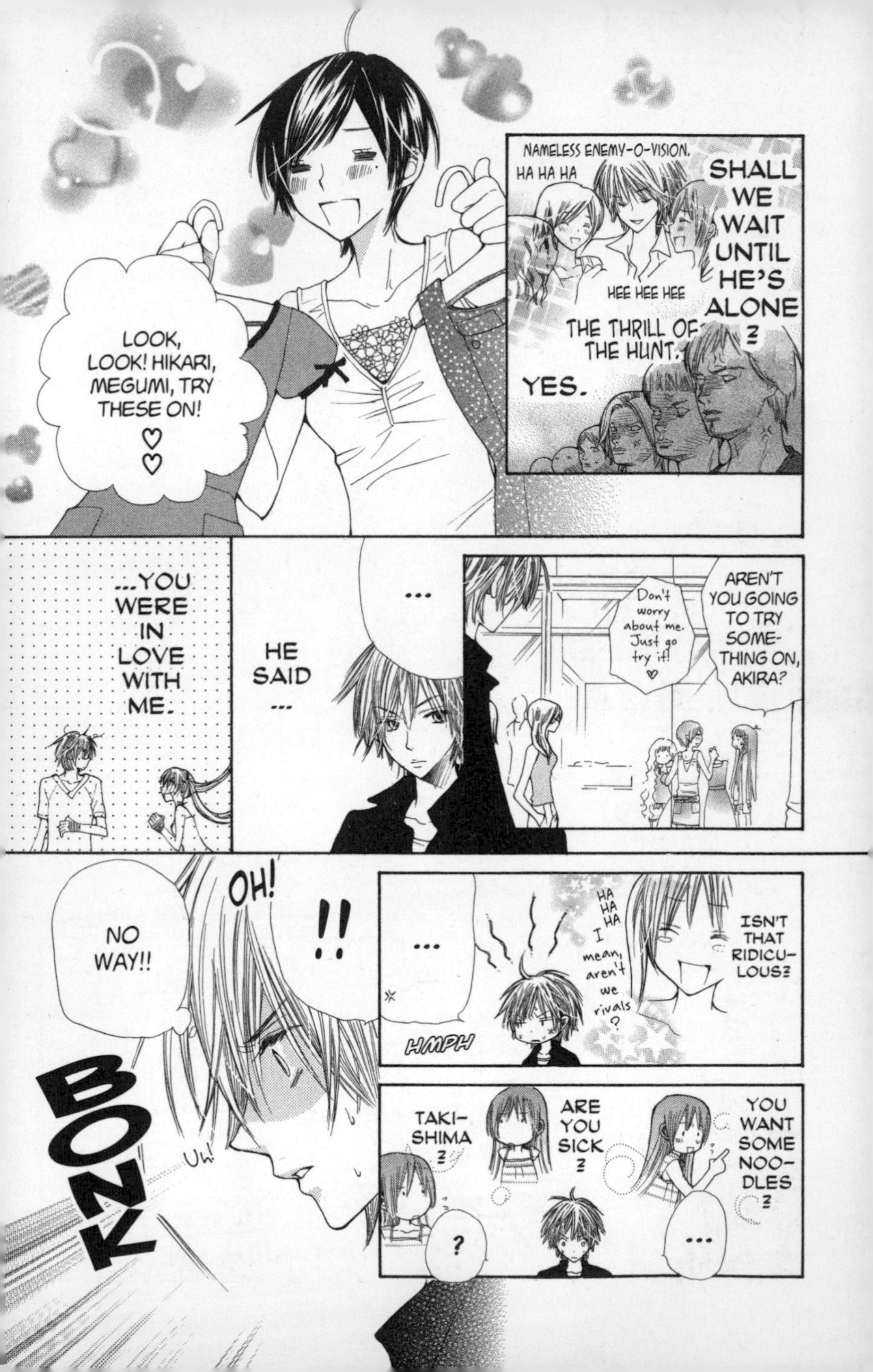
LOOK, LOOK! HIKARI, MEGUMI, TRY THESE ON! ♡ ♡
NAMELESS ENEMY-O-VISION.
SHALL WE WAIT UNTIL HE'S ALONE?
HA HA HA
HEE HEE HEE
THE THRILL OF THE HUNT.
YES.
AREN'T YOU GOING TO TRY SOME-THING ON, AKIRA?
Don't worry about me. Just go try it! ♡
...
HE SAID ...
...YOU WERE IN LOVE WITH ME.
ISN'T THAT RIDICU-LOUS?
HA HA HA
I mean, aren't we rivals?
...
HMPH
YOU WANT SOME NOO-DLES?
ARE YOU SICK?
TAKI-SHIMA?
...
?
OH!
!!
NO WAY!!
BONK
Uh!

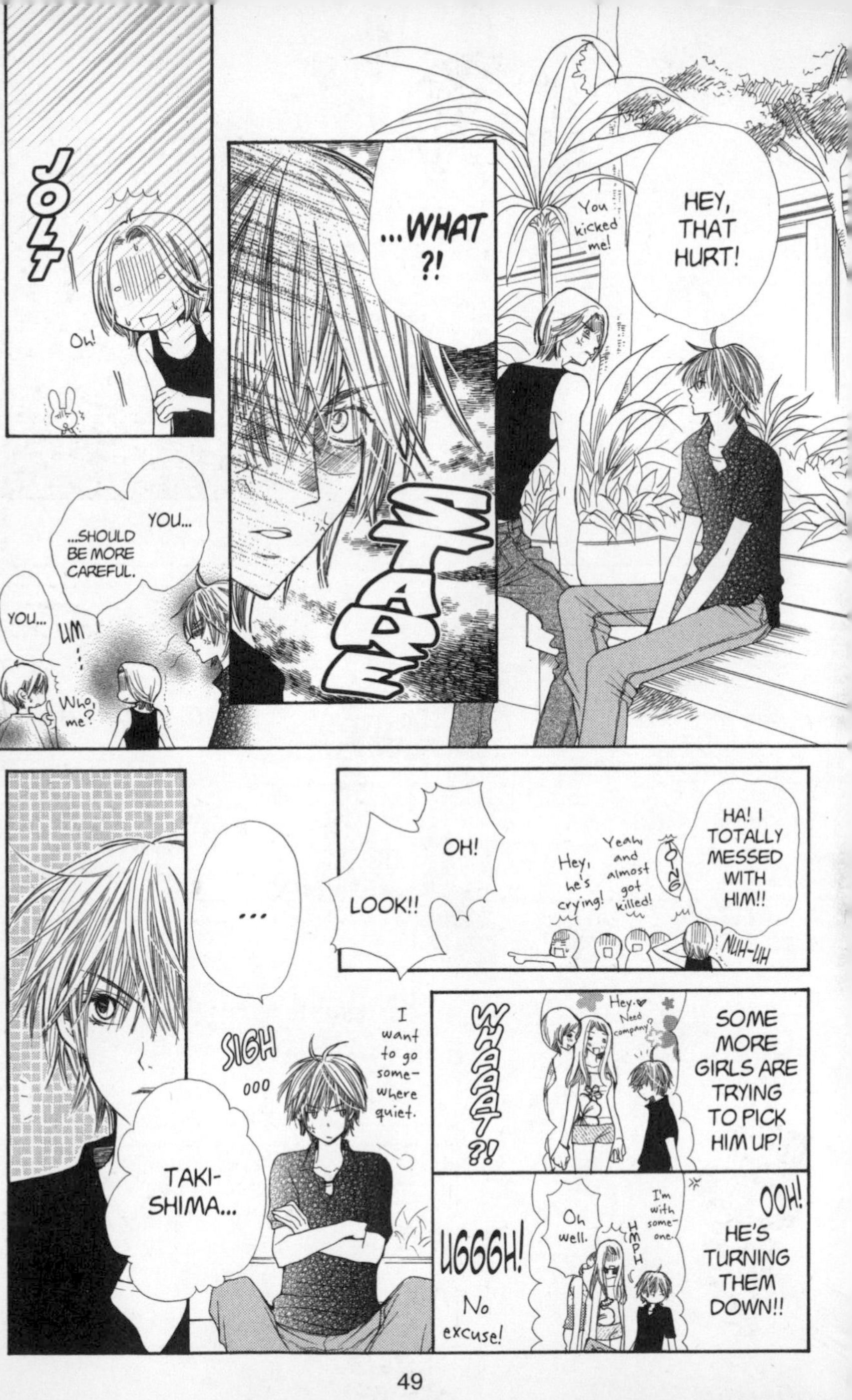
HEY, THAT HURT!
You kicked me!
...WHAT?!
STARE
JOLT
Oh!
YOU...
...SHOULD BE MORE CAREFUL.
YOU...
UM...
Who, me?
HA! I TOTALLY MESSED WITH HIM!!
TOING
NUH-UH
Yeah, and almost got killed!
Hey, he's crying!
OH!
LOOK!!
SOME MORE GIRLS ARE TRYING TO PICK HIM UP!
Hey. Need company?
WHAAAT?!
OOH!
HE'S TURNING THEM DOWN!!
I'm with someone.
HMPH
Oh well.
UGGGH!
No excuse!
...
I want to go somewhere quiet.
SIGH
ooo
TAKI-SHIMA...

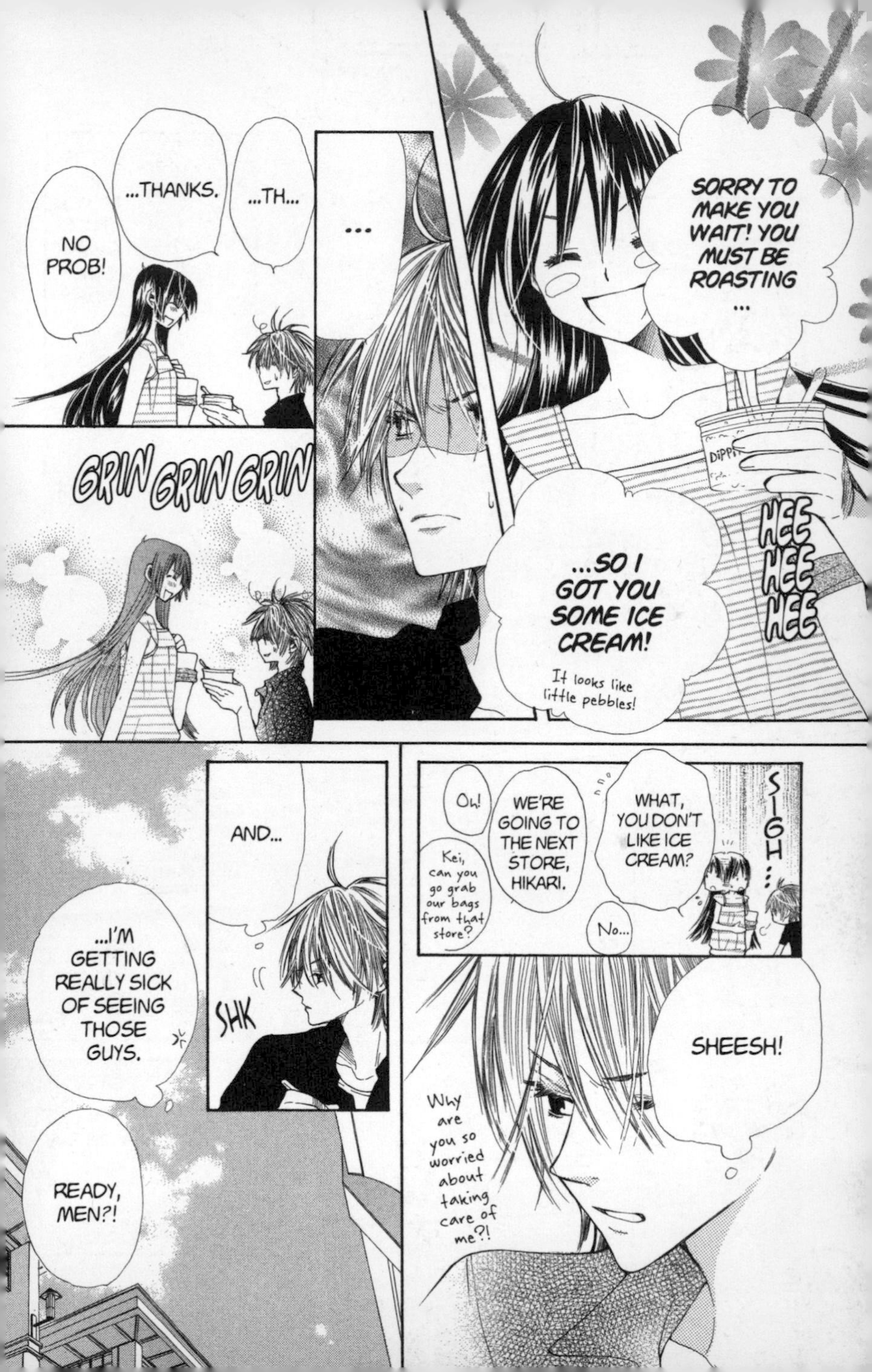
SORRY TO MAKE YOU WAIT! YOU MUST BE ROASTING ...
HEE HEE HEE
...SO I GOT YOU SOME ICE CREAM!
It looks like little pebbles!
...
...TH...
...THANKS.
NO PROB!
GRIN GRIN GRIN
SIGH...
WHAT, YOU DON'T LIKE ICE CREAM?
No...
WE'RE GOING TO THE NEXT STORE, HIKARI.
Oh!
Kei, can you go grab our bags from that store?
SHEESH!
Why are you so worried about taking care of me?!
AND...
SHK
...I'M GETTING REALLY SICK OF SEEING THOSE GUYS.
READY, MEN?!

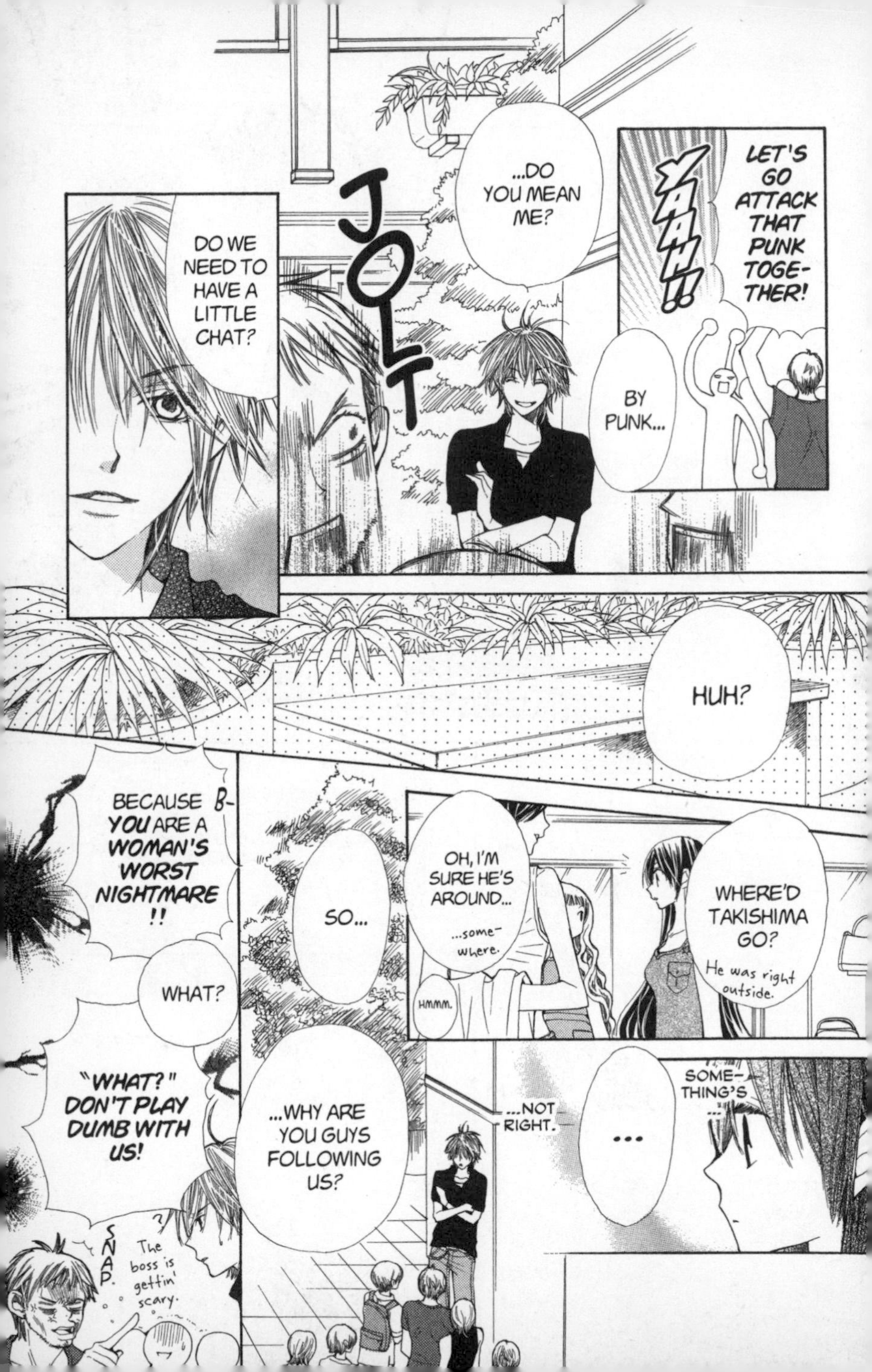
LET'S GO ATTACK THAT PUNK TOGE-THER!
BY PUNK...
...DO YOU MEAN ME?
JOLT
DO WE NEED TO HAVE A LITTLE CHAT?
HUH?
WHERE'D TAKISHIMA GO?
He was right outside.
OH, I'M SURE HE'S AROUND...
...some-where.
HMMM.
SOME-THING'S...
...
...NOT RIGHT.
SO...
B-
BECAUSE YOU ARE A WOMAN'S WORST NIGHTMARE!!
WHAT?
"WHAT?" DON'T PLAY DUMB WITH US!
...WHY ARE YOU GUYS FOLLOWING US?
SNAP.
The boss is gettin' scary.

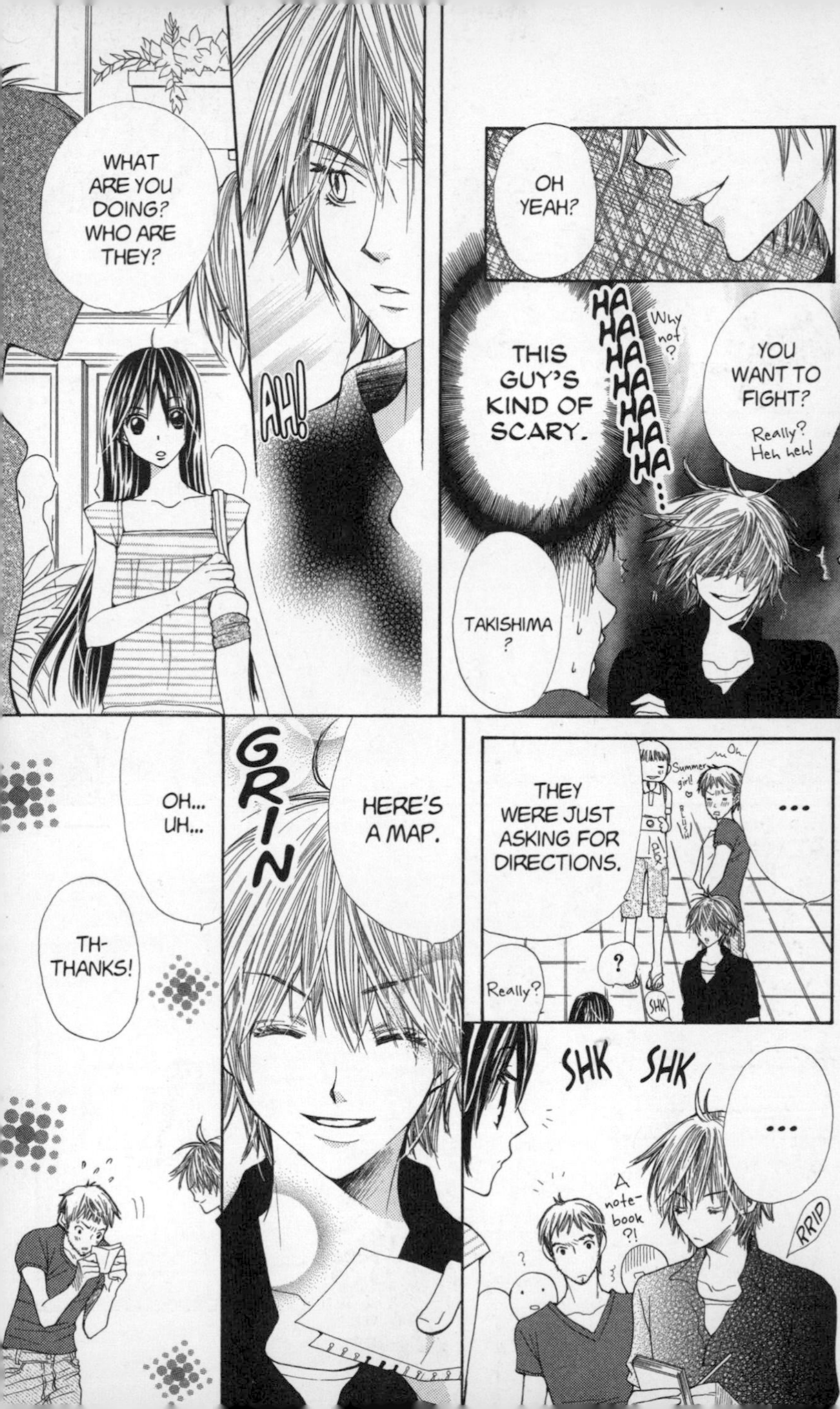
OH YEAH?
YOU WANT TO FIGHT?
Really? Heh heh!
Why not?
HAHAHAHAHAHAHA...
THIS GUY'S KIND OF SCARY.
TAKISHIMA?
AH!
WHAT ARE YOU DOING? WHO ARE THEY?
...
Oh...
Summer girl!
BLUSH
THEY WERE JUST ASKING FOR DIRECTIONS.
?
Really?
SHK
SHK SHK
...
RRIP
A notebook?!
GRIN
HERE'S A MAP.
OH... UH...
TH-THANKS!

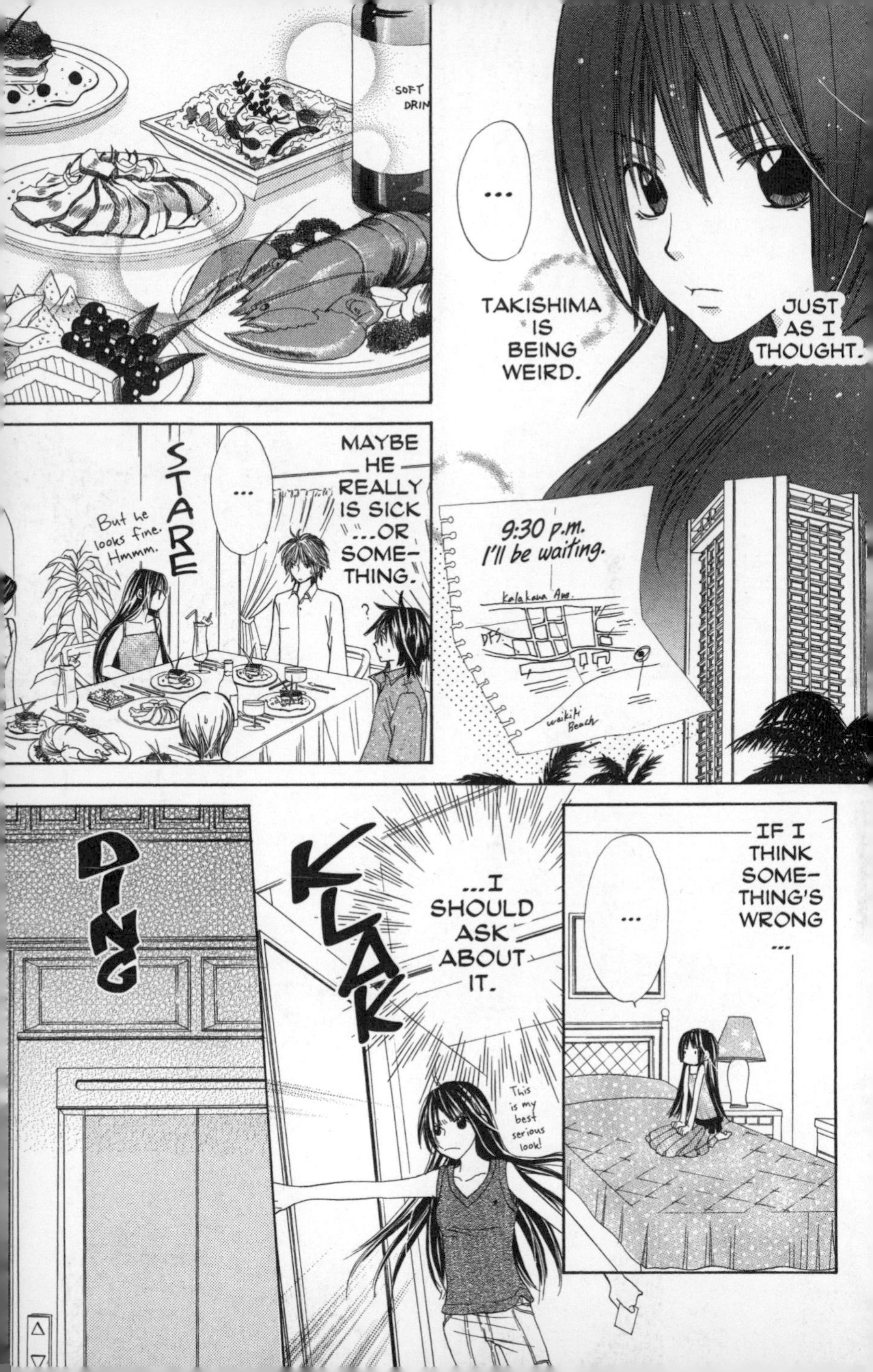
SOFT DRIN
...
JUST AS I THOUGHT.
TAKISHIMA IS BEING WEIRD.
9:30 p.m. I'll be waiting.
Kalakaua Ave.
DFS
waikiki Beach
MAYBE HE REALLY IS SICK ...OR SOME-THING.
...
STARE
But he looks fine. Hmmm.
?
IF I THINK SOME-THING'S WRONG ...
...
...I SHOULD ASK ABOUT IT.
This is my best serious look!
KLAK
DING

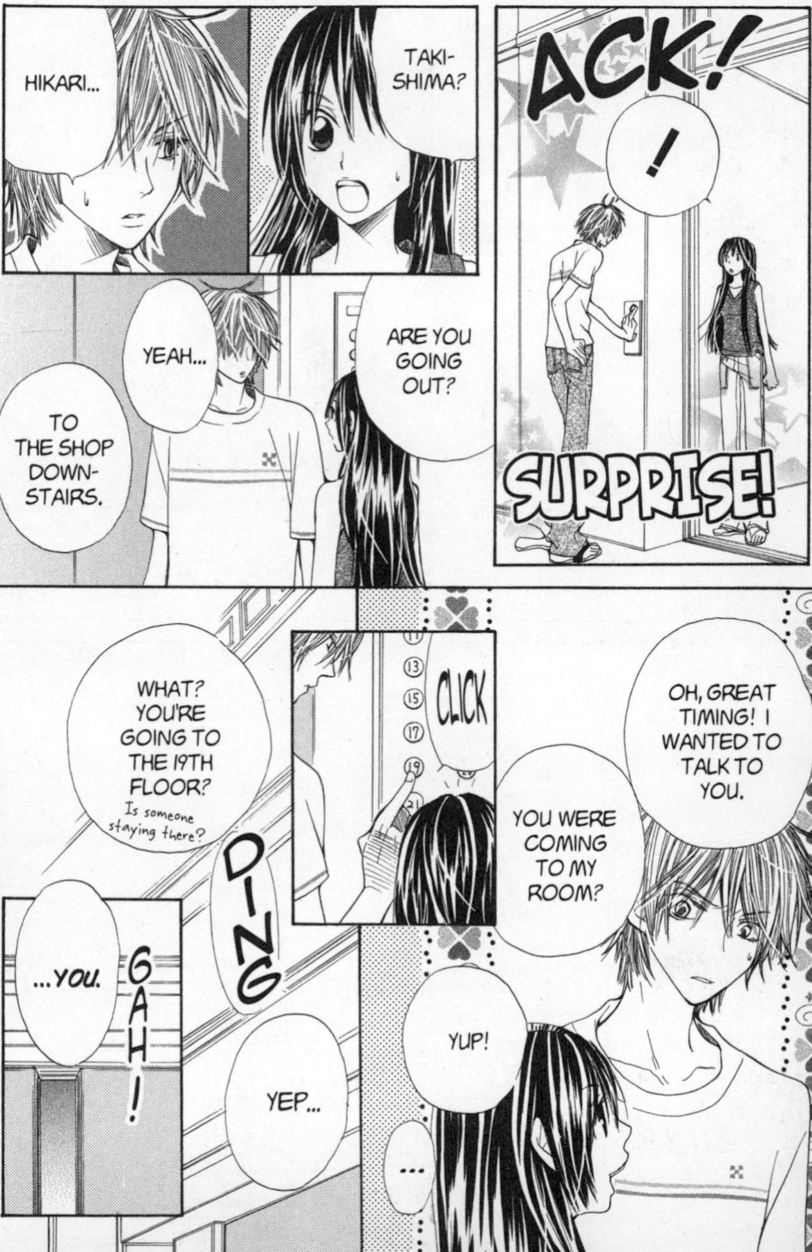
ACK!
!
SURPRISE!
TAKI-SHIMA?
HIKARI...
ARE YOU GOING OUT?
YEAH...
TO THE SHOP DOWN-STAIRS.
OH, GREAT TIMING! I WANTED TO TALK TO YOU.
YOU WERE COMING TO MY ROOM?
YUP!
...
CLICK
WHAT? YOU'RE GOING TO THE 19TH FLOOR?
Is someone staying there?
DING
YEP...
...YOU.
GAH!

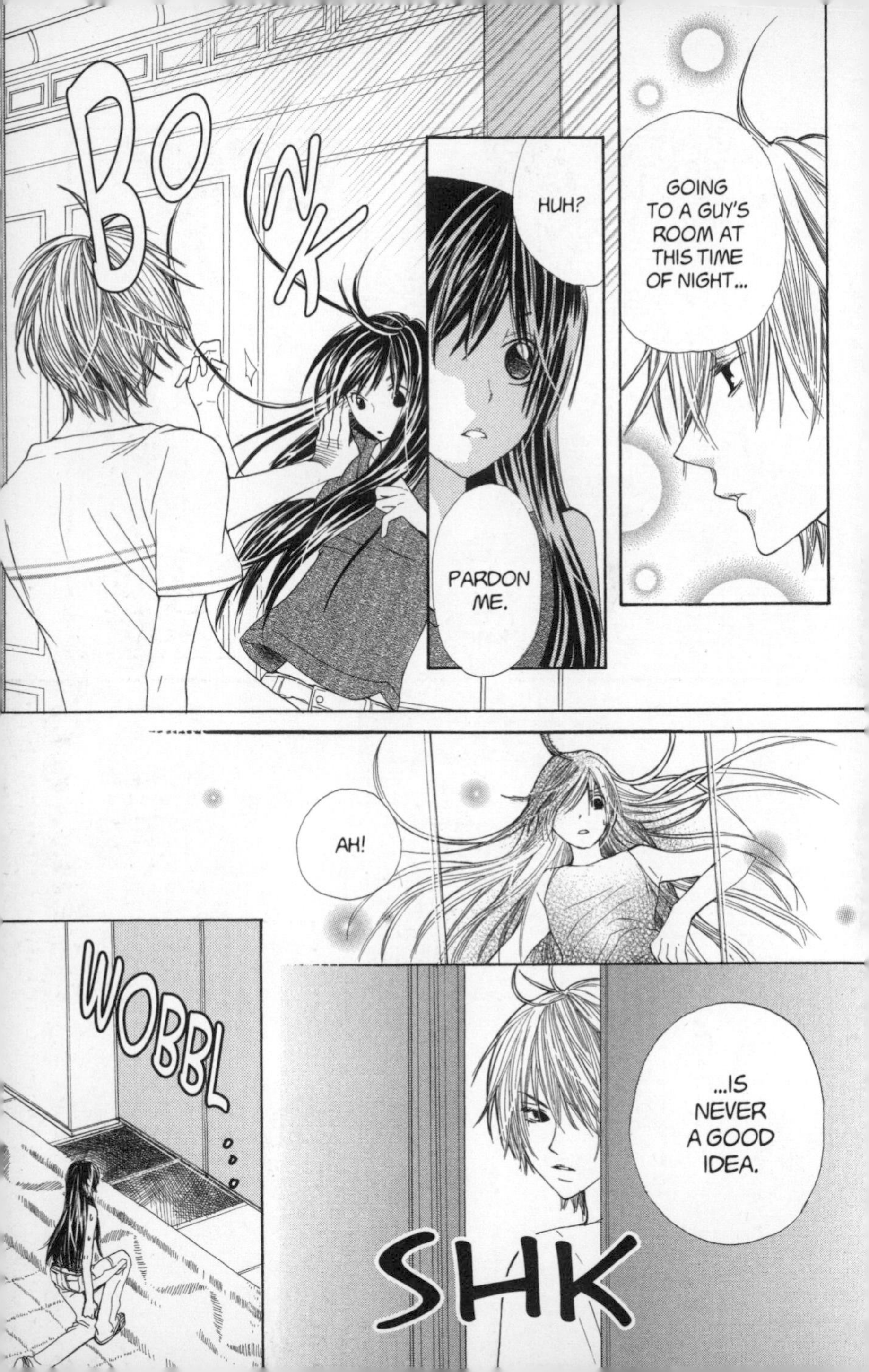
GOING TO A GUY'S ROOM AT THIS TIME OF NIGHT...
HUH?
PARDON ME.
BONK
AH!
...IS NEVER A GOOD IDEA.
SHK
WOBBL...

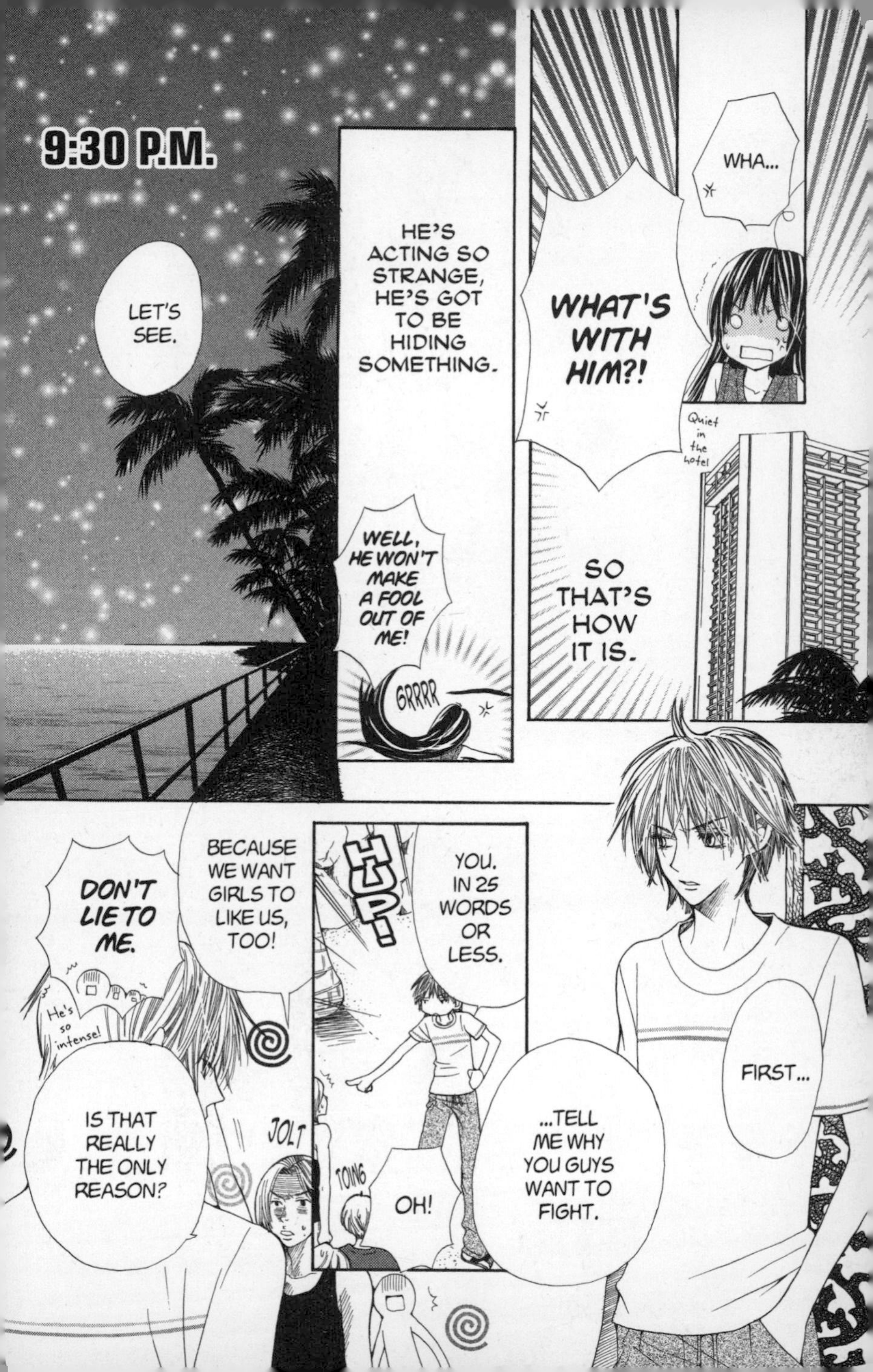
WHA...
WHAT'S WITH HIM?!
Quiet in the hotel
SO THAT'S HOW IT IS.
HE'S ACTING SO STRANGE, HE'S GOT TO BE HIDING SOMETHING.
WELL, HE WON'T MAKE A FOOL OUT OF ME!
GRRRR
9:30 P.M.
LET'S SEE.
FIRST...
...TELL ME WHY YOU GUYS WANT TO FIGHT.
YOU. IN 25 WORDS OR LESS.
HUP!
TOING
OH!
BECAUSE WE WANT GIRLS TO LIKE US, TOO!
DON'T LIE TO ME.
He's so intense!
JOLT
IS THAT REALLY THE ONLY REASON?

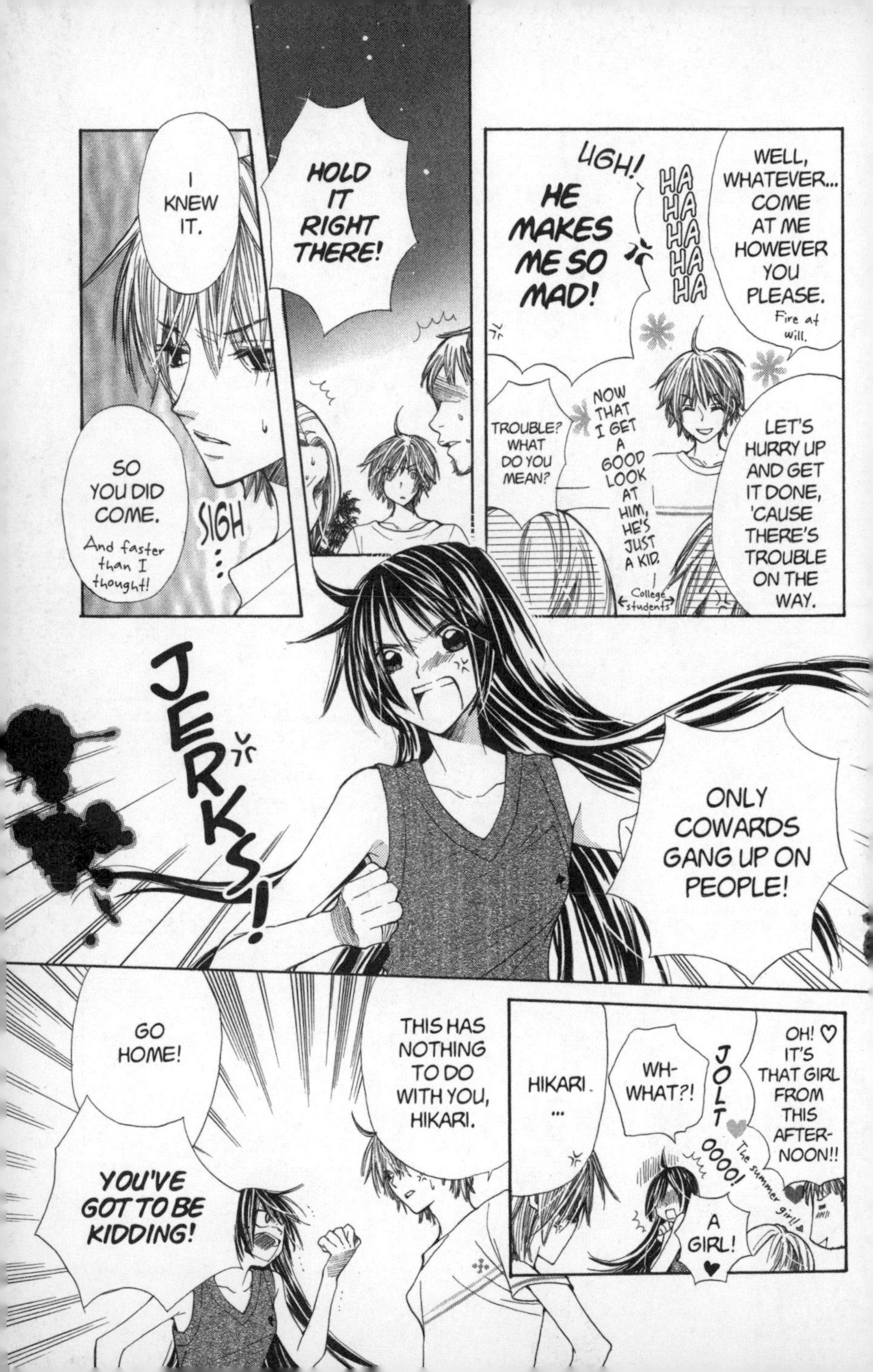
WELL, WHATEVER... COME AT ME HOWEVER YOU PLEASE.
Fire at will.
HAHAHAHAHA
UGH!
HE MAKES ME SO MAD!
LET'S HURRY UP AND GET IT DONE, 'CAUSE THERE'S TROUBLE ON THE WAY.
NOW THAT I GET A GOOD LOOK AT HIM, HE'S JUST A KID.
TROUBLE? WHAT DO YOU MEAN?
College students
HOLD IT RIGHT THERE!
I KNEW IT.
SO YOU DID COME.
SIGH...
And faster than I thought!
ONLY COWARDS GANG UP ON PEOPLE!
JERKS!
OH! ♡ IT'S THAT GIRL FROM THIS AFTERNOON!!
The summer girl!!
JOLT
WH-WHAT?!
OOOO!
A GIRL! ♥
HIKARI...
THIS HAS NOTHING TO DO WITH YOU, HIKARI.
GO HOME!
YOU'VE GOT TO BE KIDDING!

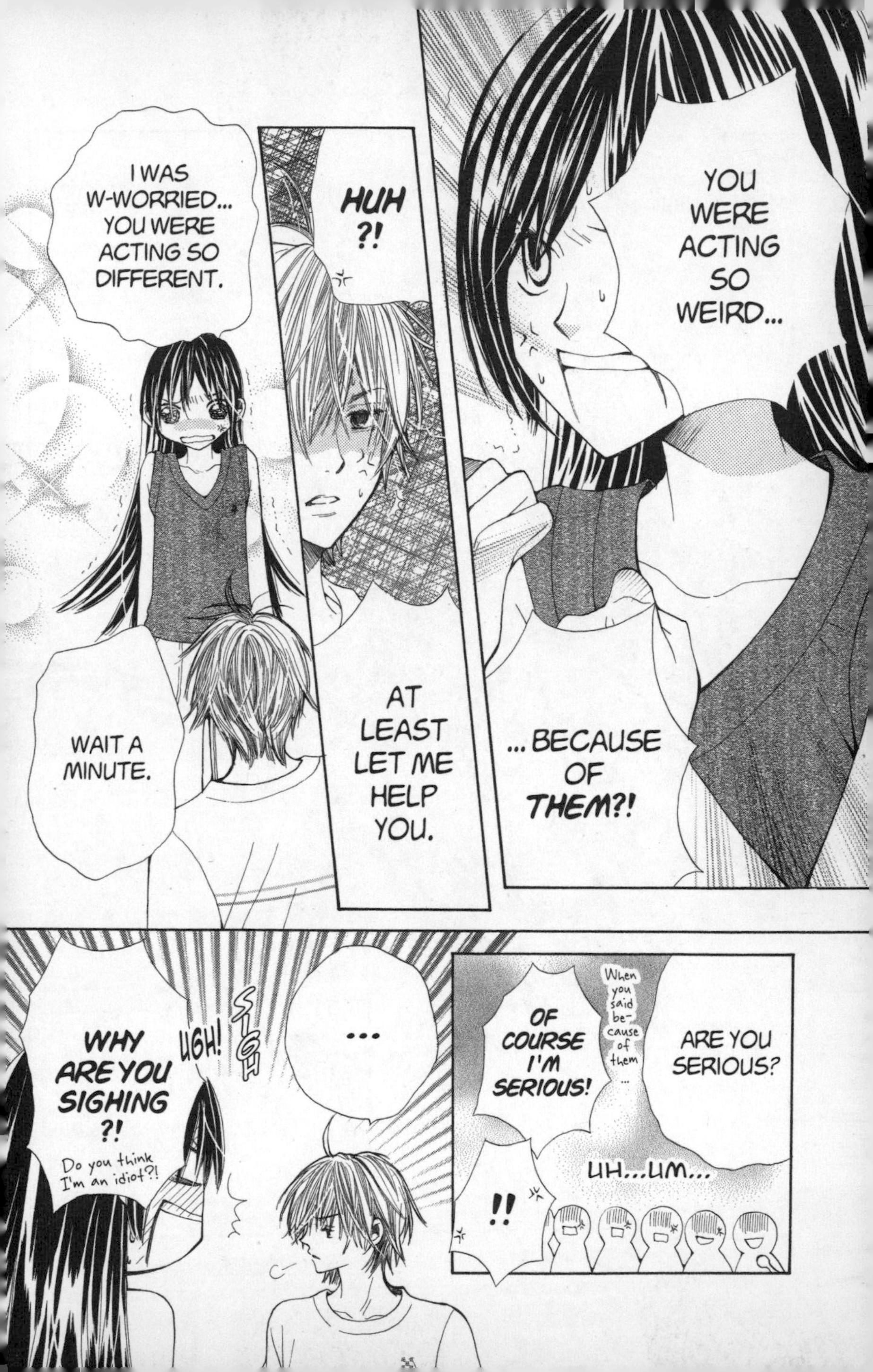
YOU WERE ACTING SO WEIRD...
...BECAUSE OF THEM?!
HUH ?!
AT LEAST LET ME HELP YOU.
I WAS W-WORRIED... YOU WERE ACTING SO DIFFERENT.
WAIT A MINUTE.
ARE YOU SERIOUS?
When you said be-cause of them ...
OF COURSE I'M SERIOUS!
UH...UM...
!!
...
SIGH
UGH!
WHY ARE YOU SIGHING ?!
Do you think I'm an idiot?!

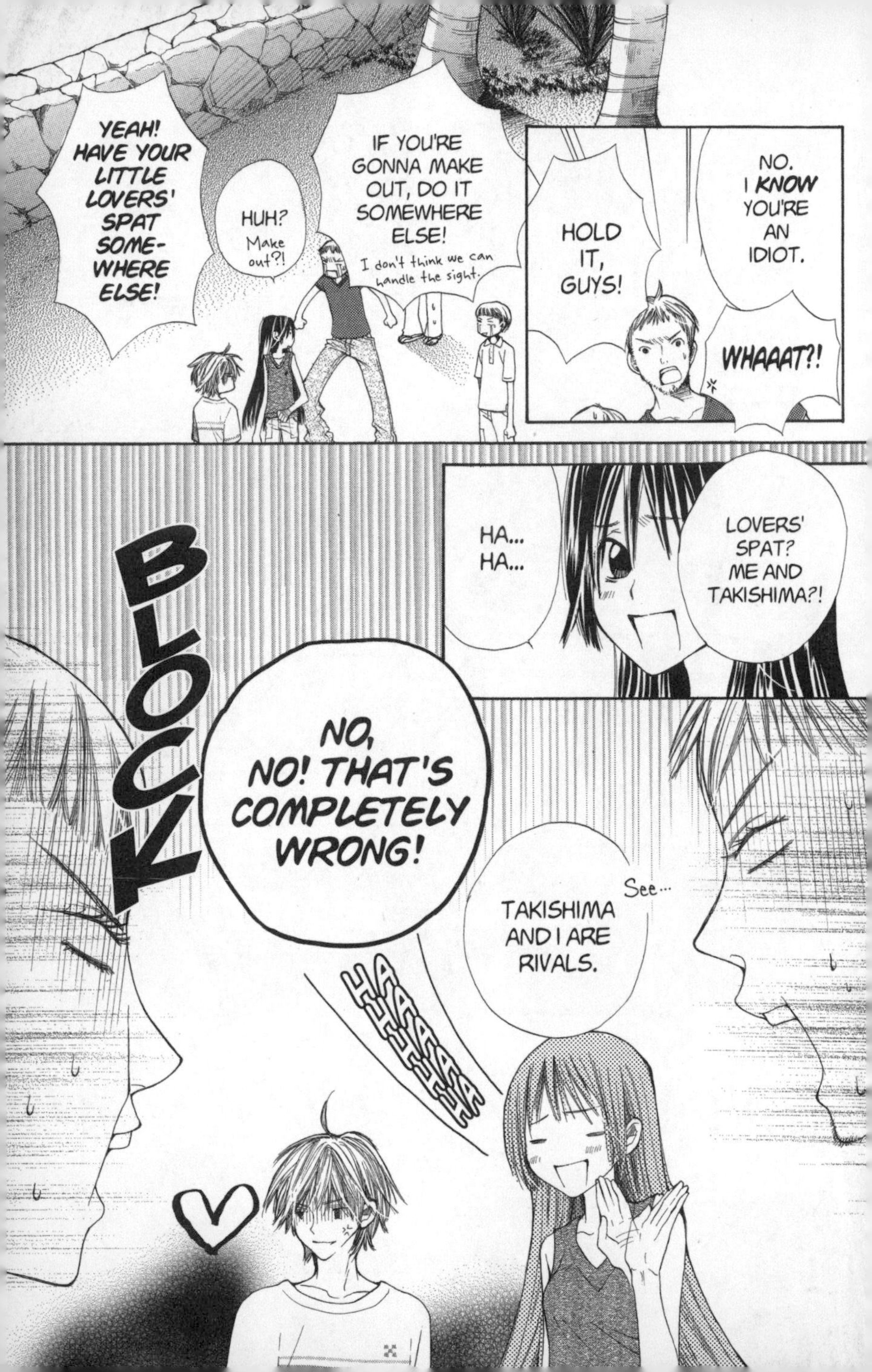
IF YOU'RE GONNA MAKE OUT, DO IT SOMEWHERE ELSE!
I don't think we can handle the sight.
HUH? Make out?!
YEAH! HAVE YOUR LITTLE LOVERS' SPAT SOME-WHERE ELSE!
HOLD IT, GUYS!
NO. I KNOW YOU'RE AN IDIOT.
WHAAAT?!
LOVERS' SPAT? ME AND TAKISHIMA?!
HA... HA...
BLOCK
NO, NO! THAT'S COMPLETELY WRONG!
See...
TAKISHIMA AND I ARE RIVALS.
HAHAHAHA

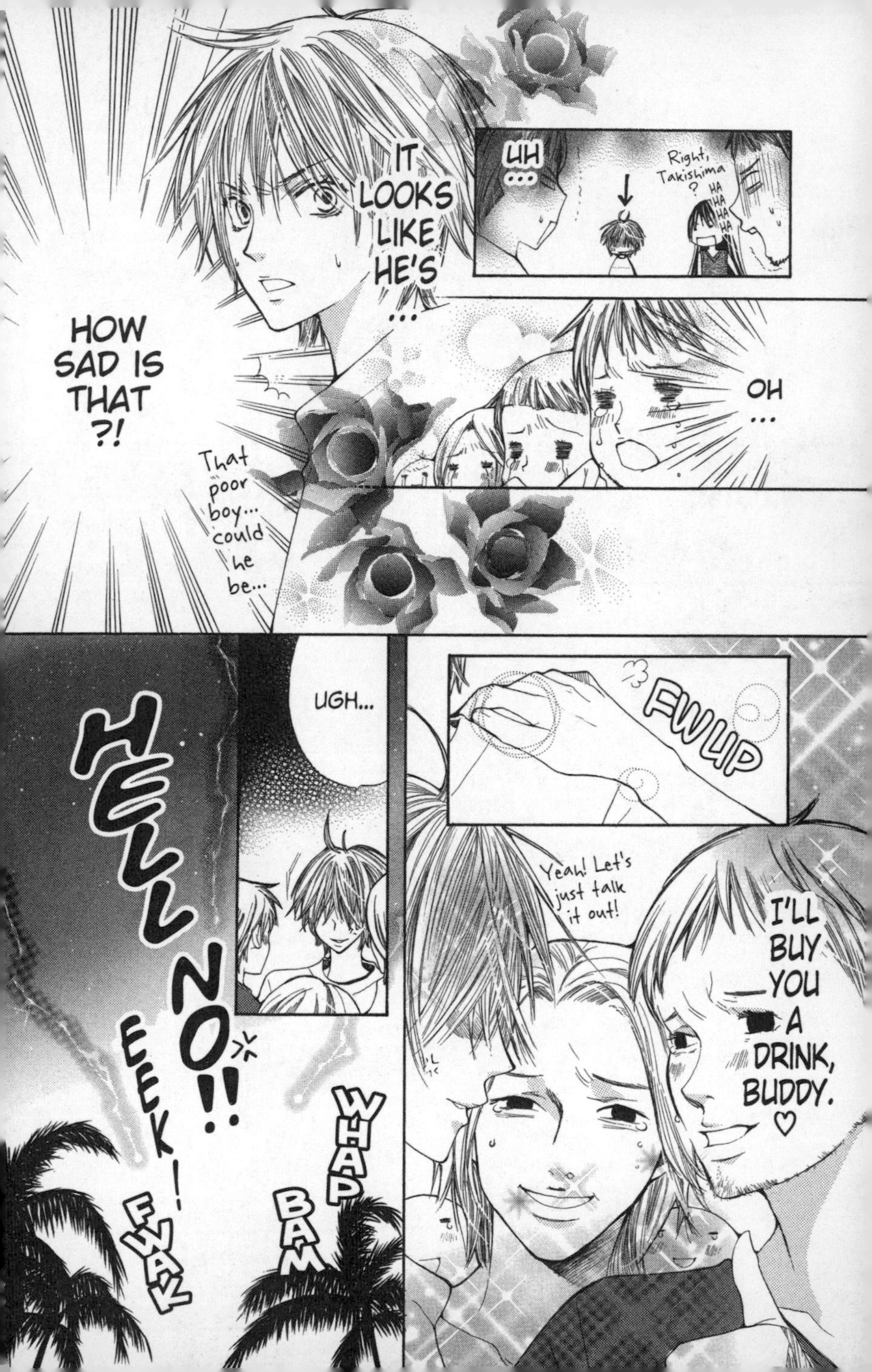
Right, Takishima?
HA HA HA HA
UH...
IT LOOKS LIKE HE'S...
OH...
HOW SAD IS THAT?!
That poor boy... could he be...
FWUP
I'LL BUY YOU A DRINK, BUDDY. ♡
Yeah! Let's just talk it out!
UGH...
HELL NO!!
EEEK!
WHAP
BAM
FWAK

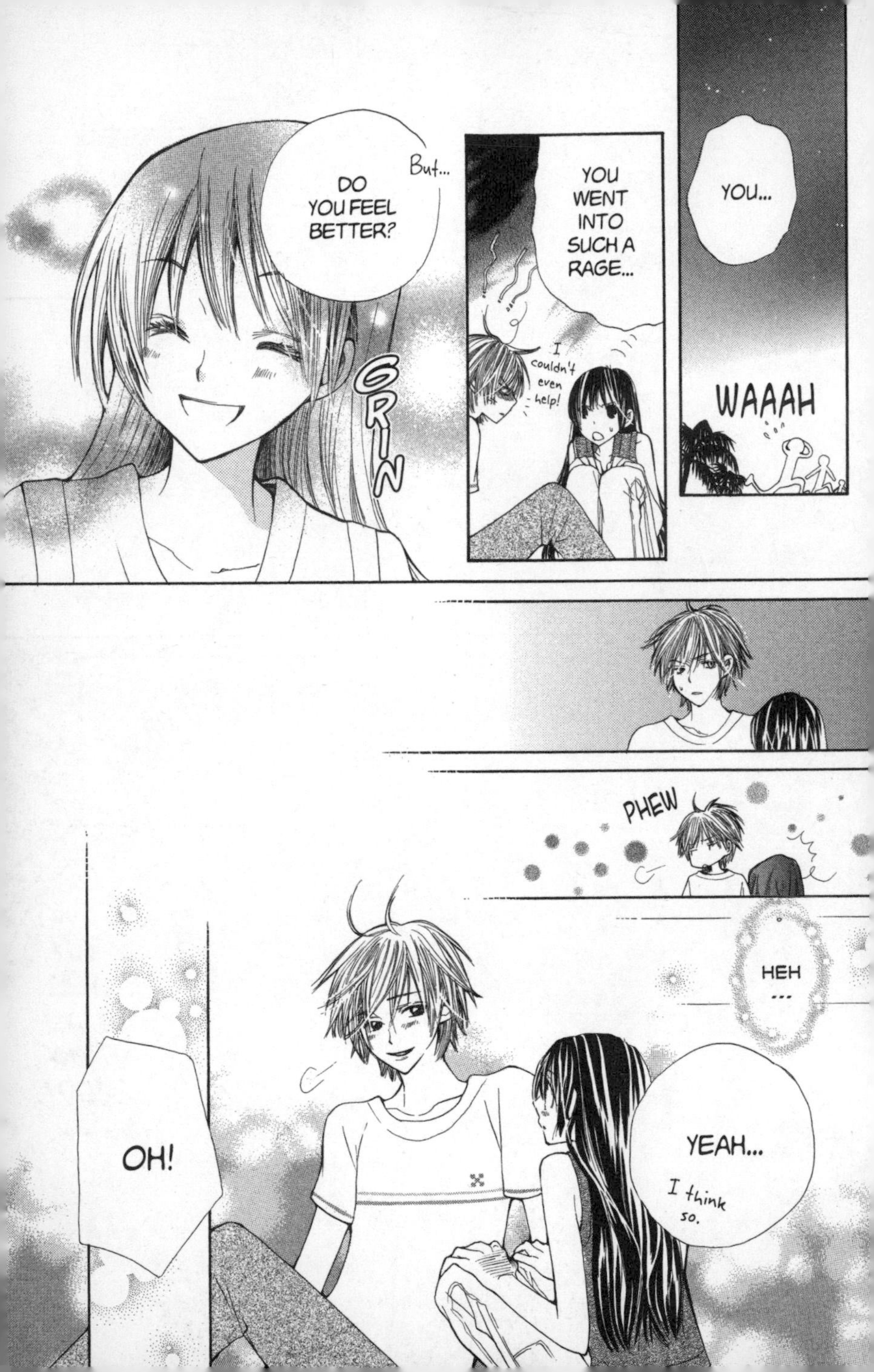
YOU...
WAAAH
YOU WENT INTO SUCH A RAGE...
I couldn't even help!
But...
DO YOU FEEL BETTER?
GRIN
PHEW
HEH...
YEAH...
I think so.
OH!

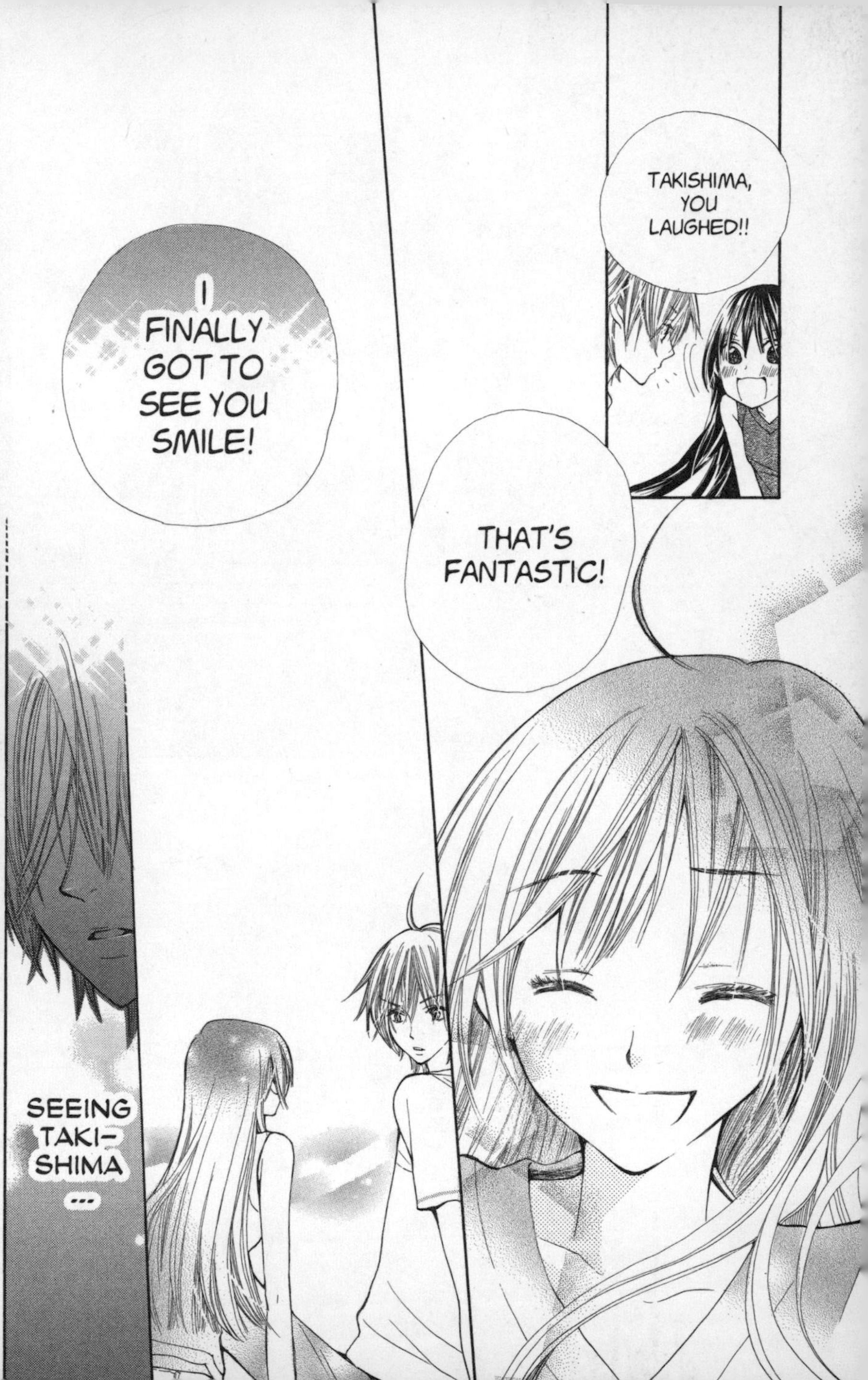
TAKISHIMA, YOU LAUGHED!!
THAT'S FANTASTIC!
I FINALLY GOT TO SEE YOU SMILE!
SEEING TAKI-SHIMA ...

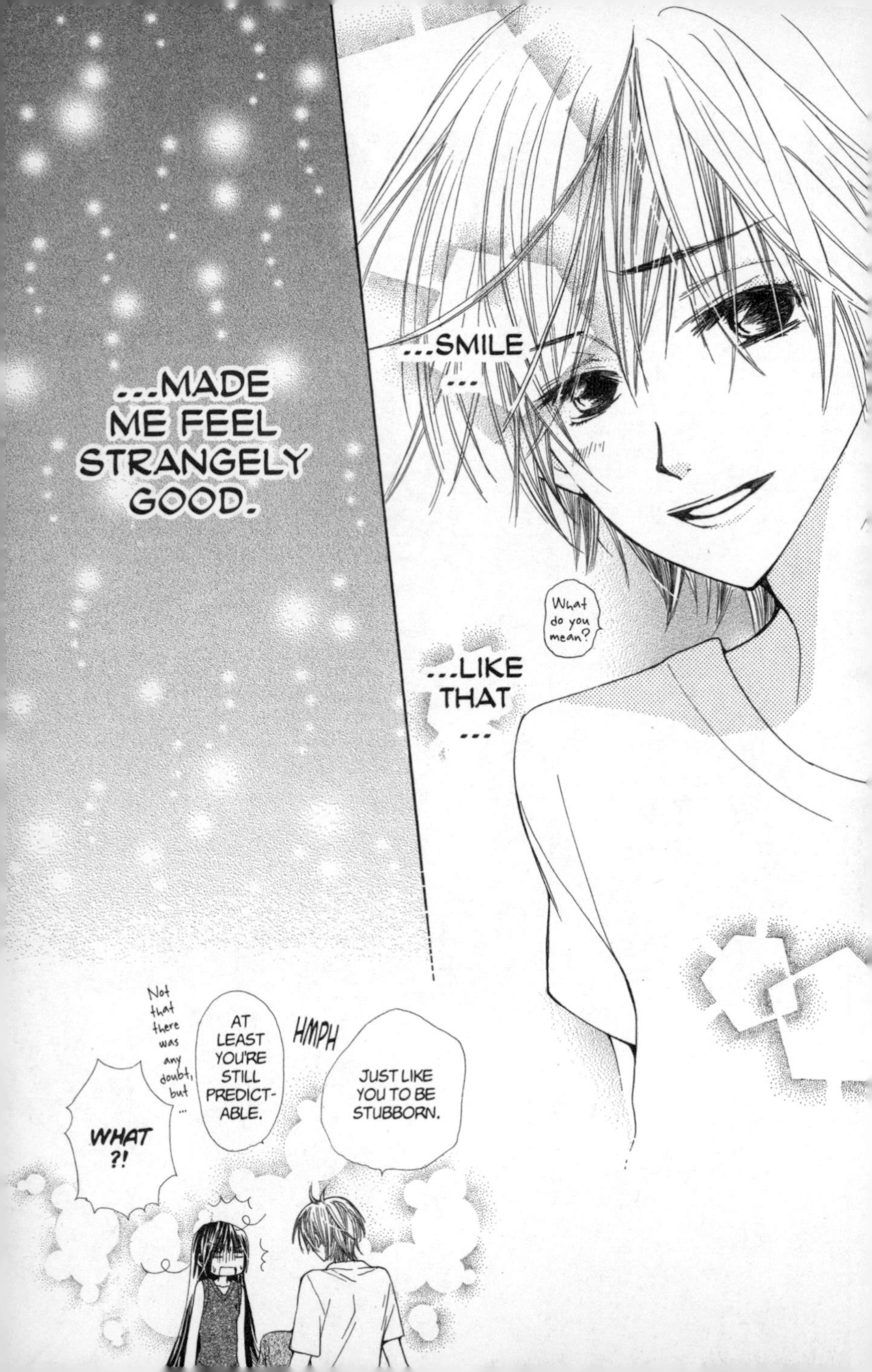
...SMILE ...
What do you mean?
...LIKE THAT ...
...MADE ME FEEL STRANGELY GOOD.
JUST LIKE YOU TO BE STUBBORN.
HMPH
AT LEAST YOU'RE STILL PREDICT-ABLE.
Not that there was any doubt, but ...
WHAT ?!

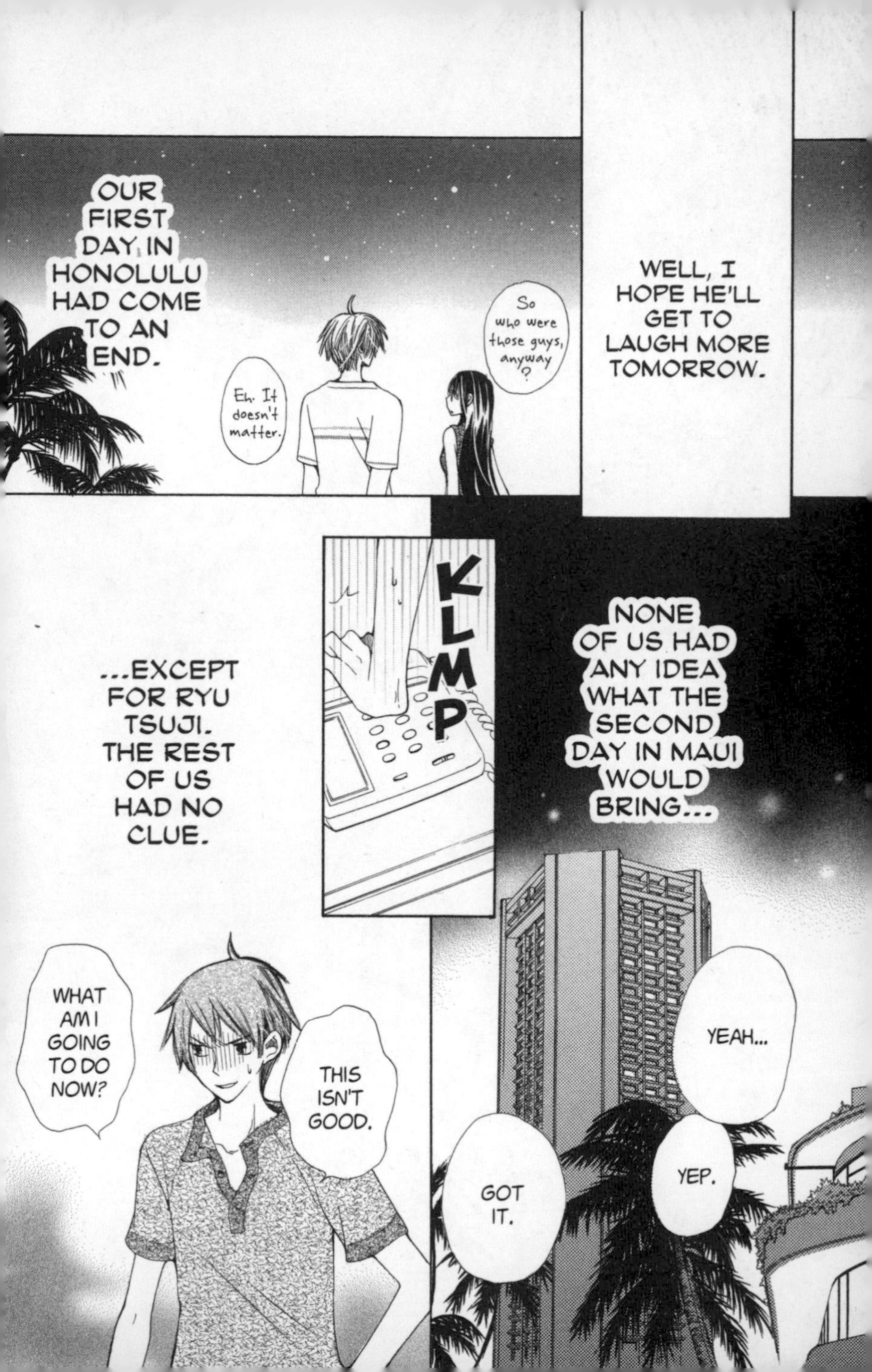
WELL, I HOPE HE'LL GET TO LAUGH MORE TOMORROW.
OUR FIRST DAY IN HONOLULU HAD COME TO AN END.
So who were those guys, anyway?
Eh. It doesn't matter.
NONE OF US HAD ANY IDEA WHAT THE SECOND DAY IN MAUI WOULD BRING...
YEAH...
YEP.
GOT IT.
KLMP
...EXCEPT FOR RYU TSUJI. THE REST OF US HAD NO CLUE.
THIS ISN'T GOOD.
WHAT AM I GOING TO DO NOW?

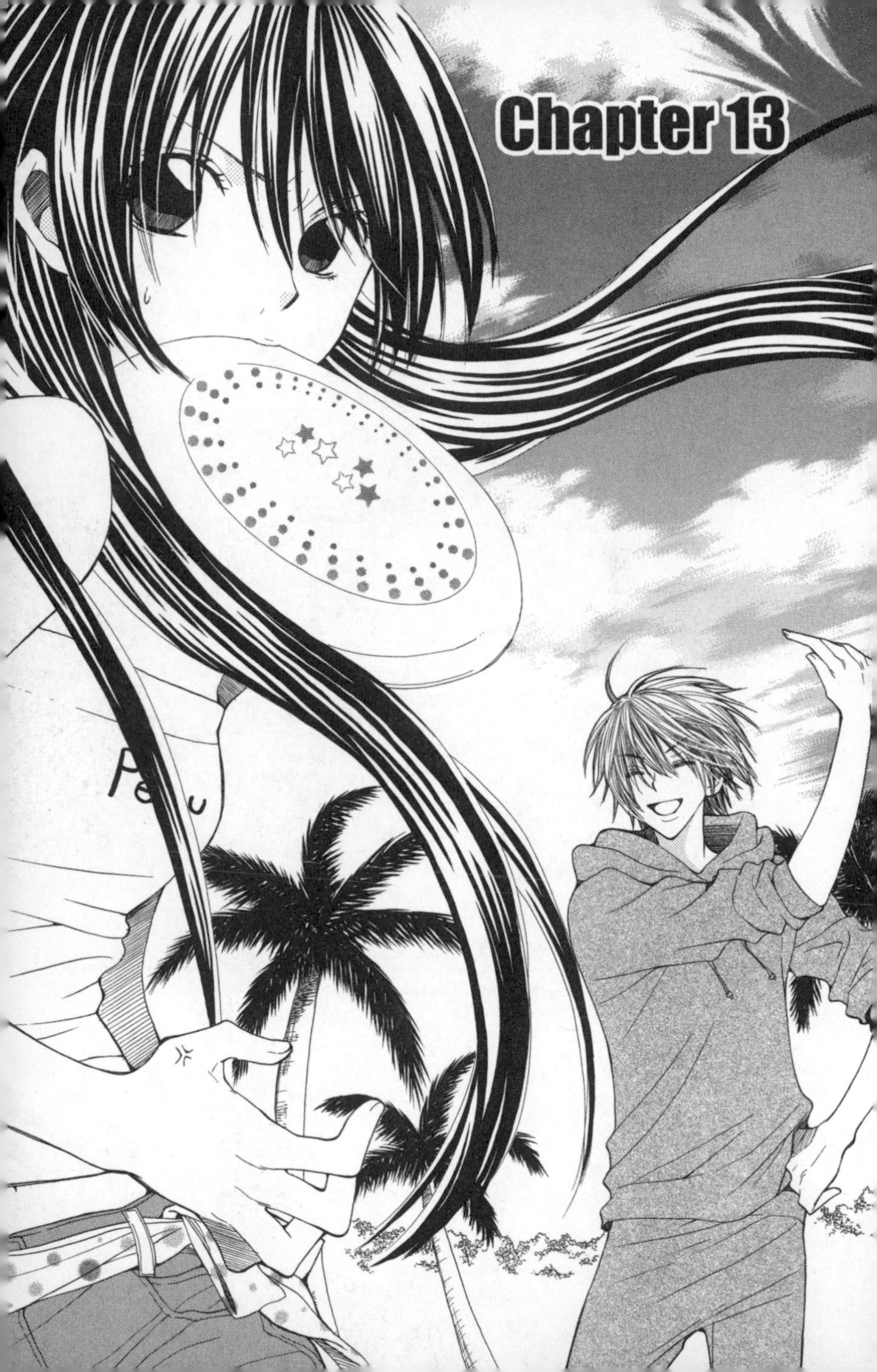
Chapter 13

ON MAUI, WE STAYED NEXT DOOR TO THE TSUJI VILLA...

...AT A RESORT NEAR KAANAPALI BEACH...

...YOUNG MAN...

...WHERE ONE...

MEGUMI YAMAMOTO	JUN YAMAMOTO
BORN: 2/14	BORN: 2/14
BLOOD TYPE: AB	BLOOD TYPE: AB
FAMILY: FATHER, MOTHER, YOUNGER BROTHER	FAMILY: FATHER, MOTHER, OLDER SISTER
FAVORITE FOODS: STRAWBERRIES, COUGH DROPS	FAVORITE FOOD: SALAD WITH ARUGULA

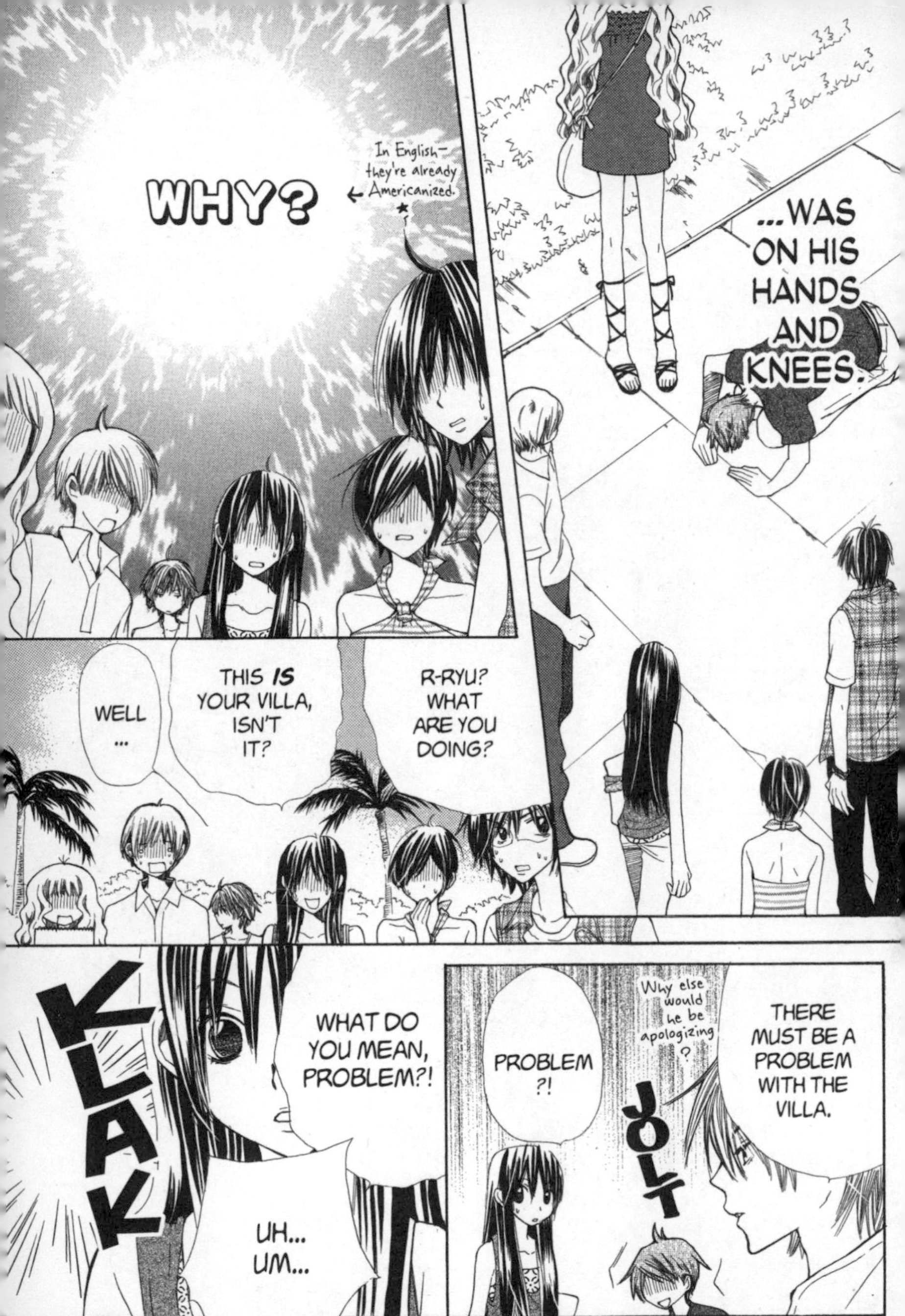
...WAS ON HIS HANDS AND KNEES.
In English—they're already Americanized.
WHY?
R-RYU? WHAT ARE YOU DOING?
THIS *IS* YOUR VILLA, ISN'T IT?
WELL...
THERE MUST BE A PROBLEM WITH THE VILLA.
Why else would he be apologizing?
JOLT
PROBLEM?!
WHAT DO YOU MEAN, PROBLEM?!
KLAK
UH... UM...

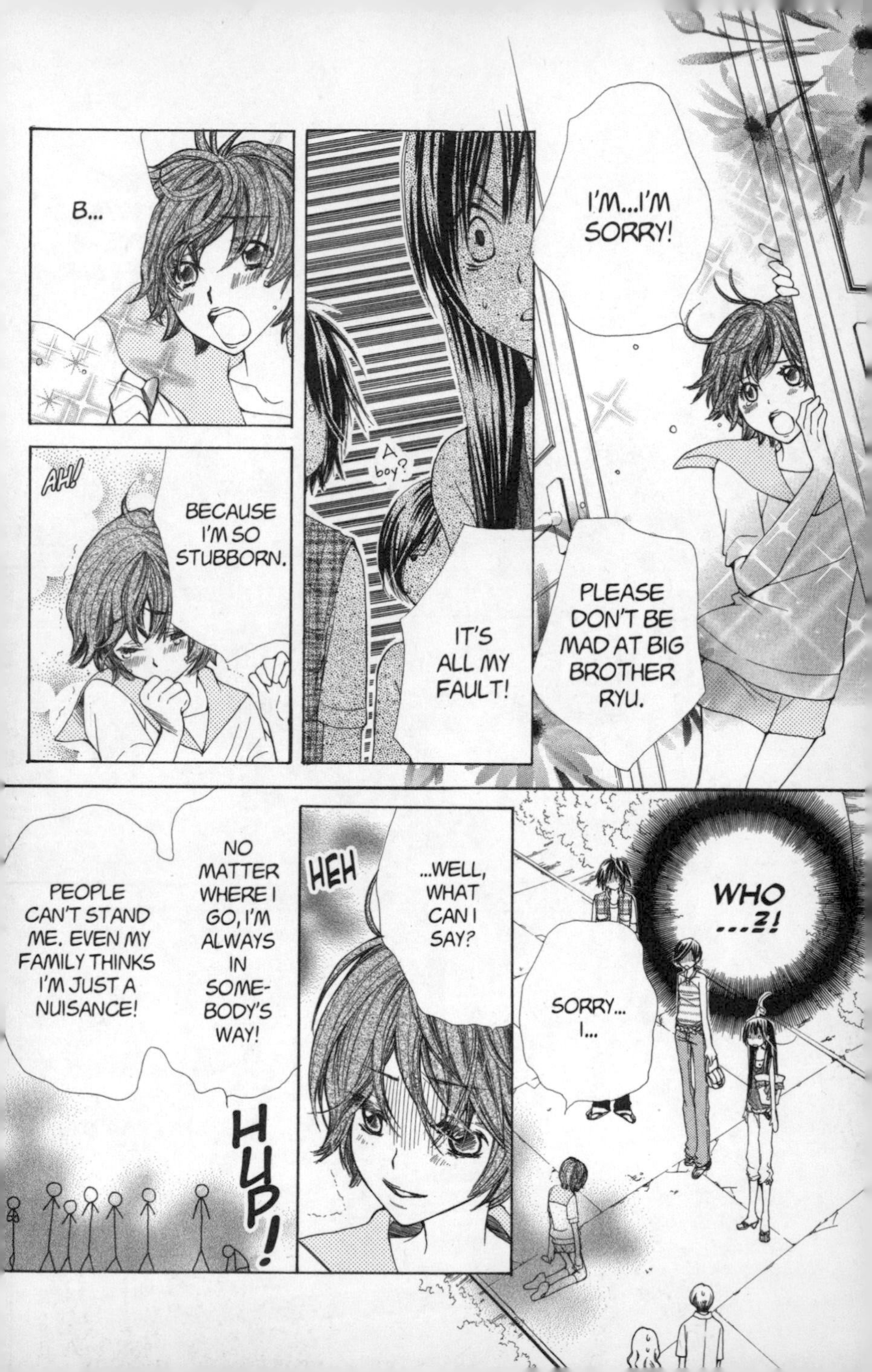
I'M...I'M SORRY!
PLEASE DON'T BE MAD AT BIG BROTHER RYU.
A boy?
IT'S ALL MY FAULT!
B...
AH!
BECAUSE I'M SO STUBBORN.
WHO ...?!
SORRY... I...
...WELL, WHAT CAN I SAY?
HEH
NO MATTER WHERE I GO, I'M ALWAYS IN SOMEBODY'S WAY!
PEOPLE CAN'T STAND ME. EVEN MY FAMILY THINKS I'M JUST A NUISANCE!
HUP!

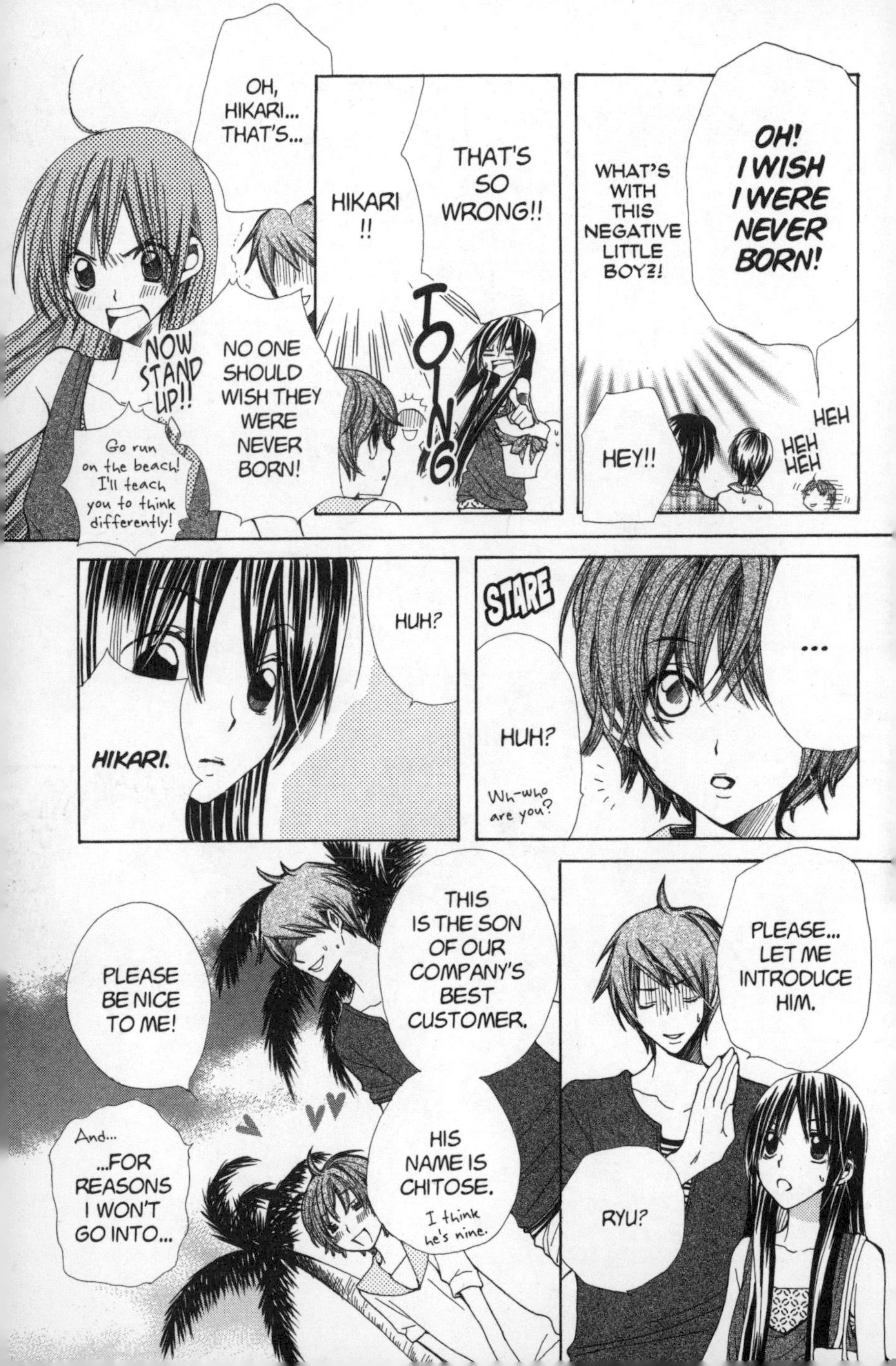
OH! I WISH I WERE NEVER BORN!
WHAT'S WITH THIS NEGATIVE LITTLE BOY?!
HEH HEH HEH
HEY!!
THAT'S SO WRONG!!
HIKARI !!
TOING
OH, HIKARI... THAT'S...
NOW STAND UP!!
NO ONE SHOULD WISH THEY WERE NEVER BORN!
Go run on the beach! I'll teach you to think differently!
STARE
...
HUH?
Wh-who are you?
HUH?
HIKARI.
PLEASE... LET ME INTRODUCE HIM.
RYU?
THIS IS THE SON OF OUR COMPANY'S BEST CUSTOMER.
PLEASE BE NICE TO ME!
HIS NAME IS CHITOSE.
I think he's nine.
And...
...FOR REASONS I WON'T GO INTO...

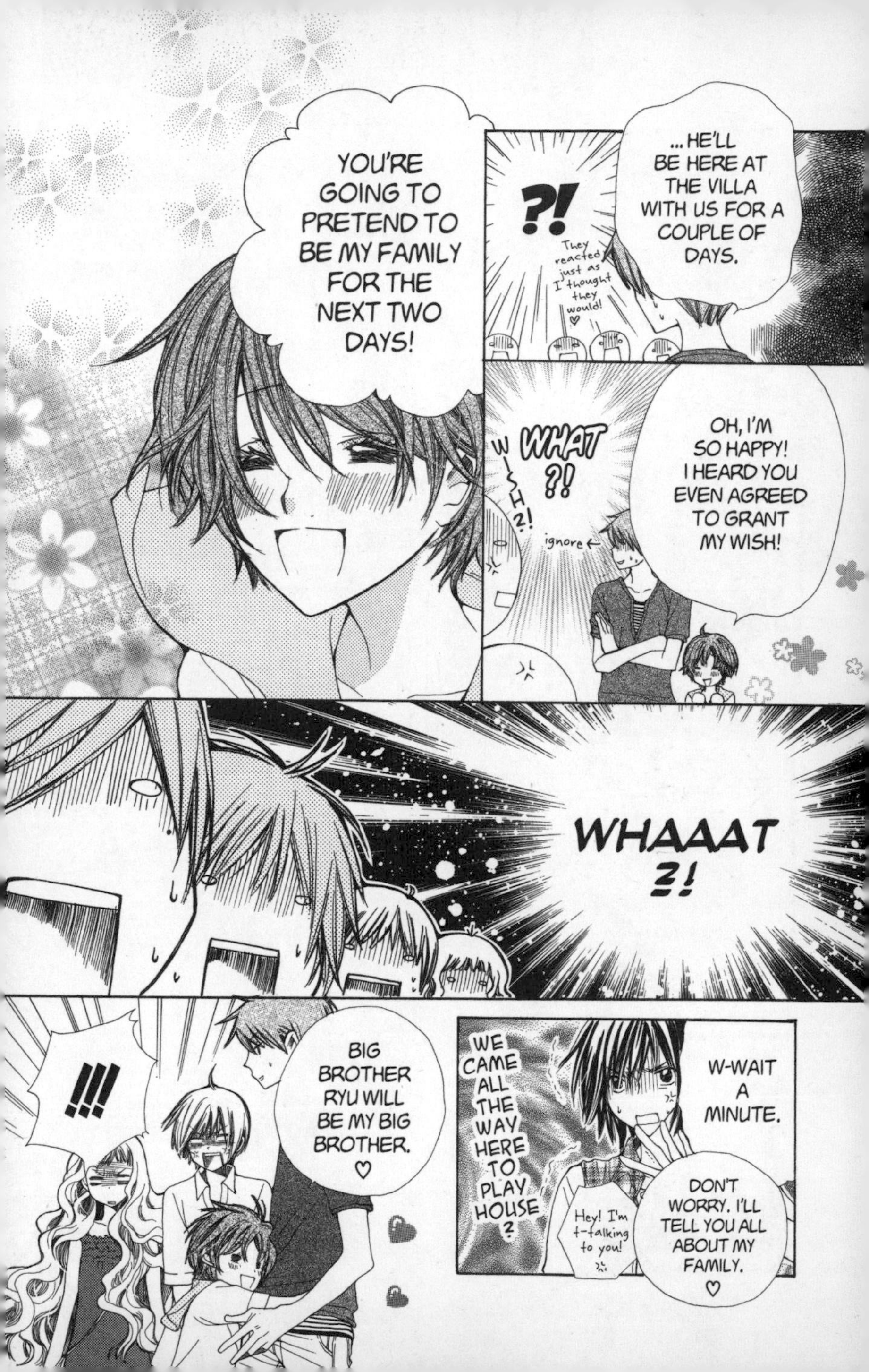
...HE'LL BE HERE AT THE VILLA WITH US FOR A COUPLE OF DAYS.
?!
They reacted just as I thought they would! ♡
OH, I'M SO HAPPY! I HEARD YOU EVEN AGREED TO GRANT MY WISH!
WHAT ?!
WISH?!
ignore ←
YOU'RE GOING TO PRETEND TO BE MY FAMILY FOR THE NEXT TWO DAYS!
WHAAAT ?!
W-WAIT A MINUTE.
WE CAME ALL THE WAY HERE TO PLAY HOUSE?
DON'T WORRY. I'LL TELL YOU ALL ABOUT MY FAMILY. ♡
Hey! I'm t-talking to you!
BIG BROTHER RYU WILL BE MY BIG BROTHER. ♡
!!!

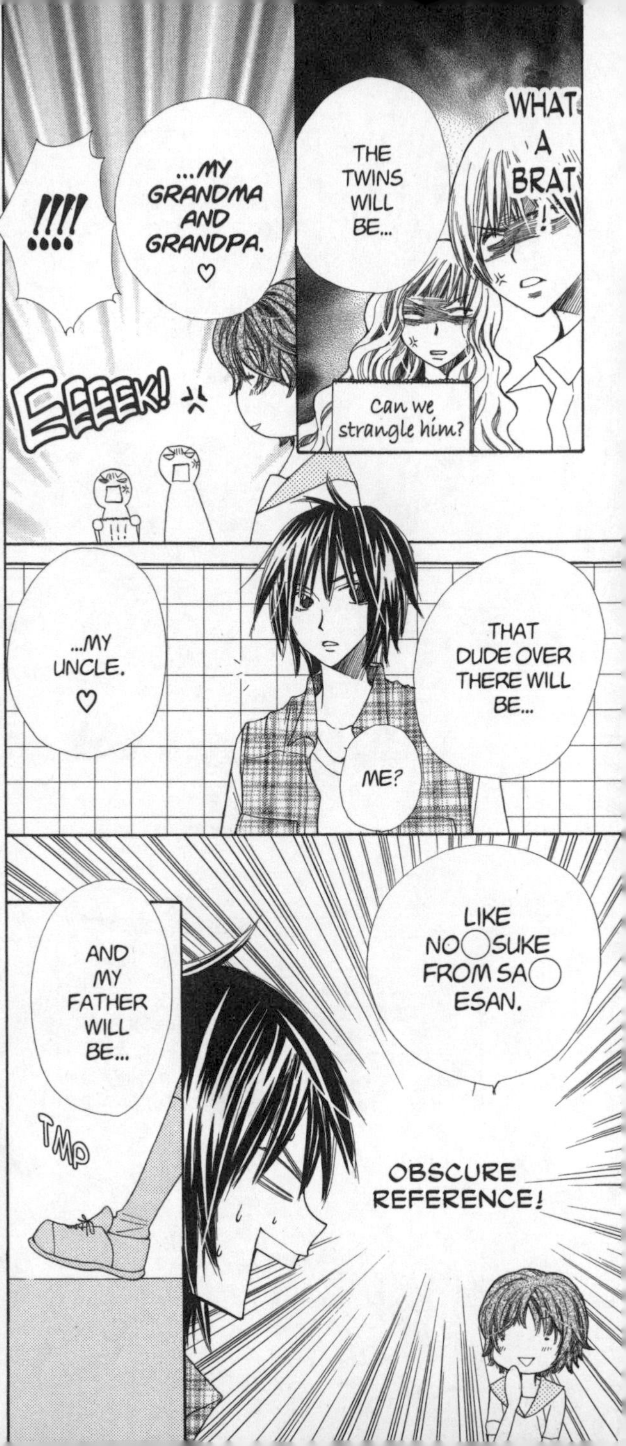
THE TWINS WILL BE...
WHAT A BRAT!
Can we strangle him?
...MY GRANDMA AND GRANDPA. ♡
!!!!
EEEEK!
THAT DUDE OVER THERE WILL BE...
ME?
...MY UNCLE. ♡
AND MY FATHER WILL BE...
TMP
LIKE NO◯SUKE FROM SA◯ ESAN.
OBSCURE REFERENCE!

3

· THINGS I'D LIKE TO TASTE ·

ARE THERE ANY FOODS YOU'D LIKE TO TRY? I HAVE LOTS! HEE HEE HEE!

THE THING I WANT TO TRY THE MOST IS THOSE DEEP-FRIED SKEWERS WITH MEATS AND VEGGIES, LIKE THEY HAVE IN OSAKA.

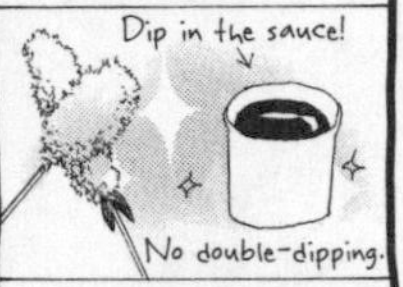
Dip in the sauce!
No double-dipping.

THEY FRY UP WHATEVER YOU PICK RIGHT THERE. IT'S SO GREAT! AND I HEAR THEY GIVE YOU ALL THE SHREDDED CABBAGE YOU WANT!

DOESN'T THAT SOUND LIKE PARADISE?!

DELICIOUS FOOD EQUALS PURE JOY!

HEE HEE HEE HA HA HA!

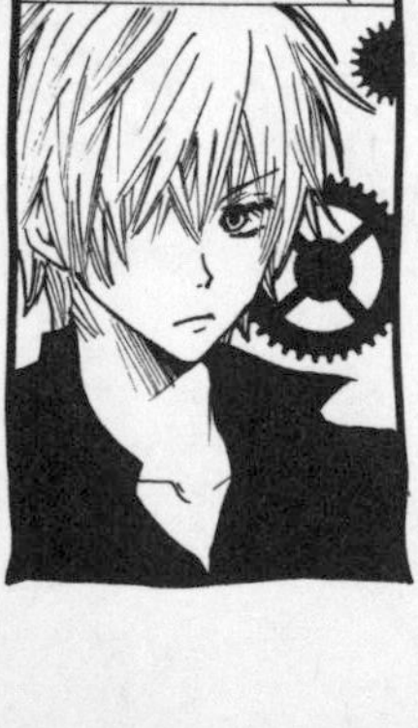

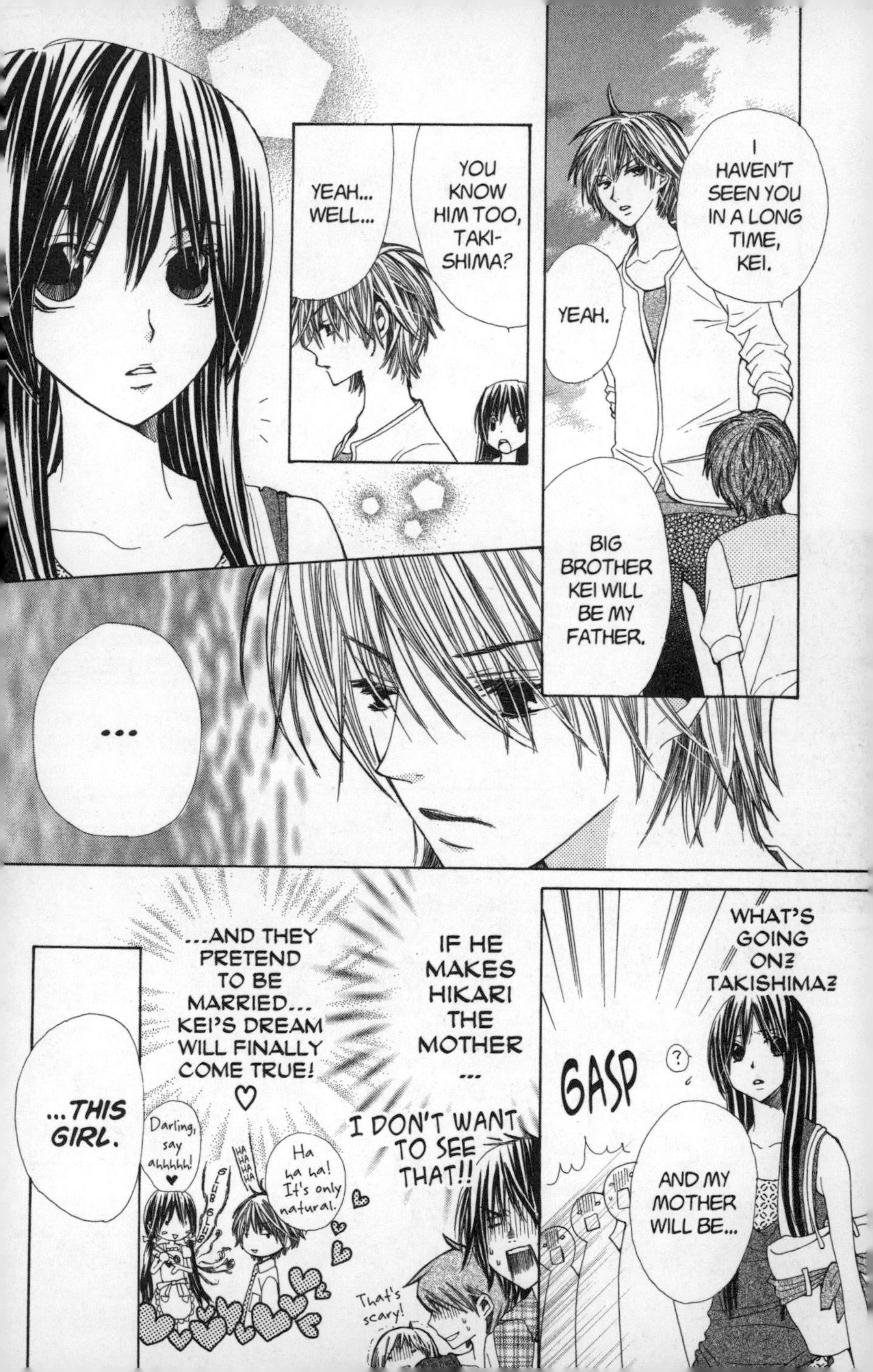

I HAVEN'T SEEN YOU IN A LONG TIME, KEI.
YEAH.
BIG BROTHER KEI WILL BE MY FATHER.
YOU KNOW HIM TOO, TAKI-SHIMA?
YEAH... WELL...
...
WHAT'S GOING ON? TAKISHIMA?
?
GASP
AND MY MOTHER WILL BE...
IF HE MAKES HIKARI THE MOTHER...
I DON'T WANT TO SEE THAT!!
That's scary!
...AND THEY PRETEND TO BE MARRIED... KEI'S DREAM WILL FINALLY COME TRUE! ♡
Ha ha ha! It's only natural.
HA HA HA HA
GLUB GLUB
Darling, say ahhhhh! ♥
...THIS GIRL.

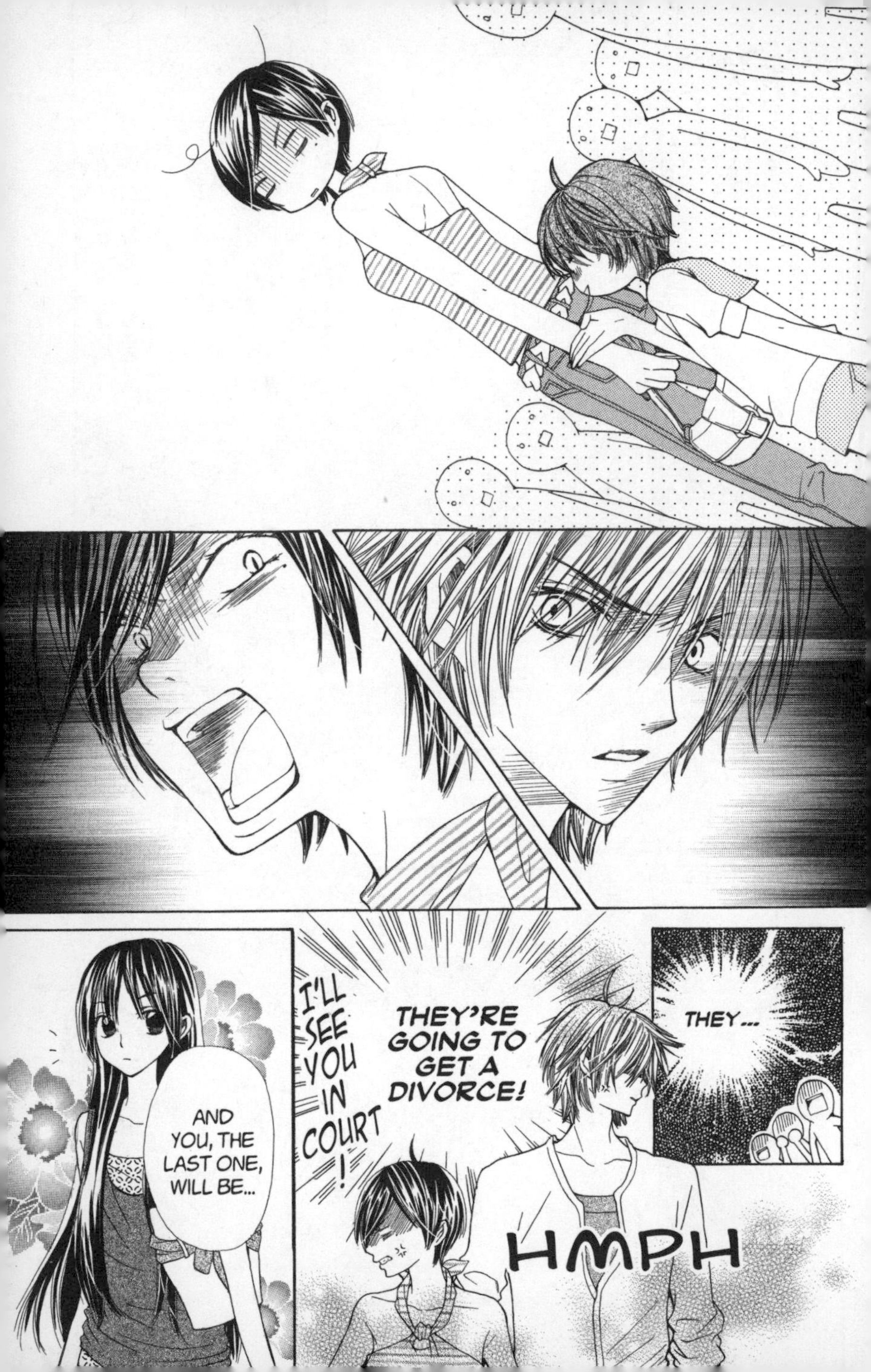
THEY...
THEY'RE GOING TO GET A DIVORCE!
I'LL SEE YOU IN COURT!
HMPH
AND YOU, THE LAST ONE, WILL BE...

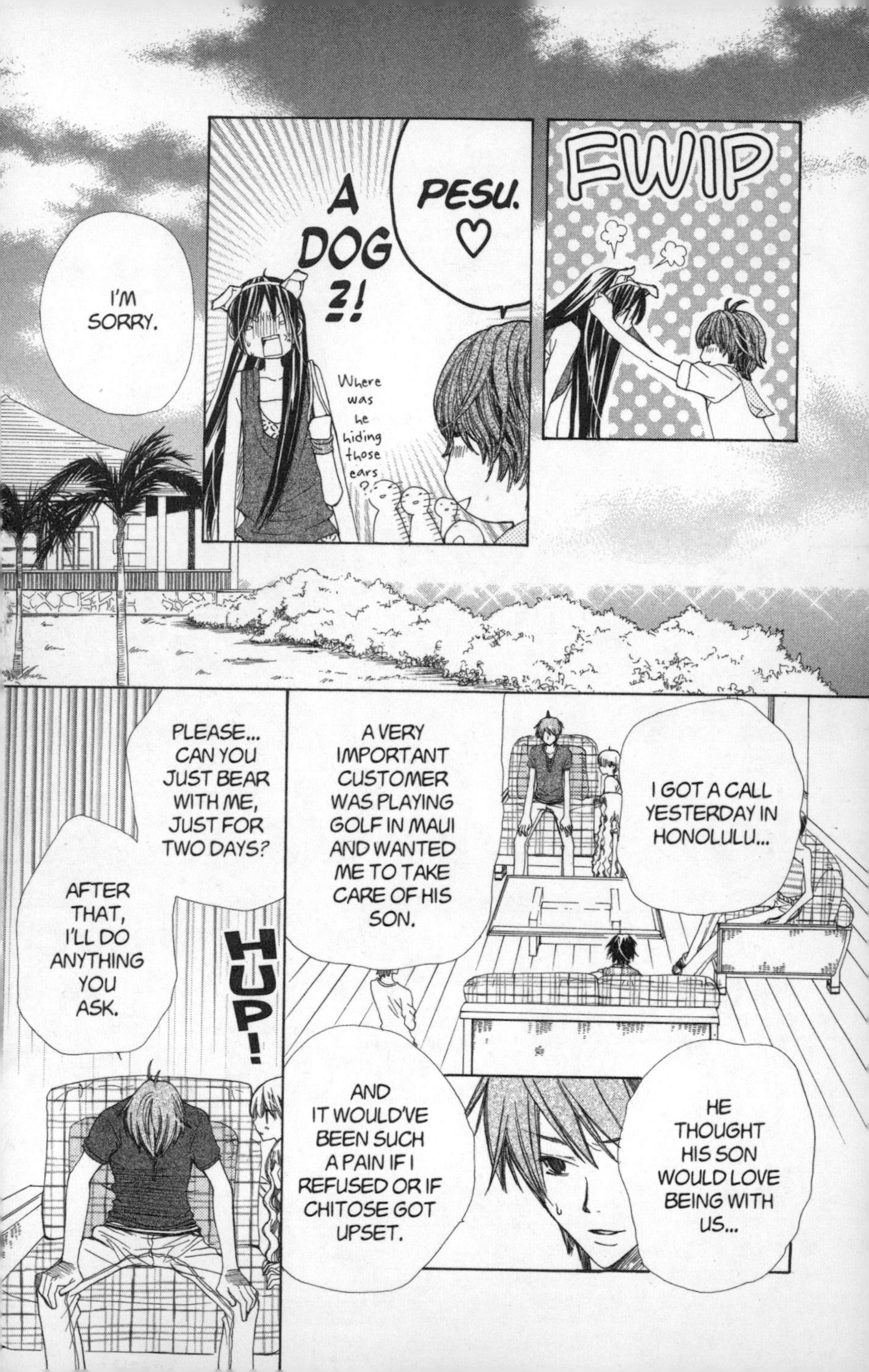
FWIP
PESU. ♥
A DOG?!
Where was he hiding those ears?
I'M SORRY.
I GOT A CALL YESTERDAY IN HONOLULU...
A VERY IMPORTANT CUSTOMER WAS PLAYING GOLF IN MAUI AND WANTED ME TO TAKE CARE OF HIS SON.
HE THOUGHT HIS SON WOULD LOVE BEING WITH US...
AND IT WOULD'VE BEEN SUCH A PAIN IF I REFUSED OR IF CHITOSE GOT UPSET.
HUP!
PLEASE... CAN YOU JUST BEAR WITH ME, JUST FOR TWO DAYS?
AFTER THAT, I'LL DO ANYTHING YOU ASK.

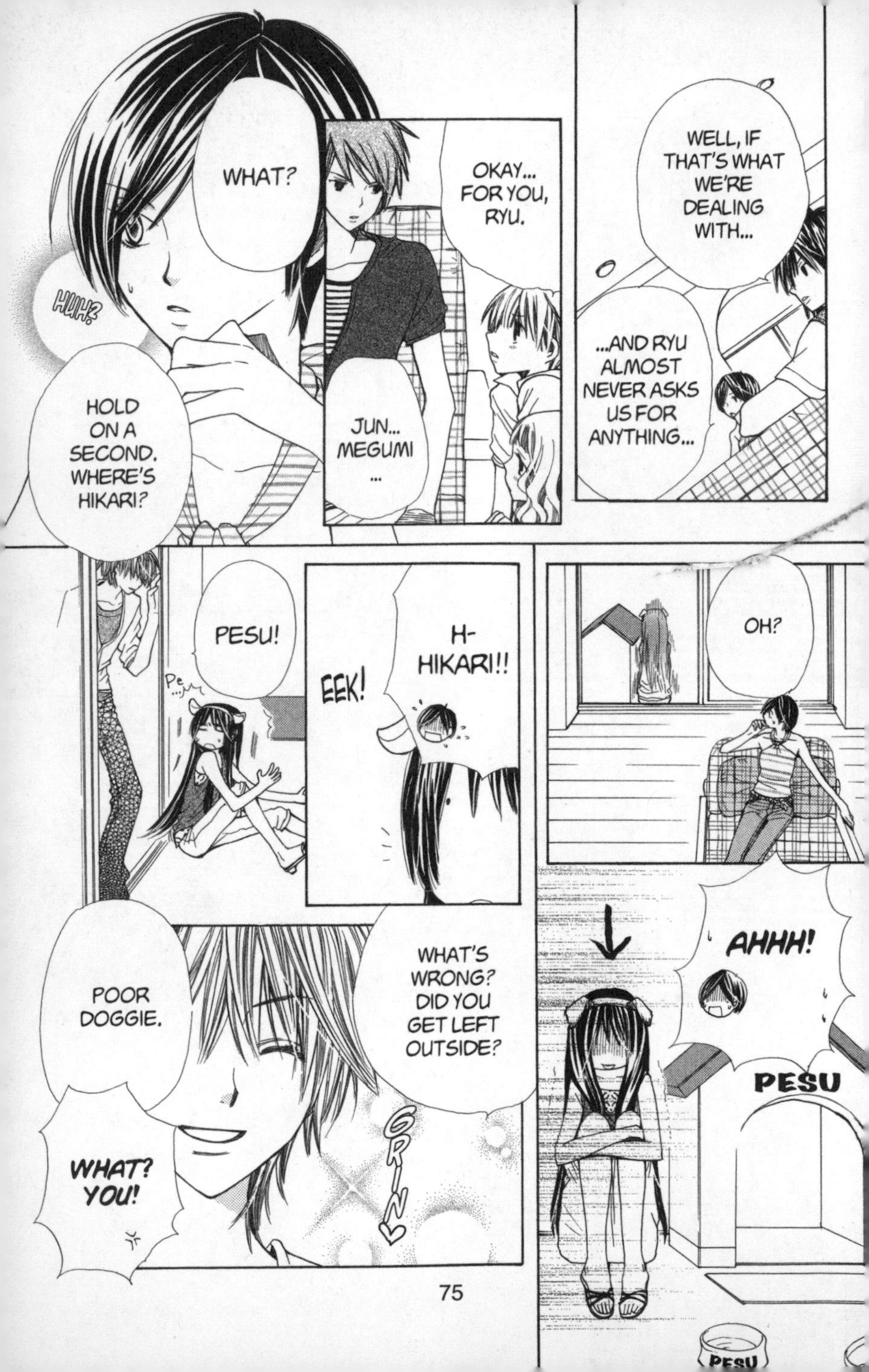

WELL, IF THAT'S WHAT WE'RE DEALING WITH...
...AND RYU ALMOST NEVER ASKS US FOR ANYTHING...
OKAY... FOR YOU, RYU.
JUN... MEGUMI ...
WHAT?
HUH?
HOLD ON A SECOND. WHERE'S HIKARI?
OH?
AHHH!
PESU
PESU
H- HIKARI!!
EEK!
PESU!
Pe...
WHAT'S WRONG? DID YOU GET LEFT OUTSIDE?
POOR DOGGIE.
GRIN
WHAT? YOU!

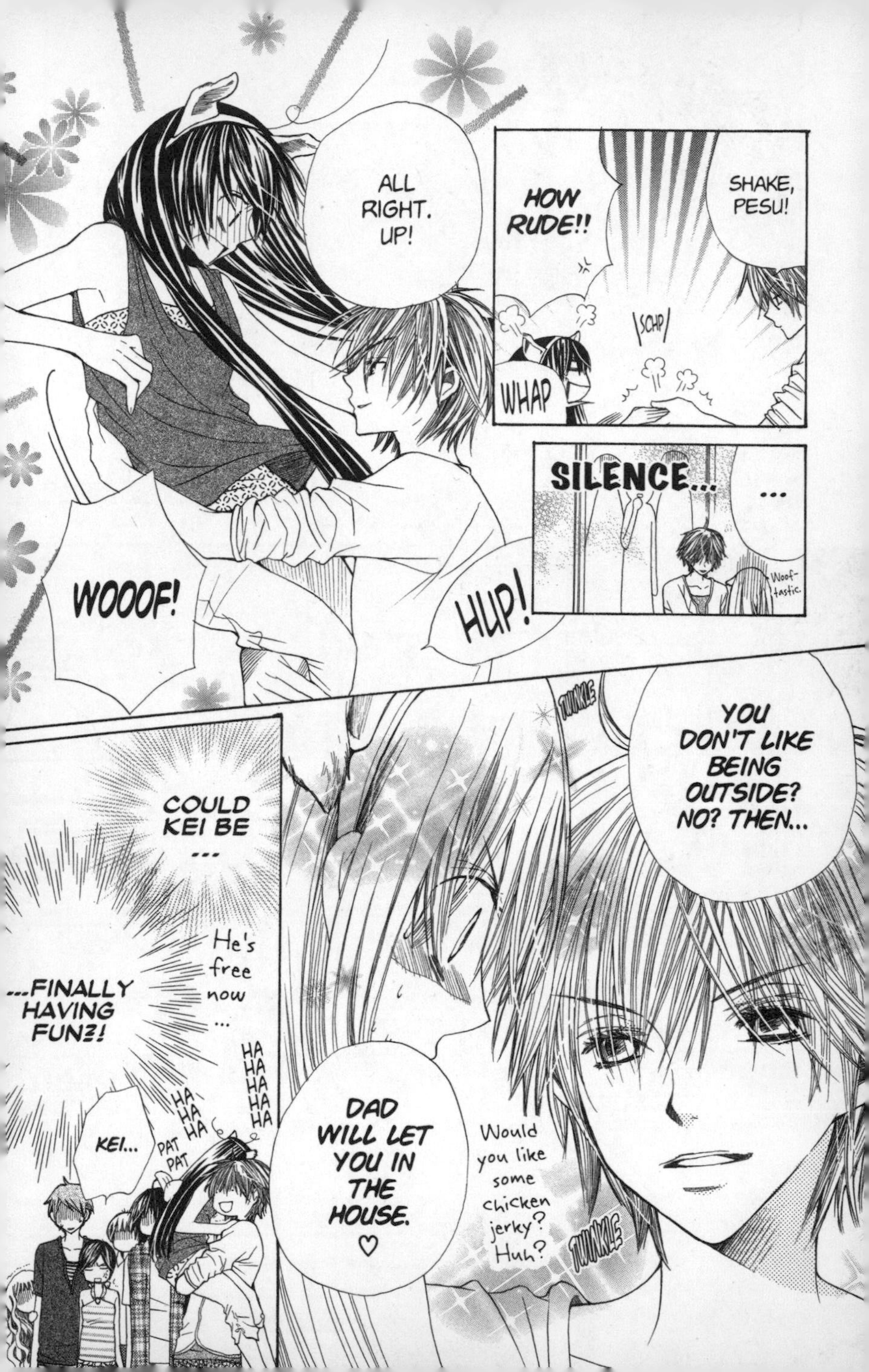
SHAKE, PESU!
HOW RUDE!!
SCHP
WHAP
...
SILENCE...
Woof-tastic.
ALL RIGHT. UP!
HUP!
WOOOF!
TWINKLE
YOU DON'T LIKE BEING OUTSIDE? NO? THEN...
Would you like some chicken jerky? Huh?
DAD WILL LET YOU IN THE HOUSE. ♡
TWINKLE
COULD KEI BE ...
He's free now ...
...FINALLY HAVING FUN?!
HA HA HA HA HA HA
HA HA HA
KEI...
PAT PAT

HUP!

TMP

FFP

THMP

KEI! WHAT ARE YOU DOING TO PESU?!

UGH!

Coconut

PESUUU!

AHH!

SHFE

ESCAPE!!

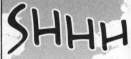

STUPID TAKISHIMA...

SPLISH

SPLISH

MAKING ME LOOK LIKE AN IDIOT!

SHHh

BUT THAT WAS KIND OF STRANGE...

HUH?

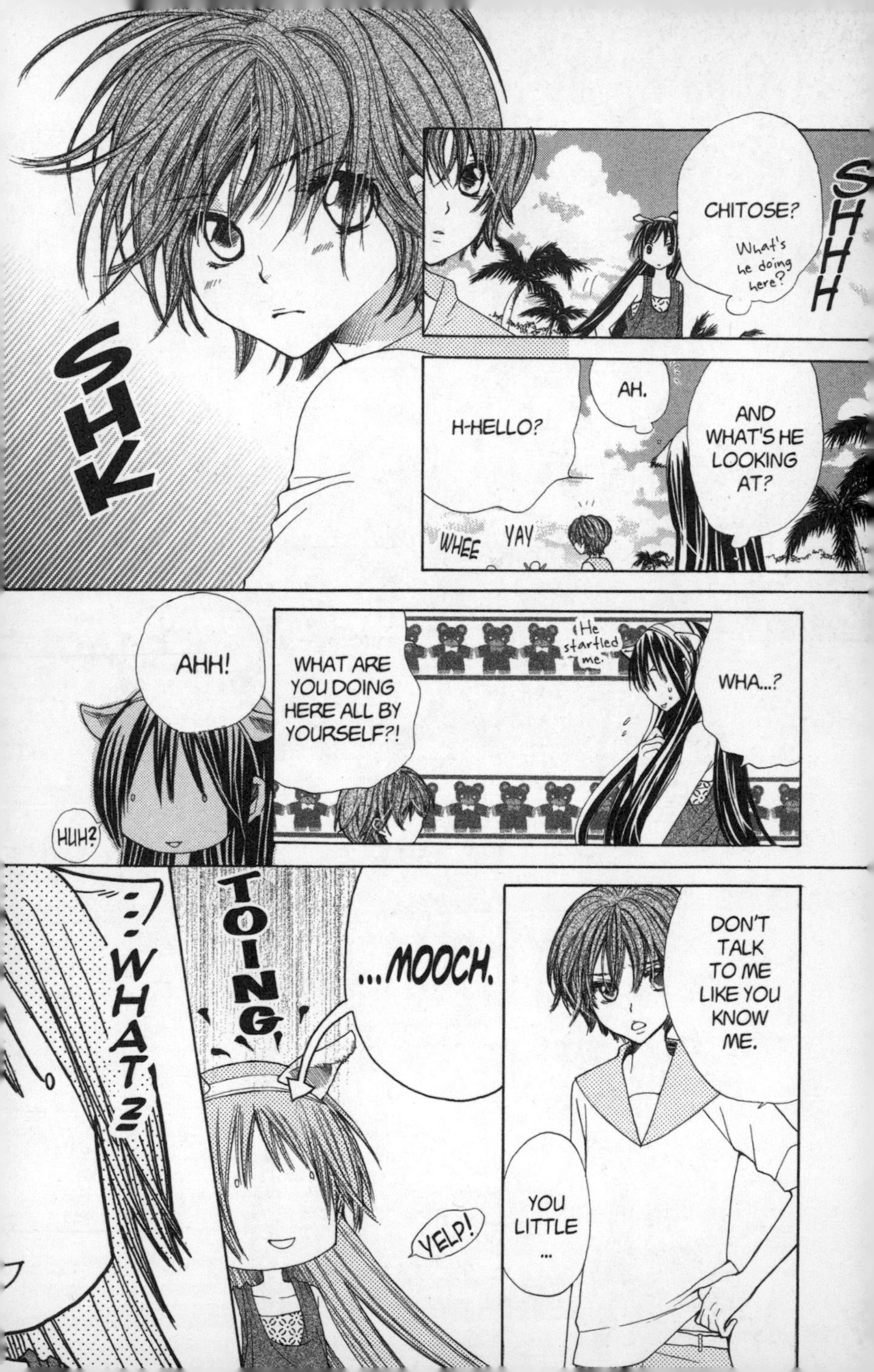
SHHHH
CHITOSE?
What's he doing here?
AND WHAT'S HE LOOKING AT?
AH.
H-HELLO?
YAY
WHEE
SHK
WHA...?
He startled me.
WHAT ARE YOU DOING HERE ALL BY YOURSELF?!
AHH!
HUH?
DON'T TALK TO ME LIKE YOU KNOW ME.
YOU LITTLE ...
...MOOCH.
TOING
YELP!
...WHAT?!

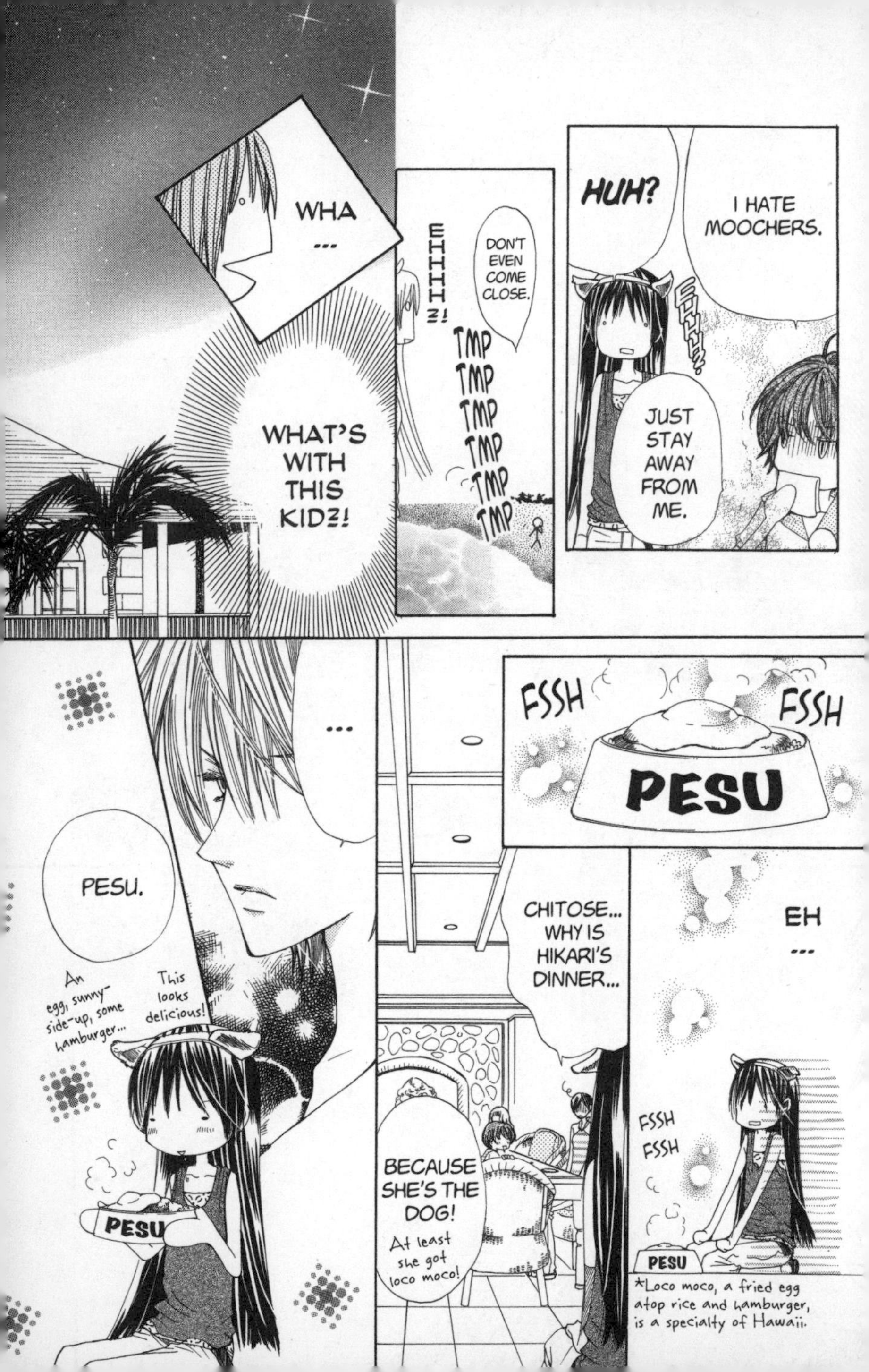
HUH?
I HATE MOOCHERS.
JUST STAY AWAY FROM ME.
EHHHH?!
DON'T EVEN COME CLOSE.
TMP TMP TMP TMP TMP TMP
WHA...
WHAT'S WITH THIS KID?!
FSSH
FSSH
PESU
EH...
FSSH FSSH
PESU
CHITOSE... WHY IS HIKARI'S DINNER...
BECAUSE SHE'S THE DOG!
At least she got loco moco!
...
PESU.
This looks delicious!
An egg, sunny-side-up, some hamburger...
PESU

*Loco moco, a fried egg atop rice and hamburger, is a specialty of Hawaii.

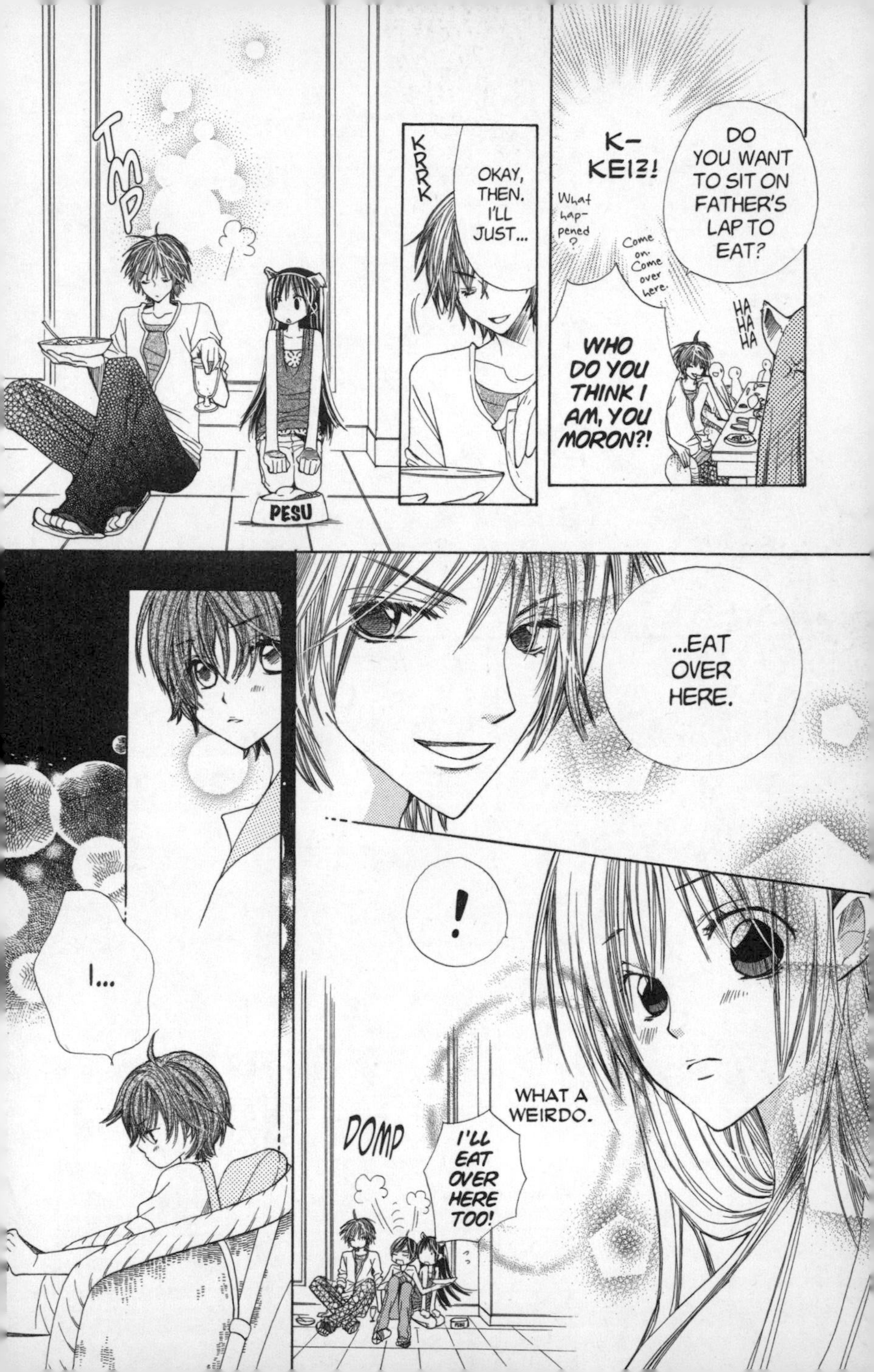
DO YOU WANT TO SIT ON FATHER'S LAP TO EAT?
K-KEI?!
What hap-pened?
Come on. Come over here.
HA HA HA
WHO DO YOU THINK I AM, YOU MORON?!
KRRK
OKAY, THEN. I'LL JUST...
TMP
PESU
...EAT OVER HERE.
!
WHAT A WEIRDO.
I'LL EAT OVER HERE TOO!
DOMP
I...

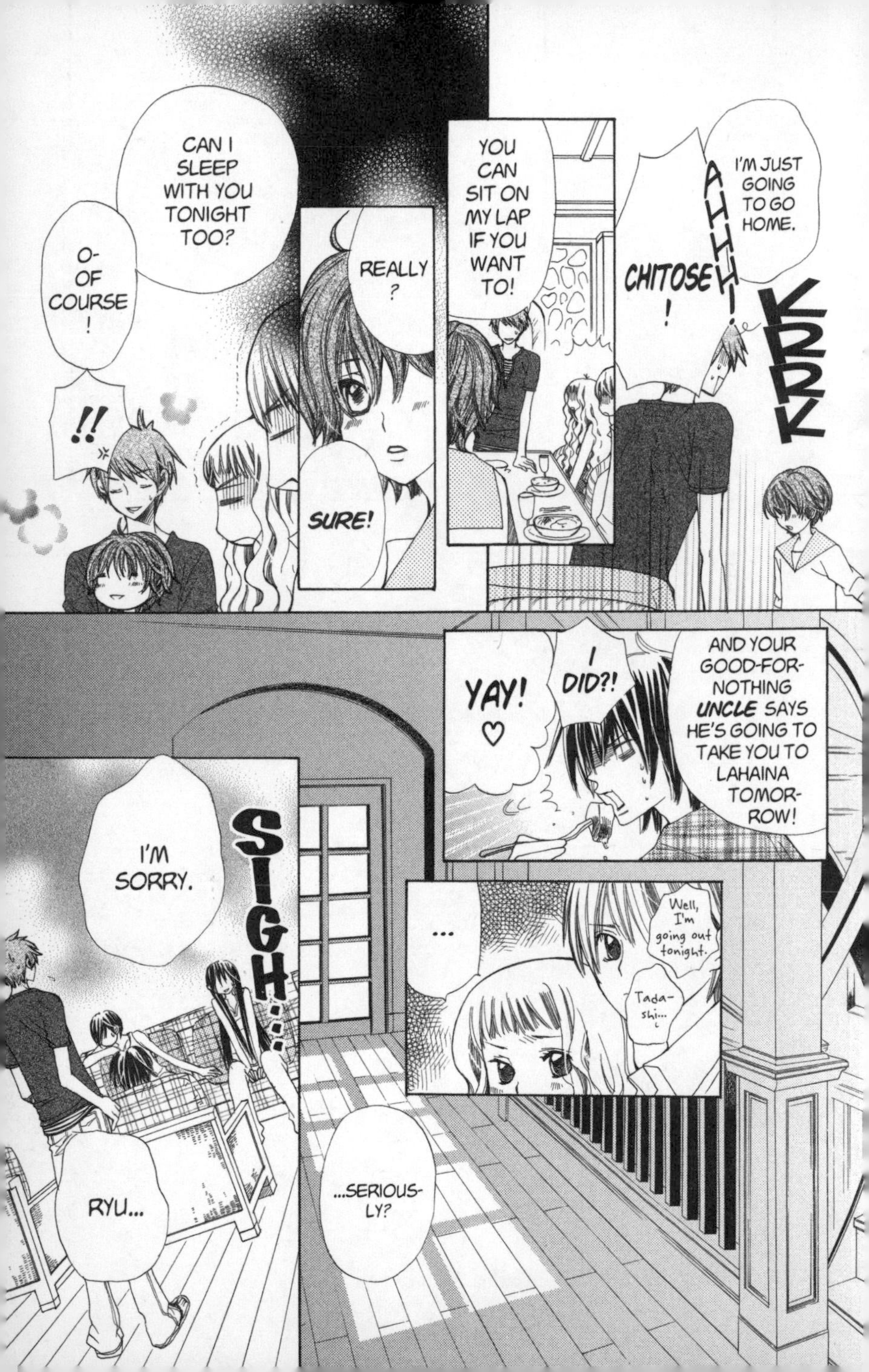
I'M JUST GOING TO GO HOME.
AHHHH!
CHITOSE!
KRRK
YOU CAN SIT ON MY LAP IF YOU WANT TO!
REALLY?
SURE!
CAN I SLEEP WITH YOU TONIGHT TOO?
O-OF COURSE!
!!
AND YOUR GOOD-FOR-NOTHING UNCLE SAYS HE'S GOING TO TAKE YOU TO LAHAINA TOMORROW!
I DID?!
YAY! ♡
Well, I'm going out tonight.
Tadashi...
...
SIGH...
I'M SORRY.
...SERIOUSLY?
RYU...

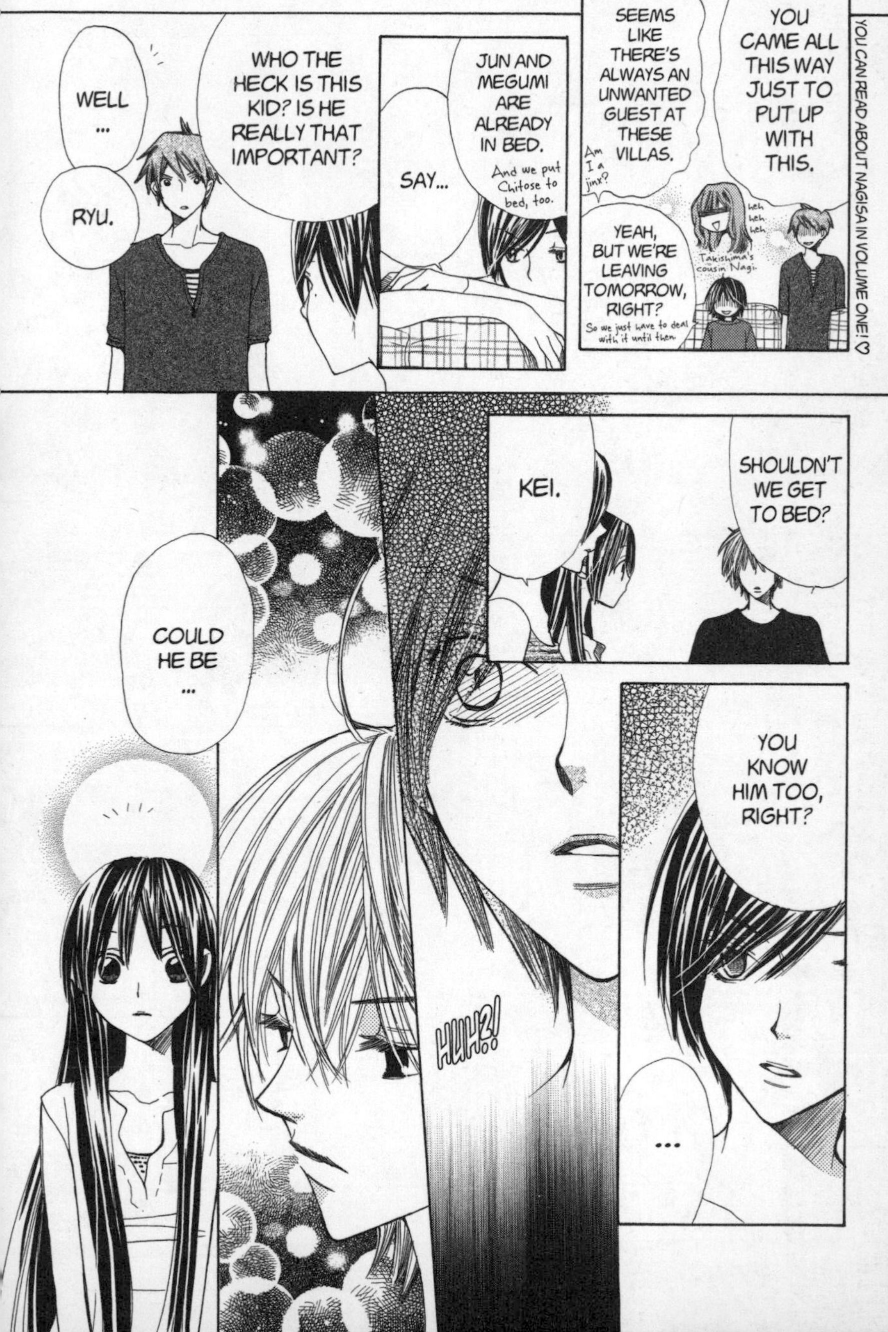
YOU CAME ALL THIS WAY JUST TO PUT UP WITH THIS.
SEEMS LIKE THERE'S ALWAYS AN UNWANTED GUEST AT THESE VILLAS.
heh heh heh
Takishima's cousin Nagi.
Am I a jinx?
YEAH, BUT WE'RE LEAVING TOMORROW, RIGHT?
So we just have to deal with it until then.
JUN AND MEGUMI ARE ALREADY IN BED.
And we put Chitose to bed, too.
SAY...
WHO THE HECK IS THIS KID? IS HE REALLY THAT IMPORTANT?
WELL ...
RYU.
SHOULDN'T WE GET TO BED?
KEI.
YOU KNOW HIM TOO, RIGHT?
...
HUH?!
COULD HE BE ...

YOU CAN READ ABOUT NAGISA IN VOLUME ONE! ♡

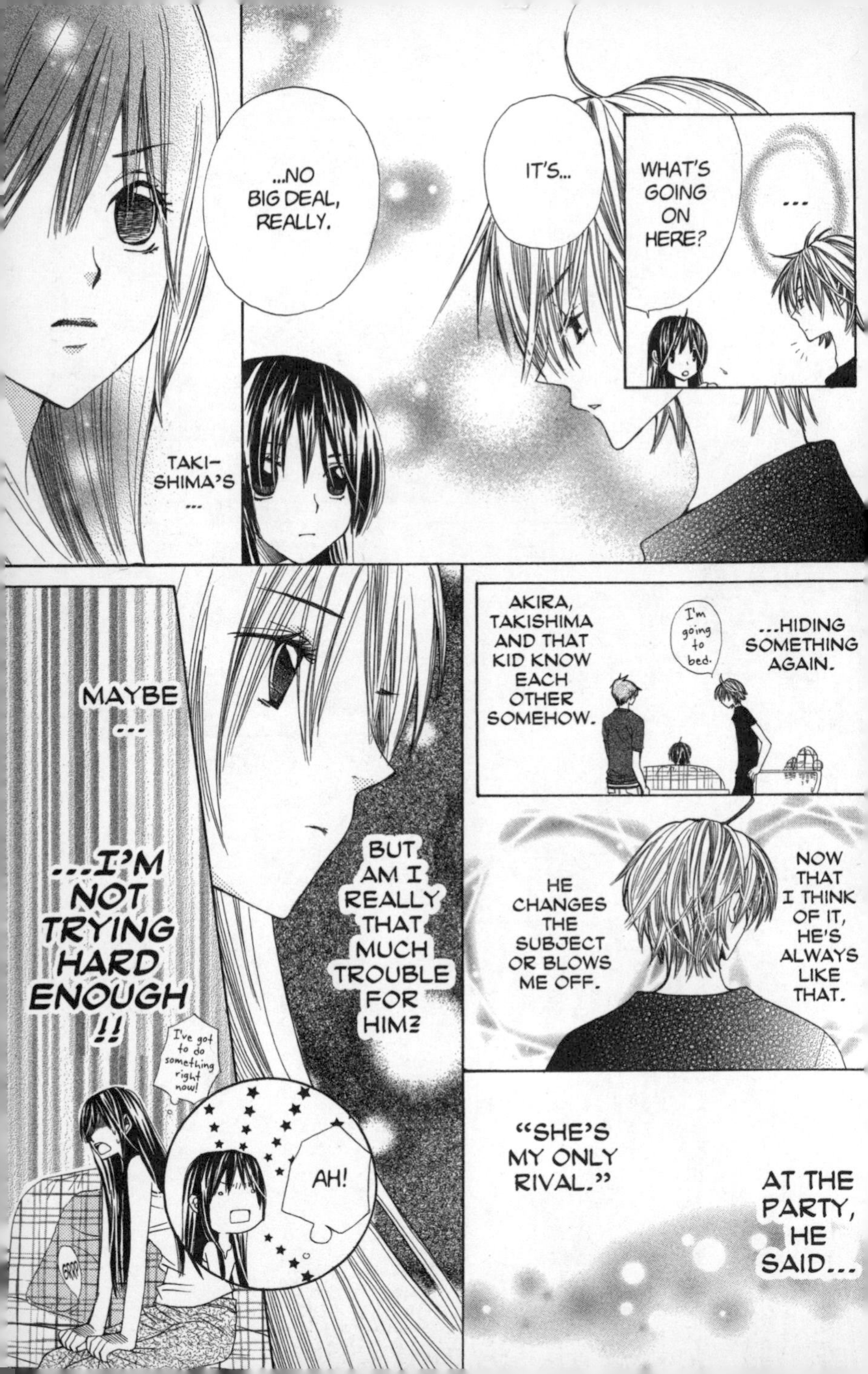
...
WHAT'S GOING ON HERE?
IT'S...
...NO BIG DEAL, REALLY.
TAKI-SHIMA'S ...
...HIDING SOMETHING AGAIN.
I'm going to bed.
AKIRA, TAKISHIMA AND THAT KID KNOW EACH OTHER SOMEHOW.
NOW THAT I THINK OF IT, HE'S ALWAYS LIKE THAT.
HE CHANGES THE SUBJECT OR BLOWS ME OFF.
AT THE PARTY, HE SAID...
“SHE'S MY ONLY RIVAL.”
BUT AM I REALLY THAT MUCH TROUBLE FOR HIM?
MAYBE ...
...I'M NOT TRYING HARD ENOUGH !!
I've got to do something right now!
AH!

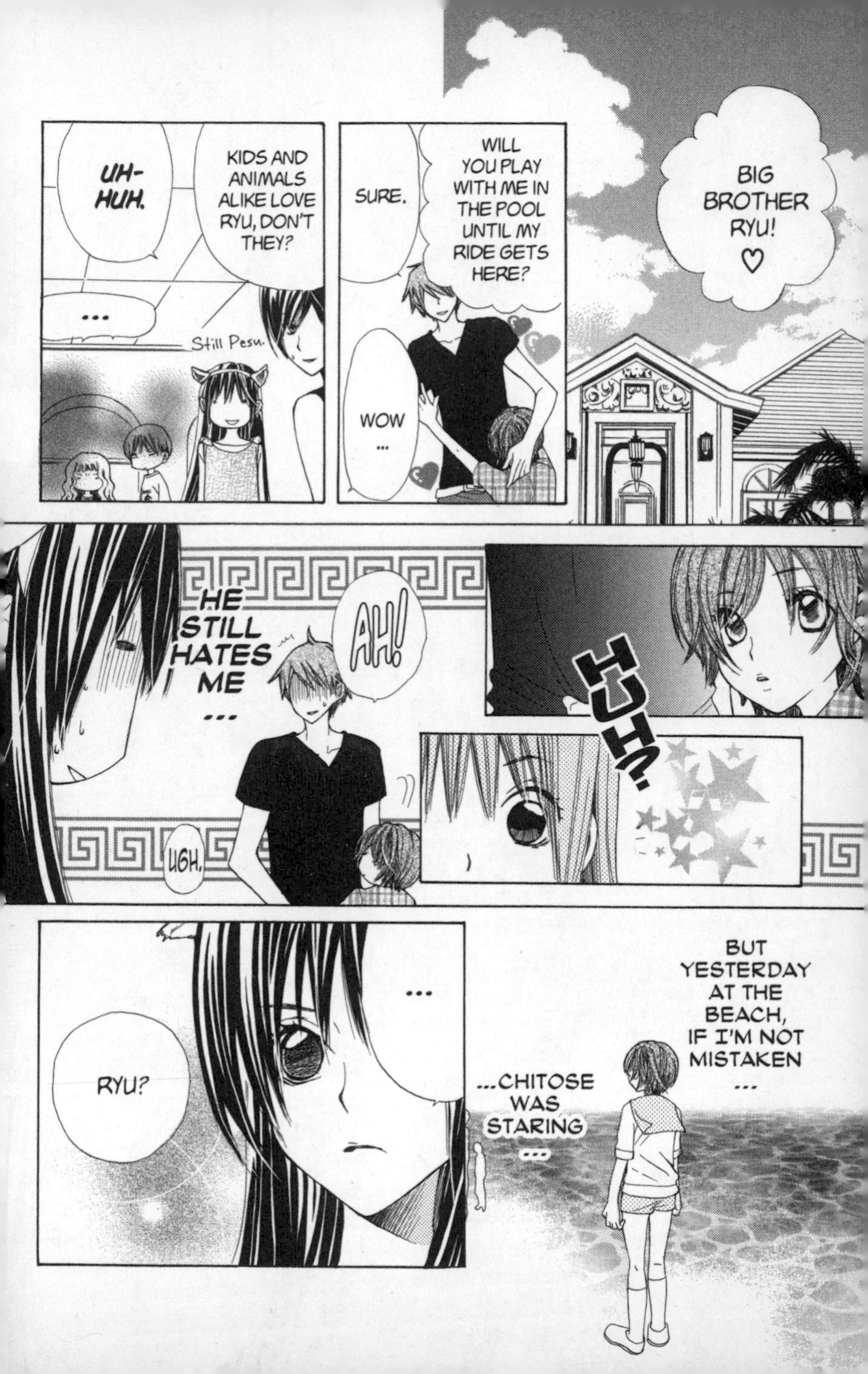
BIG BROTHER RYU! ♡
WILL YOU PLAY WITH ME IN THE POOL UNTIL MY RIDE GETS HERE?
SURE.
WOW ...
KIDS AND ANIMALS ALIKE LOVE RYU, DON'T THEY?
UH-HUH.
...
Still Pesu.
HUH?
AH!
HE STILL HATES ME ...
UGH.
BUT YESTERDAY AT THE BEACH, IF I'M NOT MISTAKEN ...
...CHITOSE WAS STARING ...
...
RYU?

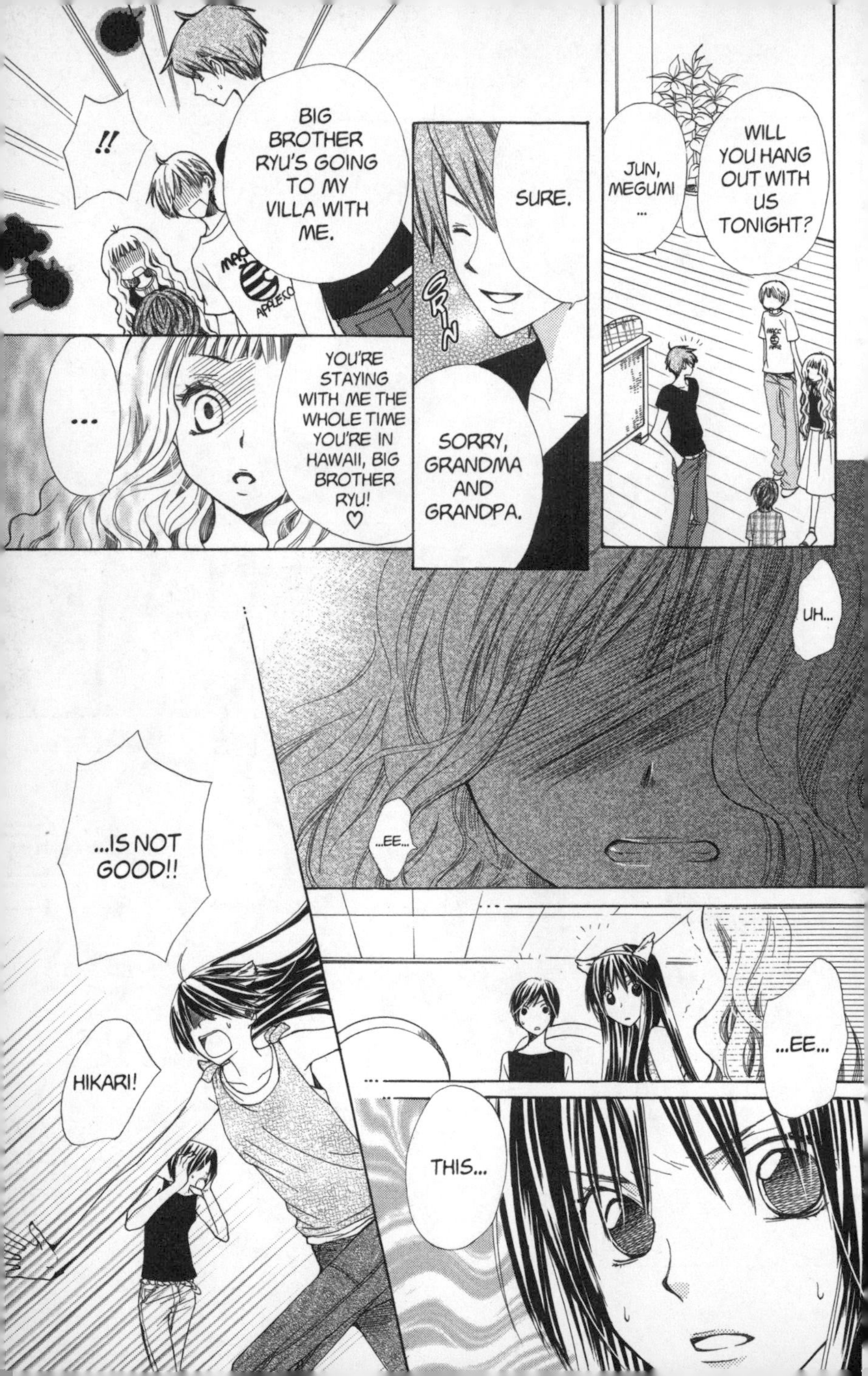
WILL YOU HANG OUT WITH US TONIGHT?
JUN, MEGUMI ...
SURE.
GRIN
SORRY, GRANDMA AND GRANDPA.
BIG BROTHER RYU'S GOING TO MY VILLA WITH ME.
!!
YOU'RE STAYING WITH ME THE WHOLE TIME YOU'RE IN HAWAII, BIG BROTHER RYU! ♡
...
UH...
...EE...
...EE...
THIS...
...IS NOT GOOD!!
HIKARI!

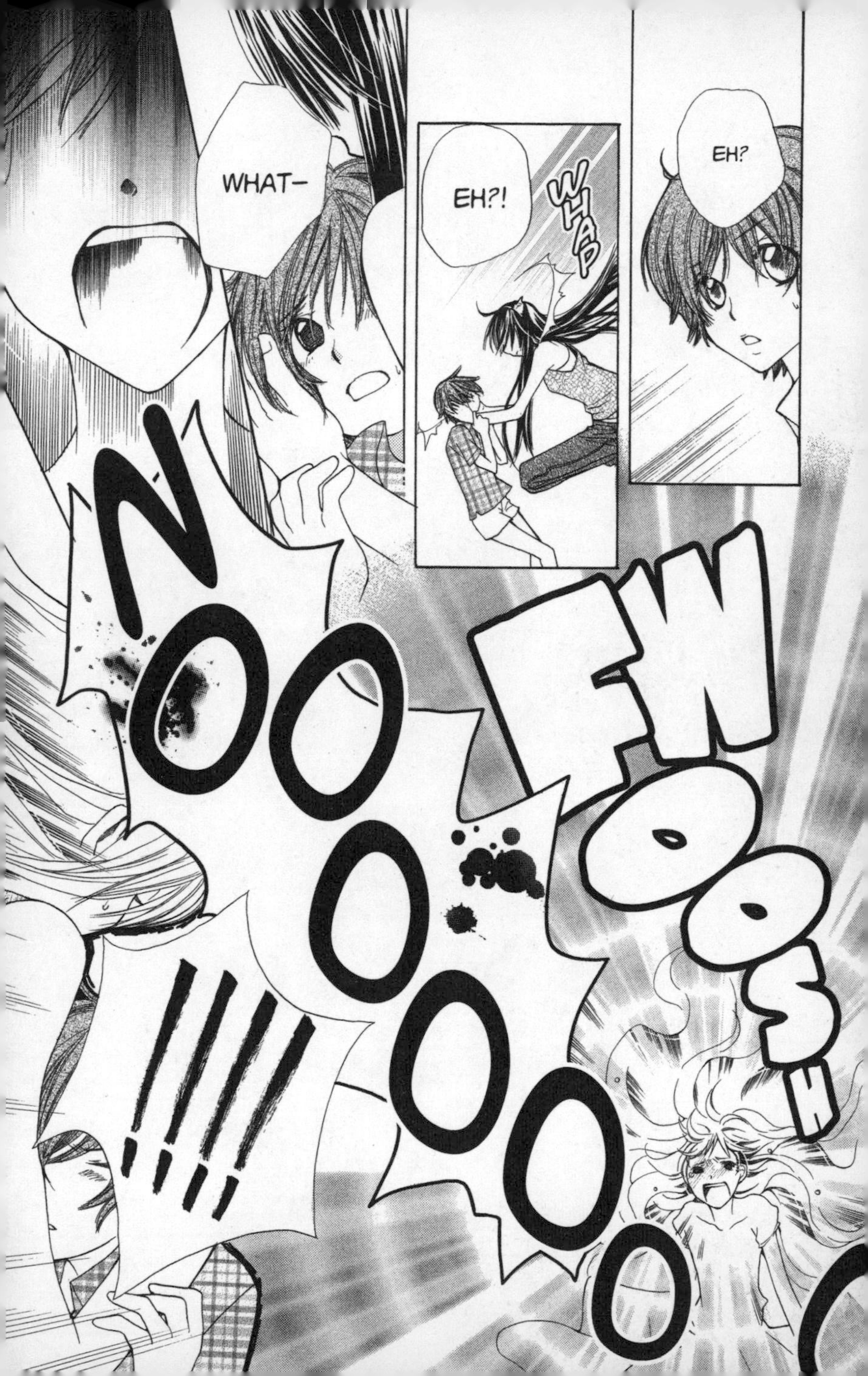
EH?
EH?!
WHAP
WHAT-
FWOOSH
NOOOOOOO!!!!

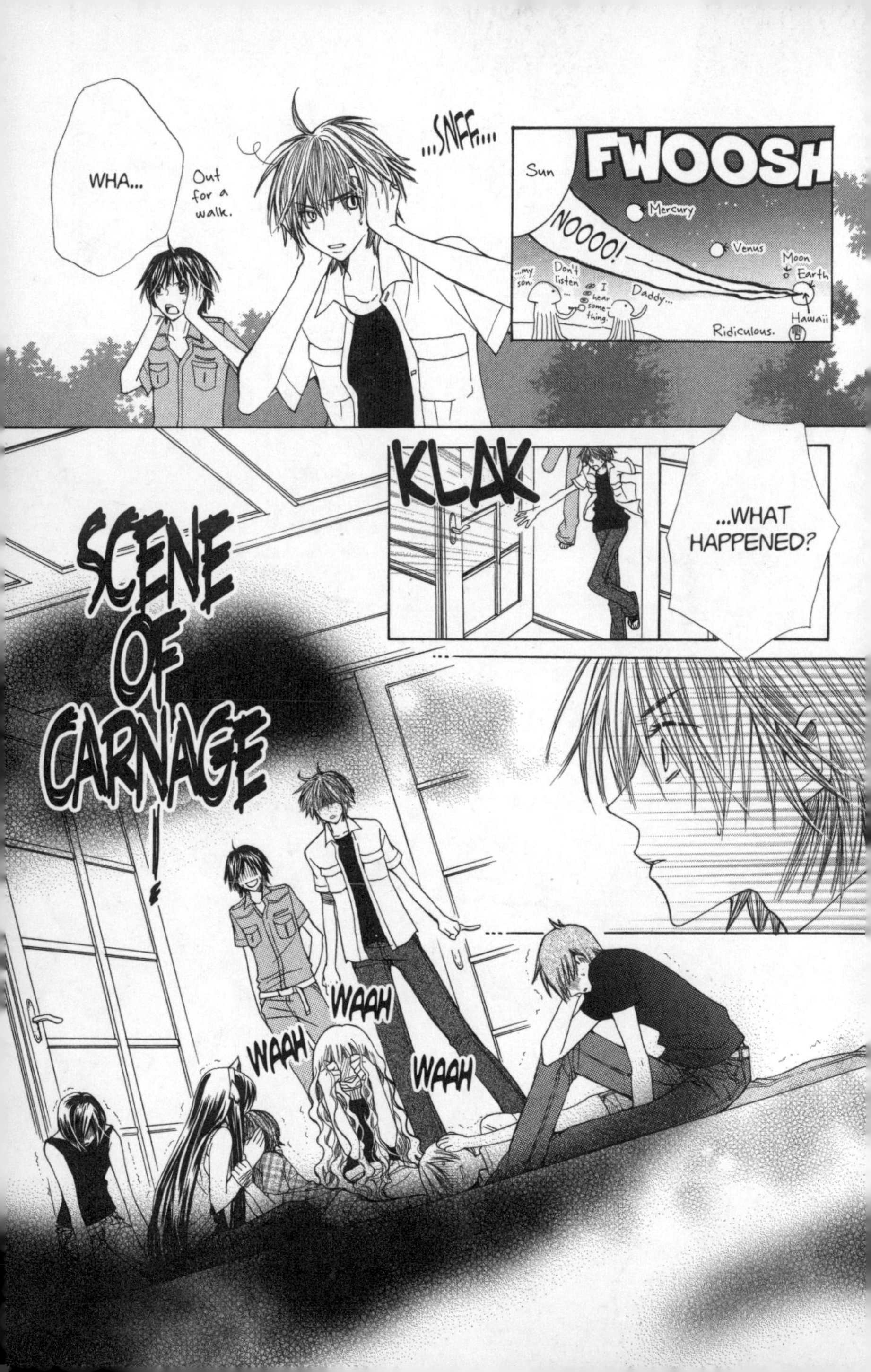
FWOOSH
Sun
Mercury
NOOOO!
Venus
Moon
Earth
Hawaii
Daddy...
I hear some-thing.
Don't listen...
...my son.
Ridiculous.
...SNFF....
Out for a walk.
WHA...
KLAK
...WHAT HAPPENED?
...
SCENE OF CARNAGE!
...
WAAH
WAAH
WAAH

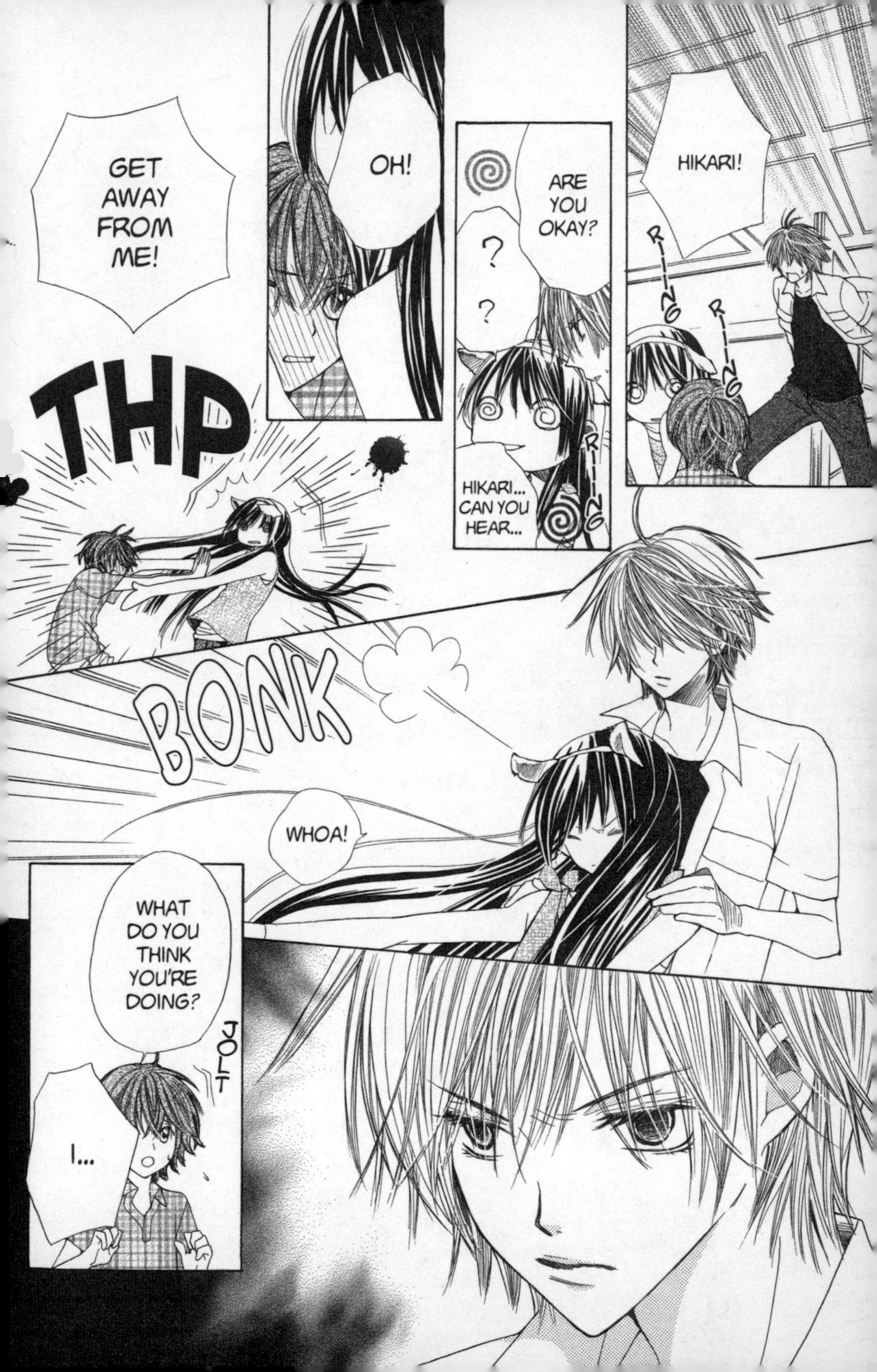
HIKARI!
RRING
RRING
ARE YOU OKAY?
?
?
RRING
HIKARI... CAN YOU HEAR...
OH!
GET AWAY FROM ME!
THP
BONK
WHOA!
WHAT DO YOU THINK YOU'RE DOING?
JOLT
I...

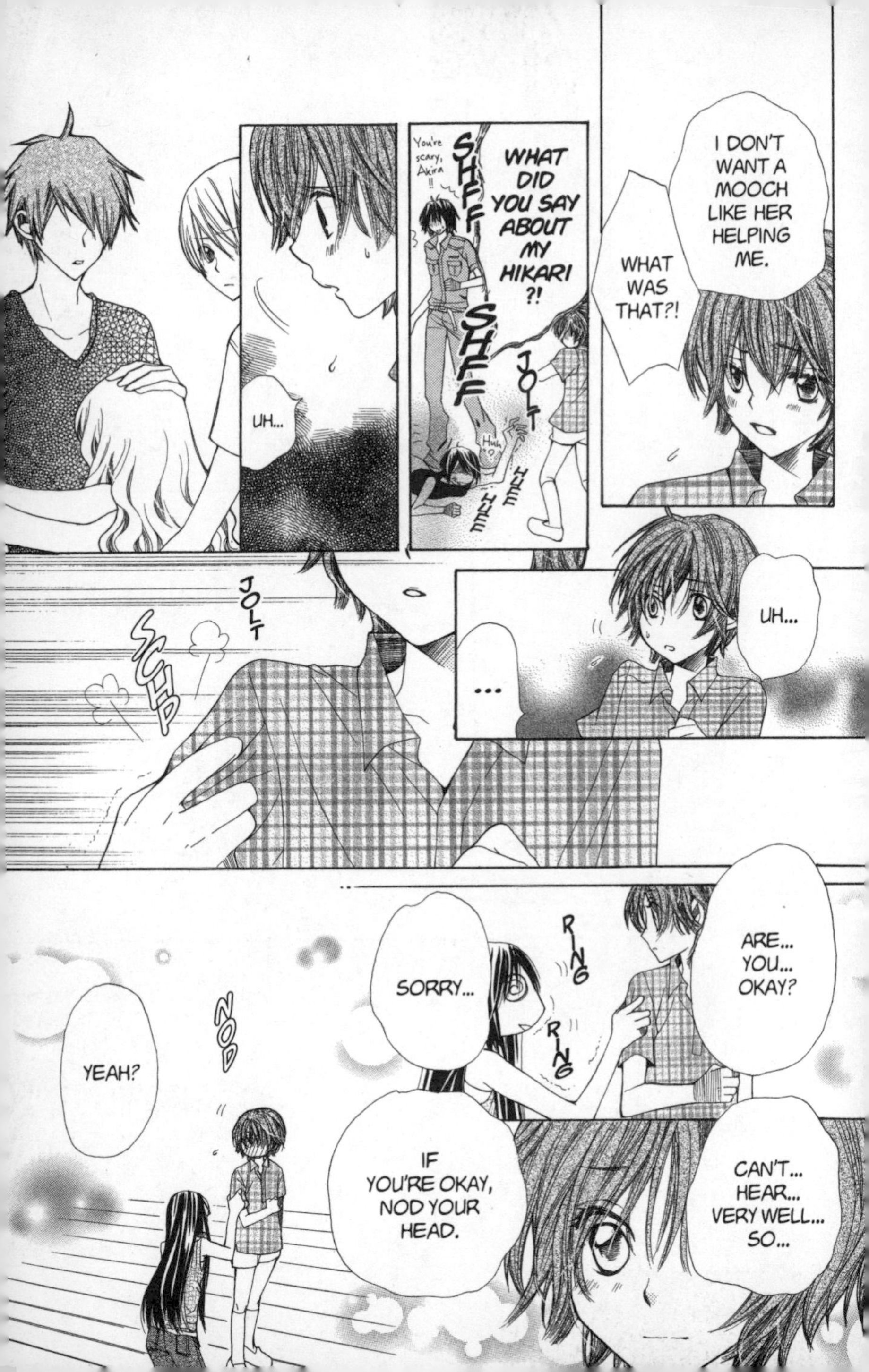
I DON'T WANT A MOOCH LIKE HER HELPING ME.
WHAT WAS THAT?!
WHAT DID YOU SAY ABOUT MY HIKARI?!
SHFF
SHFF
You're scary, Akira!!
JOLT
Huh?
HUFF HUFF
UH...
UH...
...
JOLT
SCHP
ARE... YOU... OKAY?
RING
RING
SORRY...
CAN'T... HEAR... VERY WELL... SO...
IF YOU'RE OKAY, NOD YOUR HEAD.
NOD
YEAH?

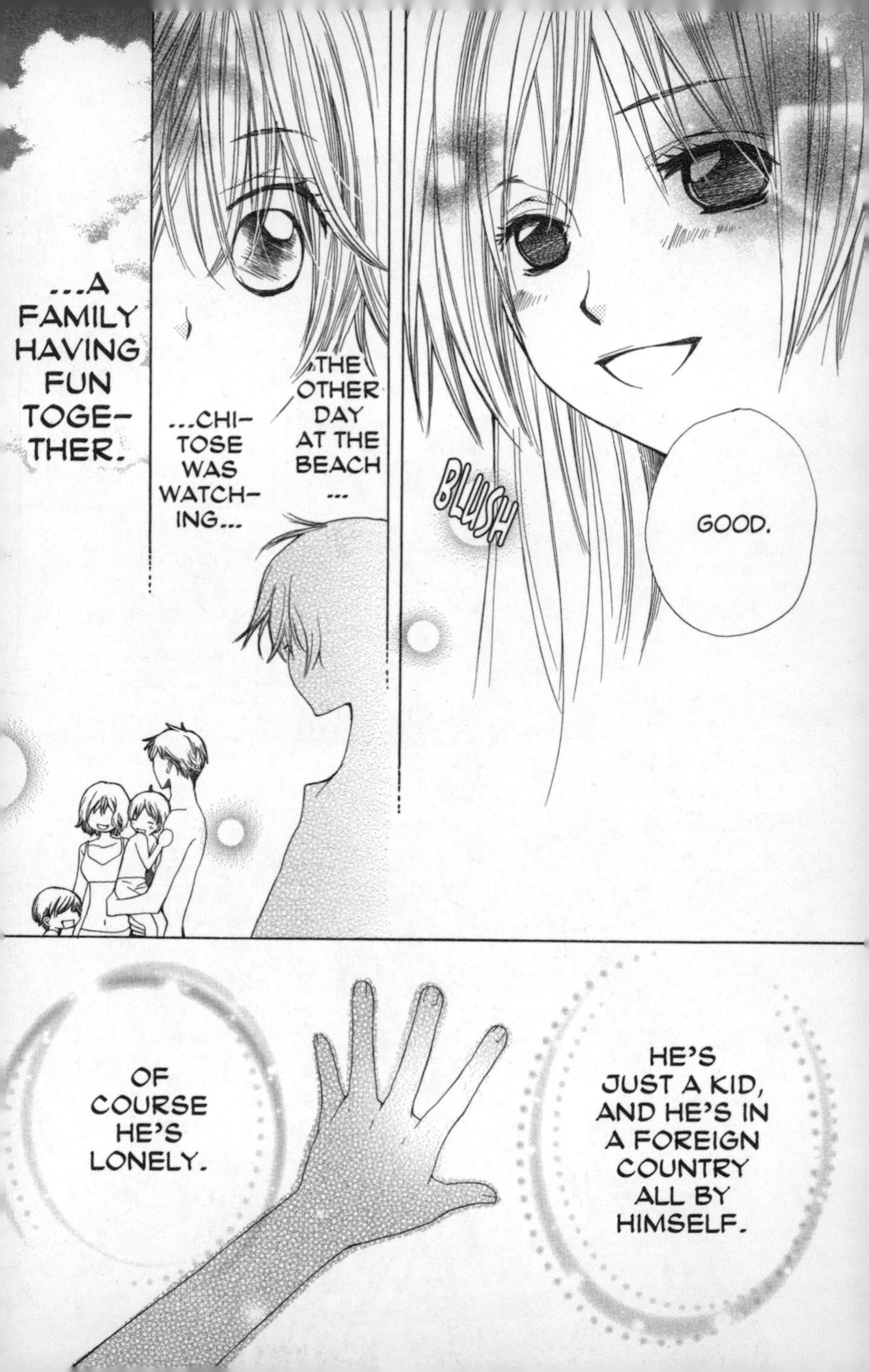

GOOD.
BLUSH
THE OTHER DAY AT THE BEACH...
...CHITOSE WAS WATCHING...
...A FAMILY HAVING FUN TOGETHER.
HE'S JUST A KID, AND HE'S IN A FOREIGN COUNTRY ALL BY HIMSELF.
OF COURSE HE'S LONELY.

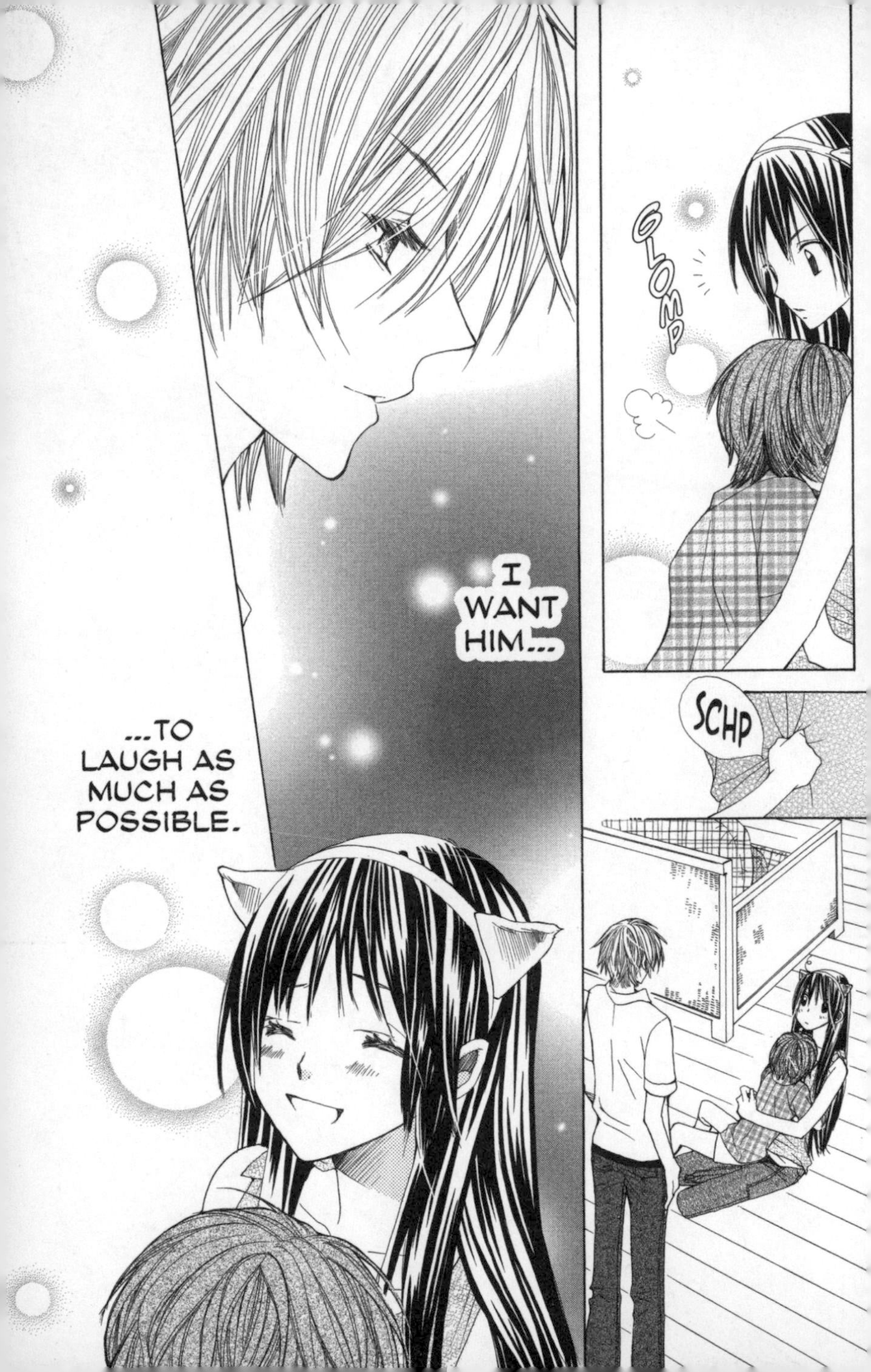
GLOMP
SCHP
I WANT HIM...
...TO LAUGH AS MUCH AS POSSIBLE.

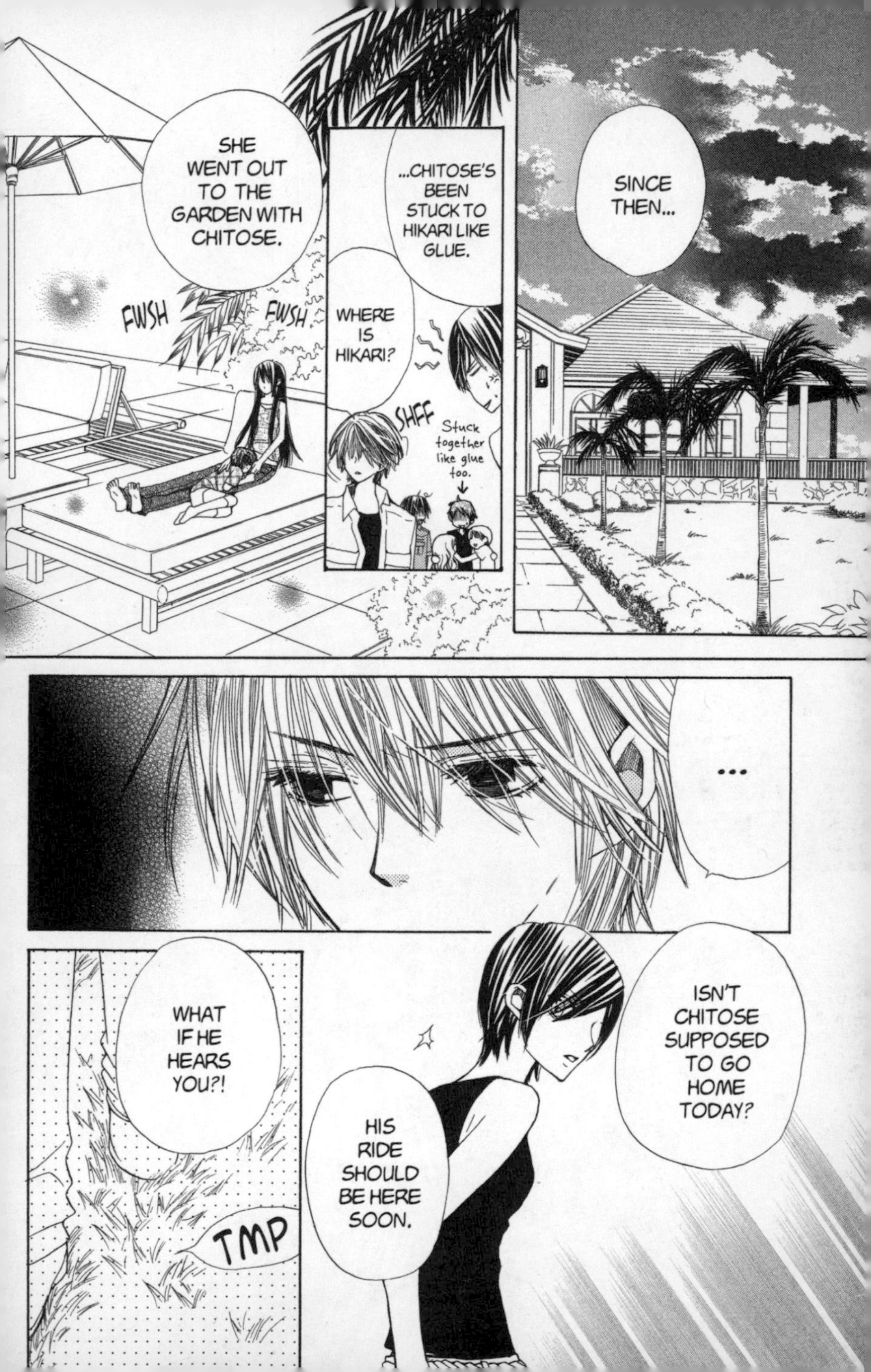
SINCE THEN...
...CHITOSE'S BEEN STUCK TO HIKARI LIKE GLUE.
WHERE IS HIKARI?
SHFF
Stuck together like glue too.
SHE WENT OUT TO THE GARDEN WITH CHITOSE.
FWSH
FWSH
...
ISN'T CHITOSE SUPPOSED TO GO HOME TODAY?
HIS RIDE SHOULD BE HERE SOON.
WHAT IF HE HEARS YOU?!
TMP

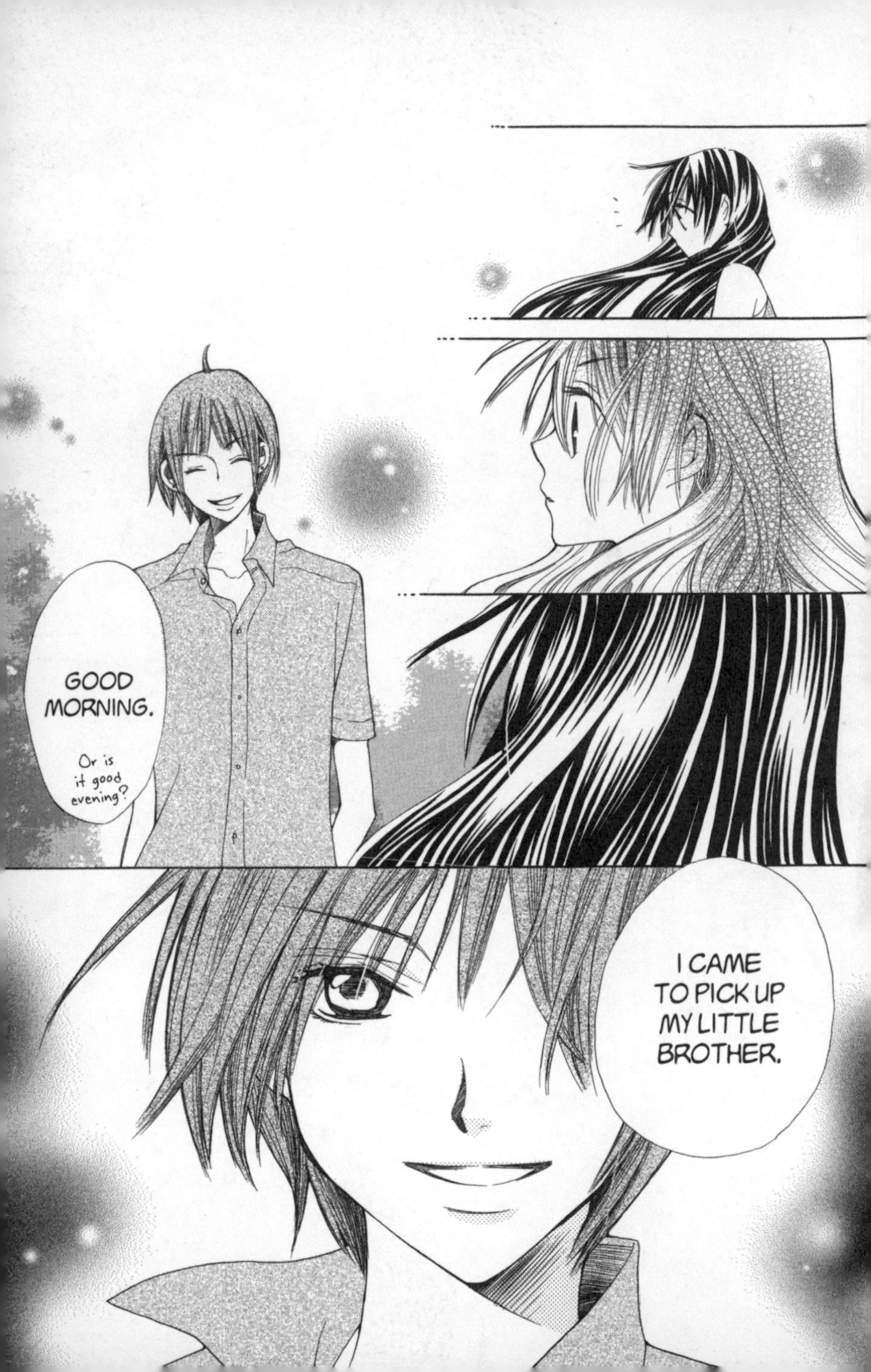
GOOD MORNING.
Or is it good evening?
I CAME TO PICK UP MY LITTLE BROTHER.

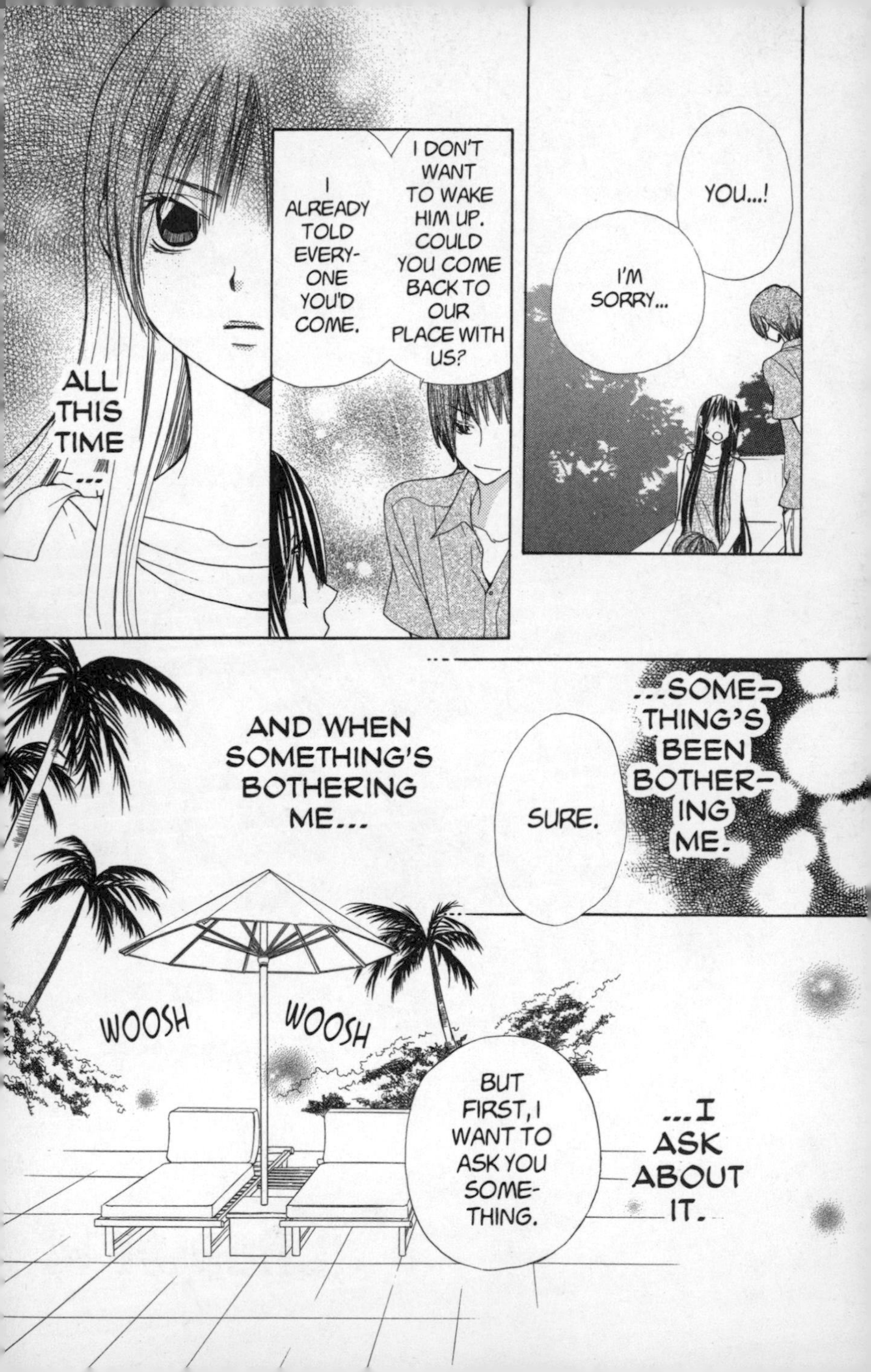
YOU...!
I'M SORRY...
I DON'T WANT TO WAKE HIM UP. COULD YOU COME BACK TO OUR PLACE WITH US?
I ALREADY TOLD EVERY-ONE YOU'D COME.
ALL THIS TIME...
...SOME-THING'S BEEN BOTHER-ING ME.
SURE.
AND WHEN SOMETHING'S BOTHERING ME...
...I ASK ABOUT IT.
BUT FIRST, I WANT TO ASK YOU SOME-THING.
WOOSH
WOOSH

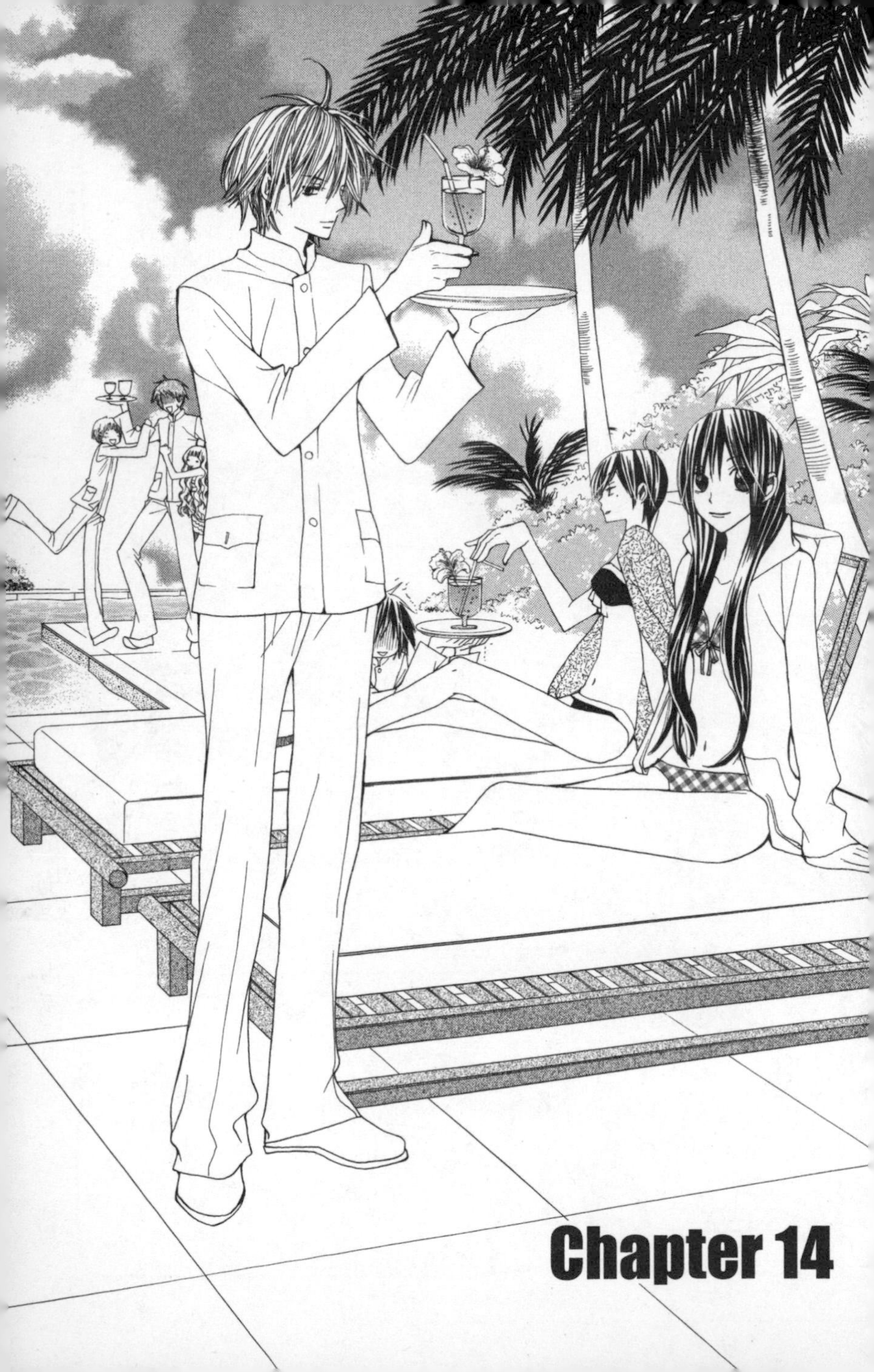

Chapter 14

SHE'S PROBABLY OVER AT YAHIRO'S.

WAIT, WHAT?!

WAAAH

YOU'VE GOT TO BE KIDDING ME! SHE'S NOWHERE!

WELL...

SOMETHING'S BEEN BOTHERING ME.

...

SPLISH

HOW CAN YOU SAY THAT SO CALMLY, KEI?

CALM?

HIKARI?!

TADASHI KARINO	AKIRA TOUDOU
BORN: 9/9	BORN: 4/19
BLOOD TYPE: B	BLOOD TYPE: B
FAMILY: FATHER, MOTHER, GRANDFATHER	FAMILY: FATHER, MOTHER
FAVORITE FOOD: ANYTHING SWEET (ESPECIALLY IF IT'S MADE BY AKIRA)	FAVORITE FOODS: CROISSANTS, ÉCLAIRS, MERINGUE

The three measures of a good pastry chef.

grin

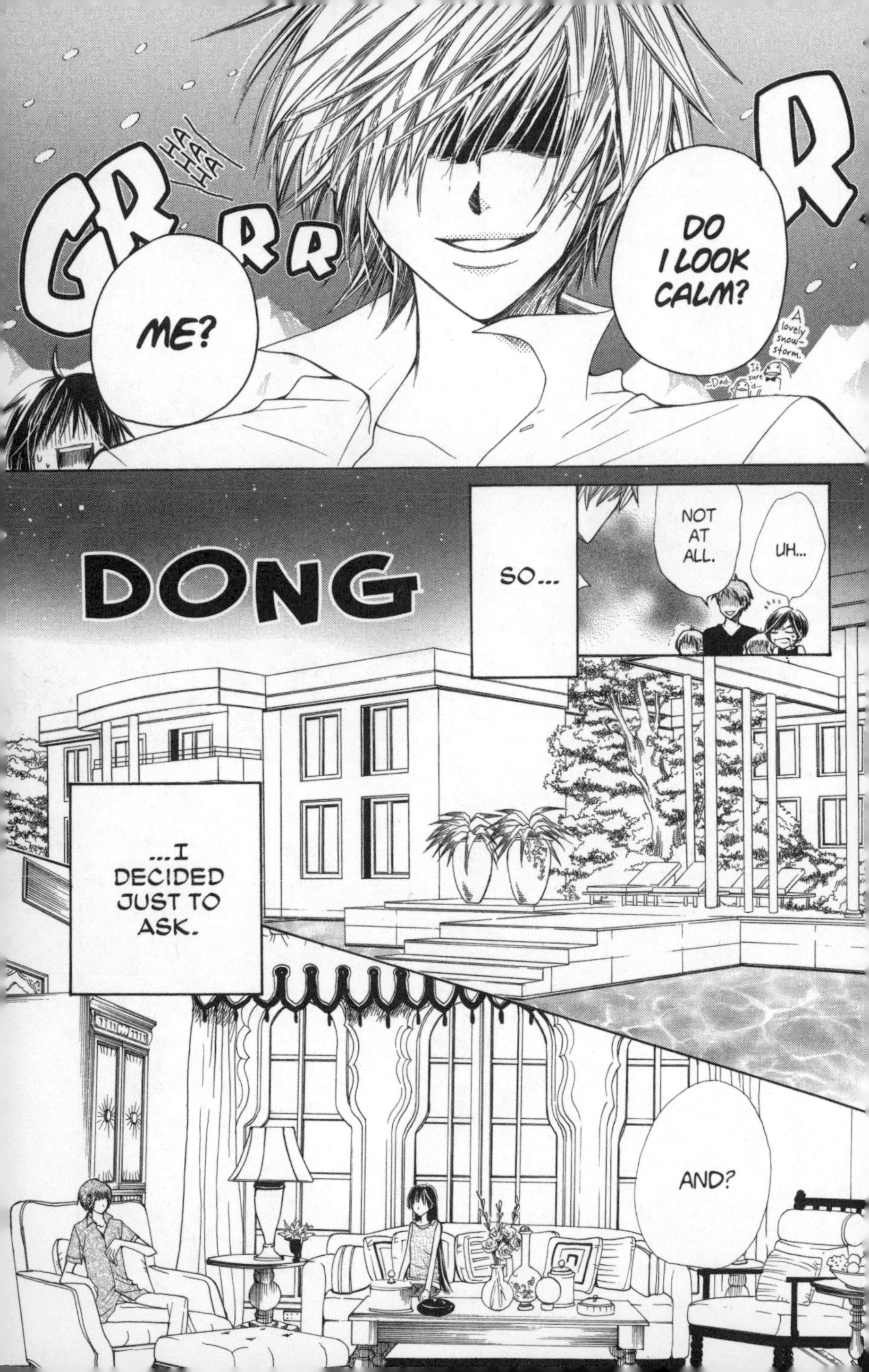
DO I LOOK CALM?
CRRRRR
HA HA HA
ME?
A lovely snowstorm.
It sure is...
...Dad.
SO...
NOT AT ALL.
UH...
DONG
...I DECIDED JUST TO ASK.
AND?

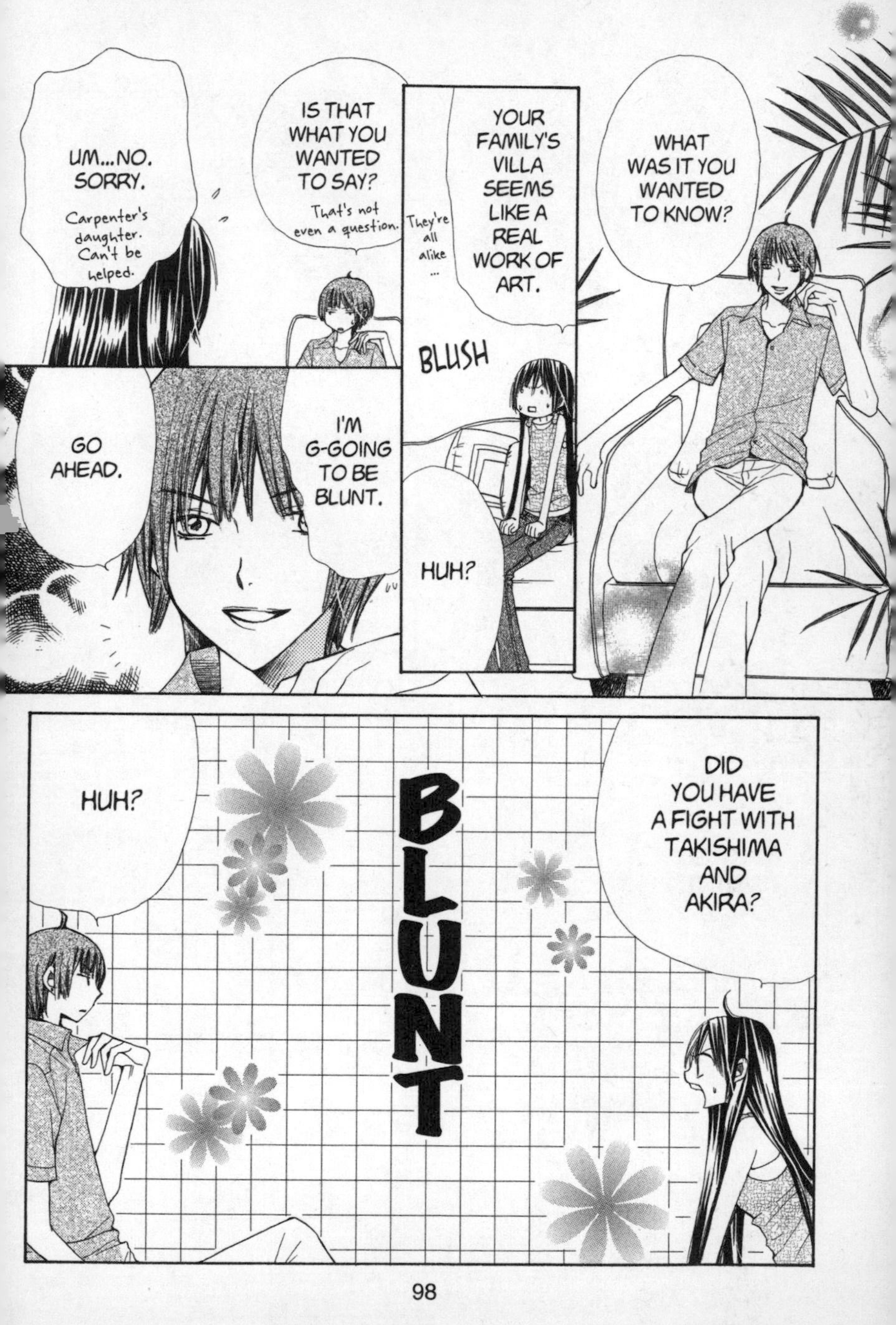
WHAT WAS IT YOU WANTED TO KNOW?
YOUR FAMILY'S VILLA SEEMS LIKE A REAL WORK OF ART.
They're all alike...
BLUSH
HUH?
IS THAT WHAT YOU WANTED TO SAY?
That's not even a question.
UM...NO. SORRY.
Carpenter's daughter. Can't be helped.
I'M G-GOING TO BE BLUNT.
GO AHEAD.
DID YOU HAVE A FIGHT WITH TAKISHIMA AND AKIRA?
BLUNT
HUH?

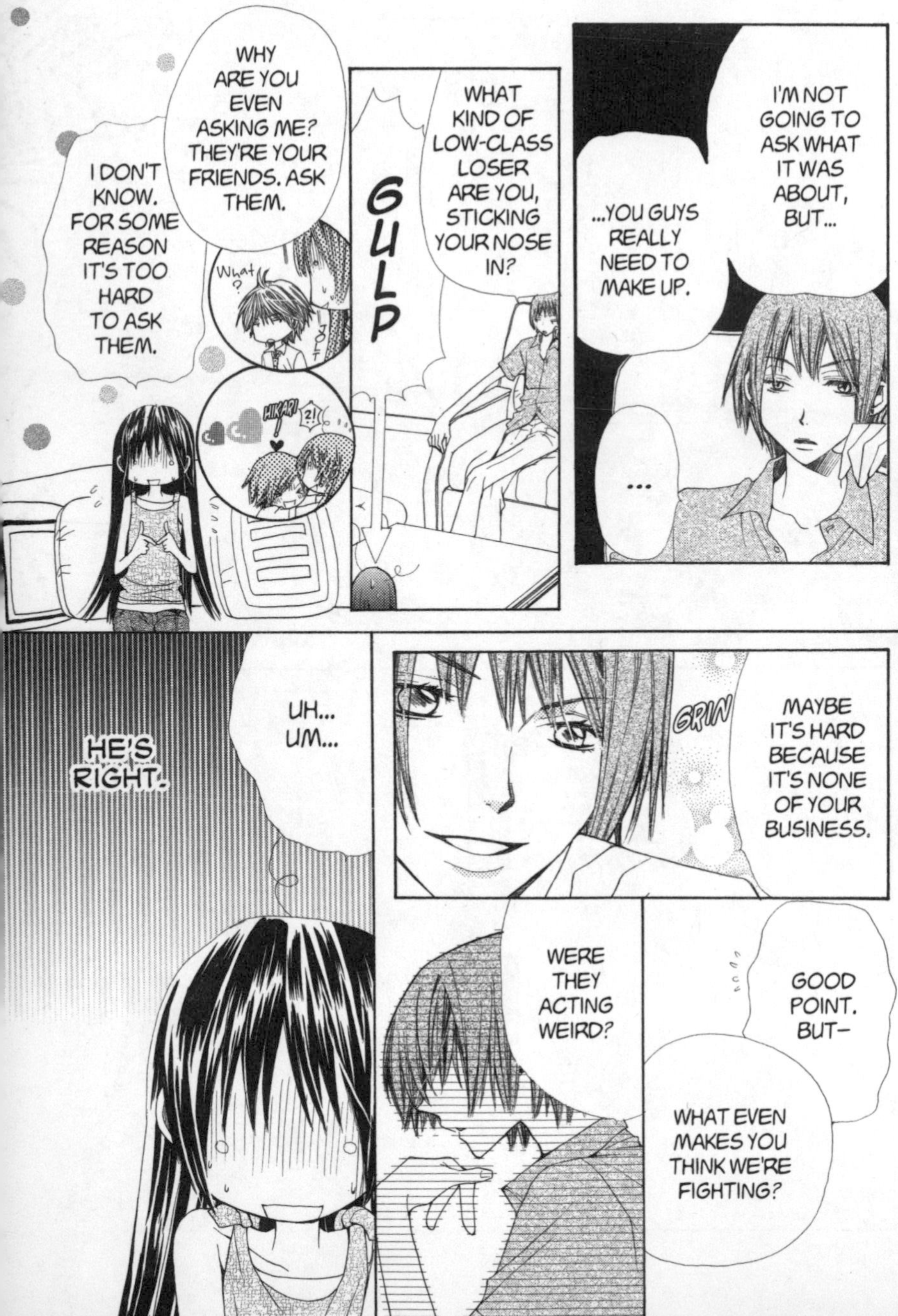
I'M NOT GOING TO ASK WHAT IT WAS ABOUT, BUT...
...YOU GUYS REALLY NEED TO MAKE UP.
...
WHAT KIND OF LOW-CLASS LOSER ARE YOU, STICKING YOUR NOSE IN?
GULP
WHY ARE YOU EVEN ASKING ME? THEY'RE YOUR FRIENDS. ASK THEM.
What?
HIKARI!
I DON'T KNOW. FOR SOME REASON IT'S TOO HARD TO ASK THEM.
GRIN
MAYBE IT'S HARD BECAUSE IT'S NONE OF YOUR BUSINESS.
GOOD POINT. BUT–
WHAT EVEN MAKES YOU THINK WE'RE FIGHTING?
WERE THEY ACTING WEIRD?
UH... UM...
HE'S RIGHT.

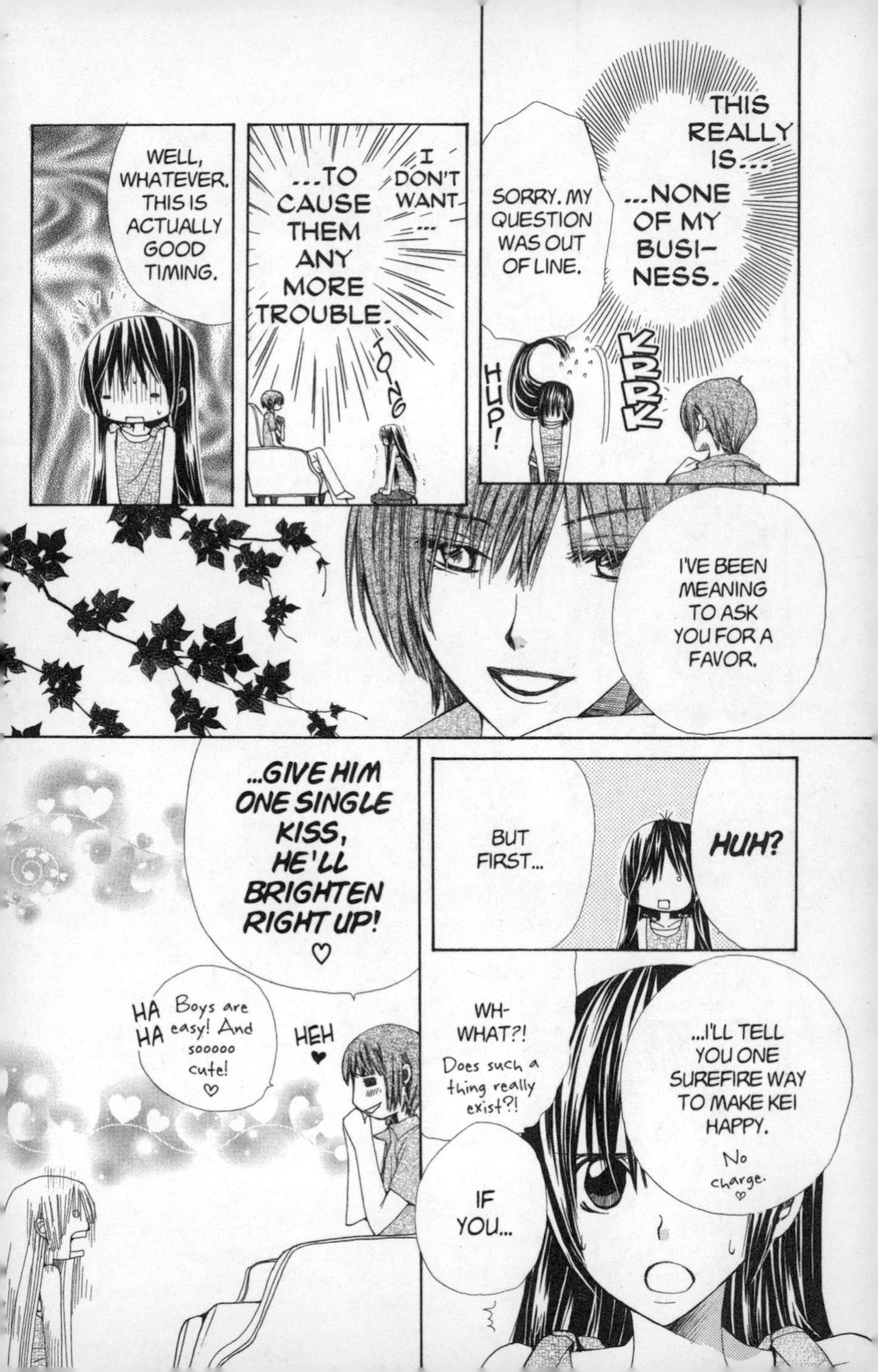
SORRY. MY QUESTION WAS OUT OF LINE.
THIS REALLY IS...
...NONE OF MY BUSINESS.
KRRK
HUP!
I DON'T WANT...
...TO CAUSE THEM ANY MORE TROUBLE.
TOING
WELL, WHATEVER. THIS IS ACTUALLY GOOD TIMING.
I'VE BEEN MEANING TO ASK YOU FOR A FAVOR.
HUH?
BUT FIRST...
...I'LL TELL YOU ONE SUREFIRE WAY TO MAKE KEI HAPPY.
No charge. ♡
WH-WHAT?!
Does such a thing really exist?!
IF YOU...
...GIVE HIM ONE SINGLE KISS, HE'LL BRIGHTEN RIGHT UP! ♡
HEH ♥
HA HA
Boys are easy! And soooooo cute! ♡

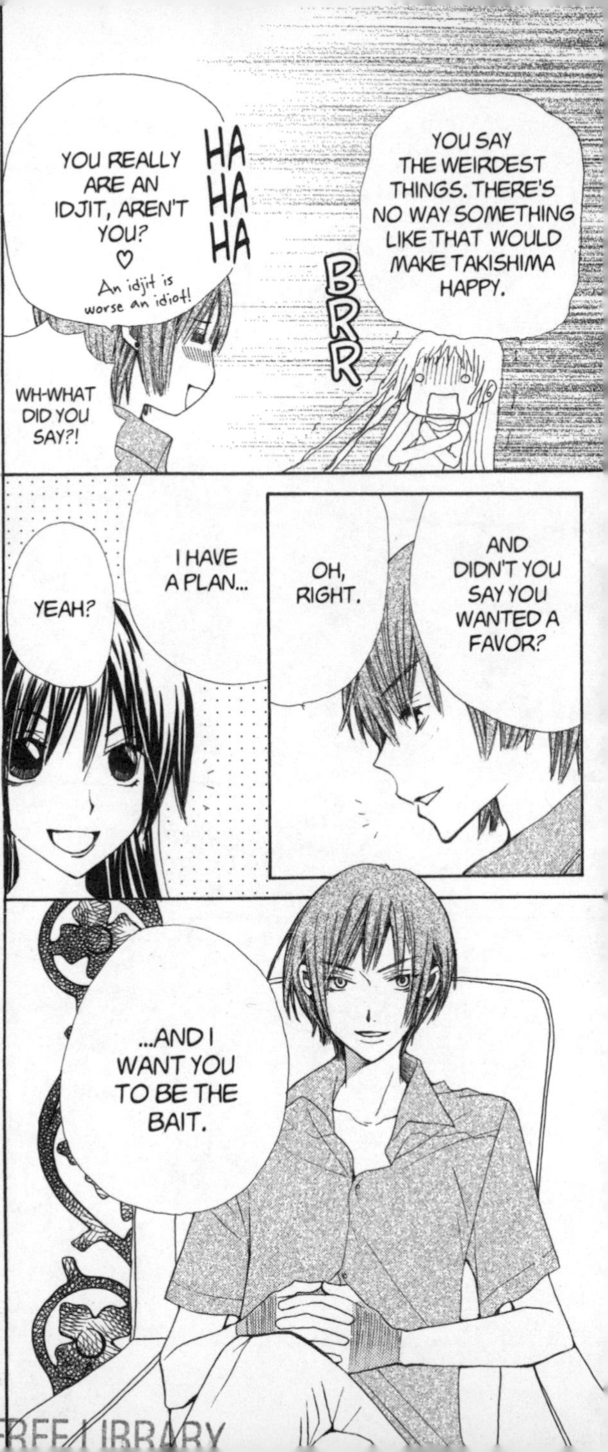
YOU SAY THE WEIRDEST THINGS. THERE'S NO WAY SOMETHING LIKE THAT WOULD MAKE TAKISHIMA HAPPY.
BRR
HA HA HA
YOU REALLY ARE AN IDJIT, AREN'T YOU? ♡
An idjit is worse an idiot!
WH-WHAT DID YOU SAY?!
AND DIDN'T YOU SAY YOU WANTED A FAVOR?
OH, RIGHT.
I HAVE A PLAN...
YEAH?
...AND I WANT YOU TO BE THE BAIT.

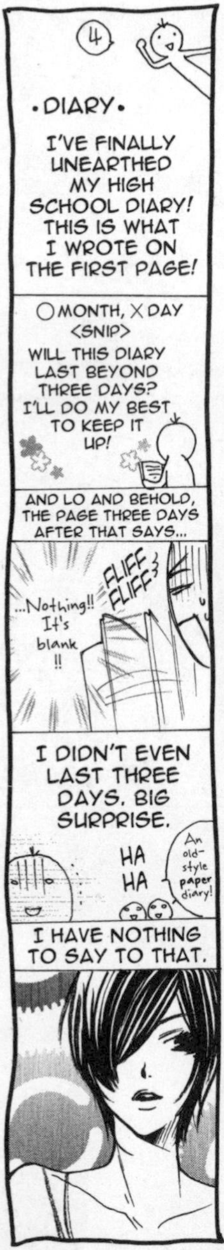
4
•DIARY•
I'VE FINALLY UNEARTHED MY HIGH SCHOOL DIARY! THIS IS WHAT I WROTE ON THE FIRST PAGE!
○MONTH, ╳DAY
<SNIP>
WILL THIS DIARY LAST BEYOND THREE DAYS? I'LL DO MY BEST TO KEEP IT UP!
AND LO AND BEHOLD, THE PAGE THREE DAYS AFTER THAT SAYS...
FLIFF FLIFF
...Nothing!! It's blank !!
I DIDN'T EVEN LAST THREE DAYS. BIG SURPRISE.
HA HA
An old-style paper diary!
I HAVE NOTHING TO SAY TO THAT.

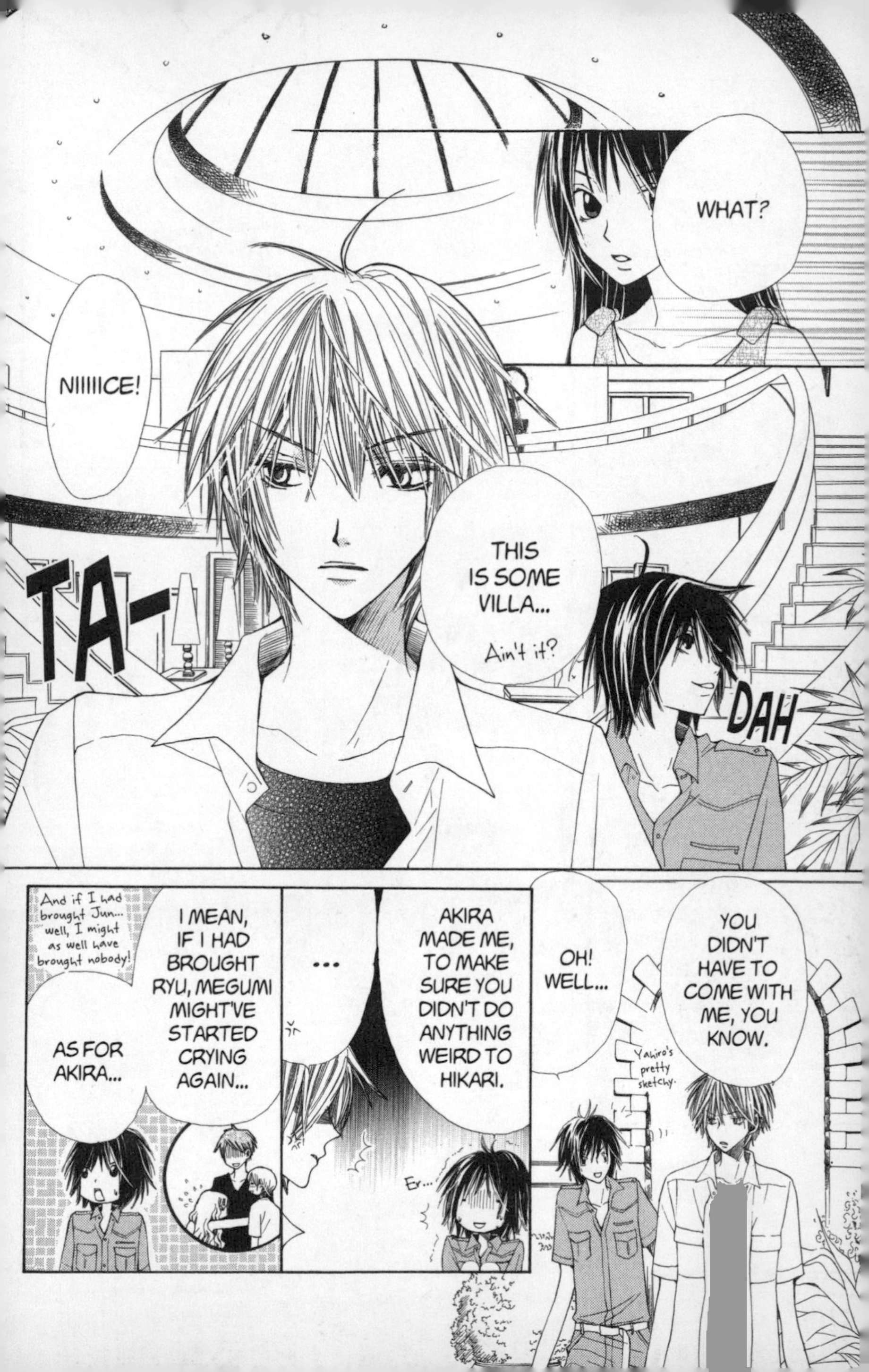
WHAT?
NIIIIICE!
THIS IS SOME VILLA...
Ain't it?
TA-
DAH
YOU DIDN'T HAVE TO COME WITH ME, YOU KNOW.
OH! WELL...
Yahiro's pretty sketchy.
AKIRA MADE ME, TO MAKE SURE YOU DIDN'T DO ANYTHING WEIRD TO HIKARI.
...
Er...
I MEAN, IF I HAD BROUGHT RYU, MEGUMI MIGHT'VE STARTED CRYING AGAIN...
And if I had brought Jun... well, I might as well have brought nobody!
AS FOR AKIRA...

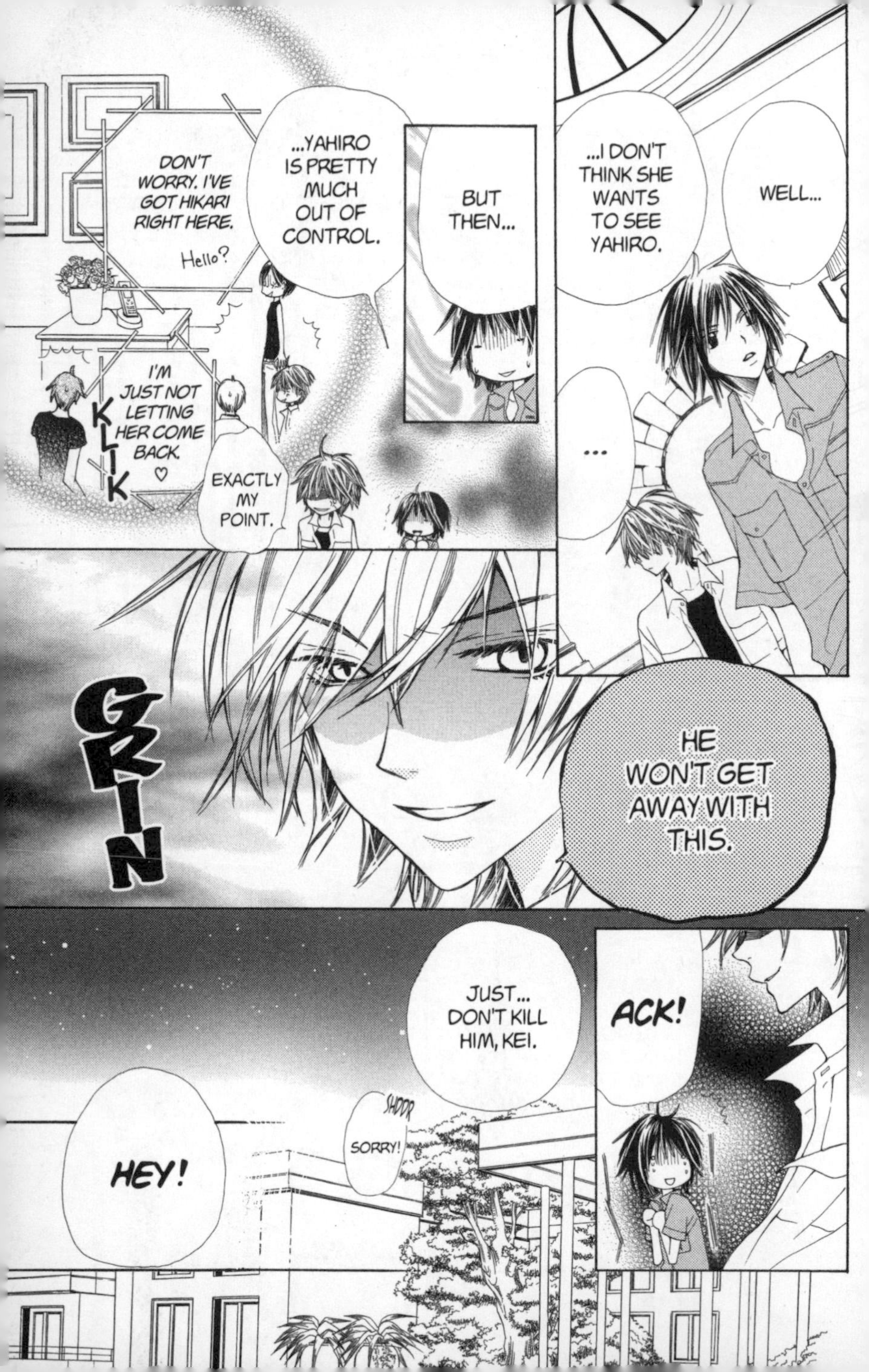
WELL...
...I DON'T THINK SHE WANTS TO SEE YAHIRO.
...
BUT THEN...
...YAHIRO IS PRETTY MUCH OUT OF CONTROL.
DON'T WORRY. I'VE GOT HIKARI RIGHT HERE.
Hello?
I'M JUST NOT LETTING HER COME BACK. ♡
KLIK
EXACTLY MY POINT.
HE WON'T GET AWAY WITH THIS.
GRIN
ACK!
JUST... DON'T KILL HIM, KEI.
SHDDR
SORRY!
HEY!

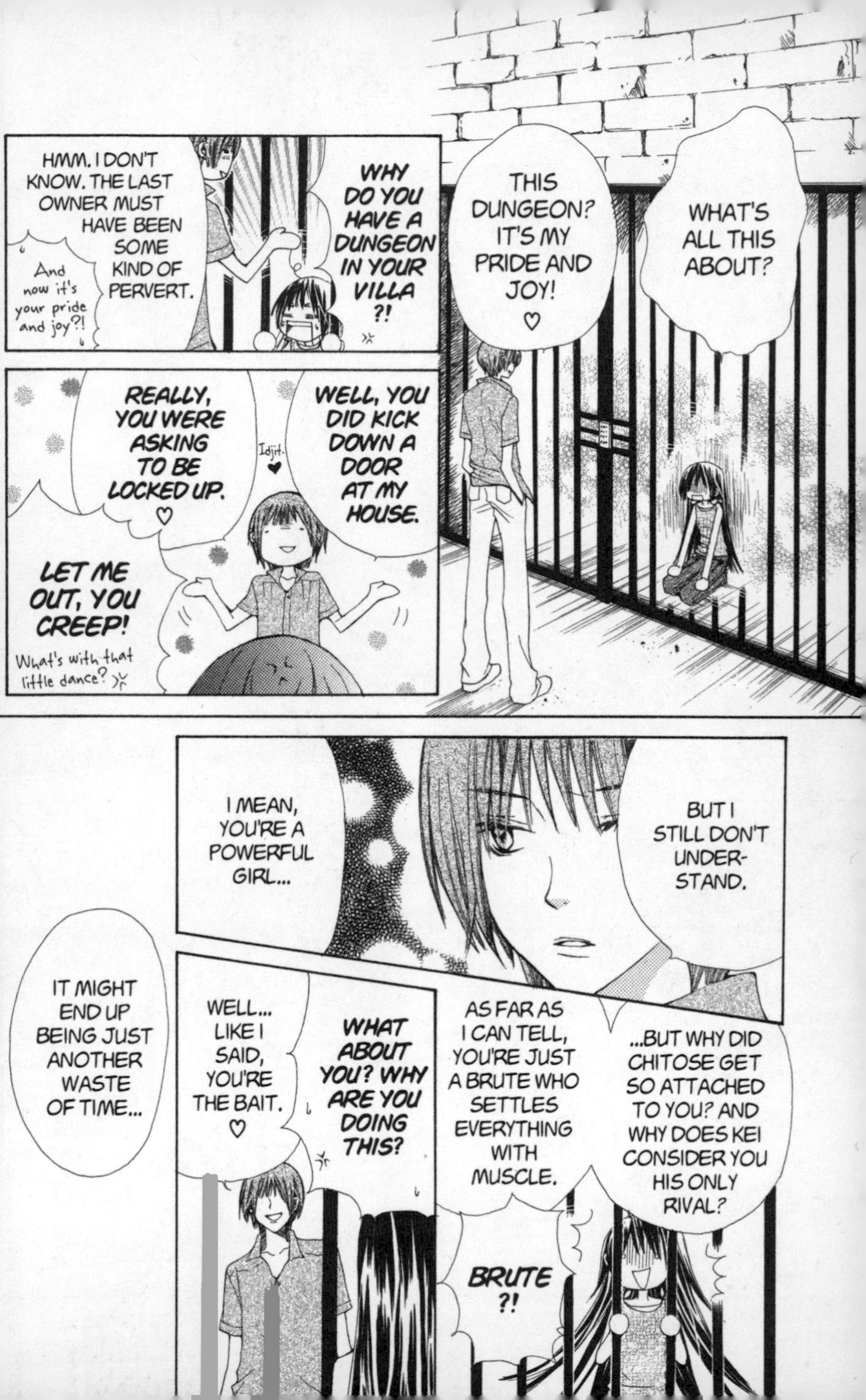
WHAT'S ALL THIS ABOUT?
THIS DUNGEON? IT'S MY PRIDE AND JOY! ♡
WHY DO YOU HAVE A DUNGEON IN YOUR VILLA?!
HMM. I DON'T KNOW. THE LAST OWNER MUST HAVE BEEN SOME KIND OF PERVERT.
And now it's your pride and joy?!
WELL, YOU DID KICK DOWN A DOOR AT MY HOUSE.
Idjit. ♥
REALLY, YOU WERE ASKING TO BE LOCKED UP. ♡
LET ME OUT, YOU CREEP!
What's with that little dance?
BUT I STILL DON'T UNDER-STAND.
I MEAN, YOU'RE A POWERFUL GIRL...
...BUT WHY DID CHITOSE GET SO ATTACHED TO YOU? AND WHY DOES KEI CONSIDER YOU HIS ONLY RIVAL?
AS FAR AS I CAN TELL, YOU'RE JUST A BRUTE WHO SETTLES EVERYTHING WITH MUSCLE.
BRUTE?!
WHAT ABOUT YOU? WHY ARE YOU DOING THIS?
WELL... LIKE I SAID, YOU'RE THE BAIT. ♡
IT MIGHT END UP BEING JUST ANOTHER WASTE OF TIME...

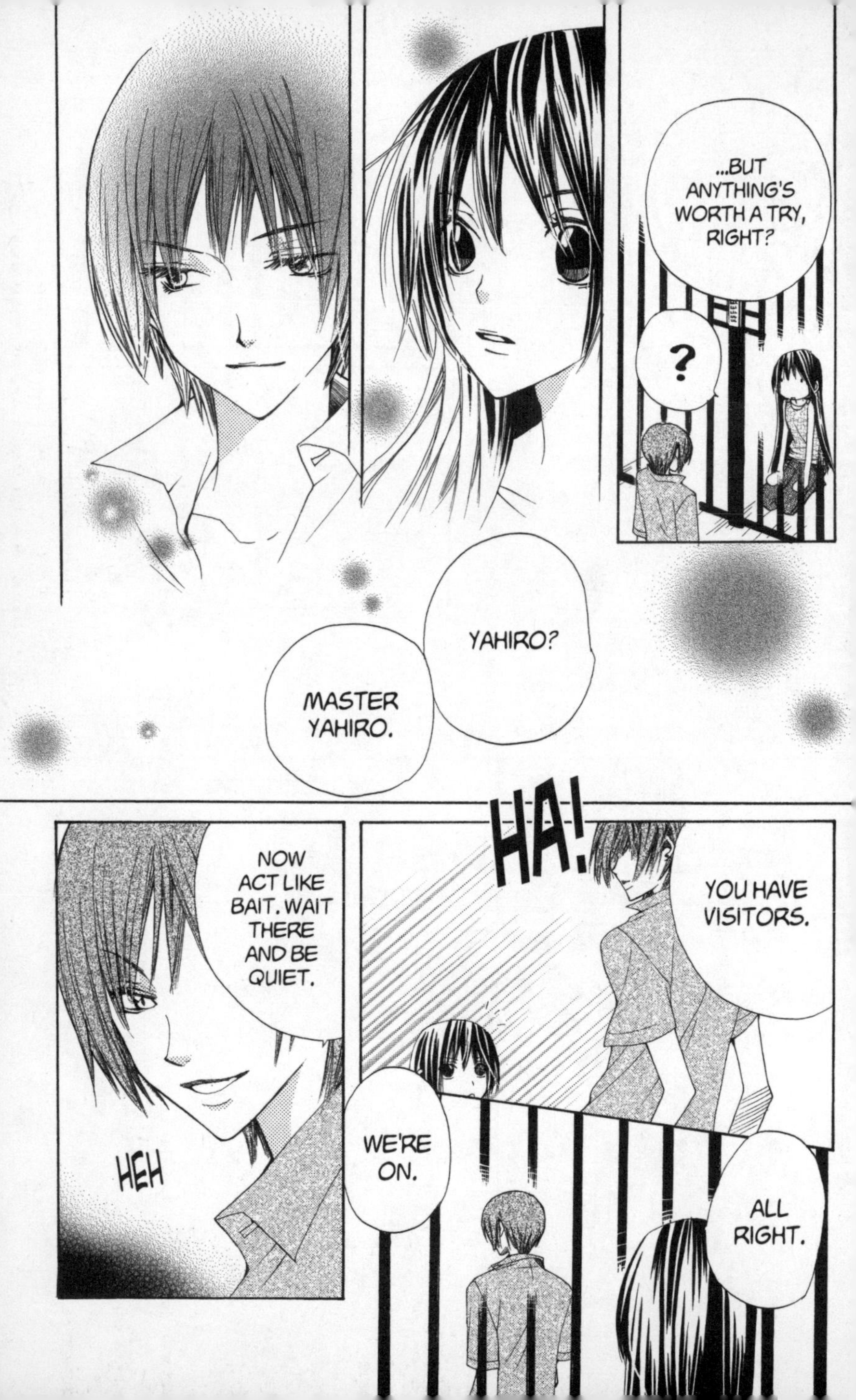
...BUT ANYTHING'S WORTH A TRY, RIGHT?
?
YAHIRO?
MASTER YAHIRO.
HA!
YOU HAVE VISITORS.
ALL RIGHT.
WE'RE ON.
NOW ACT LIKE BAIT. WAIT THERE AND BE QUIET.
HEH

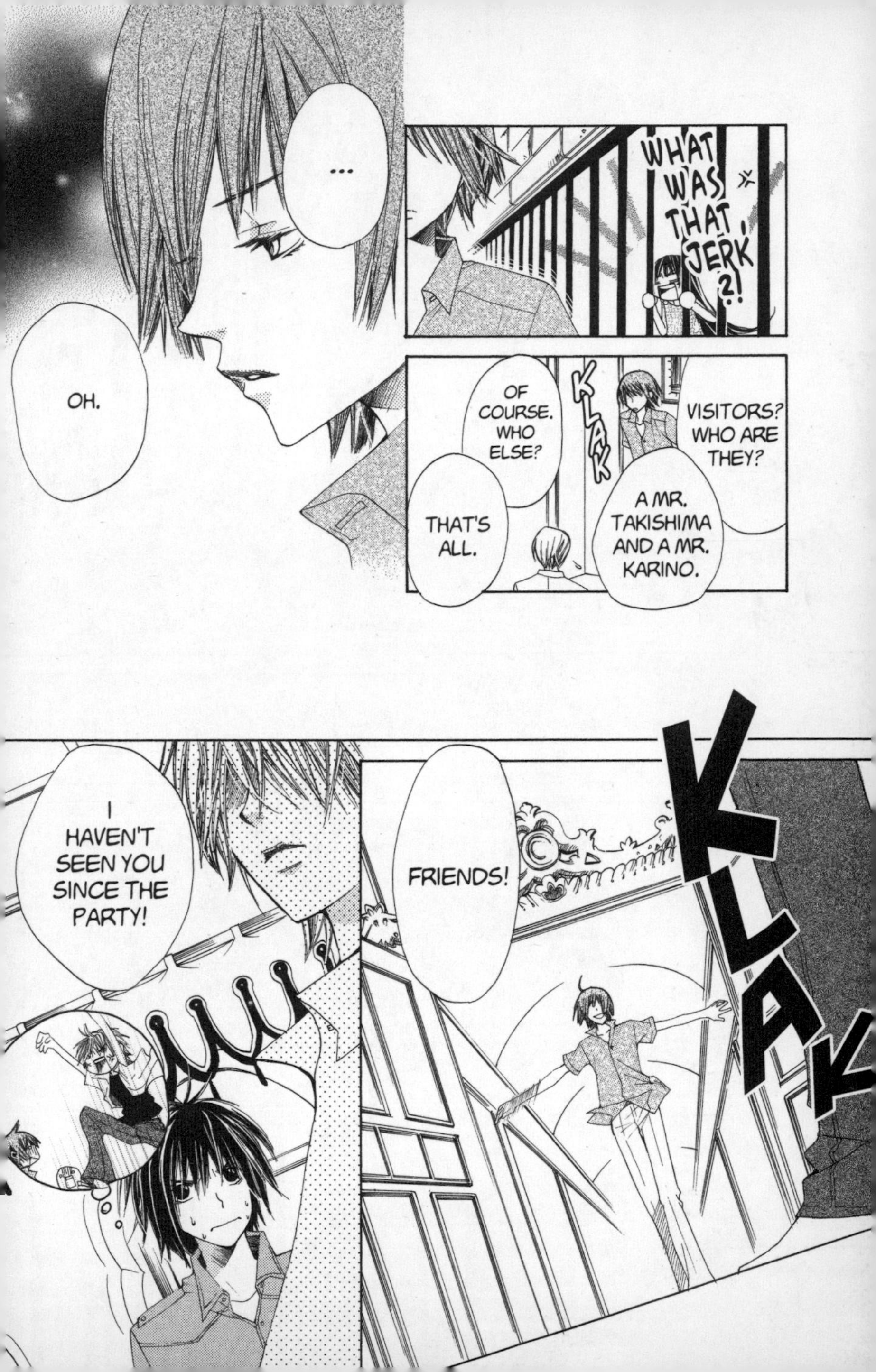
WHAT WAS THAT JERK?!
VISITORS? WHO ARE THEY?
A MR. TAKISHIMA AND A MR. KARINO.
KLAK
OF COURSE. WHO ELSE?
THAT'S ALL.
...
OH.
KLAK
FRIENDS!
I HAVEN'T SEEN YOU SINCE THE PARTY!

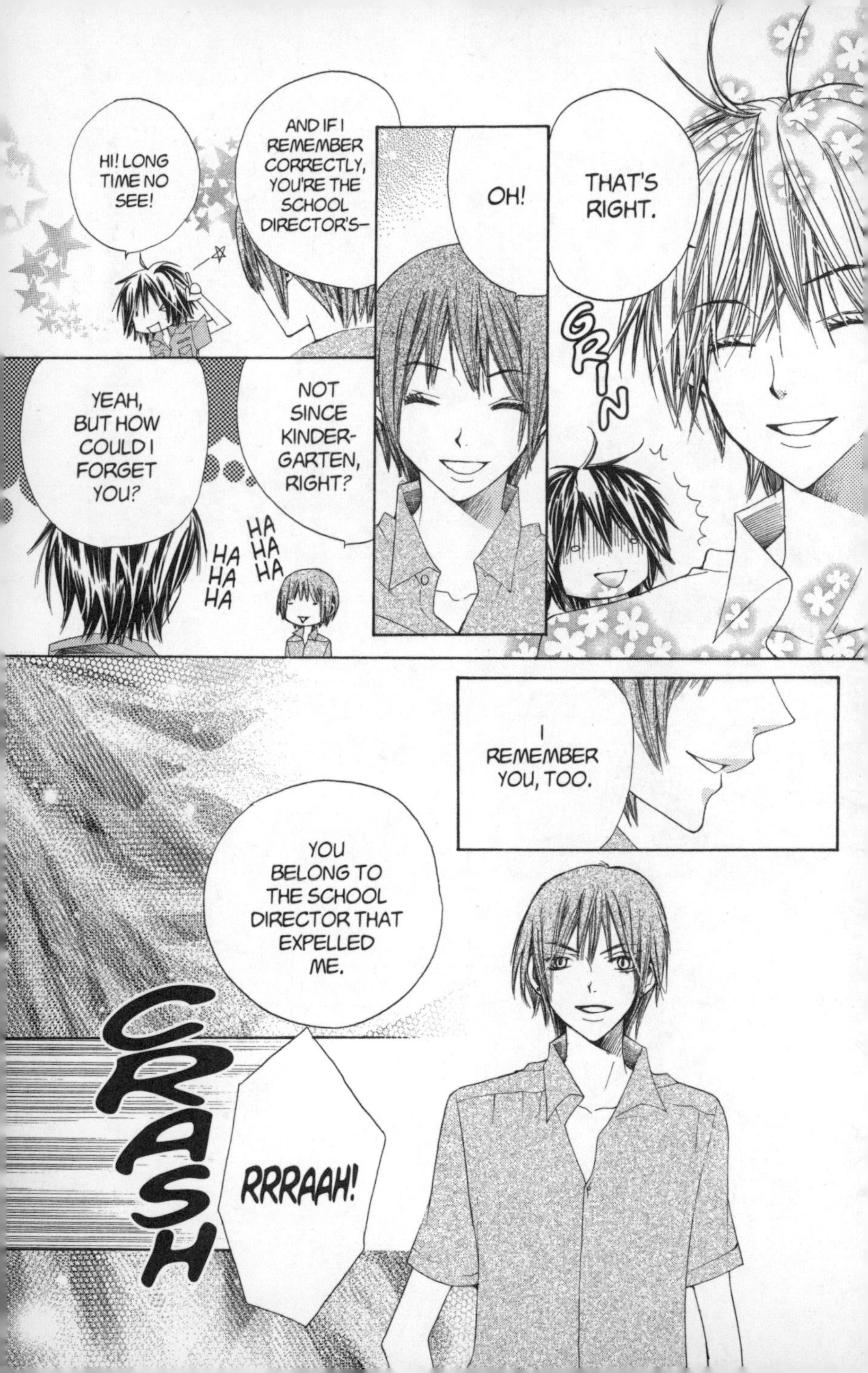
THAT'S RIGHT.
GRIN
OH!
AND IF I REMEMBER CORRECTLY, YOU'RE THE SCHOOL DIRECTOR'S—
HI! LONG TIME NO SEE!
NOT SINCE KINDER-GARTEN, RIGHT?
YEAH, BUT HOW COULD I FORGET YOU?
HA HA HA
HA HA HA
I REMEMBER YOU, TOO.
YOU BELONG TO THE SCHOOL DIRECTOR THAT EXPELLED ME.
RRRAAH!
CRASH

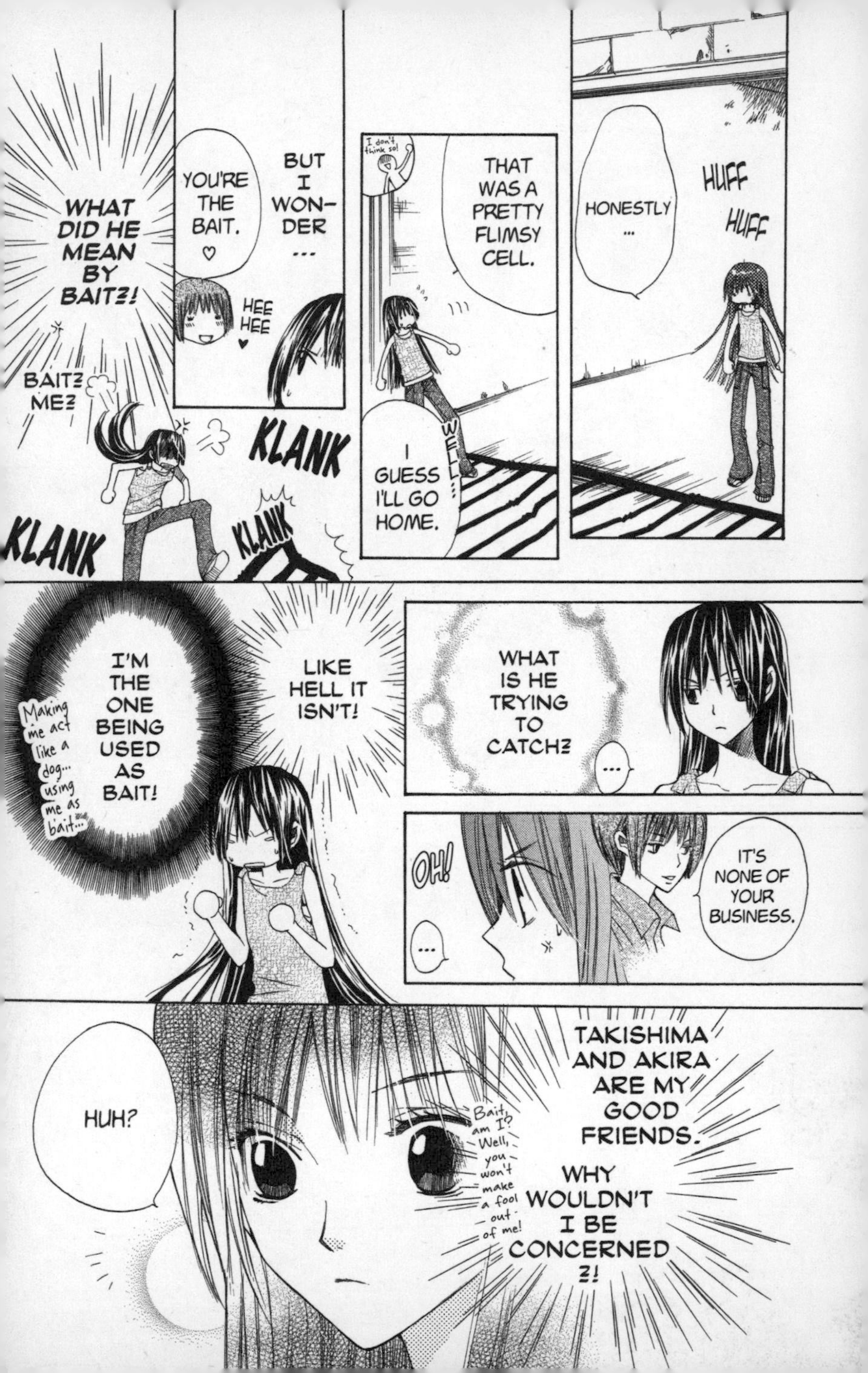
HUFF HUFF
HONESTLY ...
THAT WAS A PRETTY FLIMSY CELL.
I don't think so!
WELL...
I GUESS I'LL GO HOME.
BUT I WONDER ...
YOU'RE THE BAIT. ♡
HEE HEE ♥
WHAT DID HE MEAN BY BAIT?!
BAIT? ME?
KLANK
KLANK
KLANK
WHAT IS HE TRYING TO CATCH?
...
IT'S NONE OF YOUR BUSINESS.
OH!
...
LIKE HELL IT ISN'T!
I'M THE ONE BEING USED AS BAIT!
Making me act like a dog... using me as bait...
TAKISHIMA AND AKIRA ARE MY GOOD FRIENDS.
WHY WOULDN'T I BE CONCERNED?!
Bait, am I? Well, you won't make a fool out of me!
HUH?

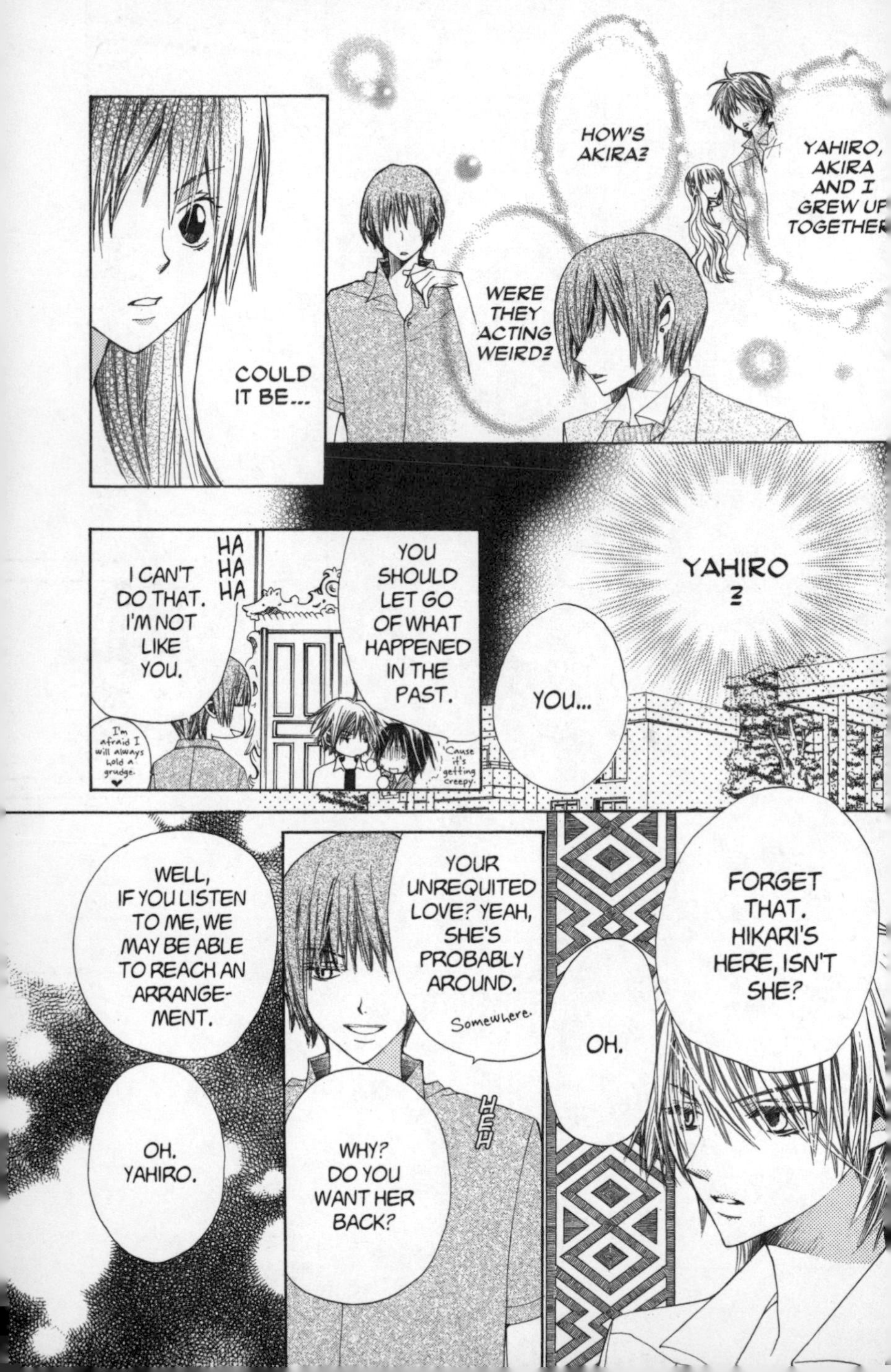
YAHIRO, AKIRA AND I GREW UP TOGETHER
HOW'S AKIRA?
WERE THEY ACTING WEIRD?
COULD IT BE...
YAHIRO?
YOU...
YOU SHOULD LET GO OF WHAT HAPPENED IN THE PAST.
'Cause it's getting creepy.
HA HA HA
I CAN'T DO THAT. I'M NOT LIKE YOU.
I'm afraid I will always hold a grudge.
FORGET THAT. HIKARI'S HERE, ISN'T SHE?
OH.
YOUR UNREQUITED LOVE? YEAH, SHE'S PROBABLY AROUND.
Somewhere.
HEH
WHY? DO YOU WANT HER BACK?
WELL, IF YOU LISTEN TO ME, WE MAY BE ABLE TO REACH AN ARRANGE-MENT.
OH. YAHIRO.

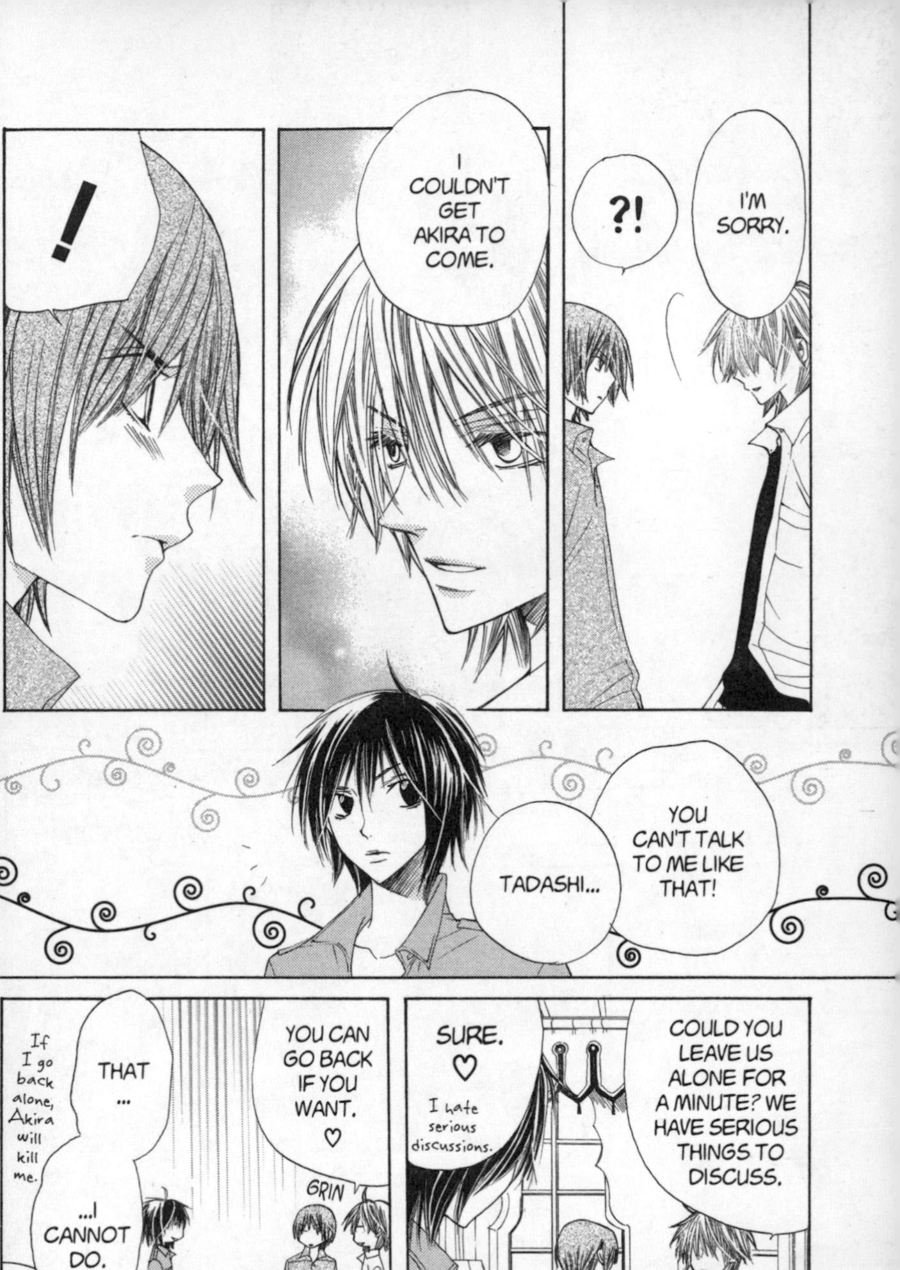
I'M SORRY.
?!
I COULDN'T GET AKIRA TO COME.
!
YOU CAN'T TALK TO ME LIKE THAT!
TADASHI...
COULD YOU LEAVE US ALONE FOR A MINUTE? WE HAVE SERIOUS THINGS TO DISCUSS.
SURE. ♡
I hate serious discussions.
YOU CAN GO BACK IF YOU WANT. ♡
GRIN
THAT ...
...I CANNOT DO.
If I go back alone, Akira will kill me.
You!!

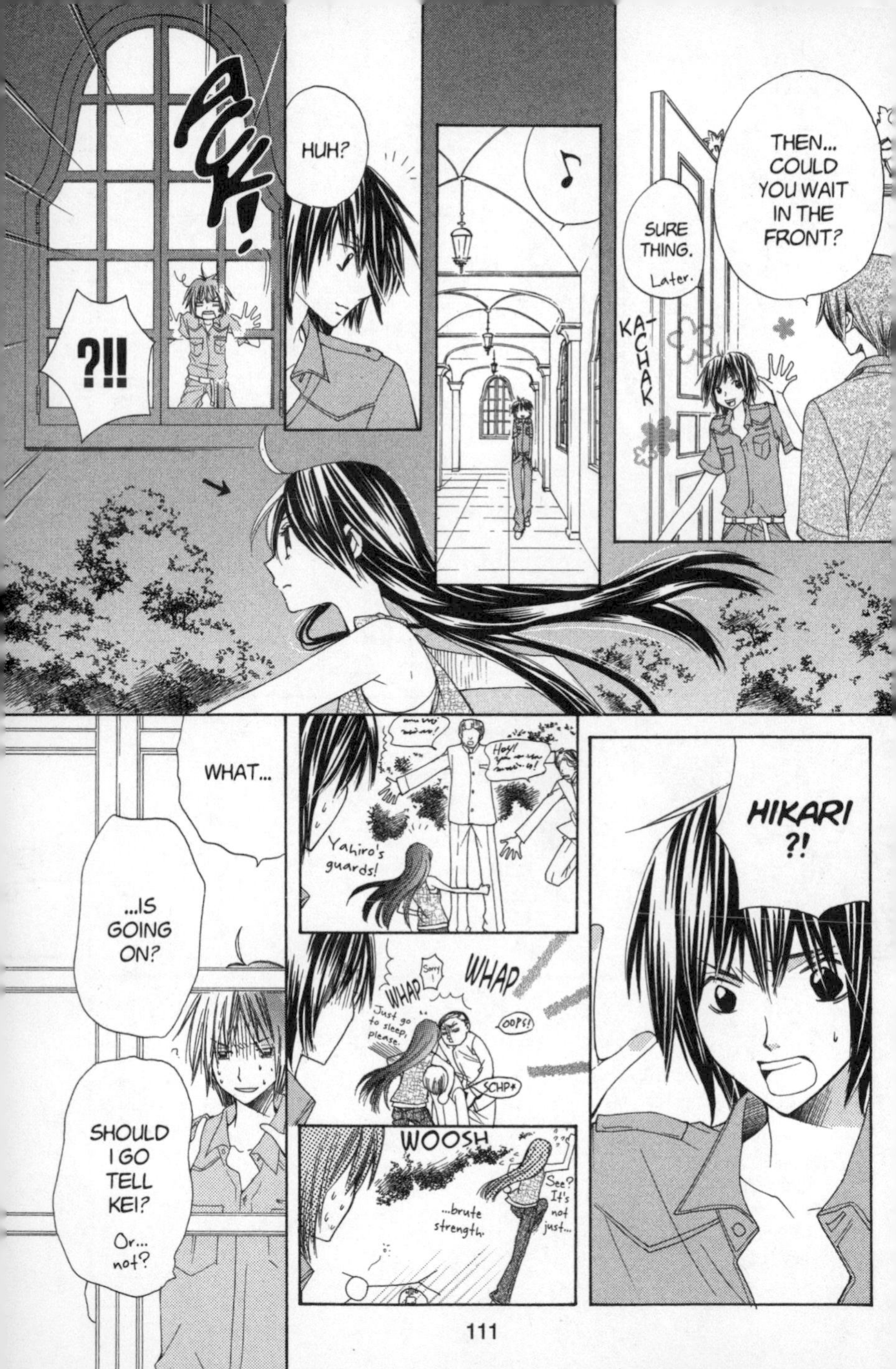
THEN... COULD YOU WAIT IN THE FRONT?
SURE THING.
Later.
KA-CHAK
♪
HUH?
POCK!
?!!
HIKARI ?!
Hey!
Yahiro's guards!
WHAP
Sorry!
WHAP
Just go to sleep, please.
OOPS!
SCHP*
WOOSH
See? It's not just...
...brute strength.
WHAT...
...IS GOING ON?
SHOULD I GO TELL KEI?
Or... not?

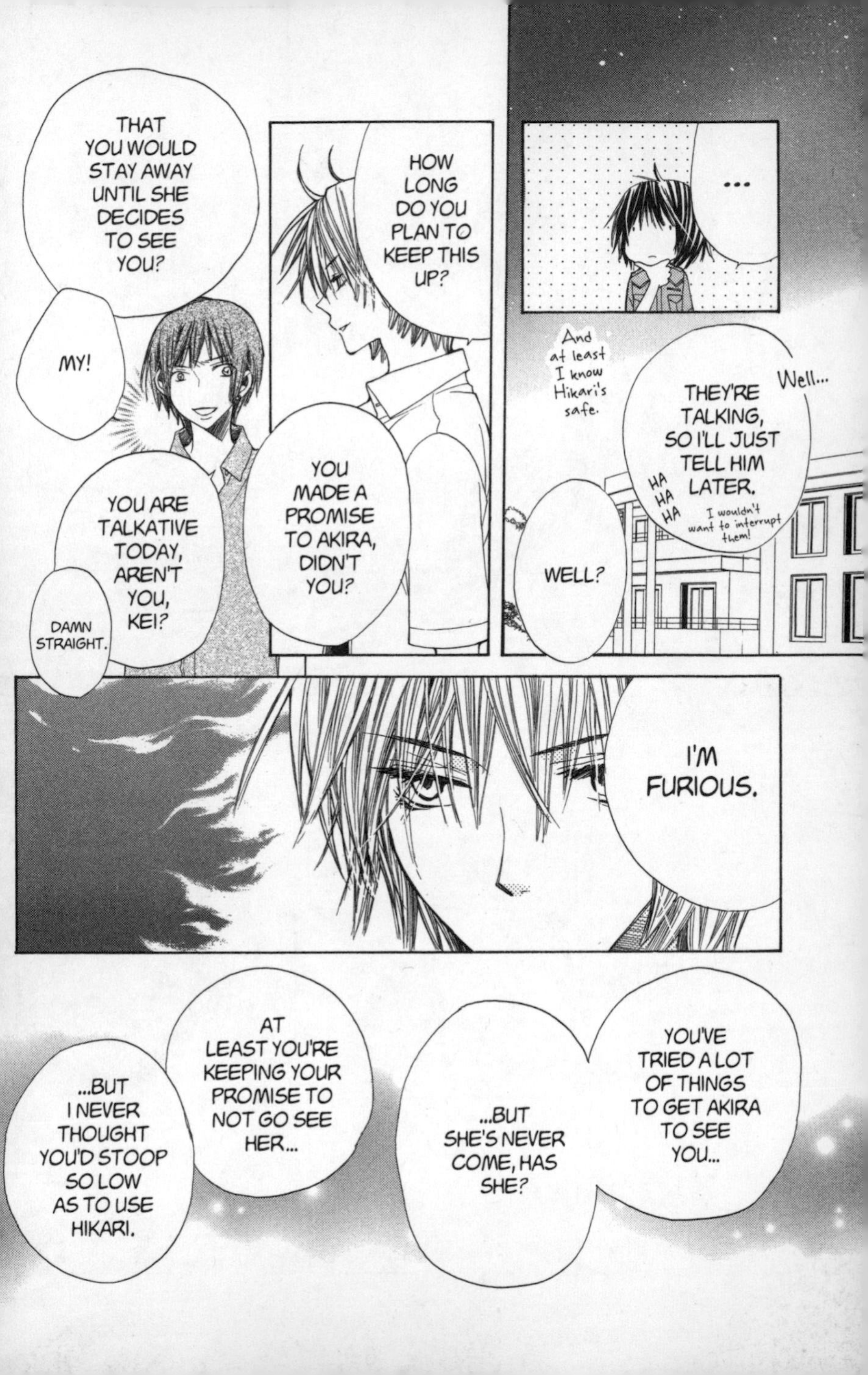
...
And at least I know Hikari's safe.
Well...
THEY'RE TALKING, SO I'LL JUST TELL HIM LATER.
HA HA HA
I wouldn't want to interrupt them!
WELL?
HOW LONG DO YOU PLAN TO KEEP THIS UP?
YOU MADE A PROMISE TO AKIRA, DIDN'T YOU?
THAT YOU WOULD STAY AWAY UNTIL SHE DECIDES TO SEE YOU?
MY!
YOU ARE TALKATIVE TODAY, AREN'T YOU, KEI?
DAMN STRAIGHT.
I'M FURIOUS.
YOU'VE TRIED A LOT OF THINGS TO GET AKIRA TO SEE YOU...
...BUT SHE'S NEVER COME, HAS SHE?
AT LEAST YOU'RE KEEPING YOUR PROMISE TO NOT GO SEE HER...
...BUT I NEVER THOUGHT YOU'D STOOP SO LOW AS TO USE HIKARI.

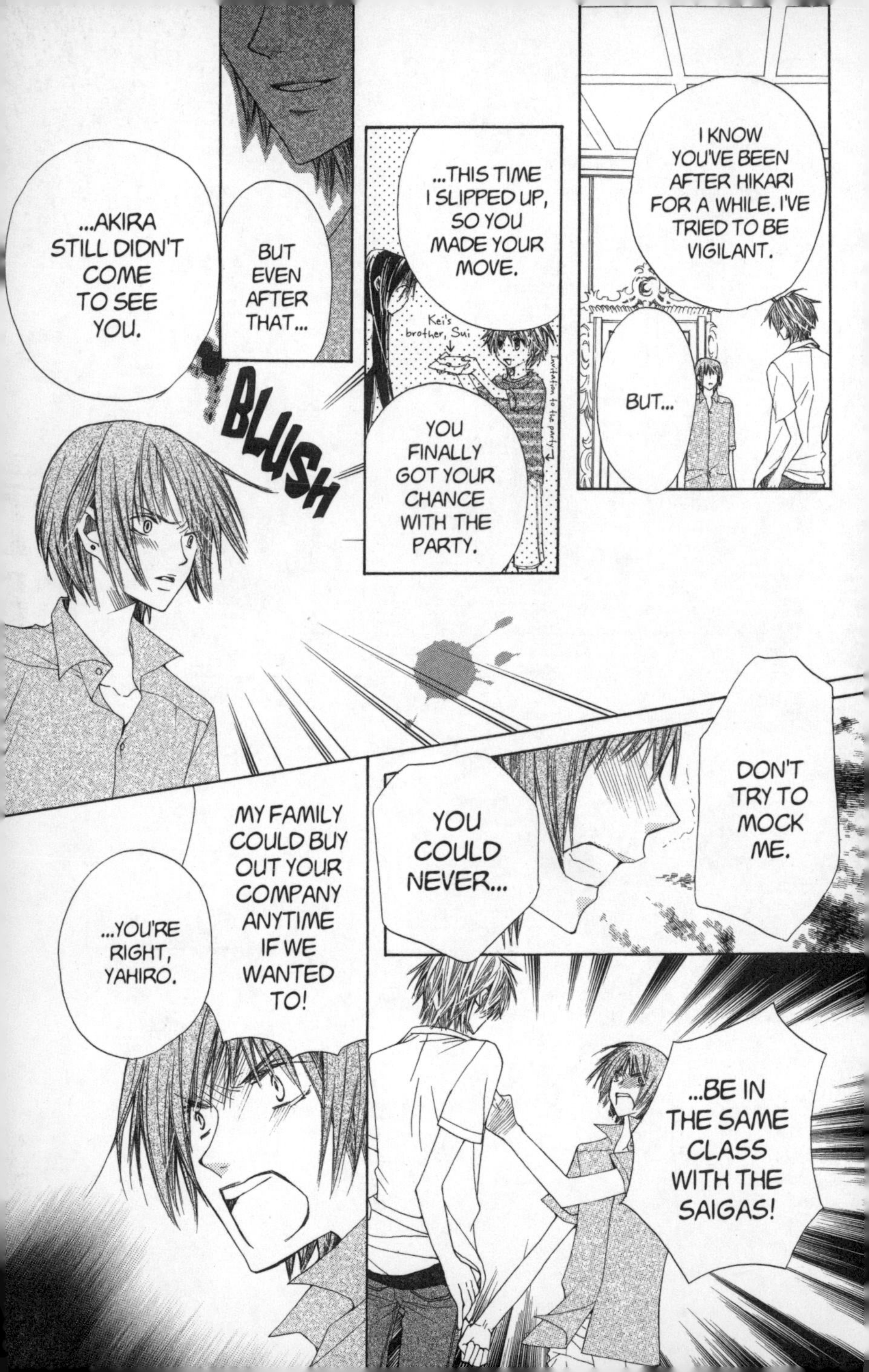
I KNOW YOU'VE BEEN AFTER HIKARI FOR A WHILE. I'VE TRIED TO BE VIGILANT.
BUT...
...THIS TIME I SLIPPED UP, SO YOU MADE YOUR MOVE.
Kei's brother, Sui
Invitation to the party
YOU FINALLY GOT YOUR CHANCE WITH THE PARTY.
BUT EVEN AFTER THAT...
...AKIRA STILL DIDN'T COME TO SEE YOU.
BLUSH
DON'T TRY TO MOCK ME.
YOU COULD NEVER...
...BE IN THE SAME CLASS WITH THE SAIGAS!
MY FAMILY COULD BUY OUT YOUR COMPANY ANYTIME IF WE WANTED TO!
...YOU'RE RIGHT, YAHIRO.

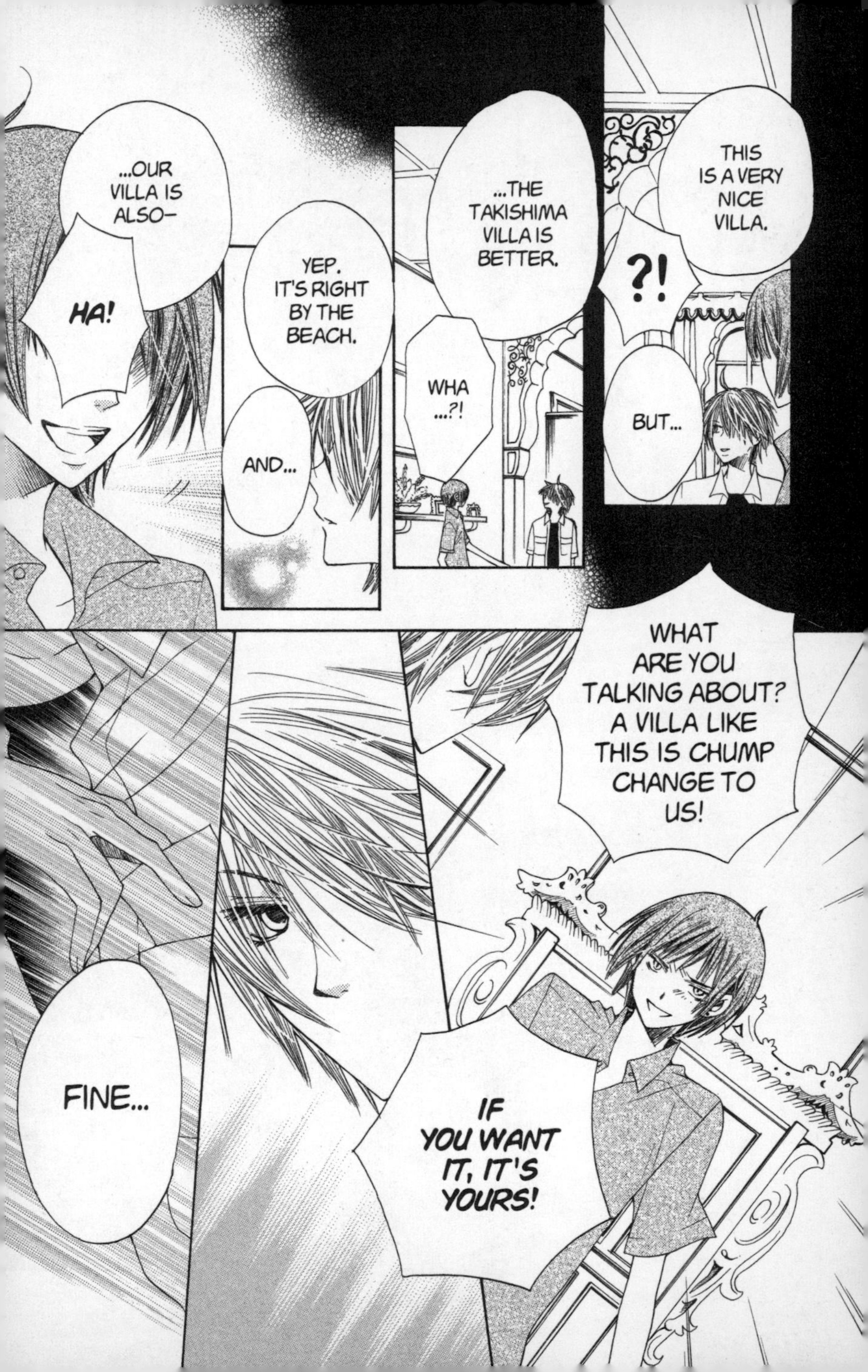
THIS IS A VERY NICE VILLA.
?!
BUT...
...THE TAKISHIMA VILLA IS BETTER.
WHA ...?!
YEP. IT'S RIGHT BY THE BEACH.
AND...
...OUR VILLA IS ALSO—
HA!
WHAT ARE YOU TALKING ABOUT? A VILLA LIKE THIS IS CHUMP CHANGE TO US!
IF YOU WANT IT, IT'S YOURS!
FINE...

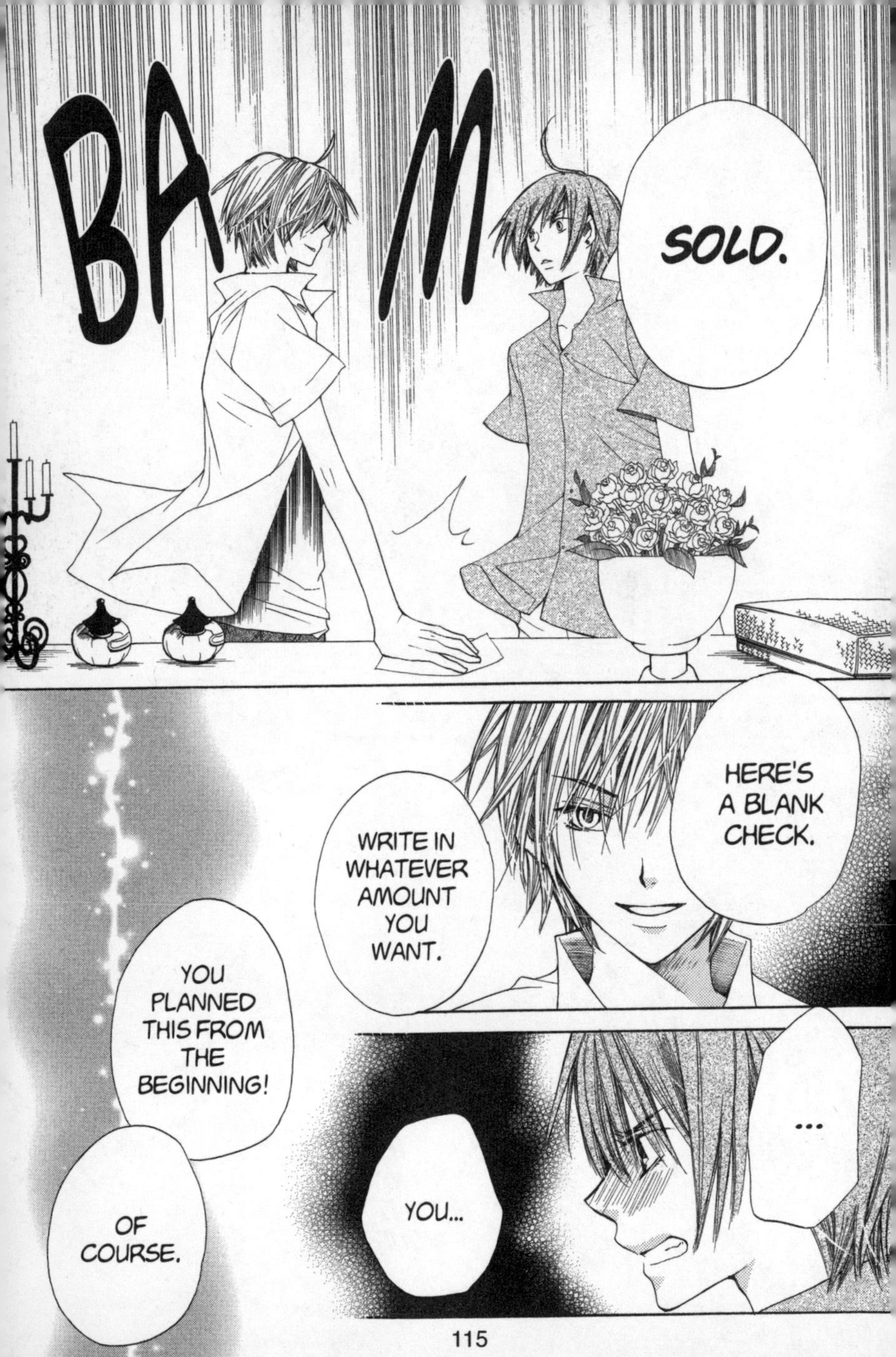
SOLD.
BAM
HERE'S A BLANK CHECK.
WRITE IN WHATEVER AMOUNT YOU WANT.
...
YOU...
YOU PLANNED THIS FROM THE BEGINNING!
OF COURSE.

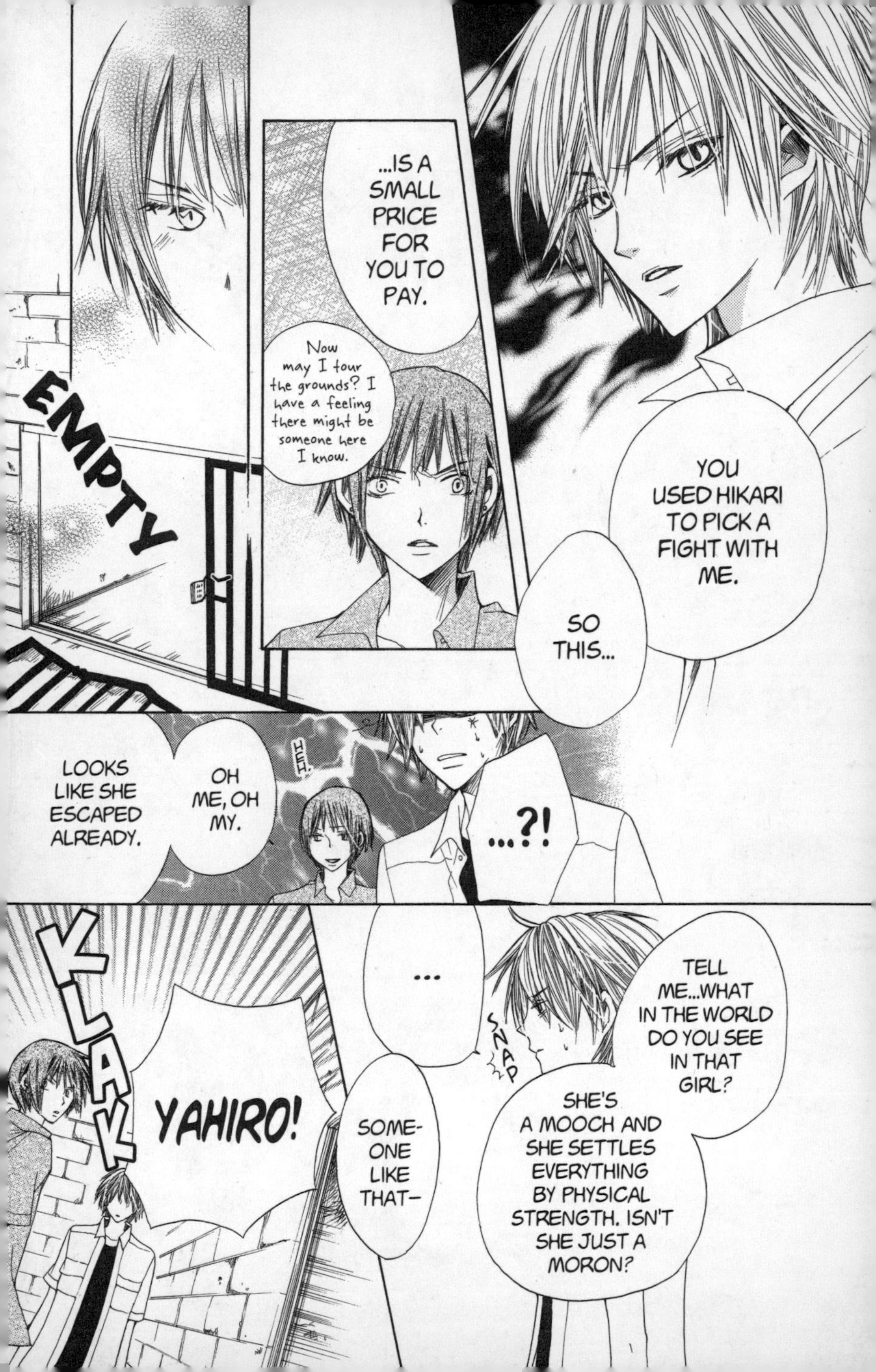
YOU USED HIKARI TO PICK A FIGHT WITH ME.
SO THIS...
...IS A SMALL PRICE FOR YOU TO PAY.
Now may I tour the grounds? I have a feeling there might be someone here I know.
EMPTY
...?!
HEH.
OH ME, OH MY.
LOOKS LIKE SHE ESCAPED ALREADY.
TELL ME...WHAT IN THE WORLD DO YOU SEE IN THAT GIRL?
SHE'S A MOOCH AND SHE SETTLES EVERYTHING BY PHYSICAL STRENGTH. ISN'T SHE JUST A MORON?
SNAP
...
SOME-ONE LIKE THAT—
KLAK
YAHIRO!

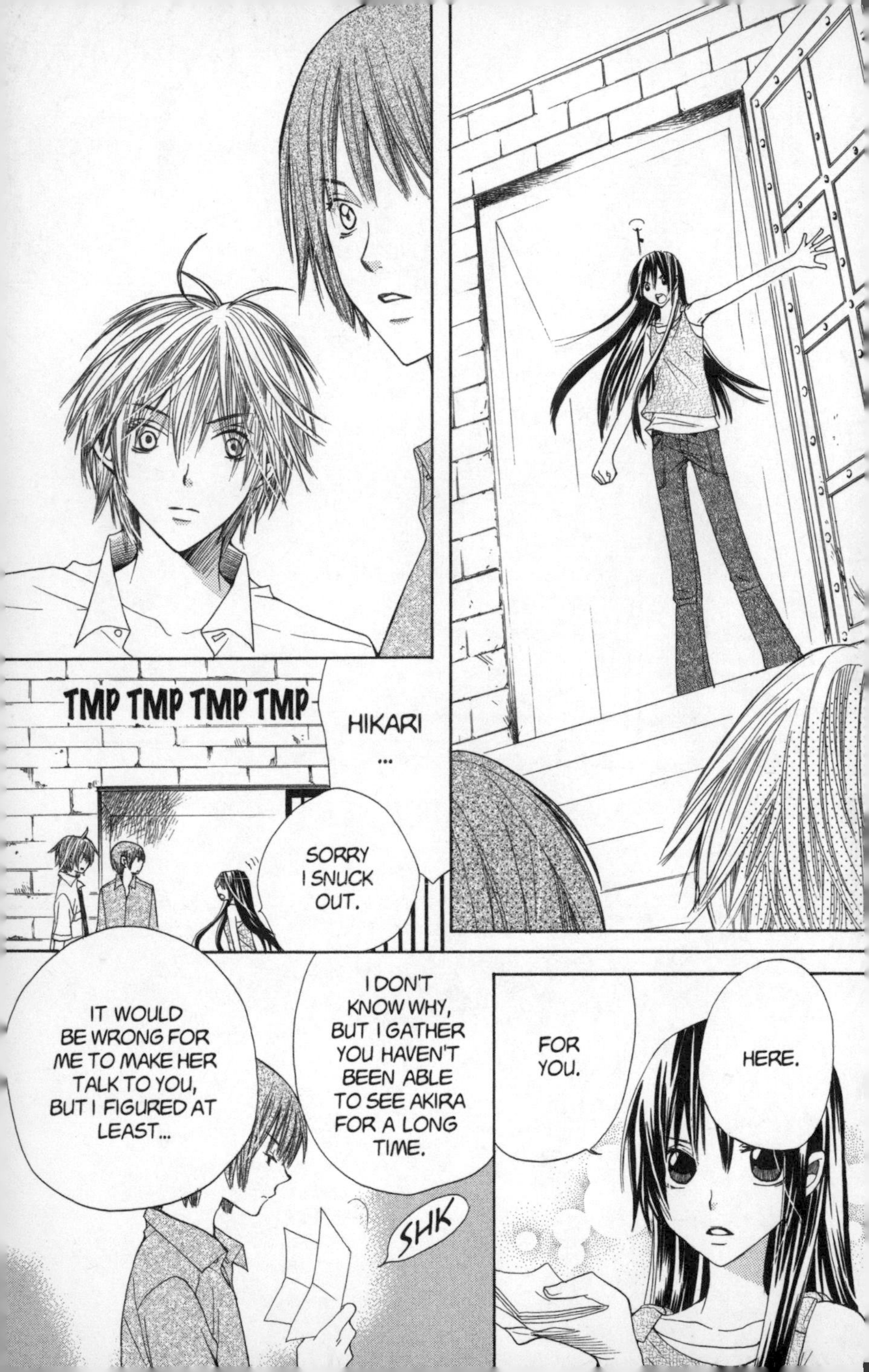
HIKARI ...
TMP TMP TMP TMP
SORRY I SNUCK OUT.
HERE.
FOR YOU.
I DON'T KNOW WHY, BUT I GATHER YOU HAVEN'T BEEN ABLE TO SEE AKIRA FOR A LONG TIME.
IT WOULD BE WRONG FOR ME TO MAKE HER TALK TO YOU, BUT I FIGURED AT LEAST...
SHK

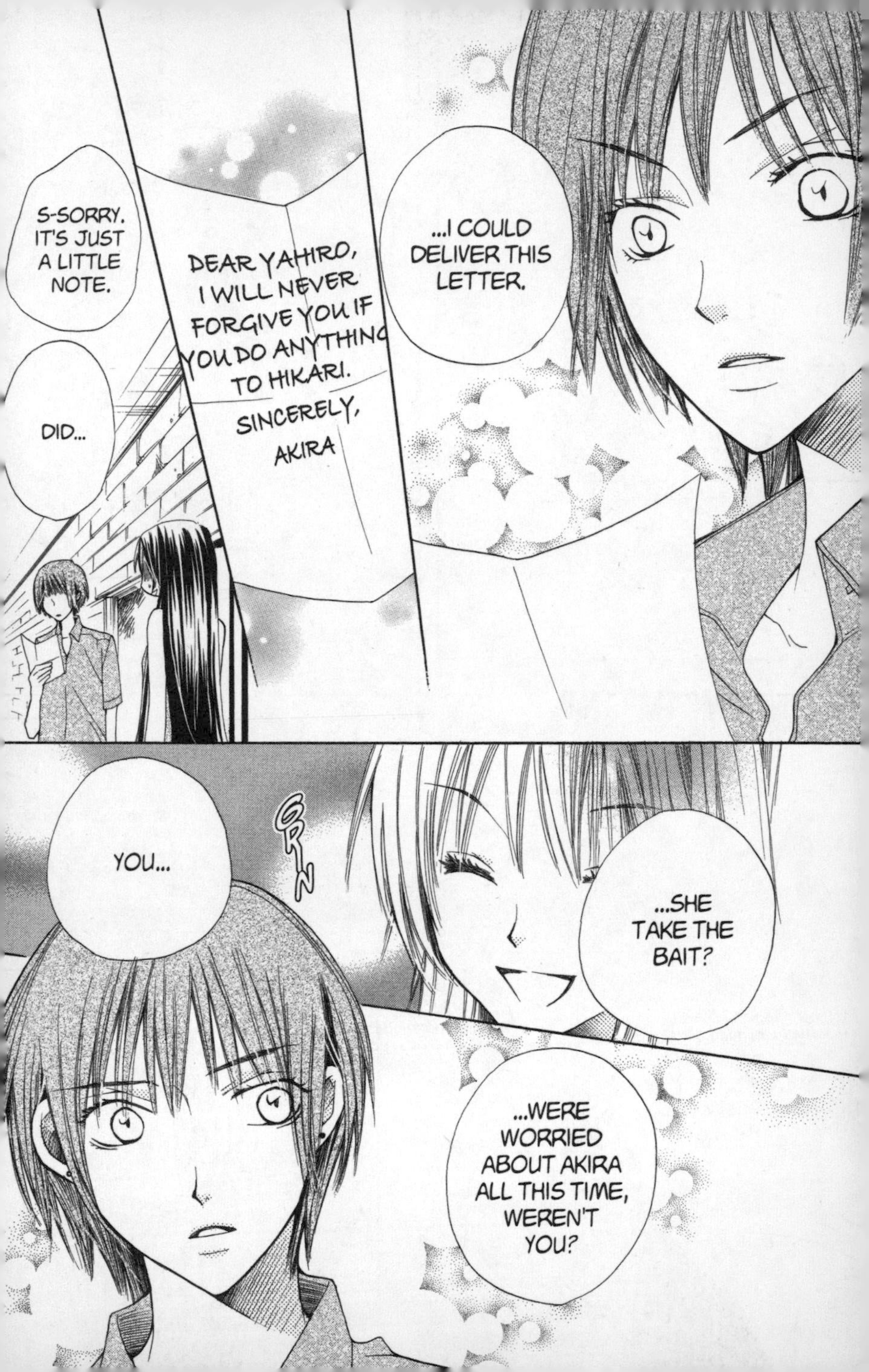
...I COULD DELIVER THIS LETTER.
DEAR YAHIRO, I WILL NEVER FORGIVE YOU IF YOU DO ANYTHING TO HIKARI. SINCERELY, AKIRA
S-SORRY. IT'S JUST A LITTLE NOTE.
DID...
...SHE TAKE THE BAIT?
GRIN
YOU...
...WERE WORRIED ABOUT AKIRA ALL THIS TIME, WEREN'T YOU?

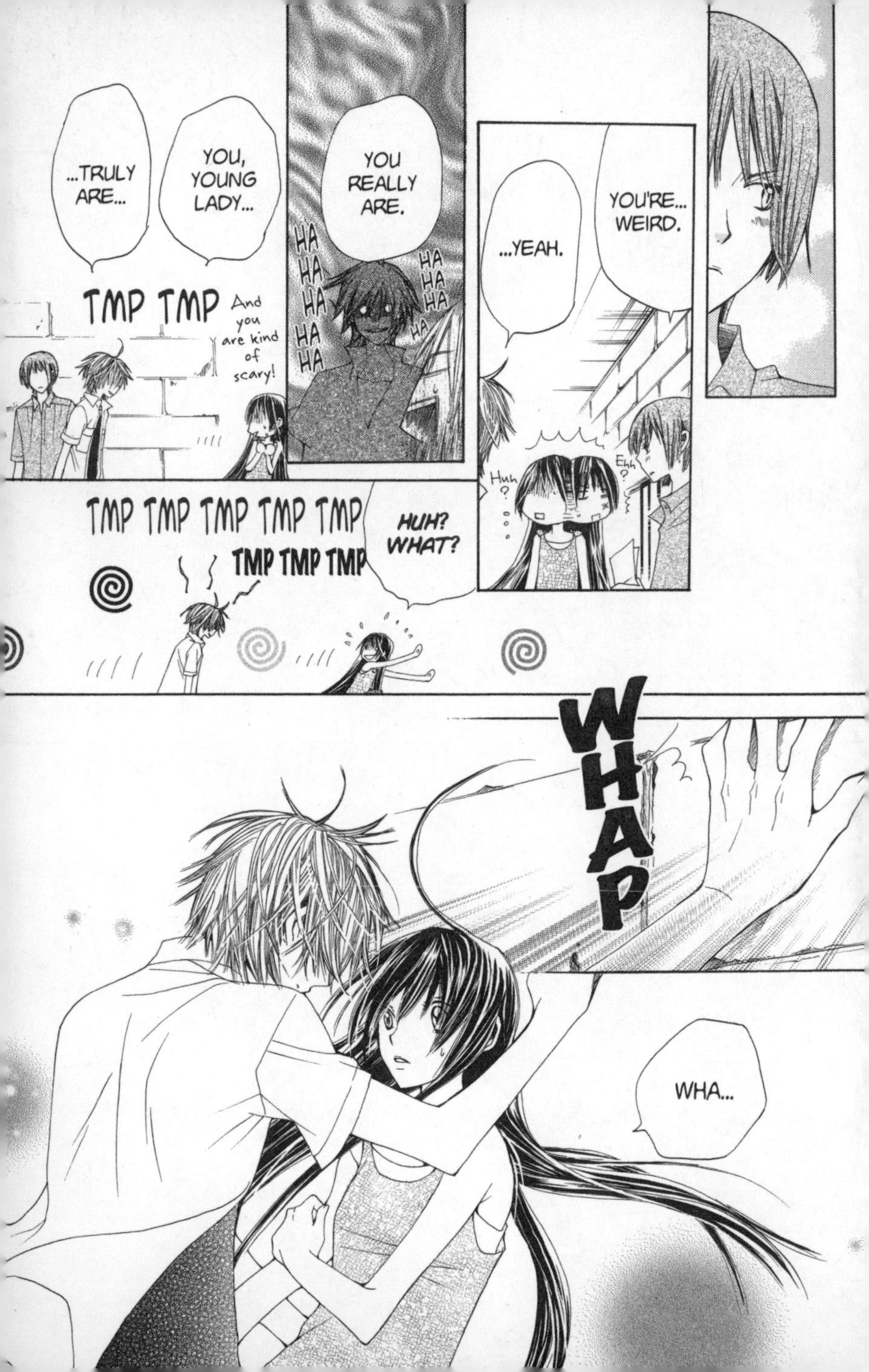
YOU'RE... WEIRD.
...YEAH.
Ehh?
Huh?
YOU REALLY ARE.
HA HA HA HA
HA HA HA HA HA
YOU, YOUNG LADY...
...TRULY ARE...
TMP TMP
And you are kind of scary!
HUH? WHAT?
TMP TMP TMP TMP TMP
TMP TMP TMP
WHAP
WHA...

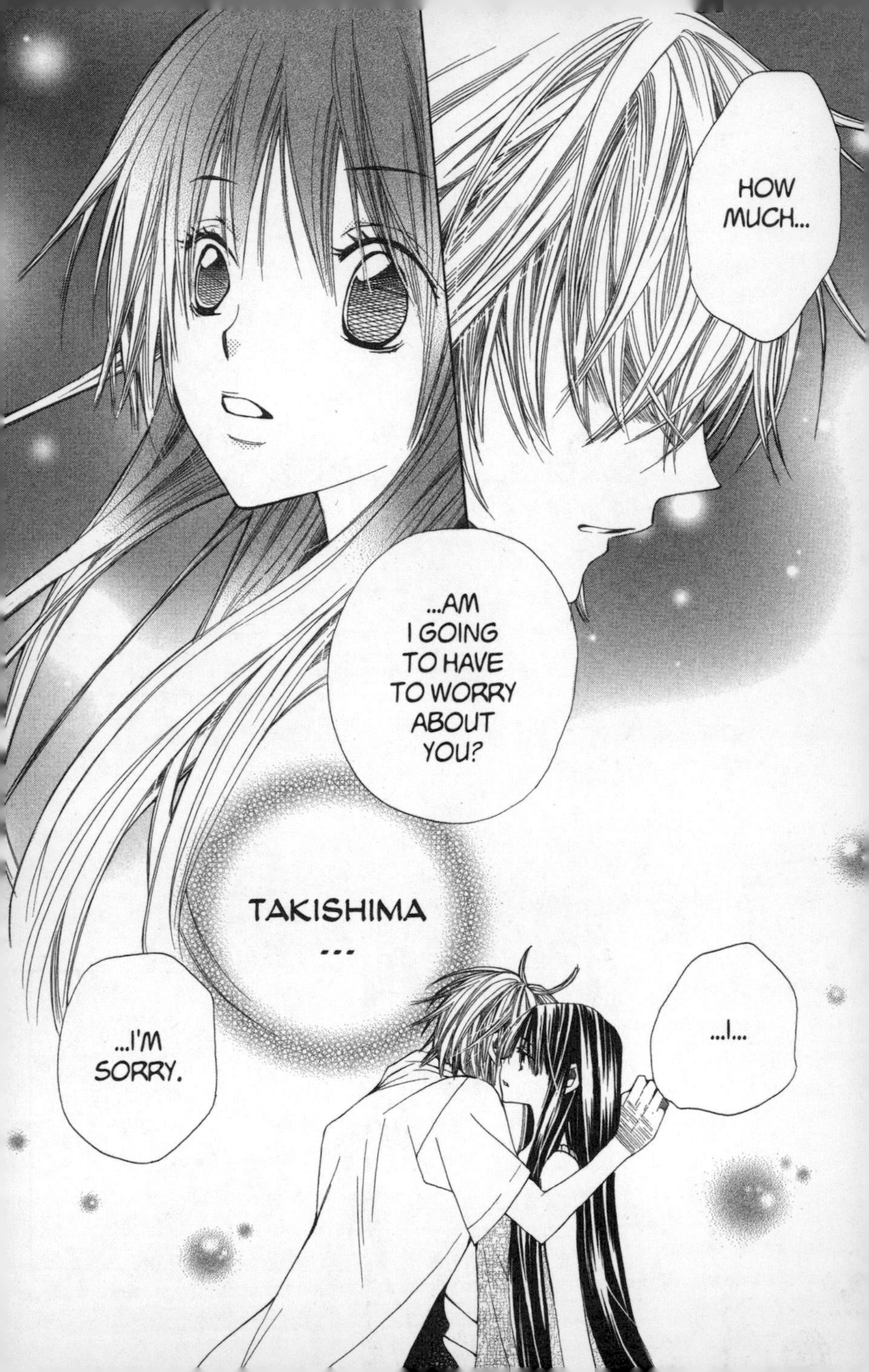
HOW MUCH...
...AM I GOING TO HAVE TO WORRY ABOUT YOU?
TAKISHIMA ...
...I...
...I'M SORRY.

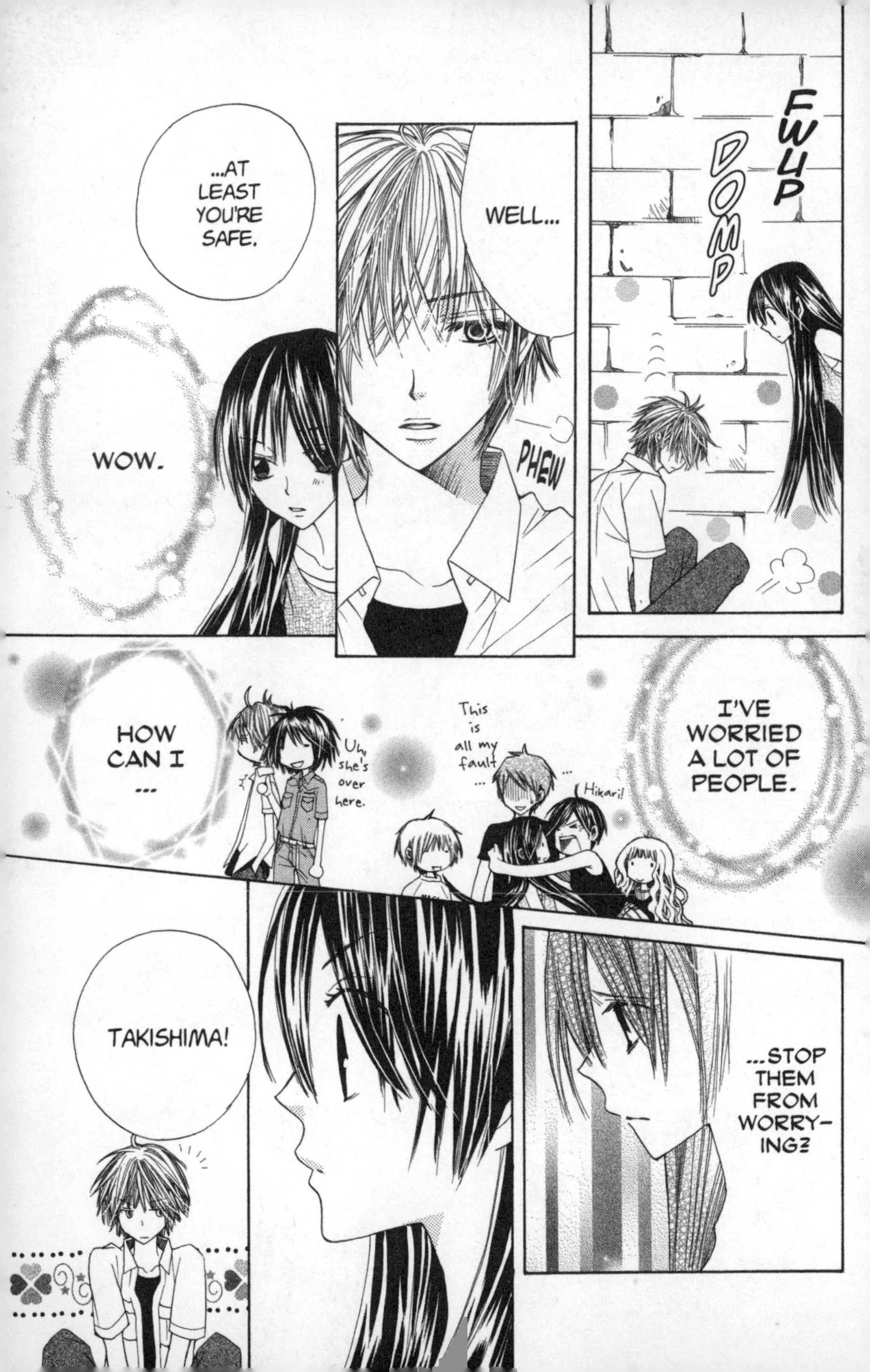
FWUP
DOMP
WELL...
PHEW
...AT LEAST YOU'RE SAFE.
WOW.
I'VE WORRIED A LOT OF PEOPLE.
Hikari!
...
This is all my fault ...
Uh she's over here.
HOW CAN I ...
...STOP THEM FROM WORRY-ING?
TAKISHIMA!

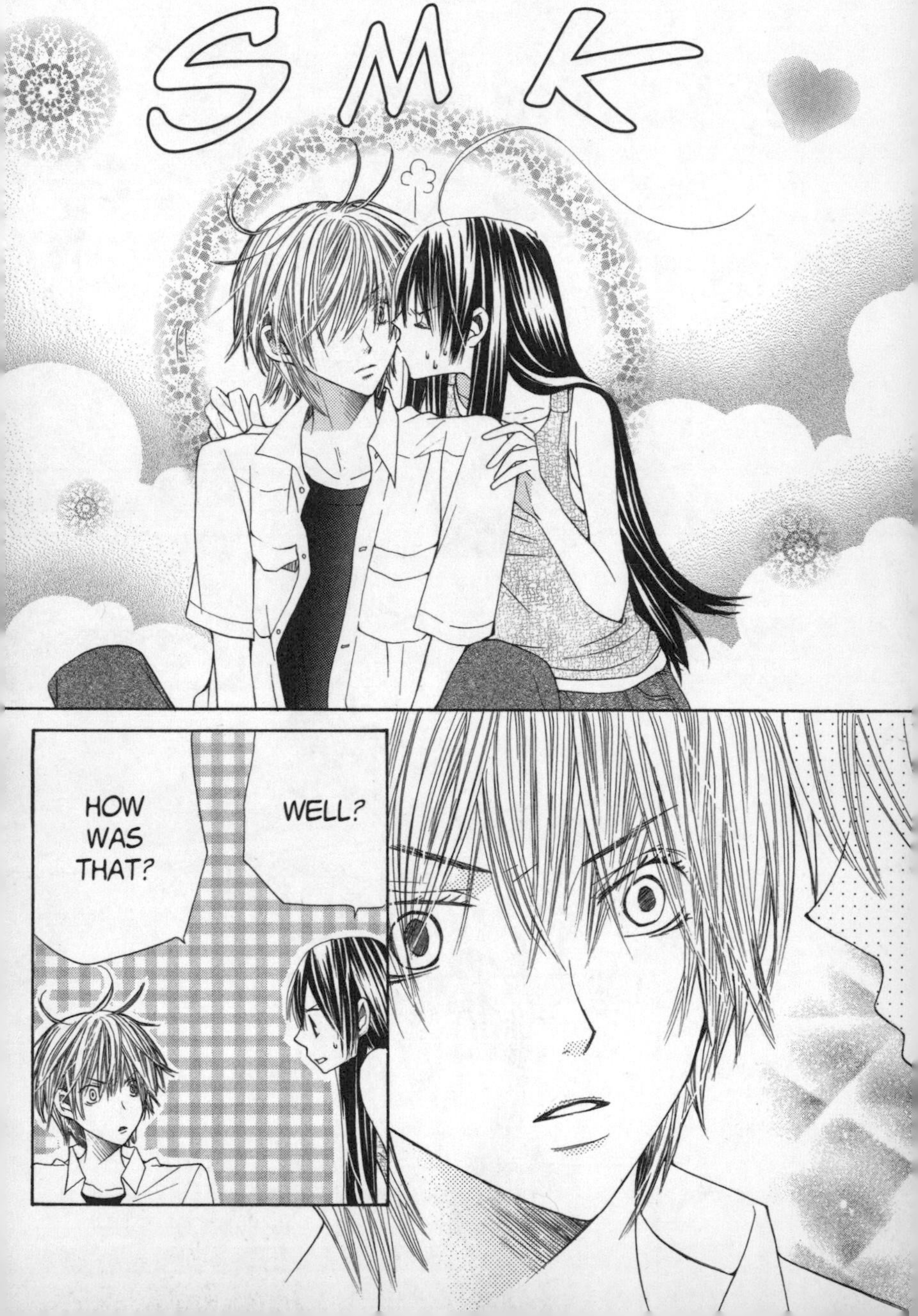
SMK
WELL?
HOW WAS THAT?

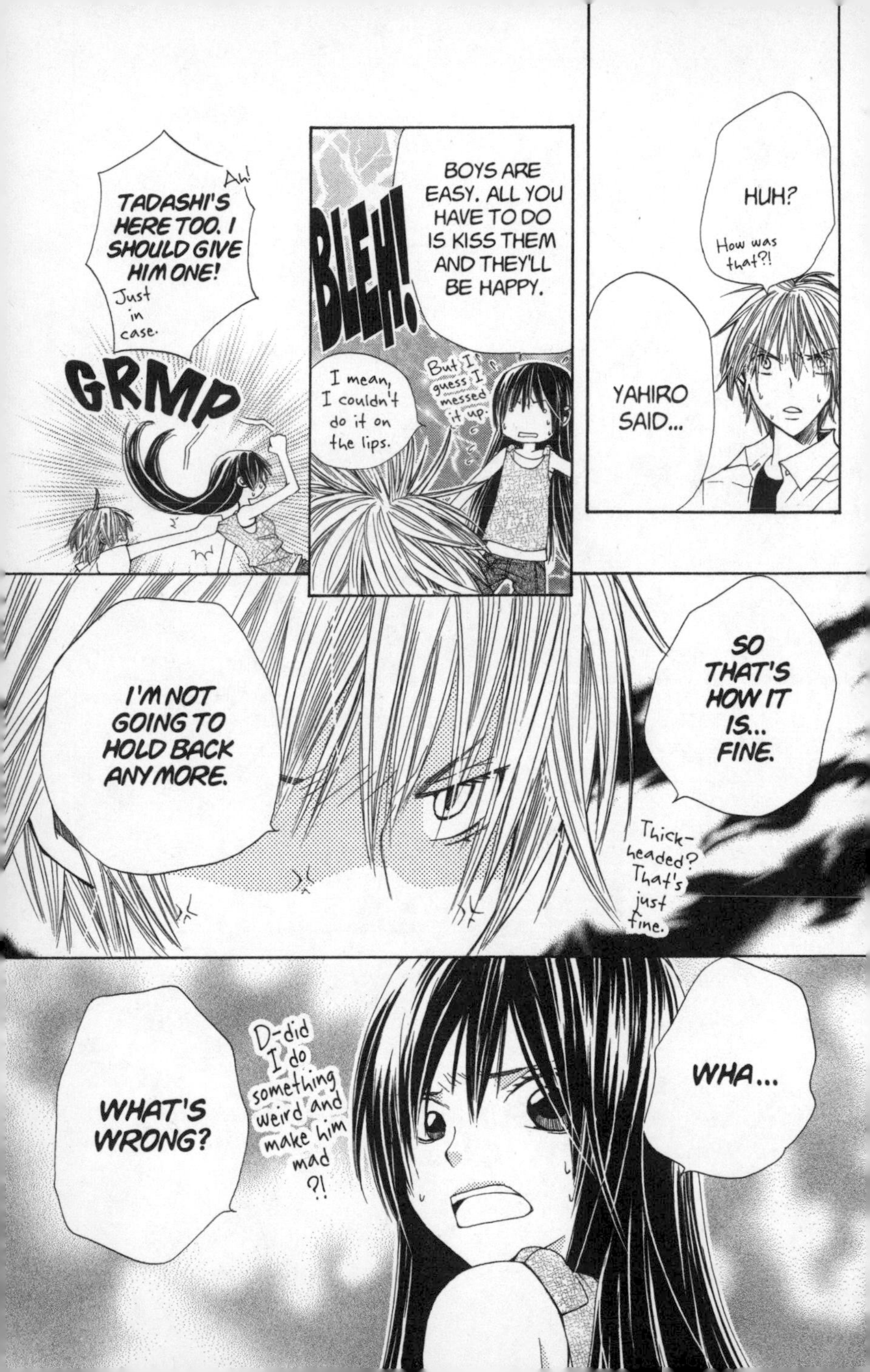
HUH?
How was that?!
YAHIRO SAID...
BOYS ARE EASY. ALL YOU HAVE TO DO IS KISS THEM AND THEY'LL BE HAPPY.
BLEH!
But I guess I messed it up.
I mean, I couldn't do it on the lips.
Ah!
TADASHI'S HERE TOO. I SHOULD GIVE HIM ONE!
Just in case.
GRMP
SO THAT'S HOW IT IS... FINE.
Thick-headed? That's just fine.
I'M NOT GOING TO HOLD BACK ANYMORE.
WHA...
D-did I do something weird and make him mad?!
WHAT'S WRONG?

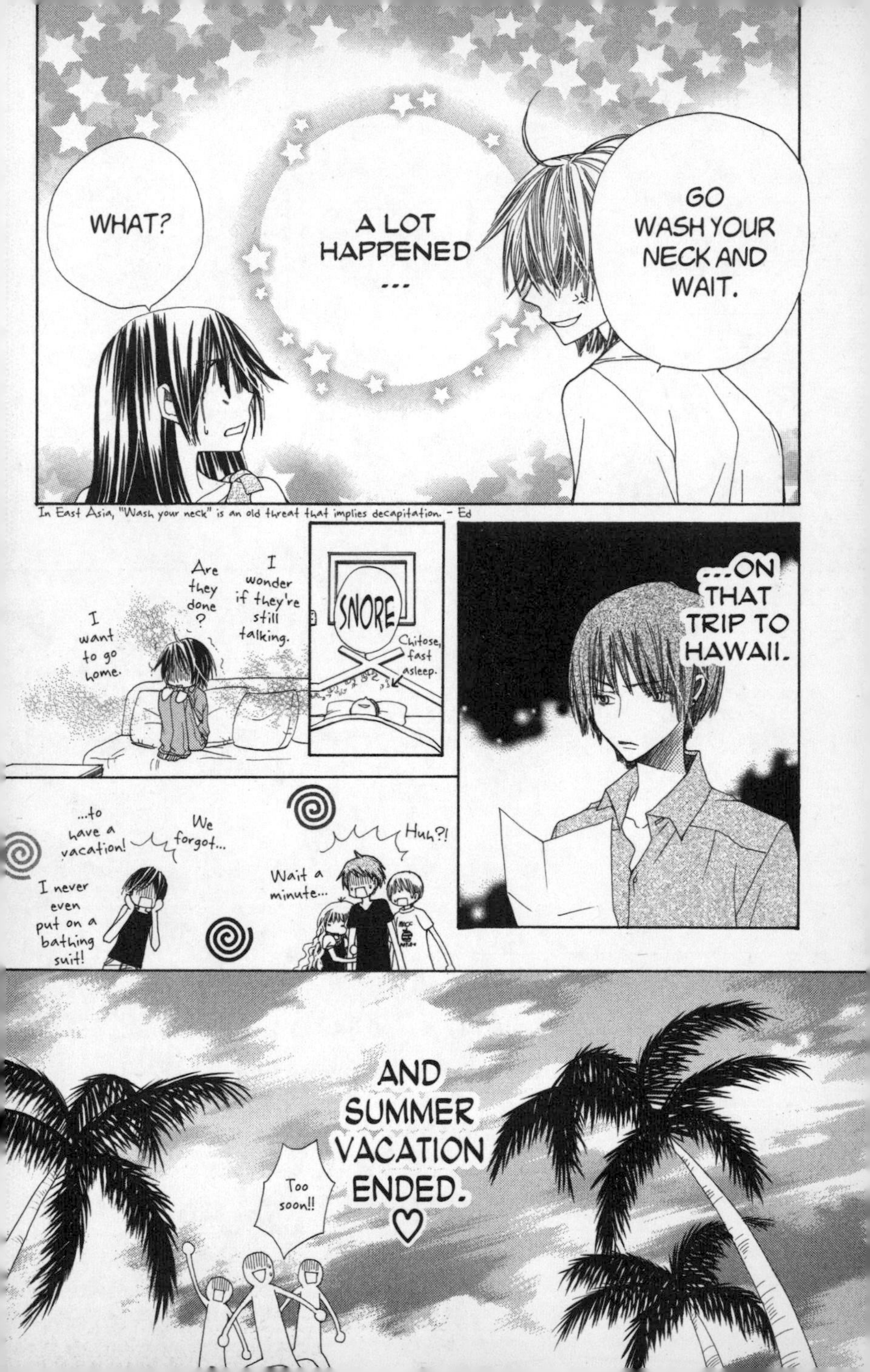
GO WASH YOUR NECK AND WAIT.
A LOT HAPPENED ...
WHAT?
In East Asia, "Wash your neck" is an old threat that implies decapitation. - Ed
...ON THAT TRIP TO HAWAII.
SNORE
Chitose, fast asleep.
I wonder if they're still talking.
Are they done?
I want to go home.
Huh?!
Wait a minute...
We forgot...
...to have a vacation!
I never even put on a bathing suit!
AND SUMMER VACATION ENDED. ♡
Too soon!!

Chapter 15

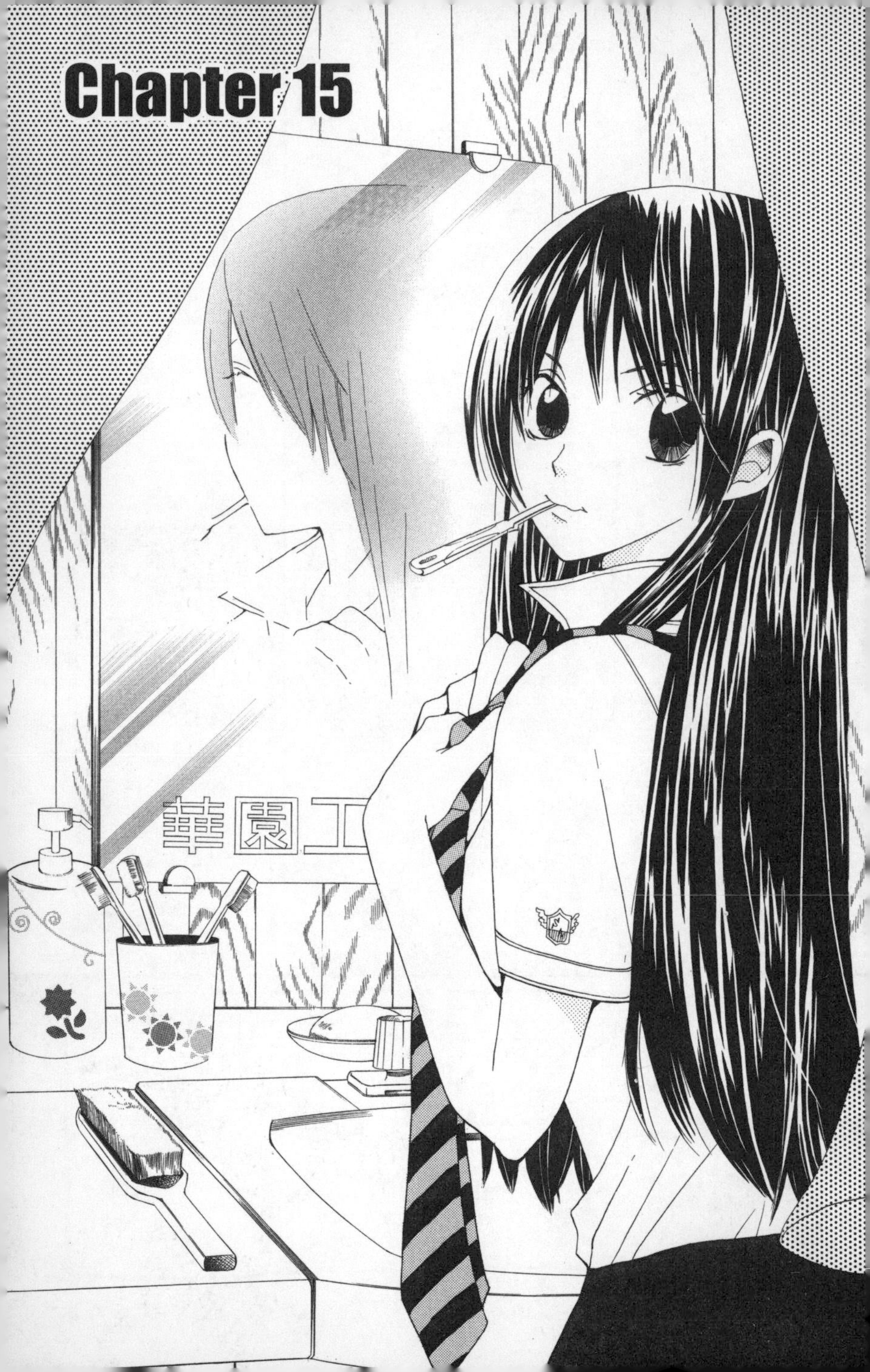
華園工

...APTITUDE TESTS.

SEEMS LIKE A LOT OF STUDENTS AREN'T HAPPY RIGHT NOW.

GO AHEAD.

Man, I haven't done anything.

Me neither! I already gave up.

HA HA HA

AT THE BEGINNING OF EACH YEAR WE HAVE LOTS OF DIFFERENT SCHOOL-WIDE EVENTS.

FWAK

IT'S FINE, SHE'S ALONE.

COME ON! GO!!

HA...

BUT FIRST WE HAVE ...

RYU TSUJI	MAKI MINAMI
BORN: 5/4	BORN: 5/20
BLOOD TYPE: A	BLOOD TYPE: AB
FAMILY: FATHER, MOTHER, YOUNGER SISTER	FAVORITE FOODS: CRAB, SWEETS, CAKES, SHREDDED SQUID, GREEN PEAS, AND... HUFF HUFF...
FAVORITE FOOD: ANYTHING SPICY	

HFF HFF

Don't tell anyone you saw me.

You're a character now?!

126

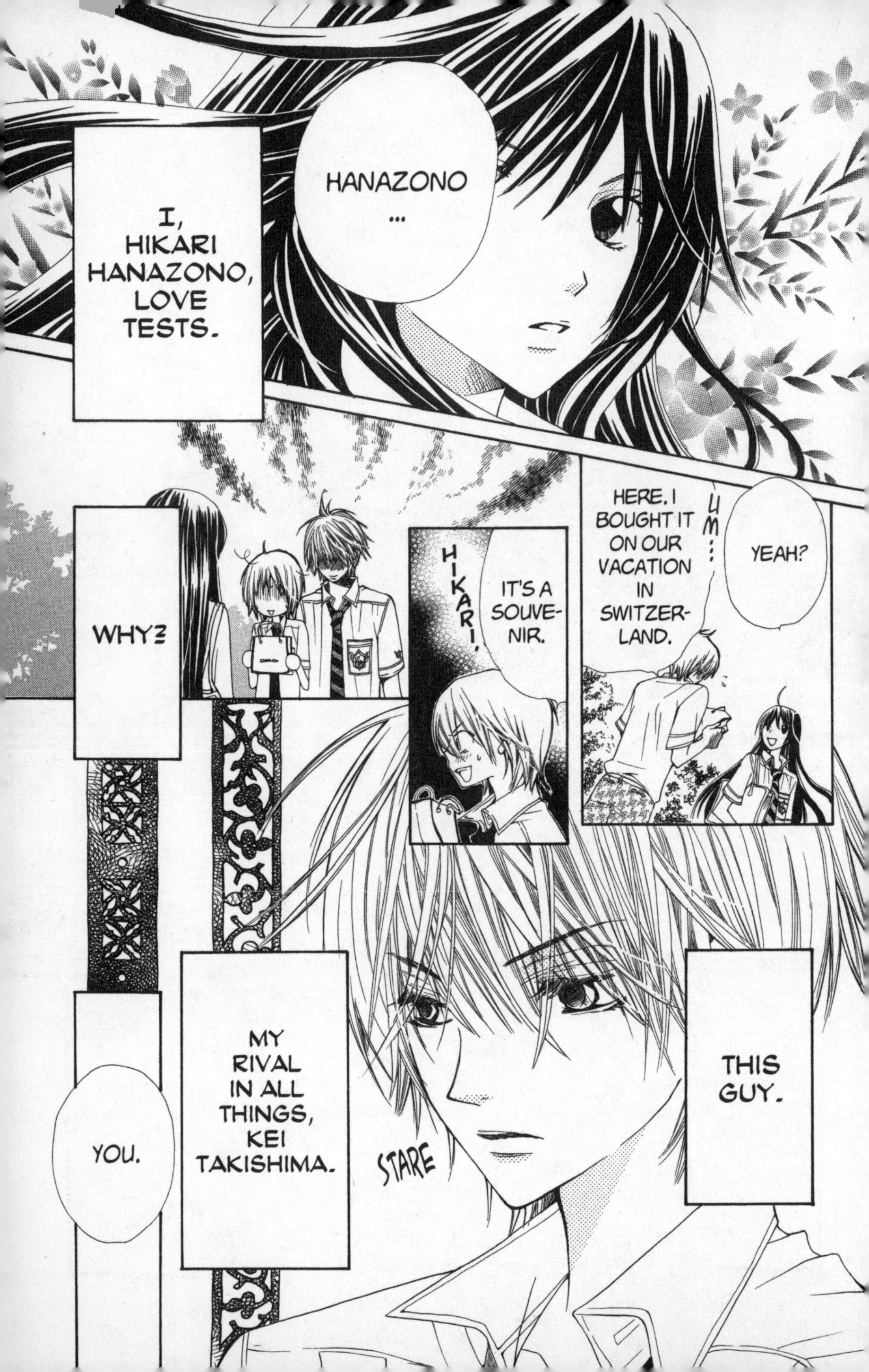
HANAZONO ...
I, HIKARI HANAZONO, LOVE TESTS.
YEAH?
UM...
HERE. I BOUGHT IT ON OUR VACATION IN SWITZER-LAND.
IT'S A SOUVE-NIR.
HIKARI,
WHY?
THIS GUY.
STARE
MY RIVAL IN ALL THINGS, KEI TAKISHIMA.
YOU.

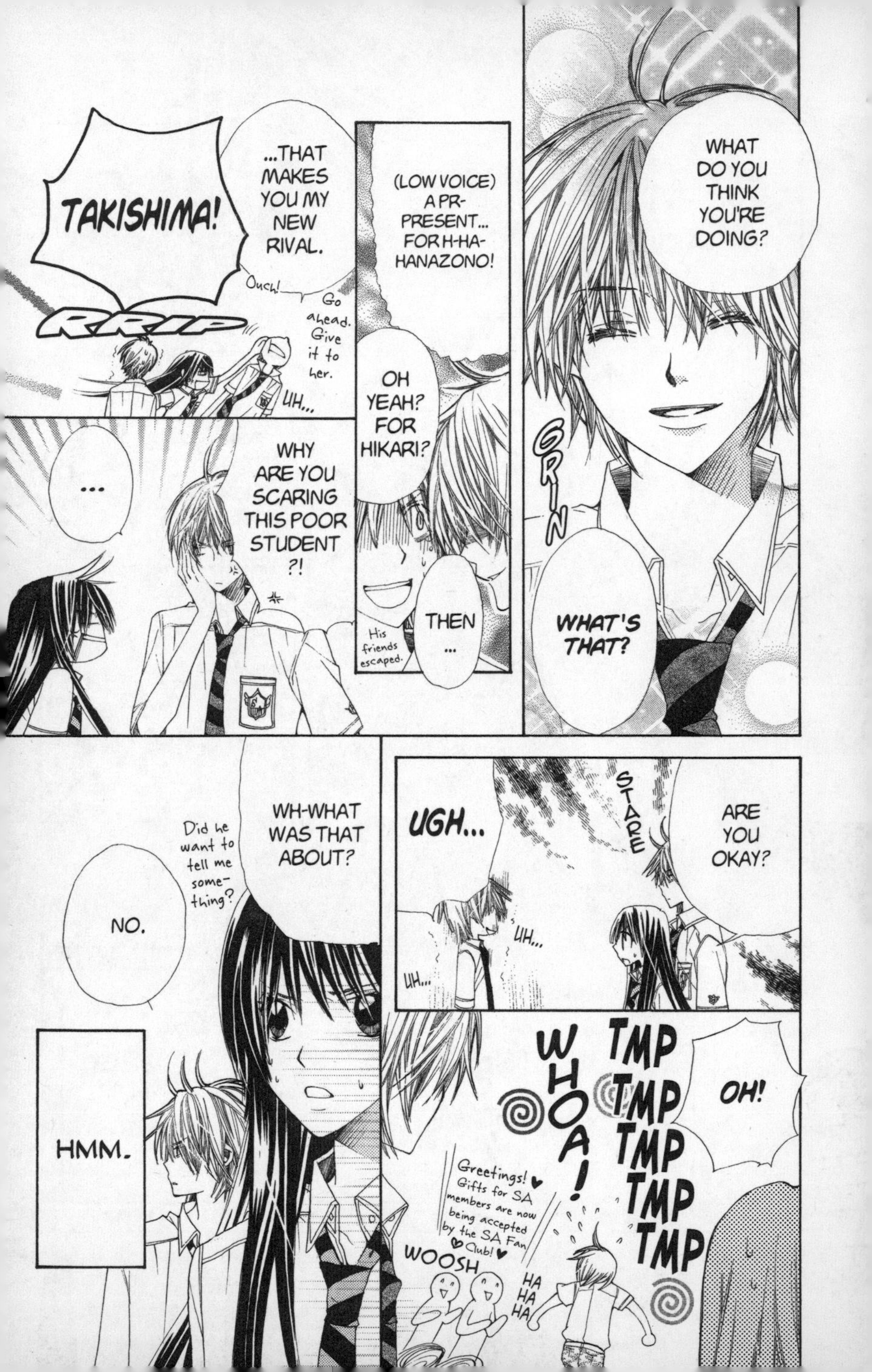
WHAT DO YOU THINK YOU'RE DOING?
GRIN
WHAT'S THAT?
(LOW VOICE) A PR-PRESENT... FOR H-HA-HANAZONO!
OH YEAH? FOR HIKARI?
THEN...
His friends escaped.
...THAT MAKES YOU MY NEW RIVAL.
TAKISHIMA!
Ouch!
Go ahead. Give it to her.
RRIP
UH...
WHY ARE YOU SCARING THIS POOR STUDENT?!
...
ARE YOU OKAY?
STARE
UGH...
UH...
UH...
OH!
TMP TMP TMP TMP TMP
WHOA!
Greetings! ♥ Gifts for SA members are now being accepted by the SA Fan ♥ Club! ♥
WOOSH
HA HA HA
WH-WHAT WAS THAT ABOUT?
Did he want to tell me some-thing?
NO.
HMM.

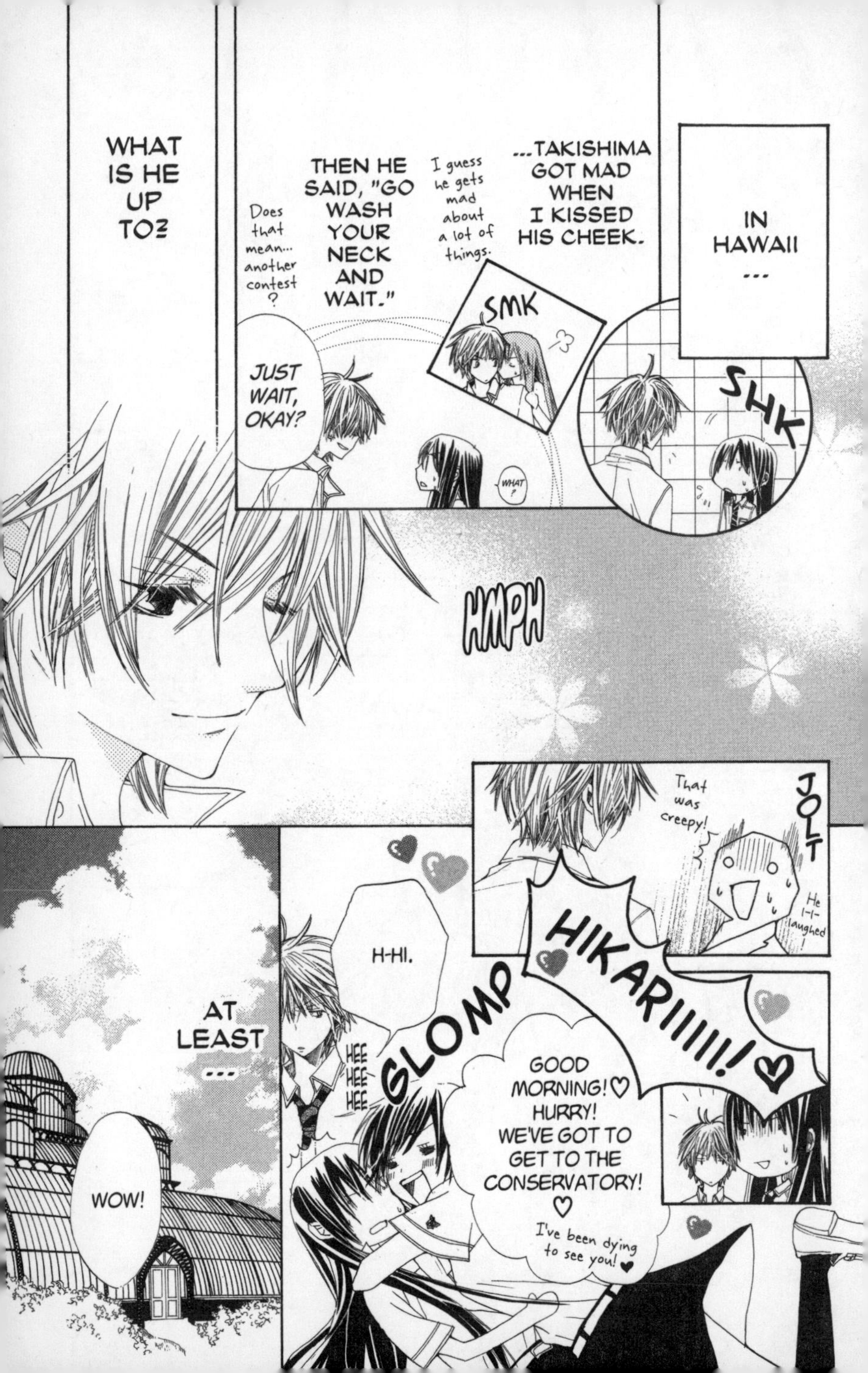
IN HAWAII...
SHK
...TAKISHIMA GOT MAD WHEN I KISSED HIS CHEEK.
I guess he gets mad about a lot of things.
SMK
THEN HE SAID, "GO WASH YOUR NECK AND WAIT."
Does that mean... another contest?
JUST WAIT, OKAY?
WHAT?
WHAT IS HE UP TO?
HMPH
JOLT
That was creepy!
He l-l-laughed!
HIKARIIIIII!
GOOD MORNING! ♡ HURRY! WE'VE GOT TO GET TO THE CONSERVATORY! ♡
I've been dying to see you! ♥
GLOMP
HEE HEE HEE
H-HI.
AT LEAST...
WOW!

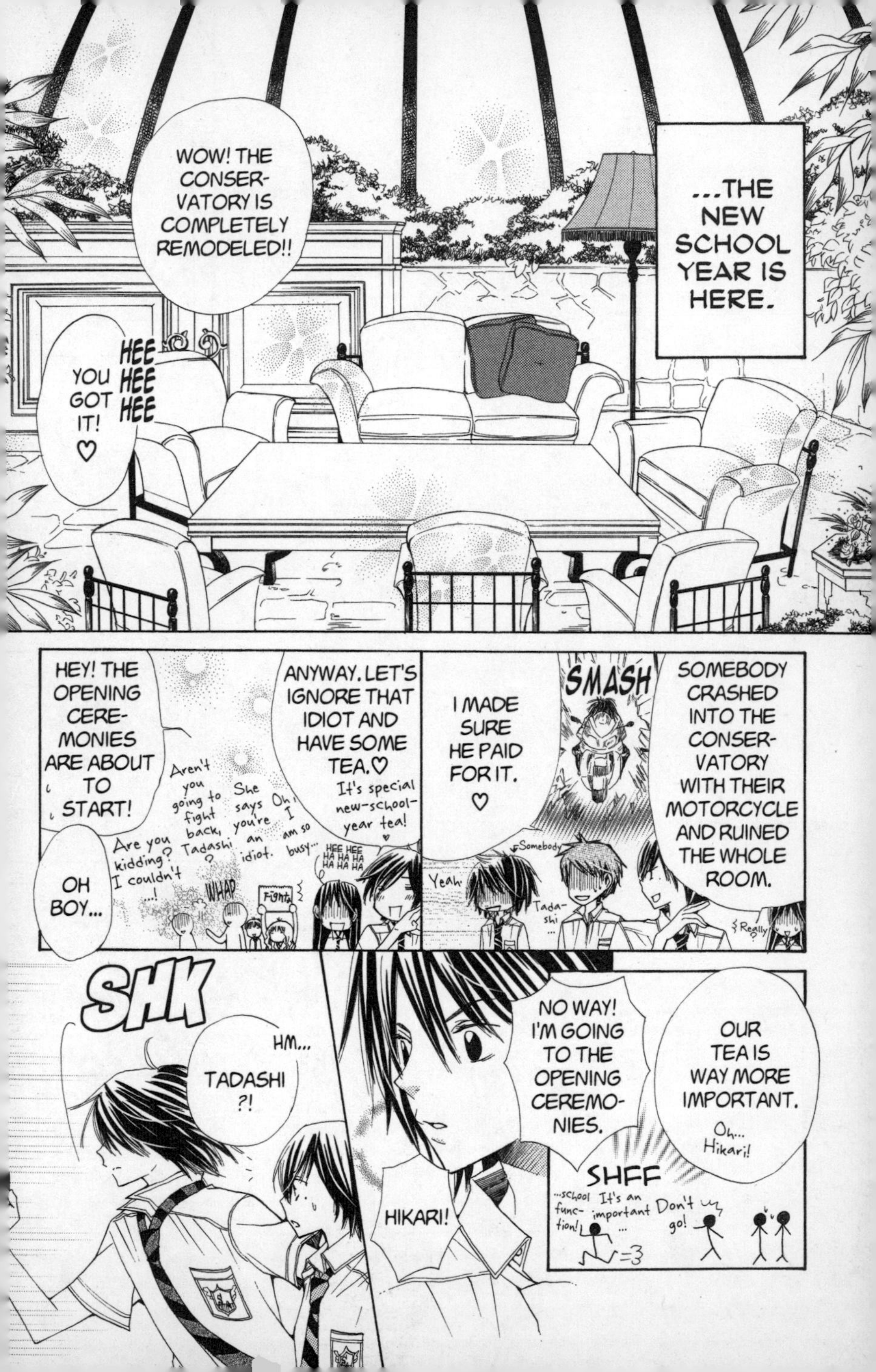
...THE NEW SCHOOL YEAR IS HERE.
WOW! THE CONSERVATORY IS COMPLETELY REMODELED!!
YOU GOT IT! ♡
HEE HEE HEE
SOMEBODY CRASHED INTO THE CONSERVATORY WITH THEIR MOTORCYCLE AND RUINED THE WHOLE ROOM.
SMASH
I MADE SURE HE PAID FOR IT. ♡
Somebody
Really
Tadashi...
Yeah
ANYWAY. LET'S IGNORE THAT IDIOT AND HAVE SOME TEA.♡
It's special new-school-year tea!
HEE HEE HA HA HA HA HA HA
Oh, I am so busy...
She says you're an idiot.
Aren't you going to fight back, Tadashi?
Are you kidding? I couldn't ...!
Fight
WHAP
HEY! THE OPENING CEREMONIES ARE ABOUT TO START!
OH BOY...
OUR TEA IS WAY MORE IMPORTANT.
Oh... Hikari!
NO WAY! I'M GOING TO THE OPENING CEREMONIES.
SHFF
Don't go!
It's an important ...
...school function!
=3
HIKARI!
HM...
TADASHI?!
SHK

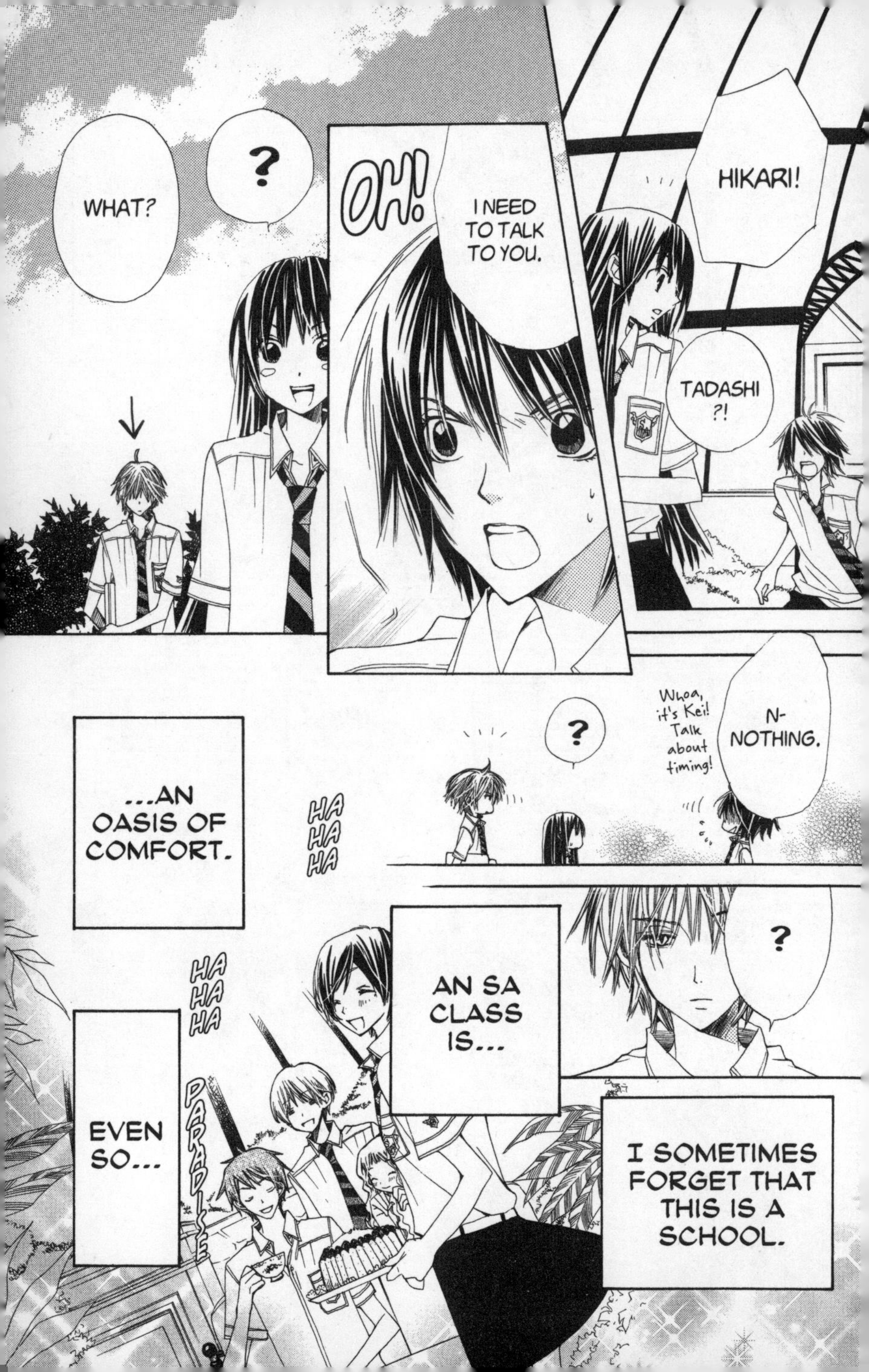
HIKARI!
TADASHI ?!
OH!
I NEED TO TALK TO YOU.
?
WHAT?
N- NOTHING.
Whoa, it's Kei! Talk about timing!
?
?
AN SA CLASS IS...
...AN OASIS OF COMFORT.
HA HA HA
HA HA HA
PARADI~SE
EVEN SO...
I SOMETIMES FORGET THAT THIS IS A SCHOOL.

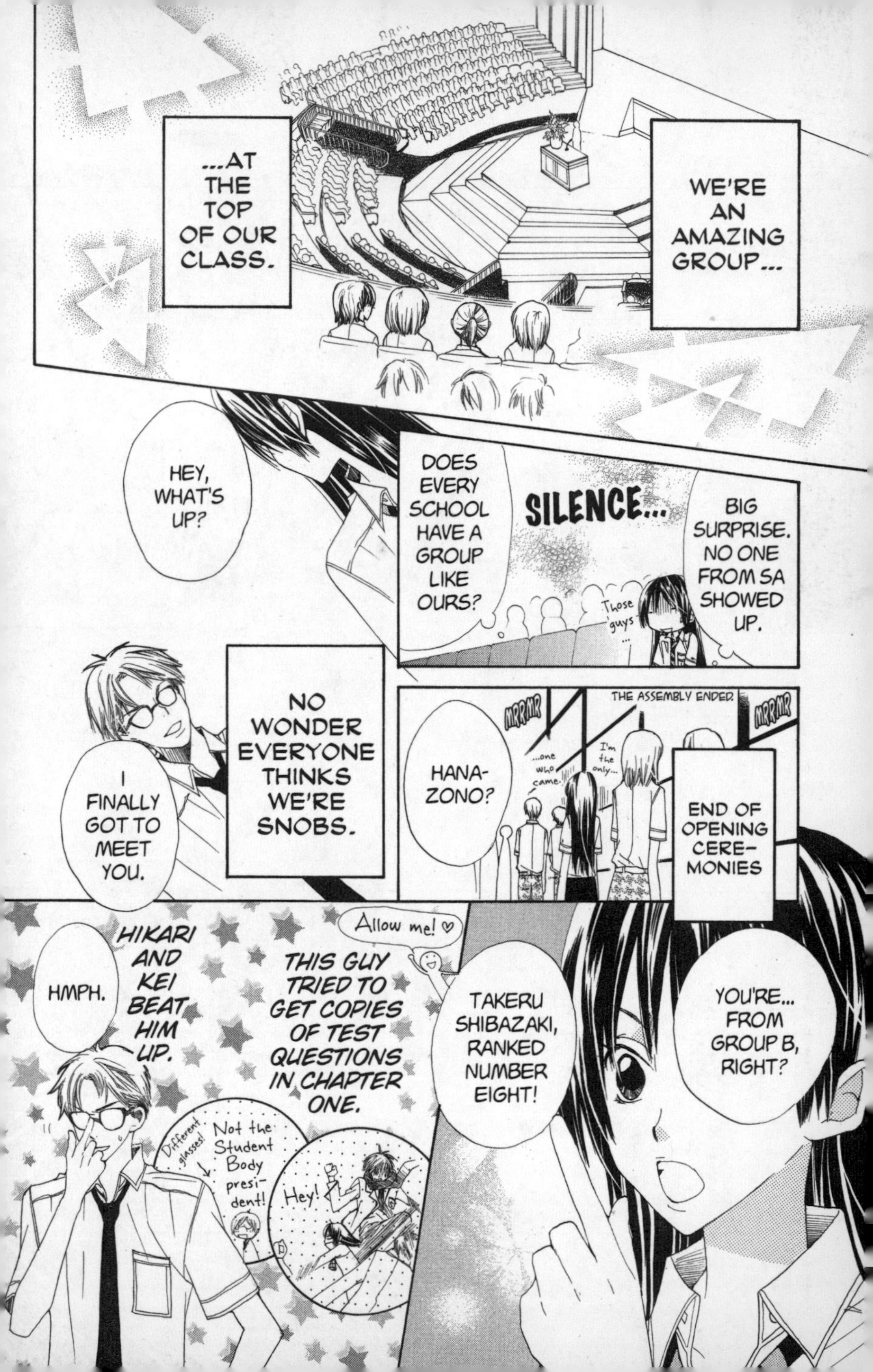
WE'RE AN AMAZING GROUP...
...AT THE TOP OF OUR CLASS.
BIG SURPRISE. NO ONE FROM SA SHOWED UP.
Those guys...
SILENCE...
DOES EVERY SCHOOL HAVE A GROUP LIKE OURS?
END OF OPENING CEREMONIES
MRRMR
THE ASSEMBLY ENDED.
I'm the only...
...one who came.
MRRMR
HANA-ZONO?
NO WONDER EVERYONE THINKS WE'RE SNOBS.
HEY, WHAT'S UP?
I FINALLY GOT TO MEET YOU.
YOU'RE... FROM GROUP B, RIGHT?
TAKERU SHIBAZAKI, RANKED NUMBER EIGHT!
Allow me! ♡
THIS GUY TRIED TO GET COPIES OF TEST QUESTIONS IN CHAPTER ONE.
HIKARI AND KEI BEAT HIM UP.
HMPH.
Not the Student Body president!
Different glasses!
Hey!

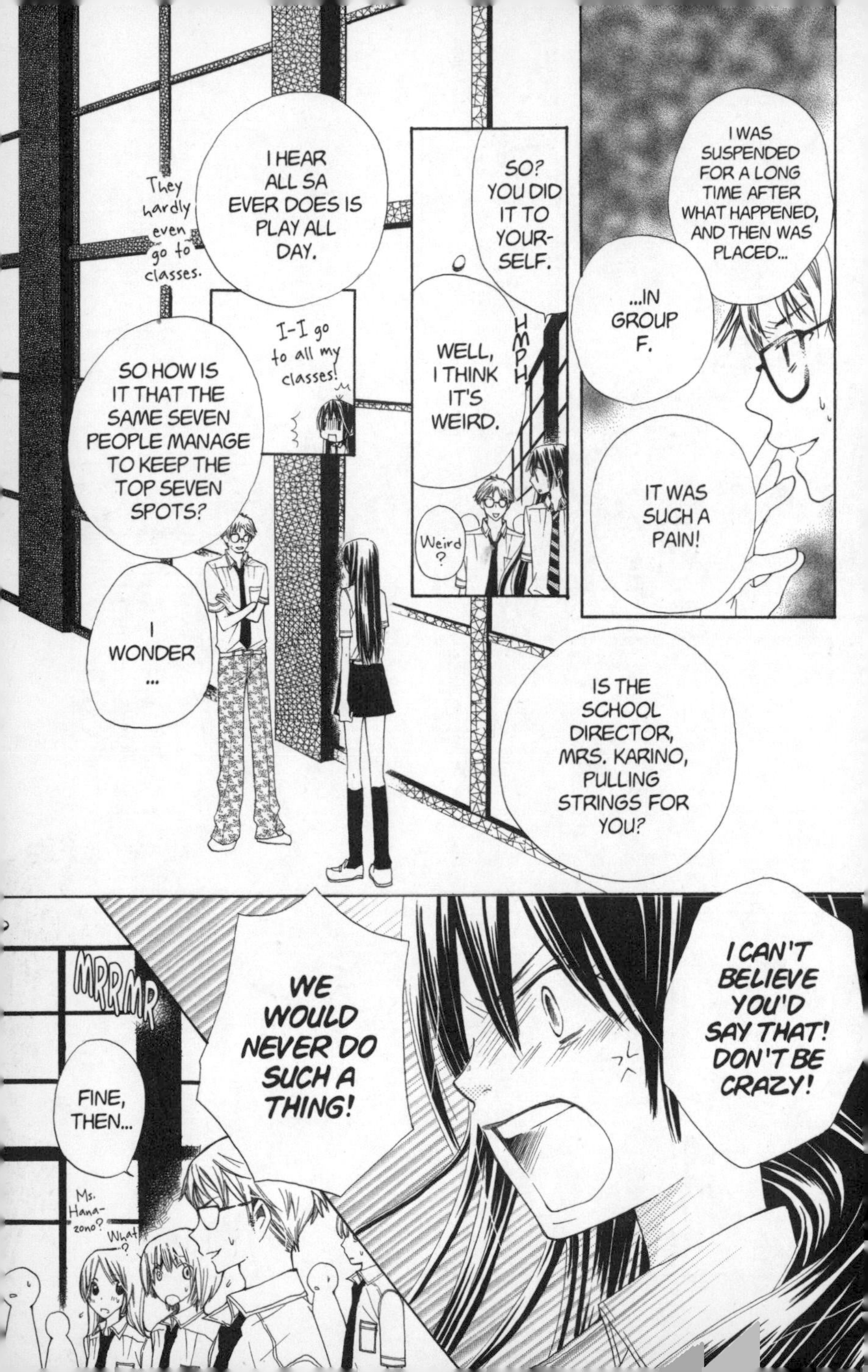
I WAS SUSPENDED FOR A LONG TIME AFTER WHAT HAPPENED, AND THEN WAS PLACED...
...IN GROUP F.
IT WAS SUCH A PAIN!
SO? YOU DID IT TO YOURSELF.
HMPH
WELL, I THINK IT'S WEIRD.
Weird?
I HEAR ALL SA EVER DOES IS PLAY ALL DAY.
They hardly even go to classes.
I-I go to all my classes!
SO HOW IS IT THAT THE SAME SEVEN PEOPLE MANAGE TO KEEP THE TOP SEVEN SPOTS?
I WONDER...
IS THE SCHOOL DIRECTOR, MRS. KARINO, PULLING STRINGS FOR YOU?
I CAN'T BELIEVE YOU'D SAY THAT! DON'T BE CRAZY!
WE WOULD NEVER DO SUCH A THING!
MRRMR
FINE, THEN...
Ms. Hana-zono?
What...?

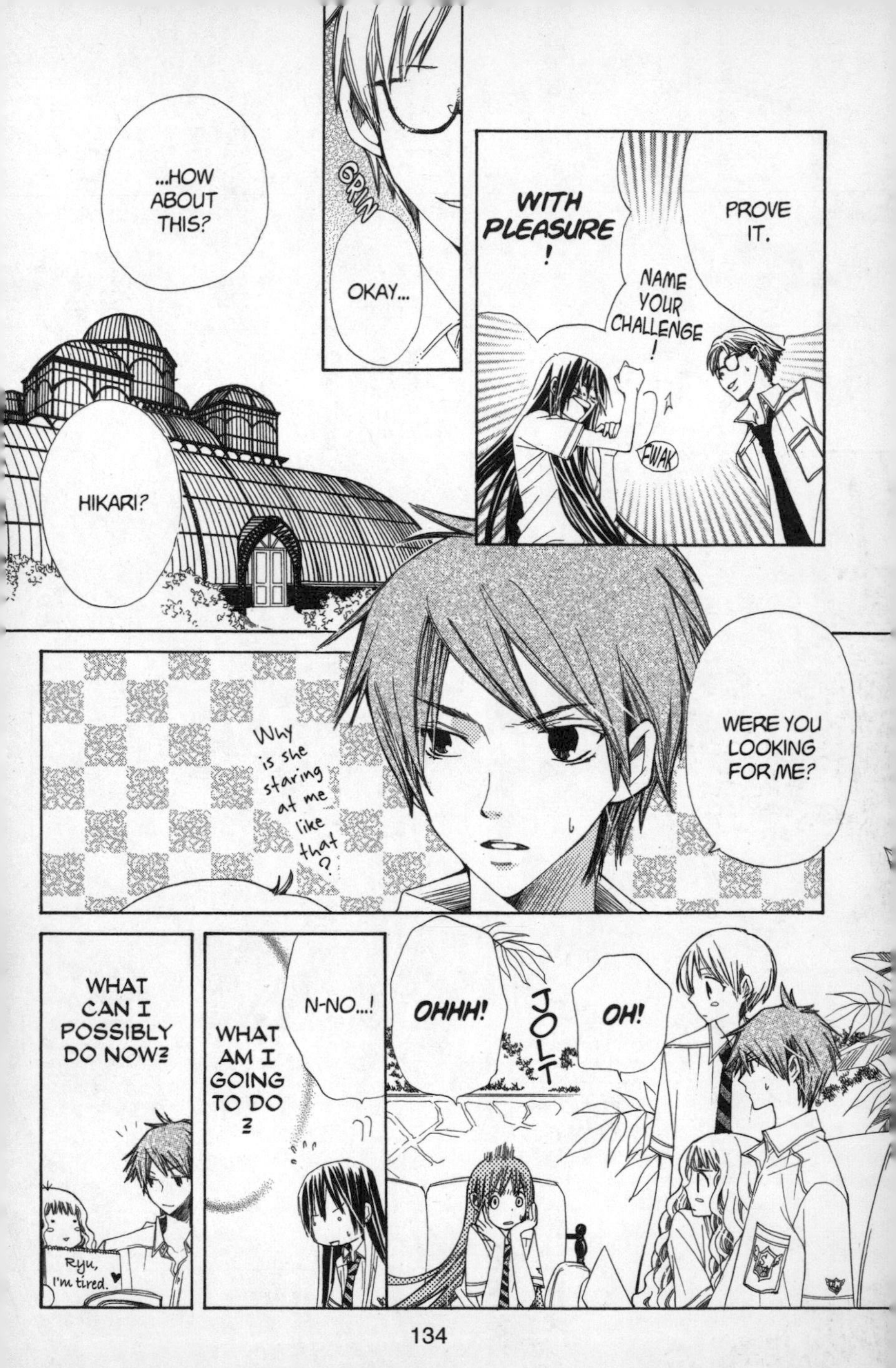

PROVE IT.
WITH PLEASURE!
NAME YOUR CHALLENGE!
FWAK
GRIN
OKAY...
...HOW ABOUT THIS?
HIKARI?
WERE YOU LOOKING FOR ME?
Why is she staring at me like that?
OH!
JOLT
OHHH!
N-NO...!
WHAT AM I GOING TO DO?
WHAT CAN I POSSIBLY DO NOW?
Ryu, I'm tired.

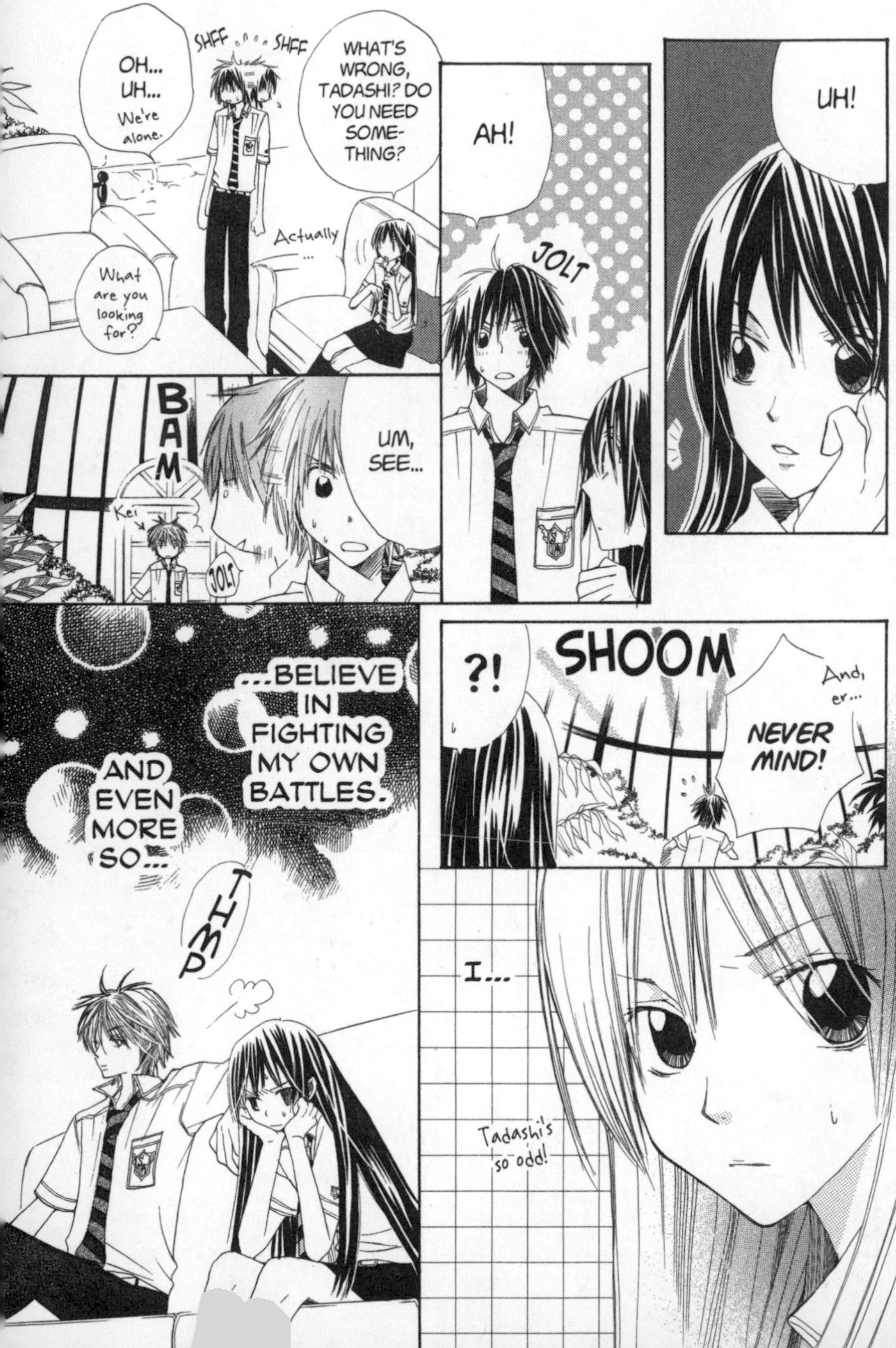
UH!
AH!
JOLT
WHAT'S WRONG, TADASHI? DO YOU NEED SOME-THING?
SHFF
SHFF
OH... UH... We're alone.
Actually ...
What are you looking for?
UM, SEE...
BAM
Kei
JOLT
And, er...
NEVER MIND!
SHOOM
?!
I...
Tadashi's so odd!
...BELIEVE IN FIGHTING MY OWN BATTLES.
AND EVEN MORE SO...
THMP

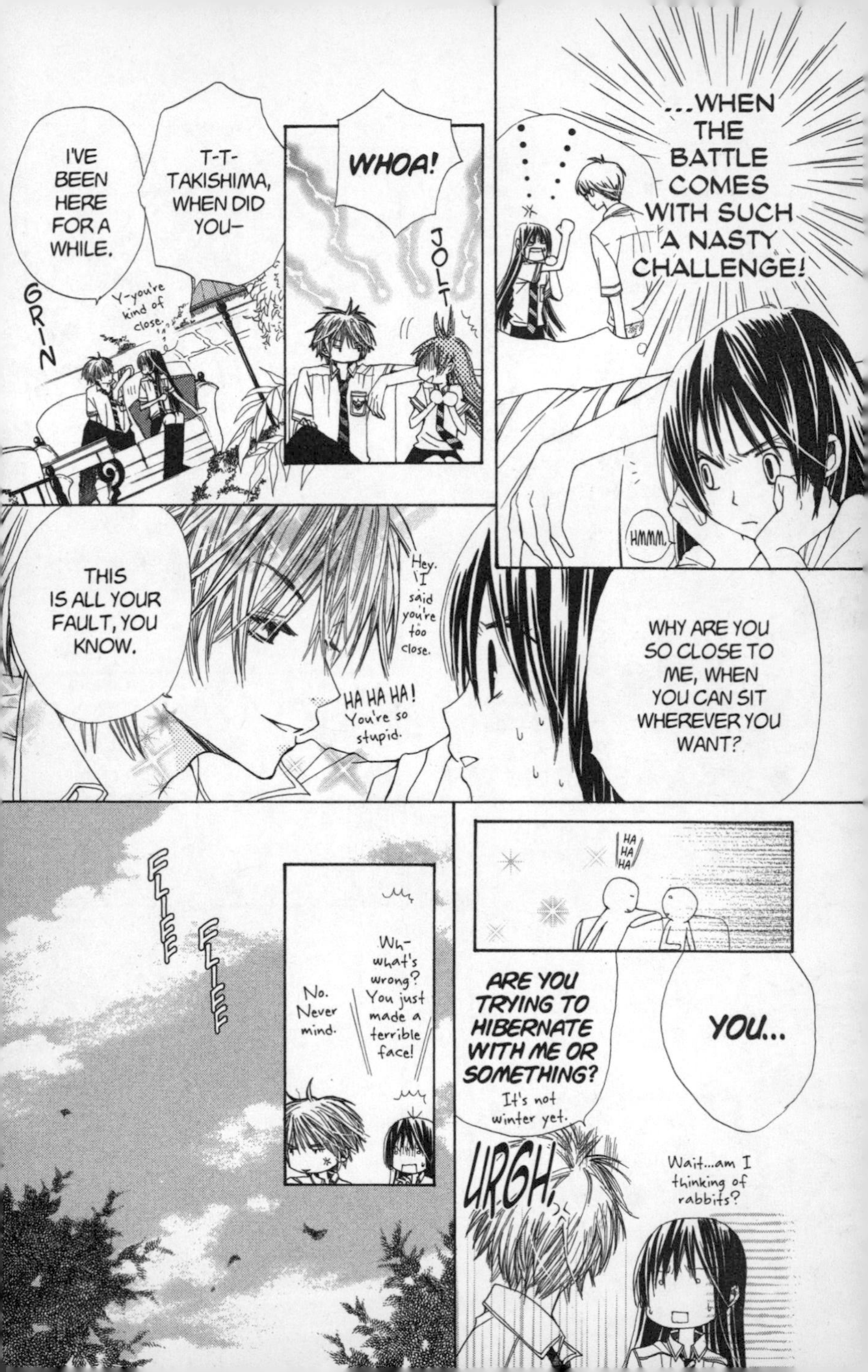
...WHEN THE BATTLE COMES WITH SUCH A NASTY CHALLENGE!
HMMM.
WHOA!
JOLT
T-T-TAKISHIMA, WHEN DID YOU—
I'VE BEEN HERE FOR A WHILE.
GRIN
Y-you're kind of close.
WHY ARE YOU SO CLOSE TO ME, WHEN YOU CAN SIT WHEREVER YOU WANT?
Hey. I said you're too close.
HA HA HA! You're so stupid.
THIS IS ALL YOUR FAULT, YOU KNOW.
HA HA HA
YOU...
ARE YOU TRYING TO HIBERNATE WITH ME OR SOMETHING?
It's not winter yet.
URGH,
Wait...am I thinking of rabbits?
Wh-what's wrong? You just made a terrible face!
No. Never mind.
FLIFF
FLIFF

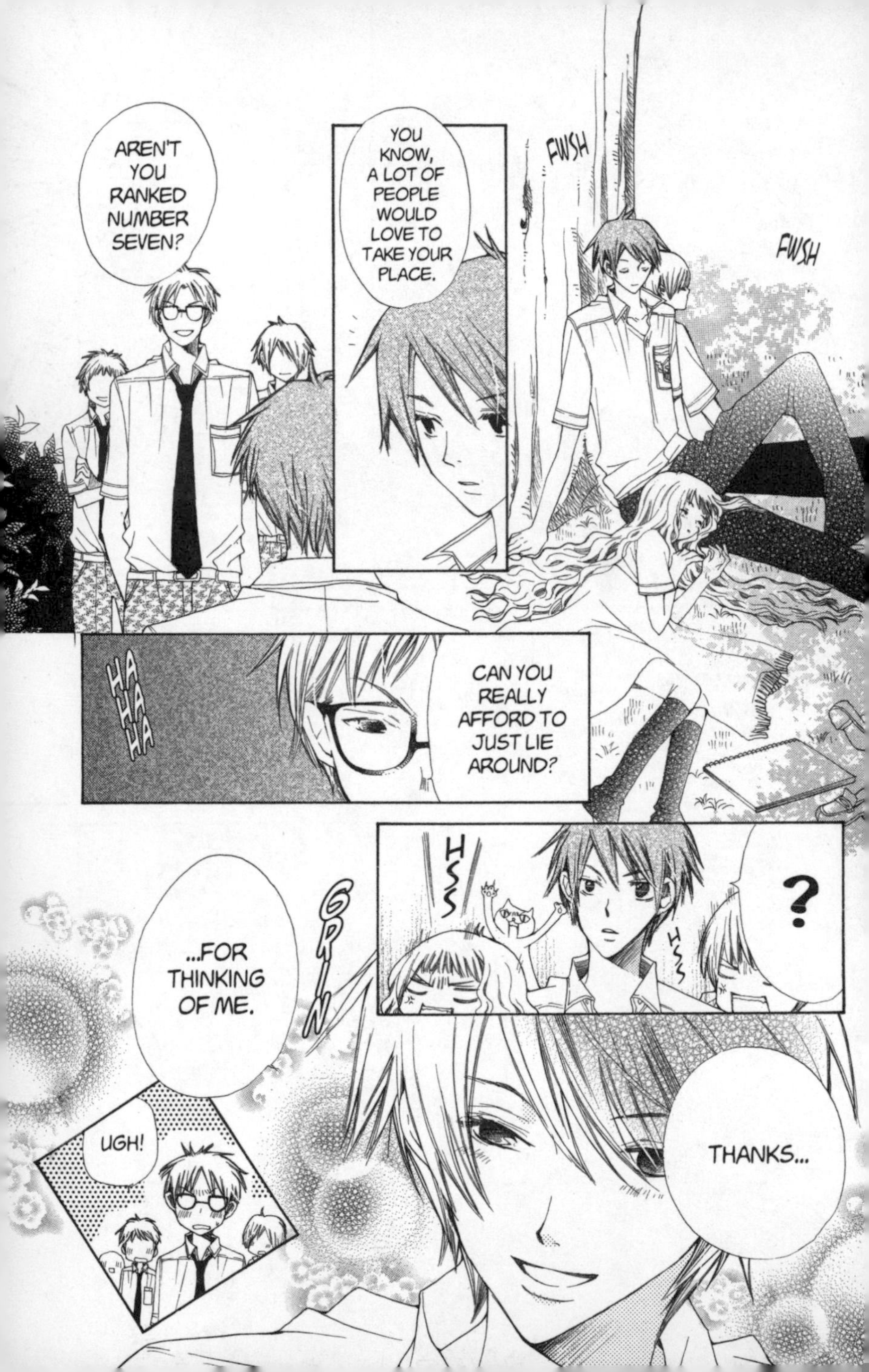
FWSH
FWSH
YOU KNOW, A LOT OF PEOPLE WOULD LOVE TO TAKE YOUR PLACE.
AREN'T YOU RANKED NUMBER SEVEN?
CAN YOU REALLY AFFORD TO JUST LIE AROUND?
HAHAHAHA
?
HSS
HSS
THANKS...
GRIN
...FOR THINKING OF ME.
UGH!

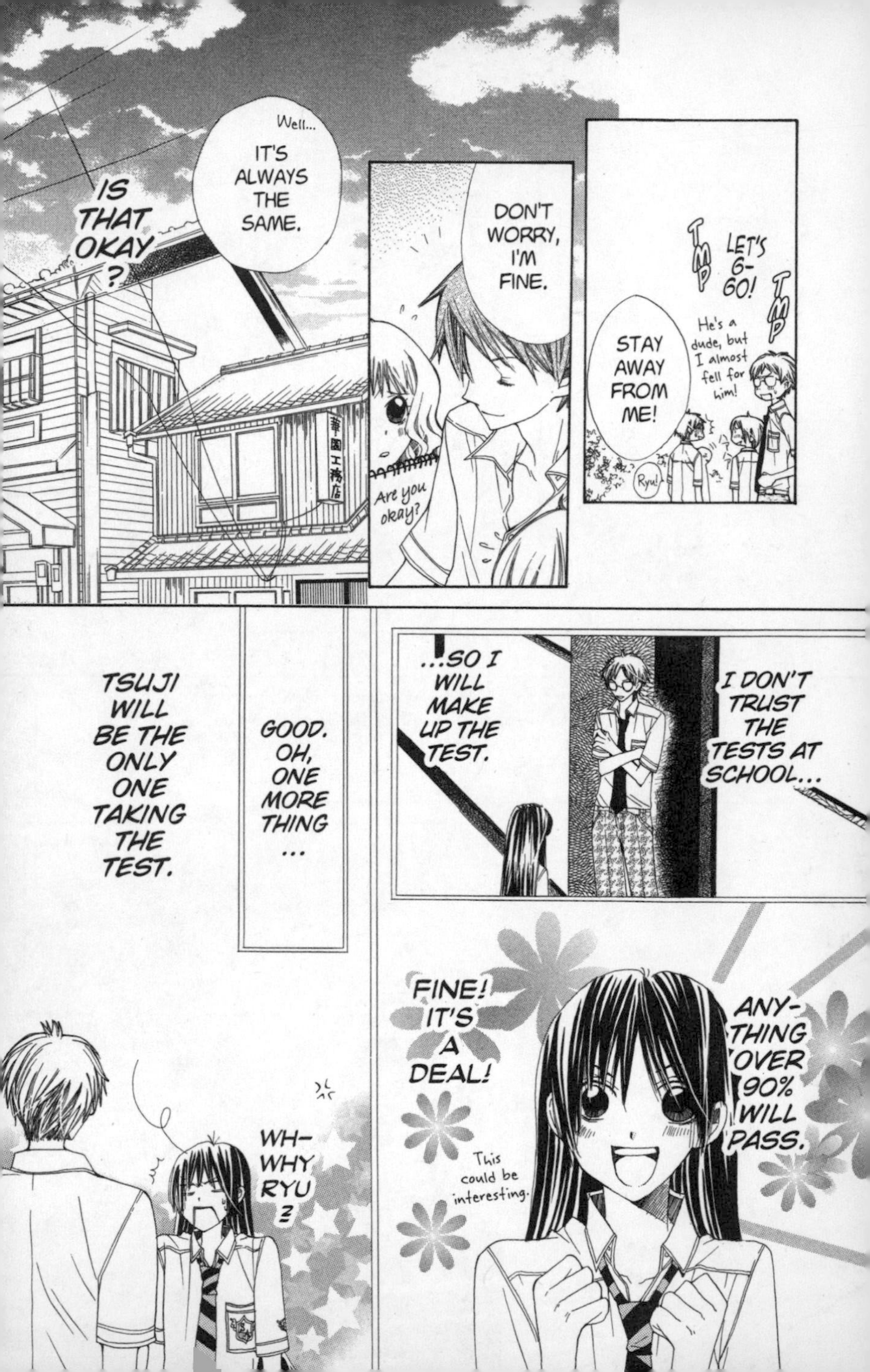
TMP
LET'S G-GO!
TMP
He's a dude, but I almost fell for him!
STAY AWAY FROM ME!
Ryu!
DON'T WORRY, I'M FINE.
Are you okay?
Well...
IT'S ALWAYS THE SAME.
華園工務店
IS THAT OKAY?
I DON'T TRUST THE TESTS AT SCHOOL...
...SO I WILL MAKE UP THE TEST.
GOOD. OH, ONE MORE THING...
TSUJI WILL BE THE ONLY ONE TAKING THE TEST.
ANY-THING OVER 90% WILL PASS.
FINE! IT'S A DEAL!
This could be interesting.
WH-WHY RYU?

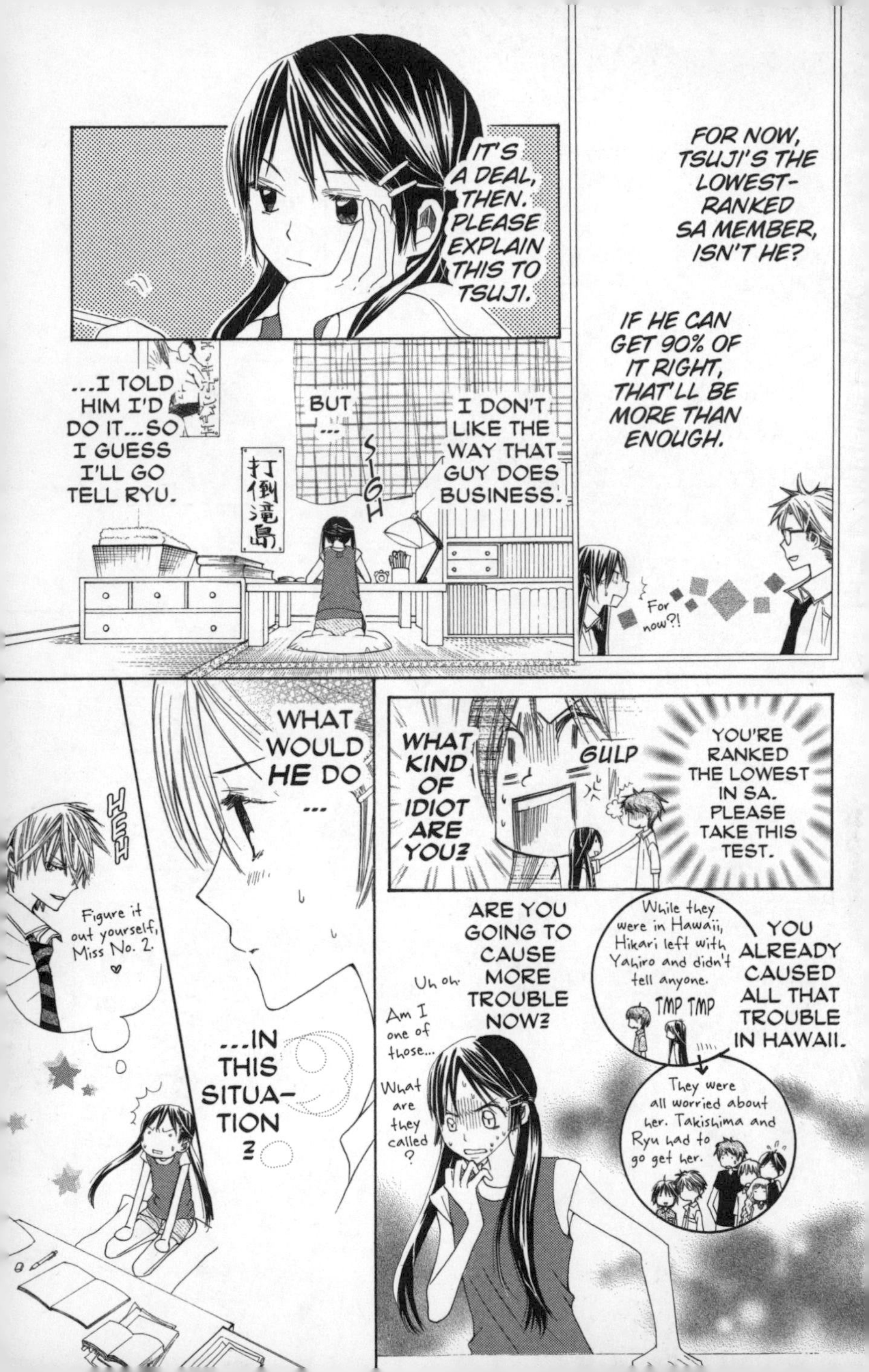

FOR NOW, TSUJI'S THE LOWEST-RANKED SA MEMBER, ISN'T HE?
IF HE CAN GET 90% OF IT RIGHT, THAT'LL BE MORE THAN ENOUGH.
For now?!
IT'S A DEAL, THEN. PLEASE EXPLAIN THIS TO TSUJI.
I DON'T LIKE THE WAY THAT GUY DOES BUSINESS.
BUT...
SIGH
打倒滝島
...I TOLD HIM I'D DO IT...SO I GUESS I'LL GO TELL RYU.
YOU'RE RANKED THE LOWEST IN SA. PLEASE TAKE THIS TEST.
GULP
WHAT KIND OF IDIOT ARE YOU?
YOU ALREADY CAUSED ALL THAT TROUBLE IN HAWAII.
While they were in Hawaii, Hikari left with Yahiro and didn't tell anyone.
TMP TMP
They were all worried about her. Takishima and Ryu had to go get her.
ARE YOU GOING TO CAUSE MORE TROUBLE NOW?
Uh oh
Am I one of those...
What are they called?
WHAT WOULD HE DO...
...IN THIS SITUATION?
HEH
Figure it out yourself, Miss No. 2.

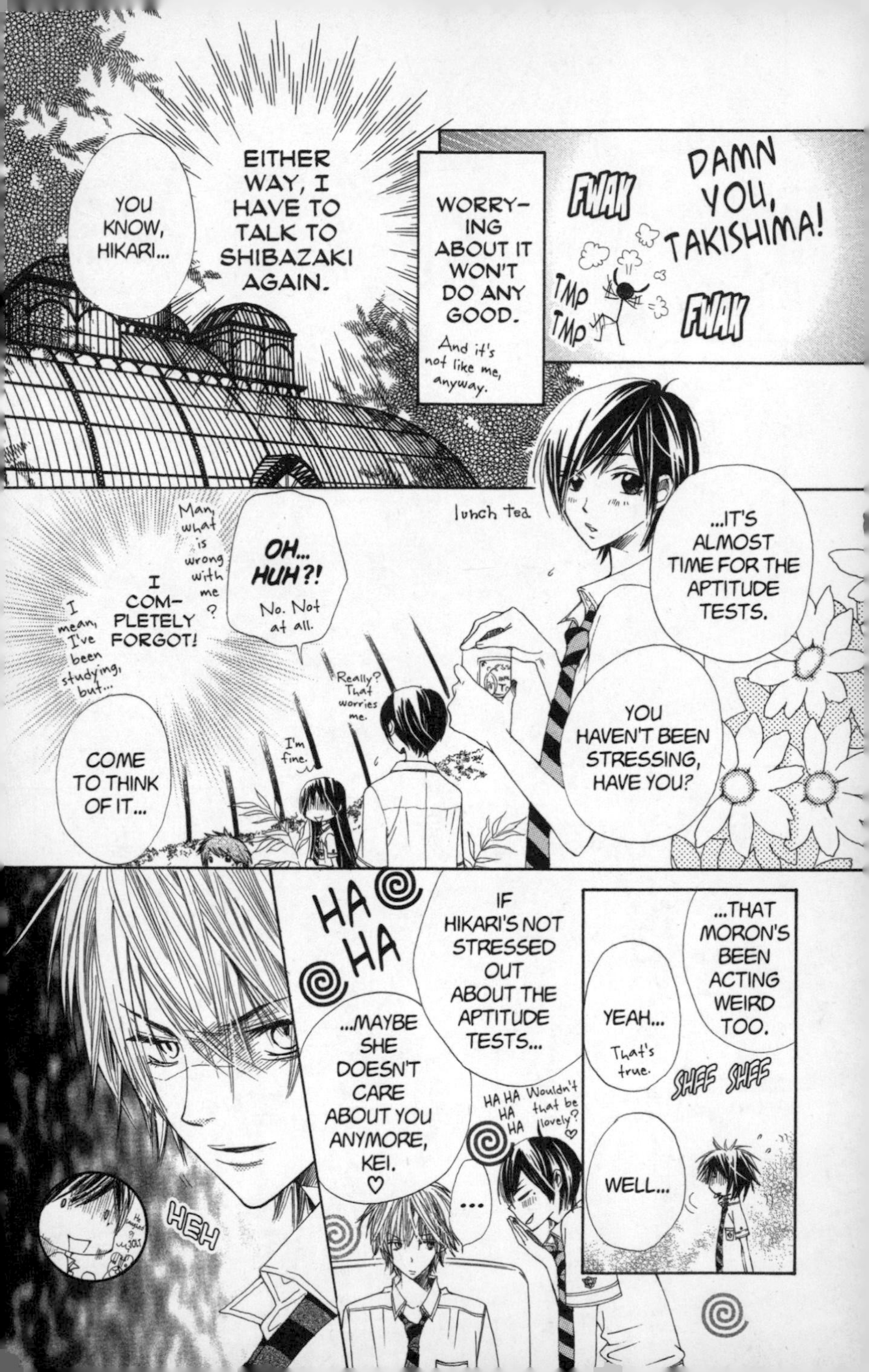
DAMN YOU, TAKISHIMA!
FWAK
FWAK
TMP TMP
WORRYING ABOUT IT WON'T DO ANY GOOD.
And it's not like me, anyway.
EITHER WAY, I HAVE TO TALK TO SHIBAZAKI AGAIN.
YOU KNOW, HIKARI...
...IT'S ALMOST TIME FOR THE APTITUDE TESTS.
lunch tea
YOU HAVEN'T BEEN STRESSING, HAVE YOU?
OH... HUH?!
No. Not at all.
Really? That worries me.
I'm fine.
Man, what is wrong with me?
I COMPLETELY FORGOT!
I mean, I've been studying, but...
COME TO THINK OF IT...
...THAT MORON'S BEEN ACTING WEIRD TOO.
SHFF SHFF
YEAH...
That's true.
WELL...
IF HIKARI'S NOT STRESSED OUT ABOUT THE APTITUDE TESTS...
HA HA
...MAYBE SHE DOESN'T CARE ABOUT YOU ANYMORE, KEI. ♡
HA HA HA HA
Wouldn't that be lovely? ♡
...
HEH

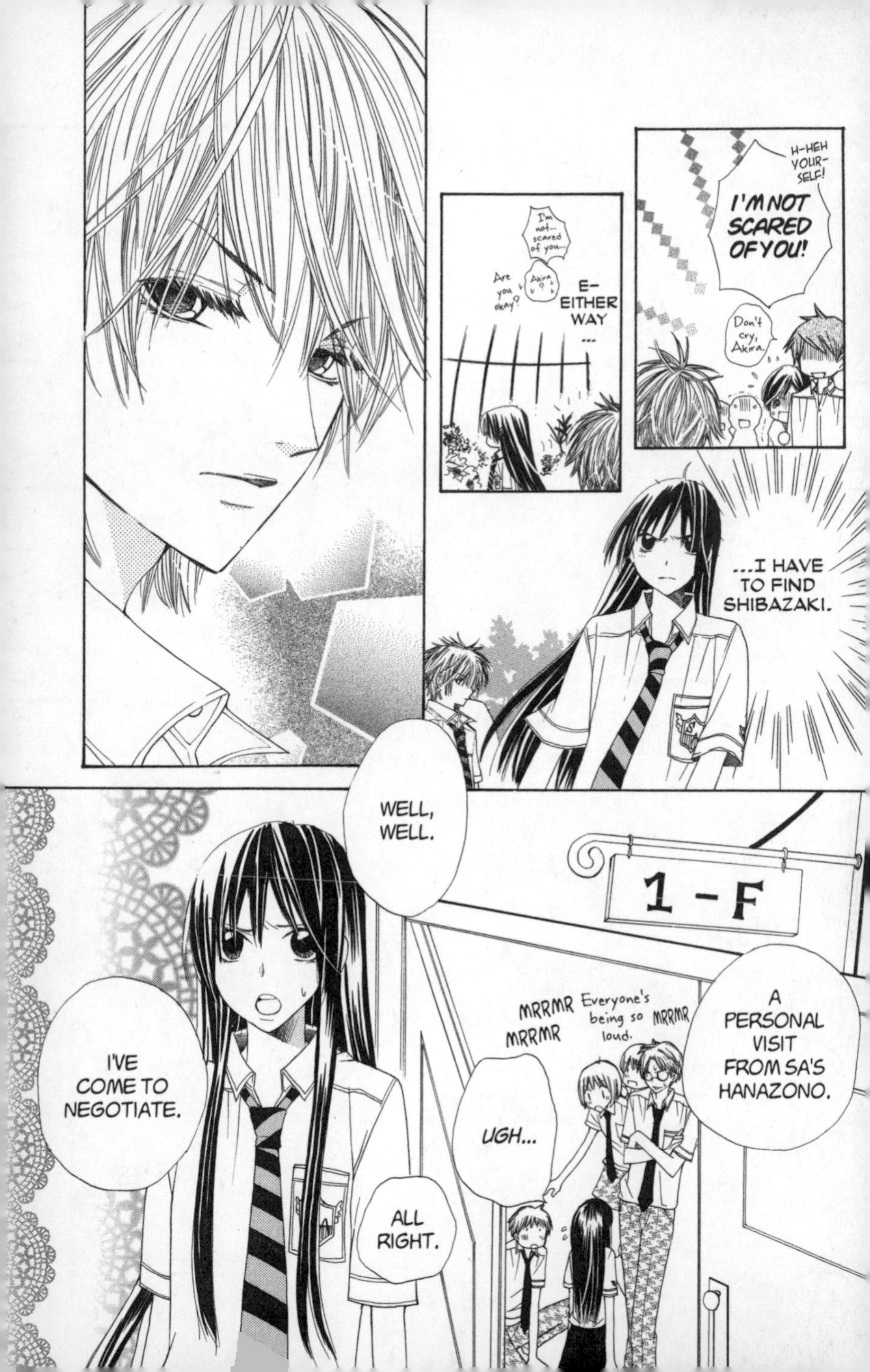
H-HEH YOURSELF!
I'M NOT SCARED OF YOU!
Don't cry, Akira.
I'm not... scared of you...
Akira?
Are you okay?
E-EITHER WAY...
...I HAVE TO FIND SHIBAZAKI.
1 - F
A PERSONAL VISIT FROM SA'S HANAZONO.
MRRMR
Everyone's being so loud.
MRRMR
MRRMR
UGH...
ALL RIGHT.
WELL, WELL.
I'VE COME TO NEGOTIATE.

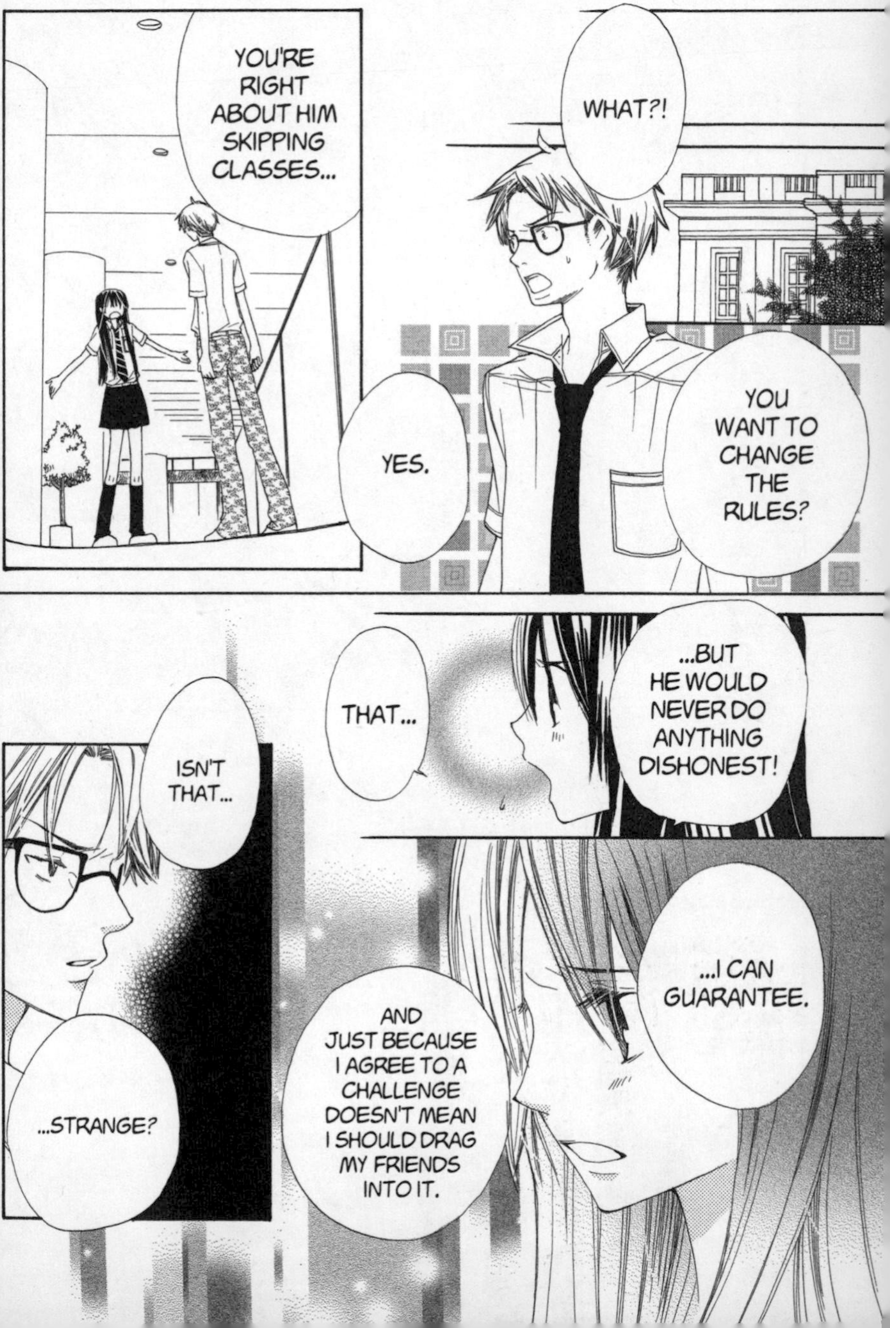
WHAT?!
YOU WANT TO CHANGE THE RULES?
YES.
YOU'RE RIGHT ABOUT HIM SKIPPING CLASSES...
...BUT HE WOULD NEVER DO ANYTHING DISHONEST!
THAT...
...I CAN GUARANTEE.
AND JUST BECAUSE I AGREE TO A CHALLENGE DOESN'T MEAN I SHOULD DRAG MY FRIENDS INTO IT.
ISN'T THAT...
...STRANGE?

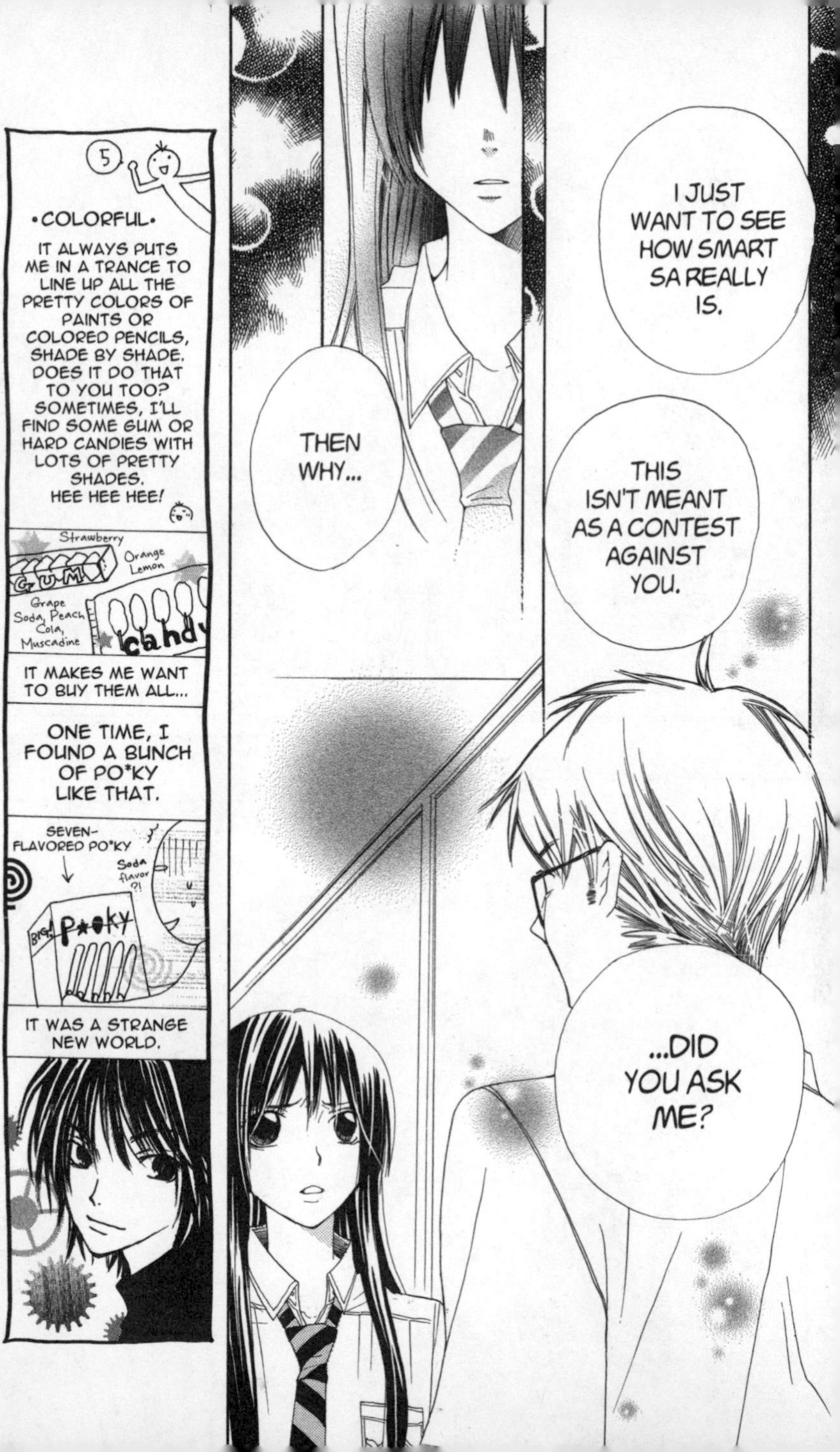
I JUST WANT TO SEE HOW SMART SA REALLY IS.
THIS ISN'T MEANT AS A CONTEST AGAINST YOU.
THEN WHY...
...DID YOU ASK ME?
5
•COLORFUL•
IT ALWAYS PUTS ME IN A TRANCE TO LINE UP ALL THE PRETTY COLORS OF PAINTS OR COLORED PENCILS, SHADE BY SHADE. DOES IT DO THAT TO YOU TOO? SOMETIMES, I'LL FIND SOME GUM OR HARD CANDIES WITH LOTS OF PRETTY SHADES. HEE HEE HEE!
Strawberry
Orange Lemon
GUM
Grape Soda, Peach Cola, Muscadine
candy
IT MAKES ME WANT TO BUY THEM ALL...
ONE TIME, I FOUND A BUNCH OF PO*KY LIKE THAT.
SEVEN-FLAVORED PO*KY
Soda flavor ?!
BIG! P*oky
IT WAS A STRANGE NEW WORLD.

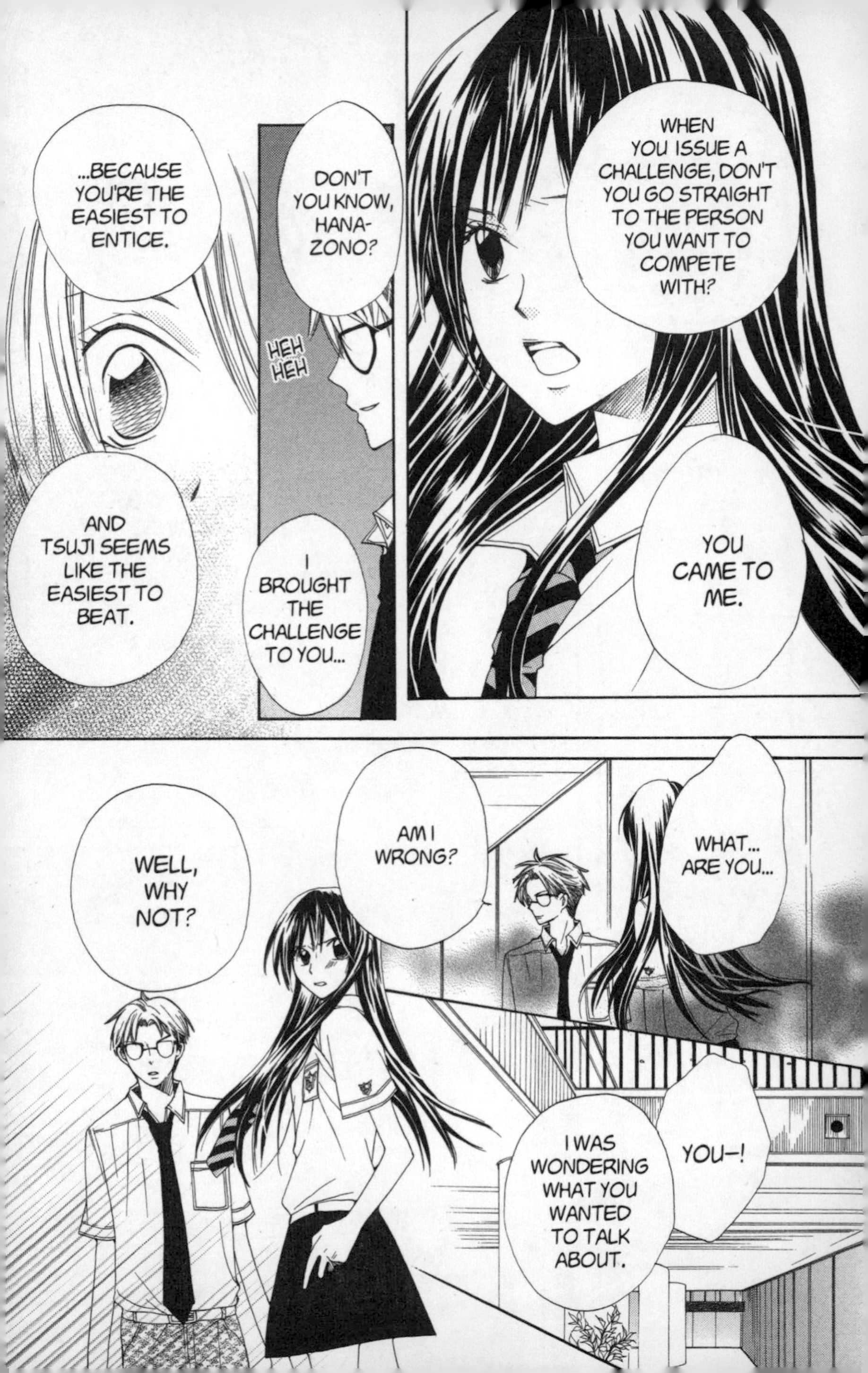
WHEN YOU ISSUE A CHALLENGE, DON'T YOU GO STRAIGHT TO THE PERSON YOU WANT TO COMPETE WITH?
YOU CAME TO ME.
DON'T YOU KNOW, HANA-ZONO?
HEH HEH
I BROUGHT THE CHALLENGE TO YOU...
...BECAUSE YOU'RE THE EASIEST TO ENTICE.
AND TSUJI SEEMS LIKE THE EASIEST TO BEAT.
WHAT... ARE YOU...
AM I WRONG?
YOU—!
I WAS WONDERING WHAT YOU WANTED TO TALK ABOUT.
WELL, WHY NOT?

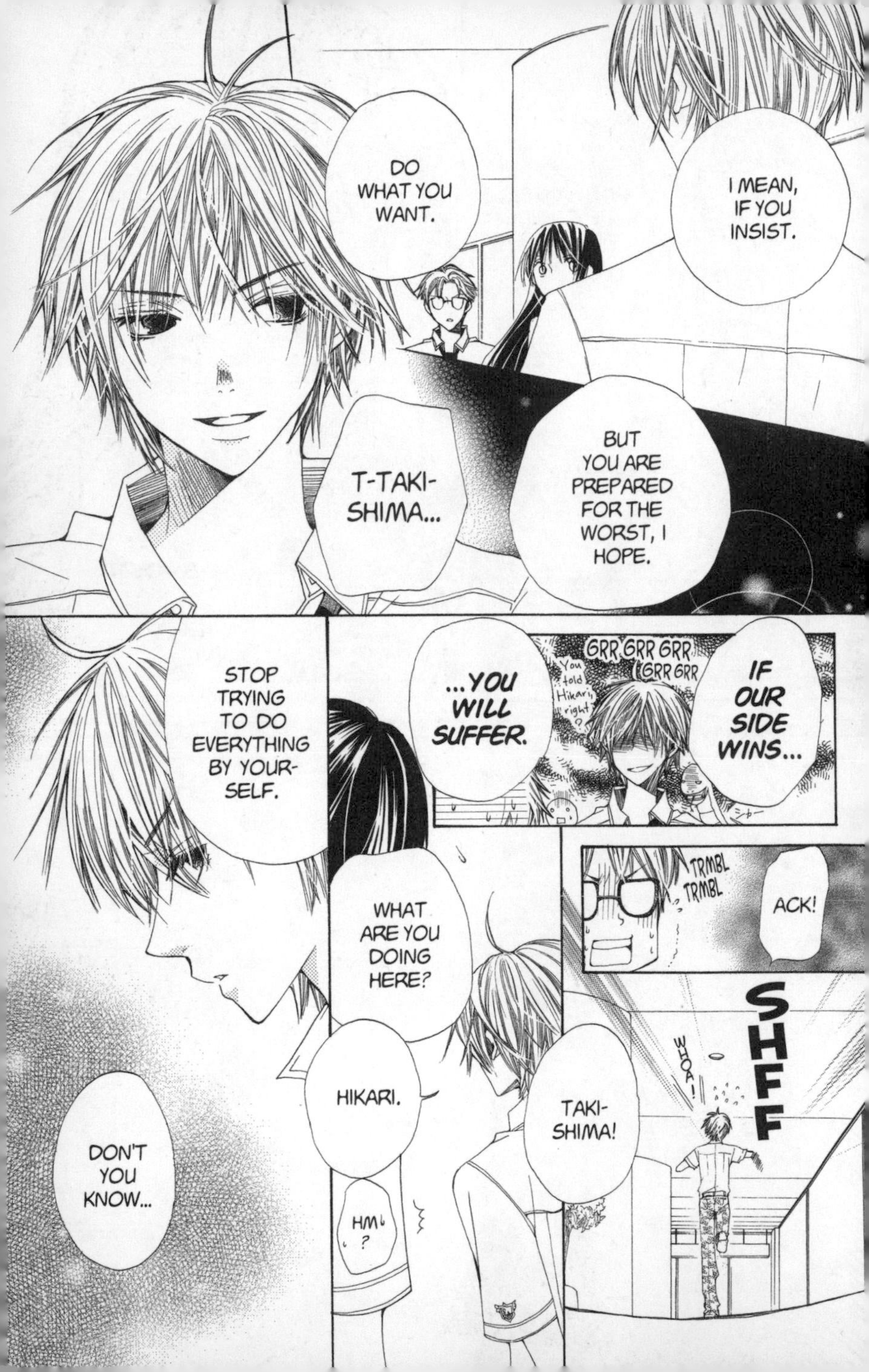
I MEAN, IF YOU INSIST.
DO WHAT YOU WANT.
BUT YOU ARE PREPARED FOR THE WORST, I HOPE.
T-TAKI-SHIMA...
IF OUR SIDE WINS...
GRR GRR GRR GRR GRR
You told Hikari, right?
...YOU WILL SUFFER.
ACK!
TRMBL TRMBL
SHFF
WHOA!
TAKI-SHIMA!
WHAT ARE YOU DOING HERE?
HIKARI.
HM?
STOP TRYING TO DO EVERYTHING BY YOUR-SELF.
DON'T YOU KNOW...

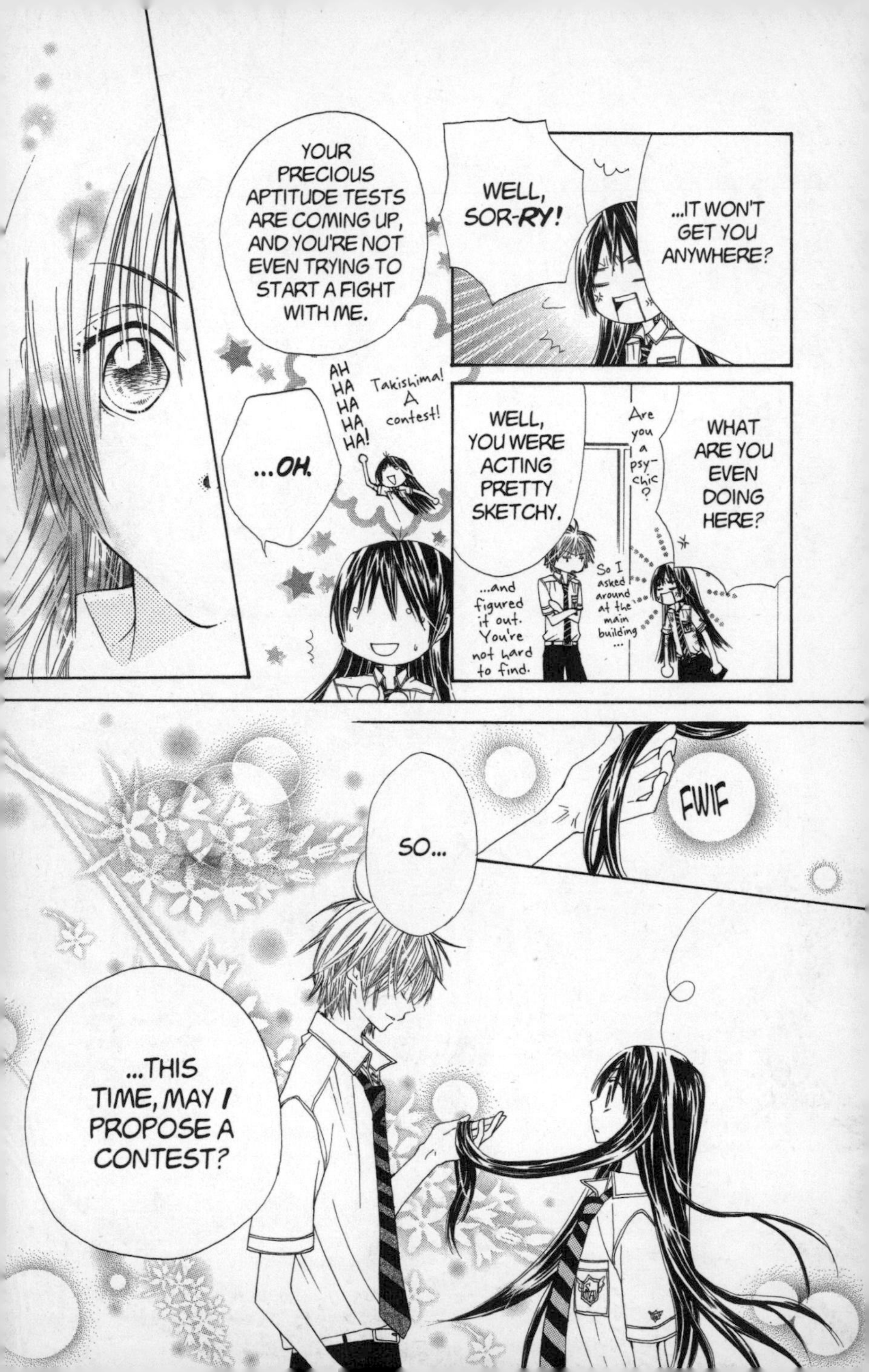
...IT WON'T GET YOU ANYWHERE?
WELL, SOR-*RY*!
WHAT ARE YOU EVEN DOING HERE?
Are you a psy-chic?
WELL, YOU WERE ACTING PRETTY SKETCHY.
So I asked around at the main building...
...and figured it out. You're not hard to find.
YOUR PRECIOUS APTITUDE TESTS ARE COMING UP, AND YOU'RE NOT EVEN TRYING TO START A FIGHT WITH ME.
AH HA HA HA HA!
Takishima! A contest!
...*OH.*
FWIF
SO...
...THIS TIME, MAY *I* PROPOSE A CONTEST?

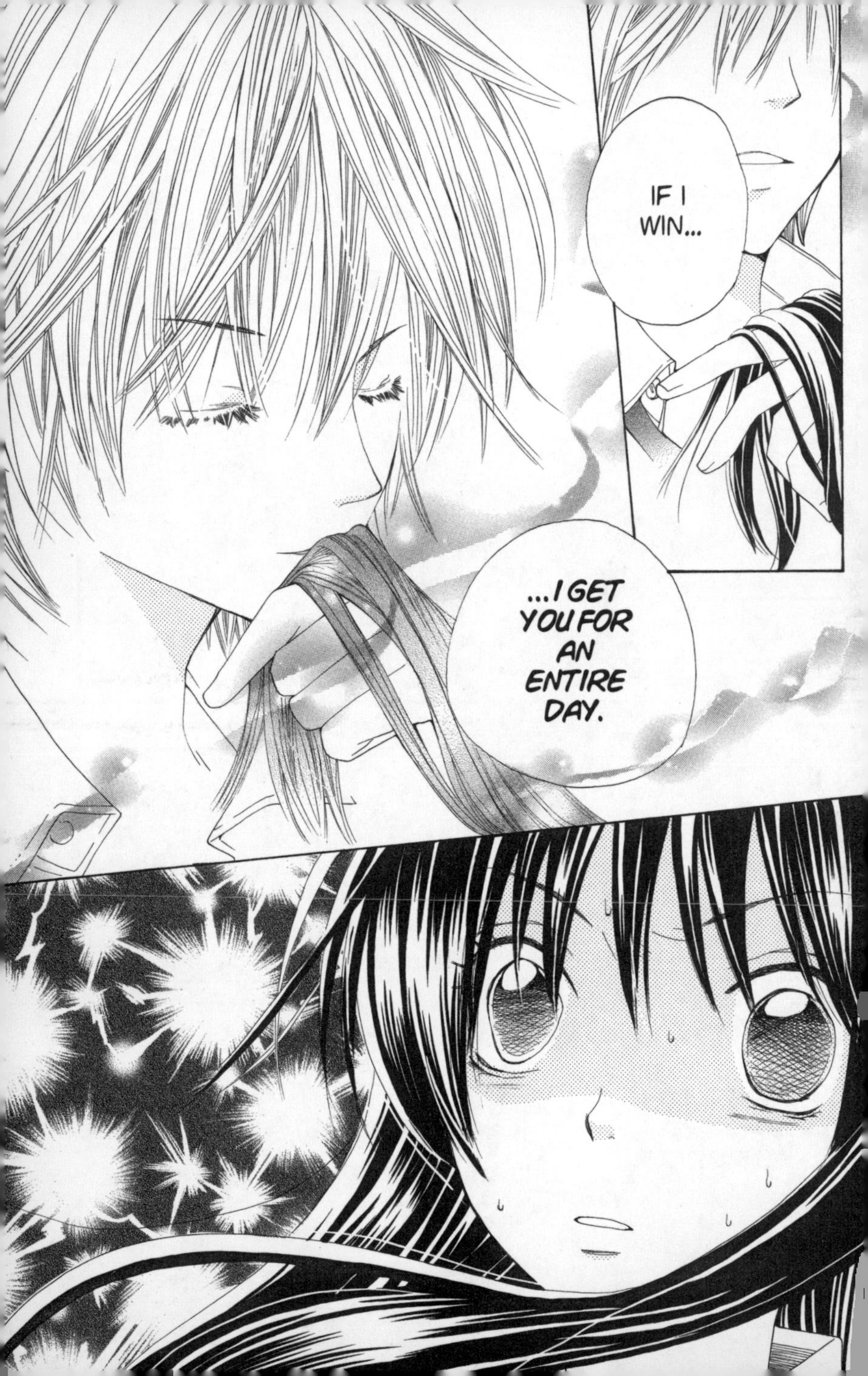
IF I WIN...
...I GET YOU FOR AN ENTIRE DAY.

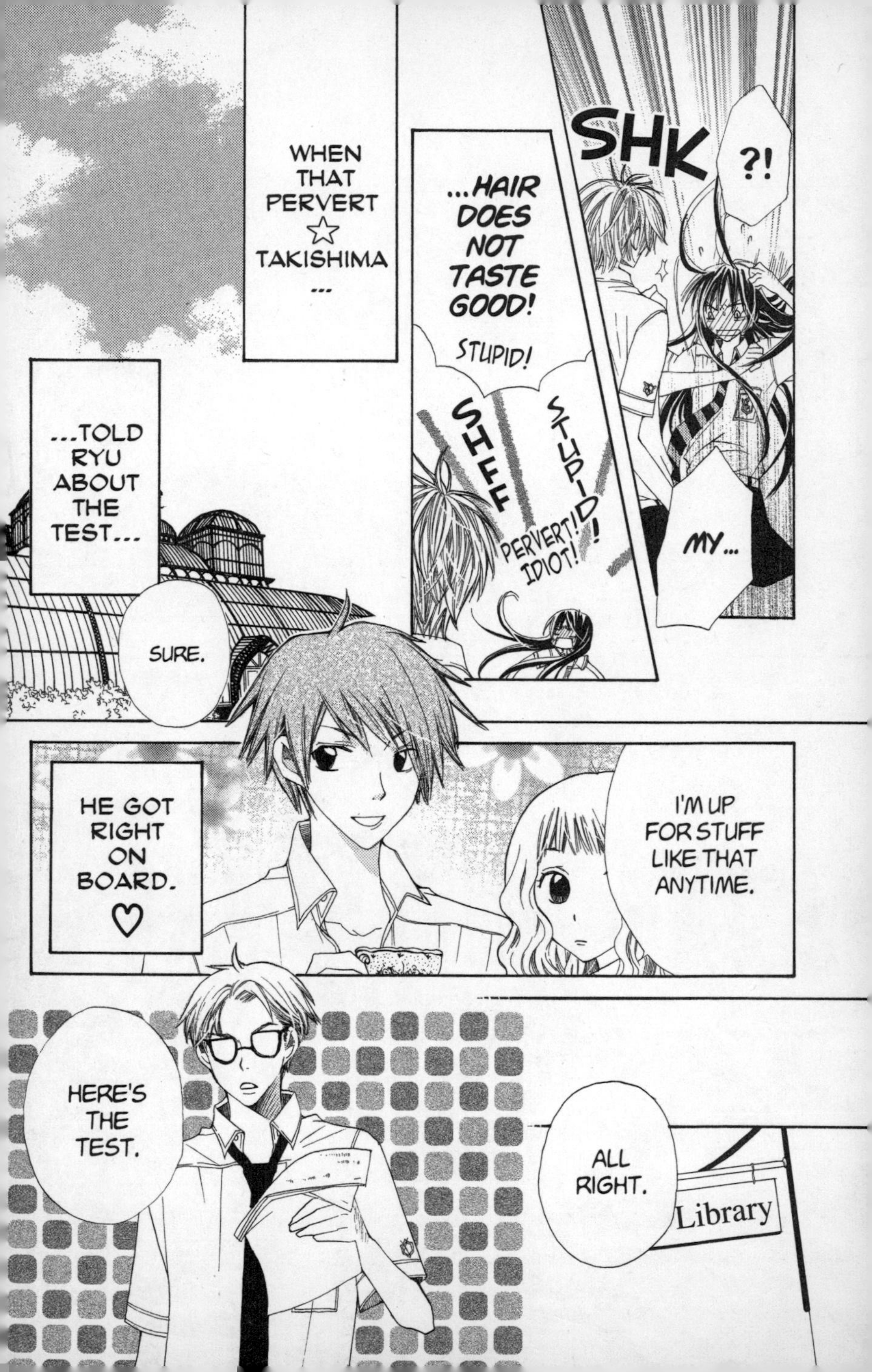
SHK
?!
MY...
...HAIR DOES NOT TASTE GOOD!
STUPID!
SHFF
STUPID!
PERVERT! IDIOT!
WHEN THAT PERVERT ☆ TAKISHIMA ...
...TOLD RYU ABOUT THE TEST...
SURE.
I'M UP FOR STUFF LIKE THAT ANYTIME.
HE GOT RIGHT ON BOARD. ♡
ALL RIGHT.
Library
HERE'S THE TEST.

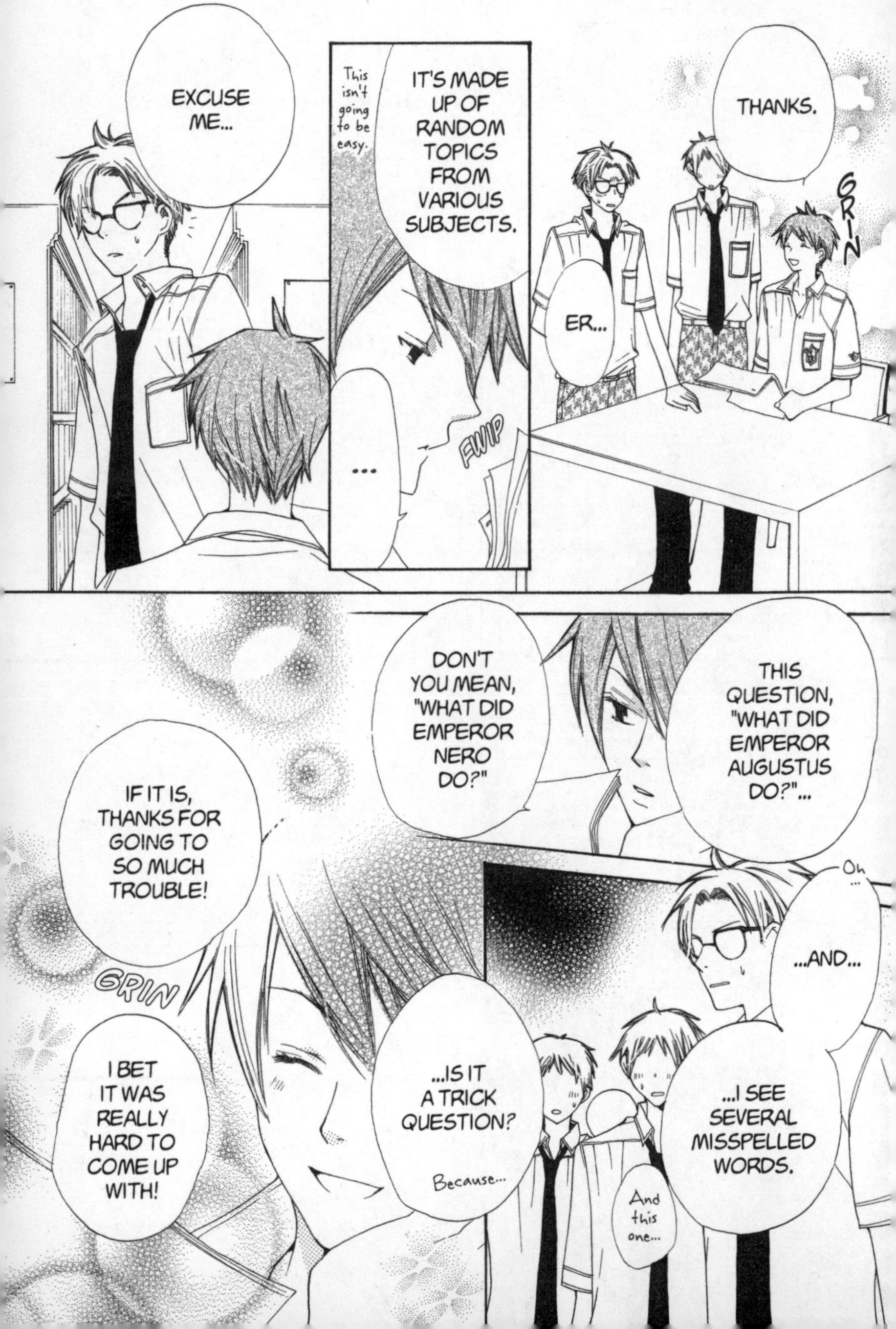
THANKS.
GRIN
ER...
IT'S MADE UP OF RANDOM TOPICS FROM VARIOUS SUBJECTS.
This isn't going to be easy.
FWIP
...
EXCUSE ME...
THIS QUESTION, "WHAT DID EMPEROR AUGUSTUS DO?"...
DON'T YOU MEAN, "WHAT DID EMPEROR NERO DO?"
Oh...
...AND...
...I SEE SEVERAL MISSPELLED WORDS.
And this one...
...IS IT A TRICK QUESTION?
Because...
IF IT IS, THANKS FOR GOING TO SO MUCH TROUBLE!
GRIN
I BET IT WAS REALLY HARD TO COME UP WITH!

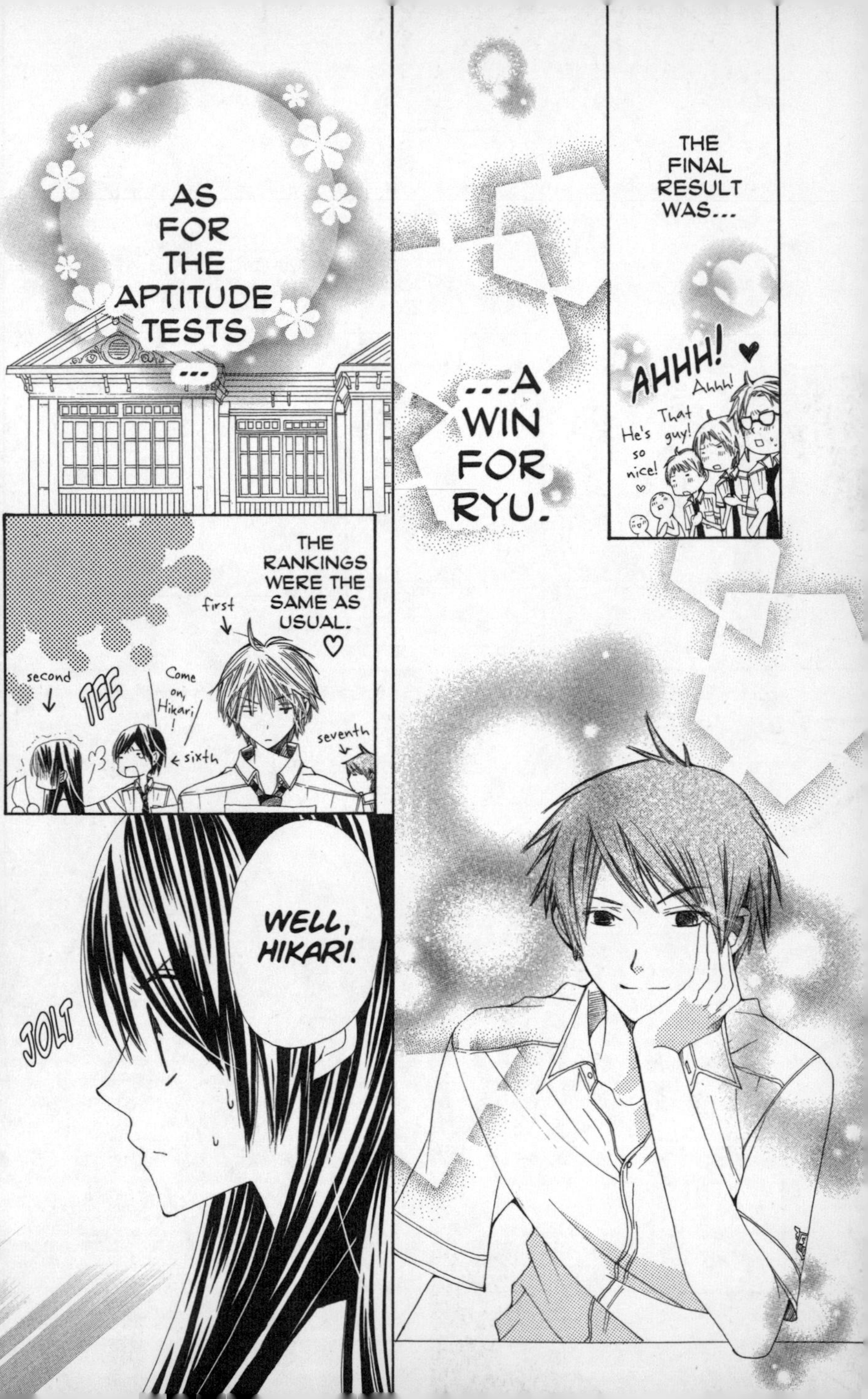
THE FINAL RESULT WAS...
AHHH!
Ahhh!
That guy!
He's so nice!
...A WIN FOR RYU.
AS FOR THE APTITUDE TESTS...
THE RANKINGS WERE THE SAME AS USUAL.
first
Come on, Hikari!
TFF
second
sixth
seventh
WELL, HIKARI.
JOLT

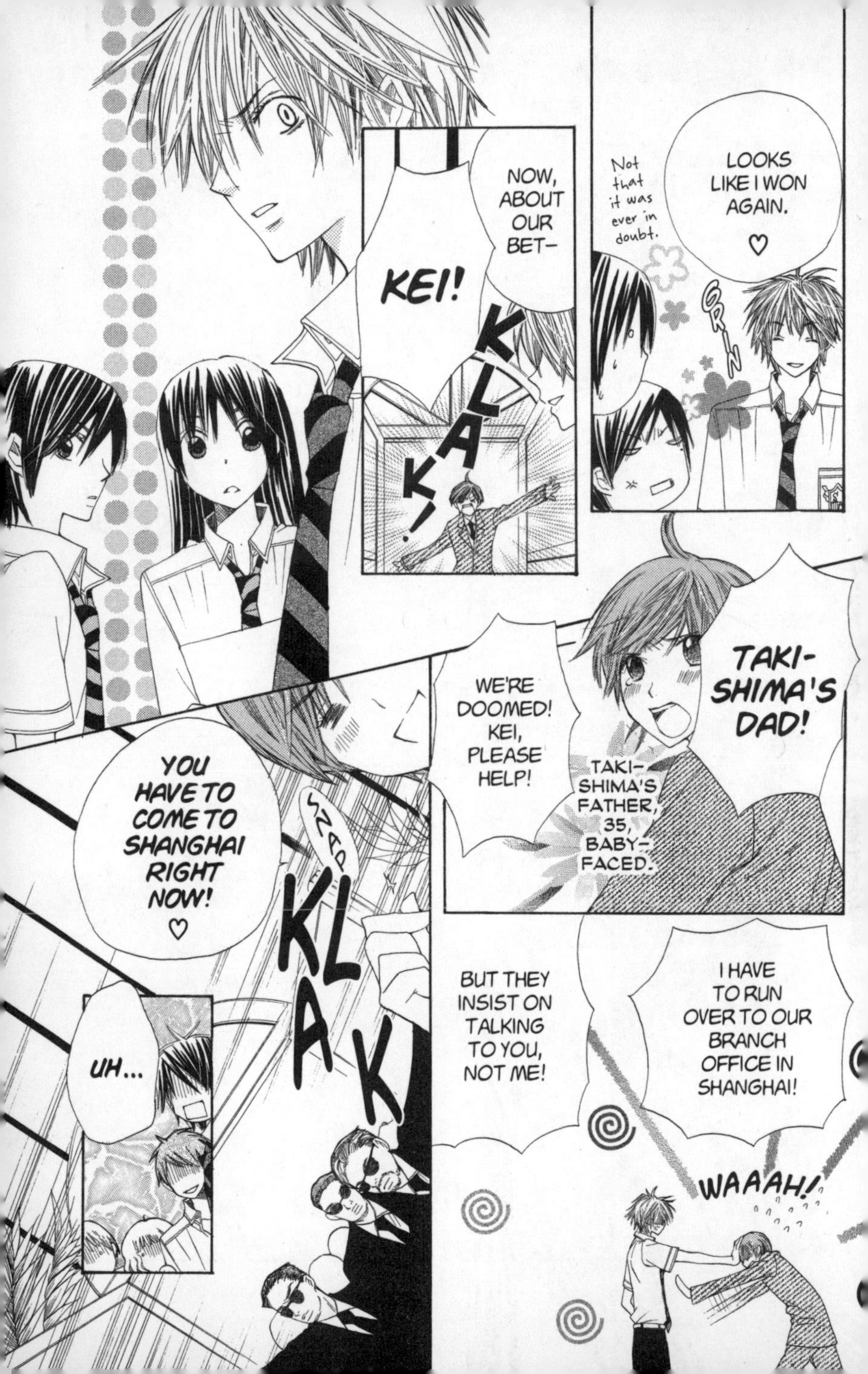

LOOKS LIKE I WON AGAIN. ♡
Not that it was ever in doubt.
GRIN
NOW, ABOUT OUR BET—
KEI!
KLAK!
TAKI-SHIMA'S DAD!
WE'RE DOOMED! KEI, PLEASE HELP!
TAKI-SHIMA'S FATHER, 35, BABY-FACED.
YOU HAVE TO COME TO SHANGHAI RIGHT NOW! ♡
I HAVE TO RUN OVER TO OUR BRANCH OFFICE IN SHANGHAI!
BUT THEY INSIST ON TALKING TO YOU, NOT ME!
WAAAH!
KLAK
UH...

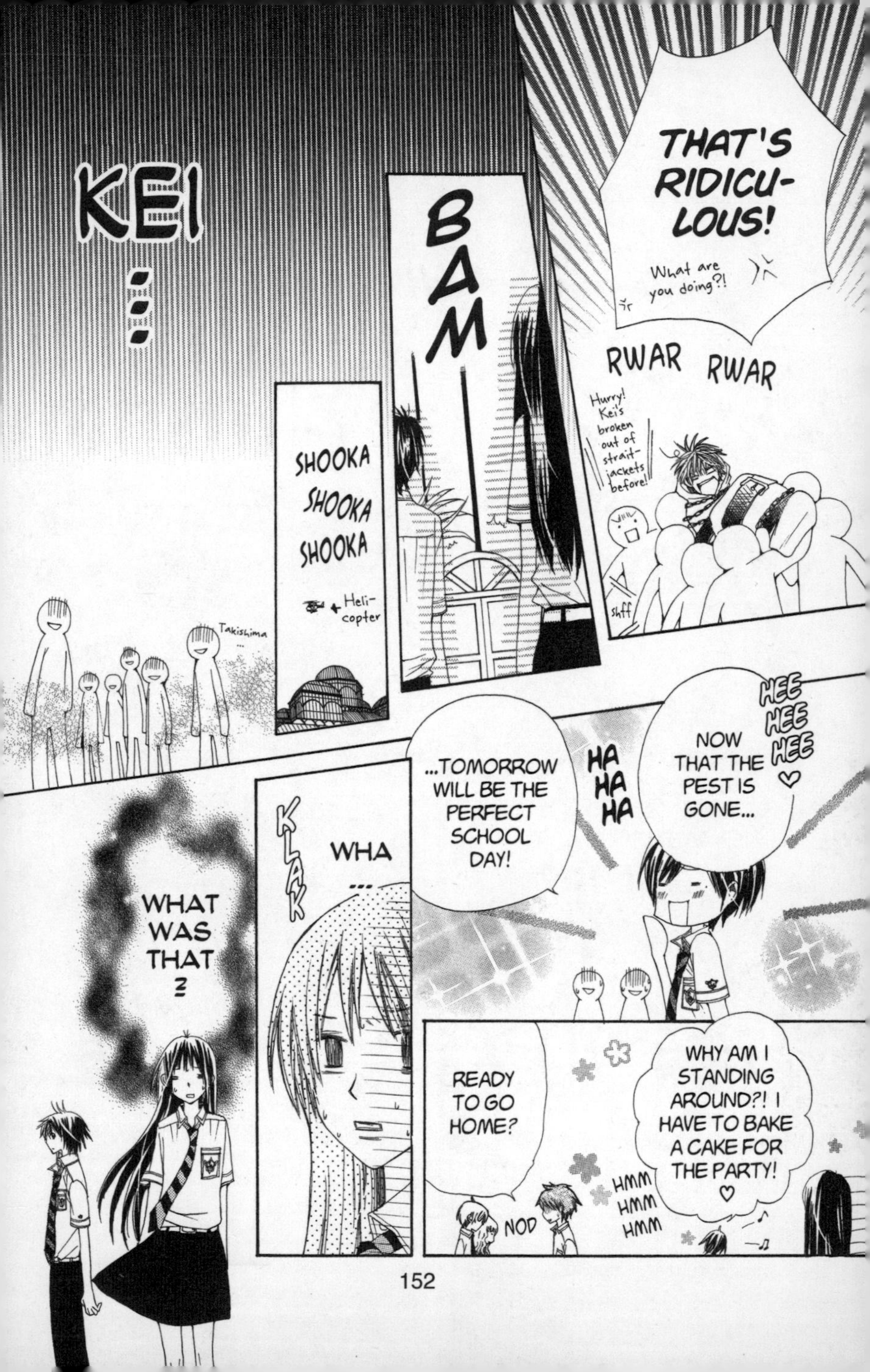
THAT'S RIDICULOUS!
What are you doing?!
RWAR RWAR
Hurry! Kei's broken out of strait-jackets before!
shff
BAM
SHOOKA SHOOKA SHOOKA
Heli-copter
KEI...
Takishima...
NOW THAT THE PEST IS GONE...
HEE HEE HEE
HA HA HA
...TOMORROW WILL BE THE PERFECT SCHOOL DAY!
WHY AM I STANDING AROUND?! I HAVE TO BAKE A CAKE FOR THE PARTY! ♡
HMM HMM HMM
READY TO GO HOME?
NOD
WHA...
KLAK
WHAT WAS THAT?

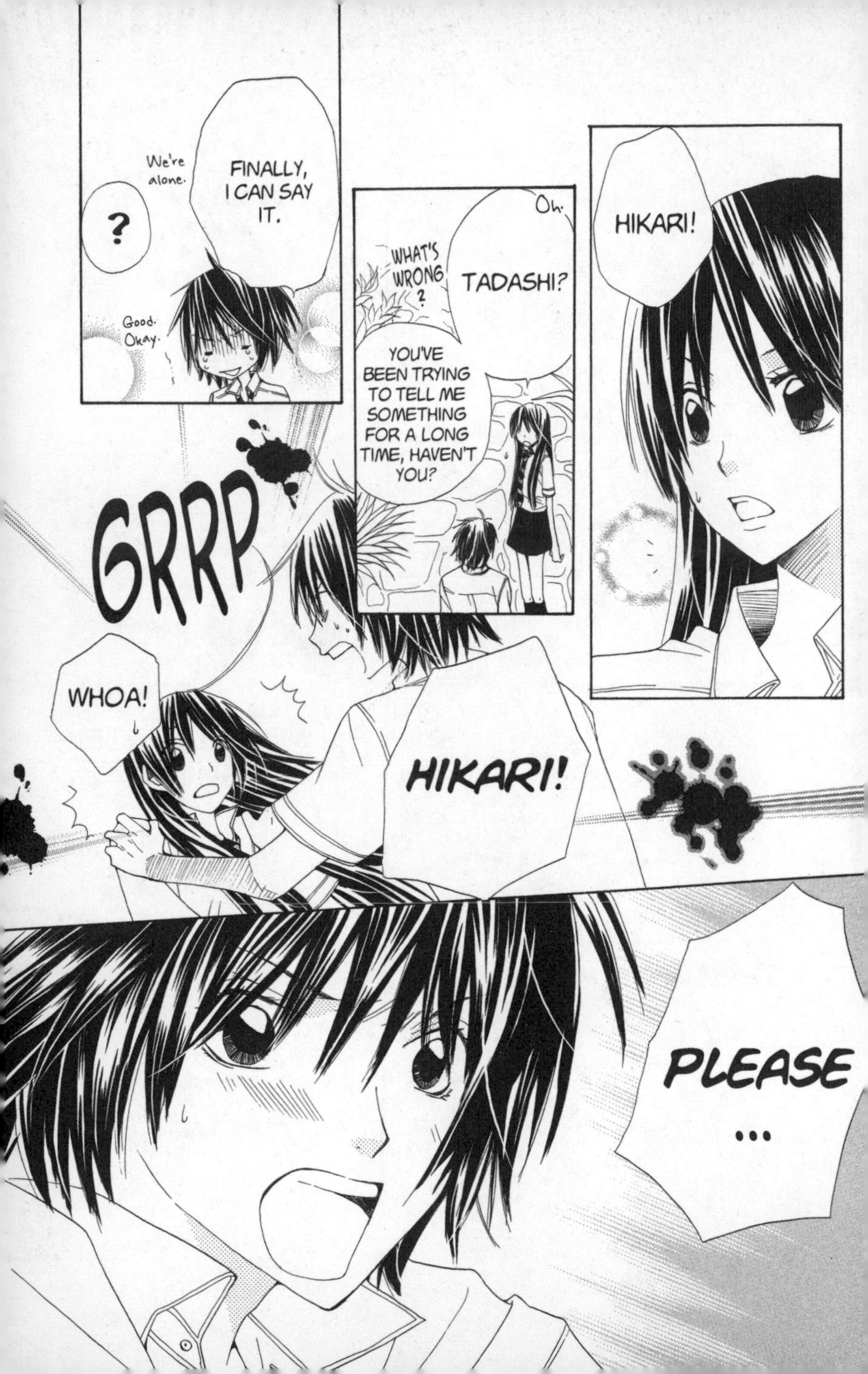
HIKARI!
Oh.
TADASHI?
WHAT'S WRONG?
YOU'VE BEEN TRYING TO TELL ME SOMETHING FOR A LONG TIME, HAVEN'T YOU?
FINALLY, I CAN SAY IT.
We're alone.
?
Good. Okay.
HIKARI!
GRRP
WHOA!
PLEASE ...

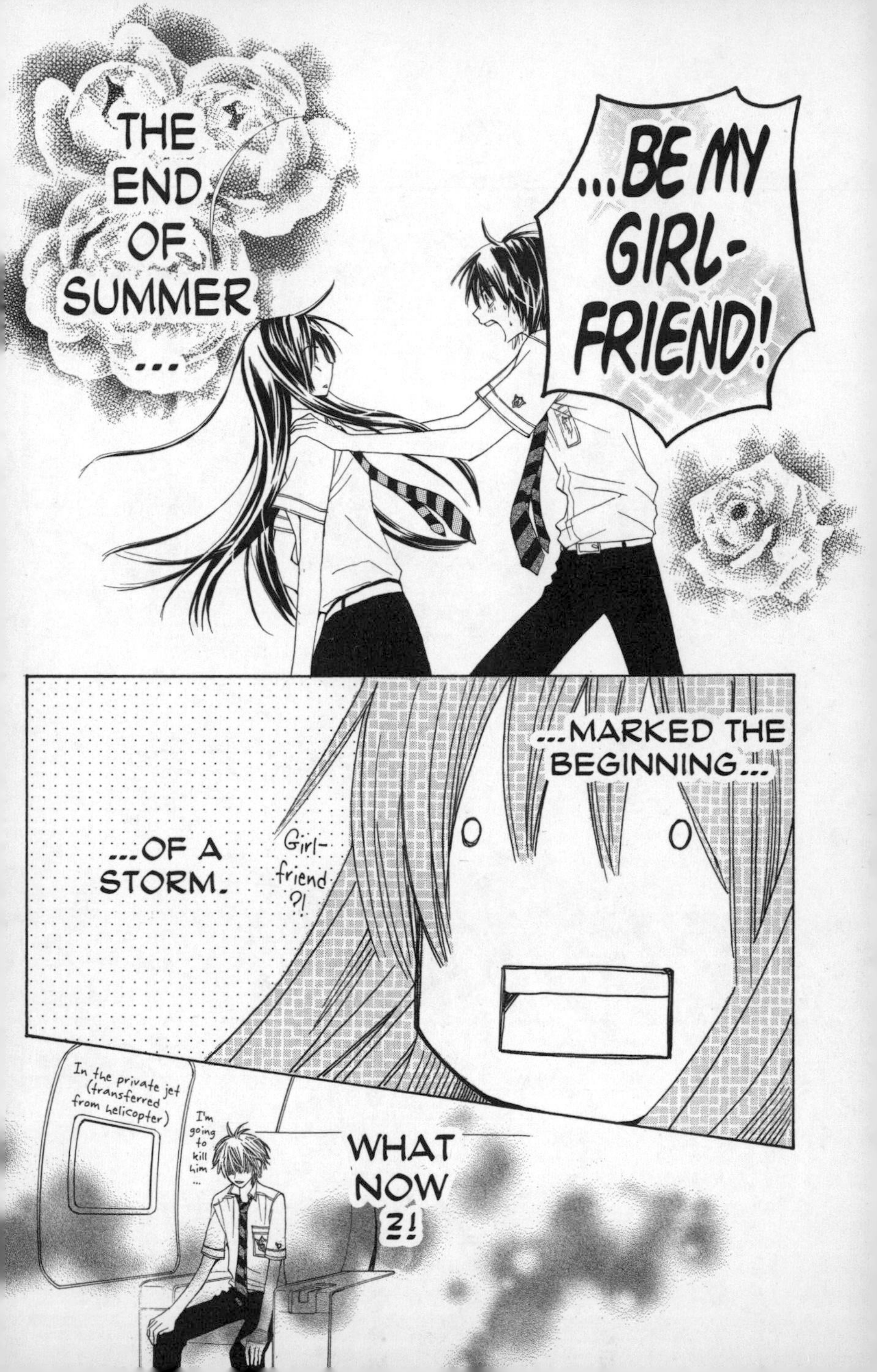
...BE MY GIRL-FRIEND!
THE END OF SUMMER ...
...MARKED THE BEGINNING...
Girl-friend ?!
...OF A STORM.
In the private jet (transferred from helicopter)
WHAT NOW ?!
I'm going to kill him ...

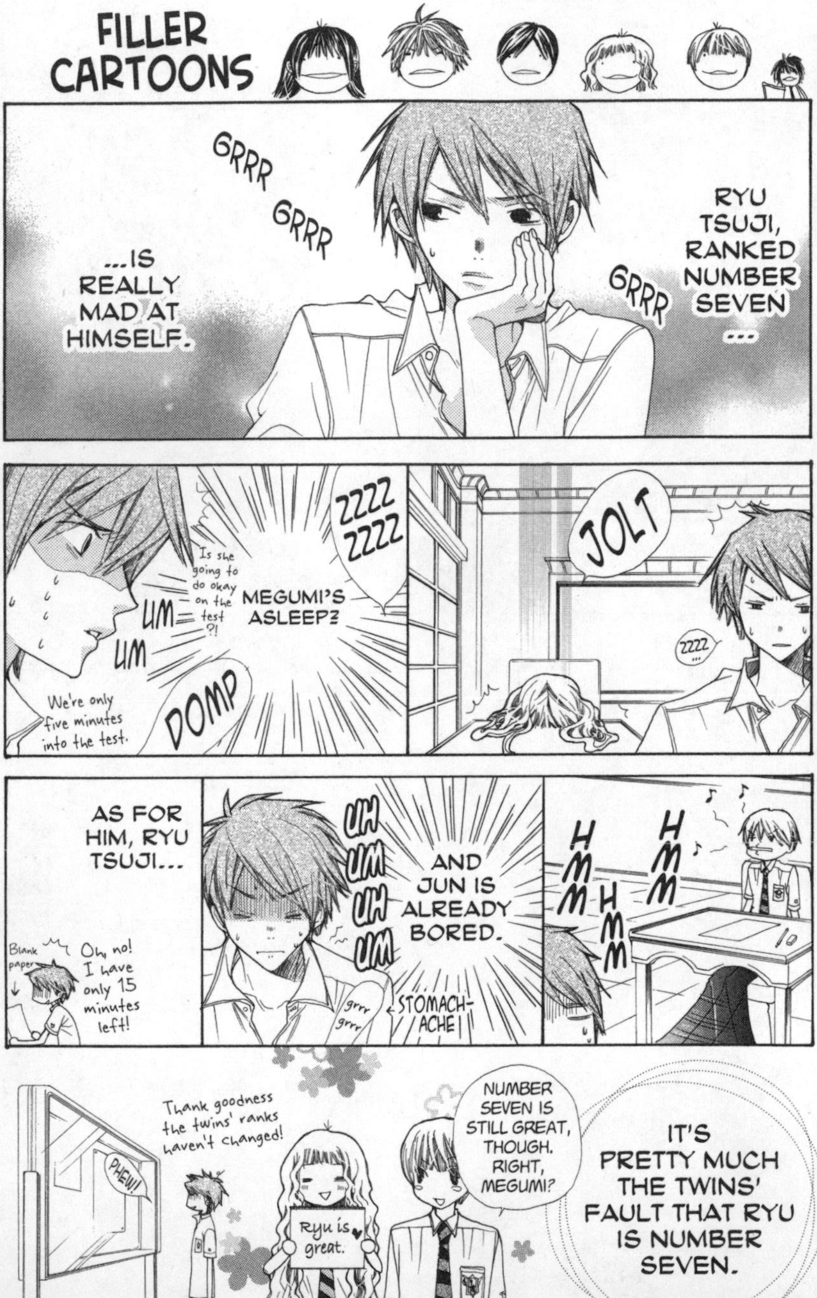
FILLER CARTOONS
RYU TSUJI, RANKED NUMBER SEVEN ...
GRRR
GRRR
GRRR
...IS REALLY MAD AT HIMSELF.
JOLT
ZZZZ ...
ZZZZ ZZZZ
MEGUMI'S ASLEEP?
Is she going to do okay on the test ?!
UM
UM
DOMP
We're only five minutes into the test.
HMM
HMM
HMM
AND JUN IS ALREADY BORED.
UH UM UH UM
STOMACHACHE
grrr grrr
AS FOR HIM, RYU TSUJI...
Blank paper
Oh, no! I have only 15 minutes left!
IT'S PRETTY MUCH THE TWINS' FAULT THAT RYU IS NUMBER SEVEN.
NUMBER SEVEN IS STILL GREAT, THOUGH. RIGHT, MEGUMI?
Ryu is great.
Thank goodness the twins' ranks haven't changed!
PHEW!

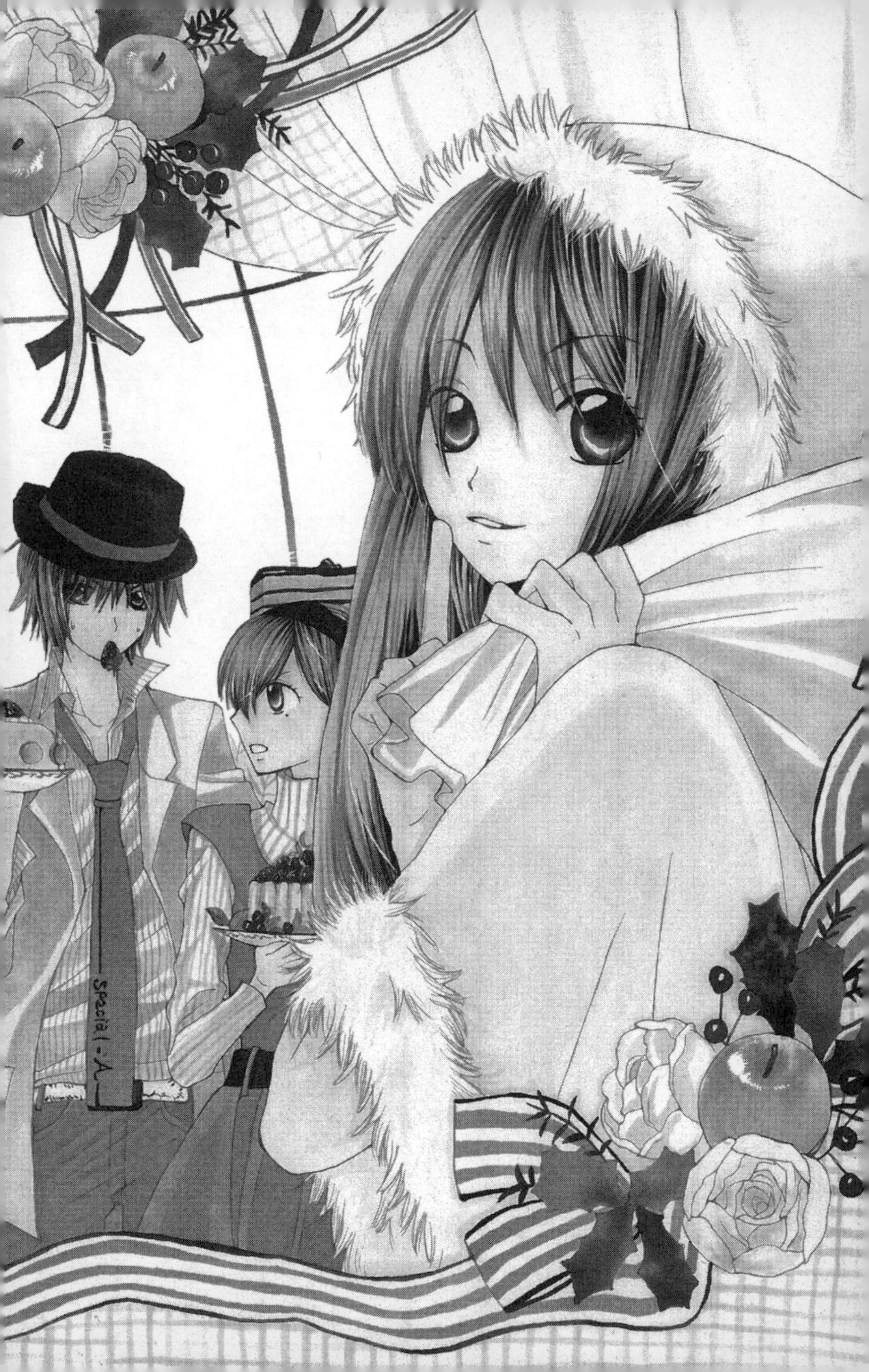
Special-A

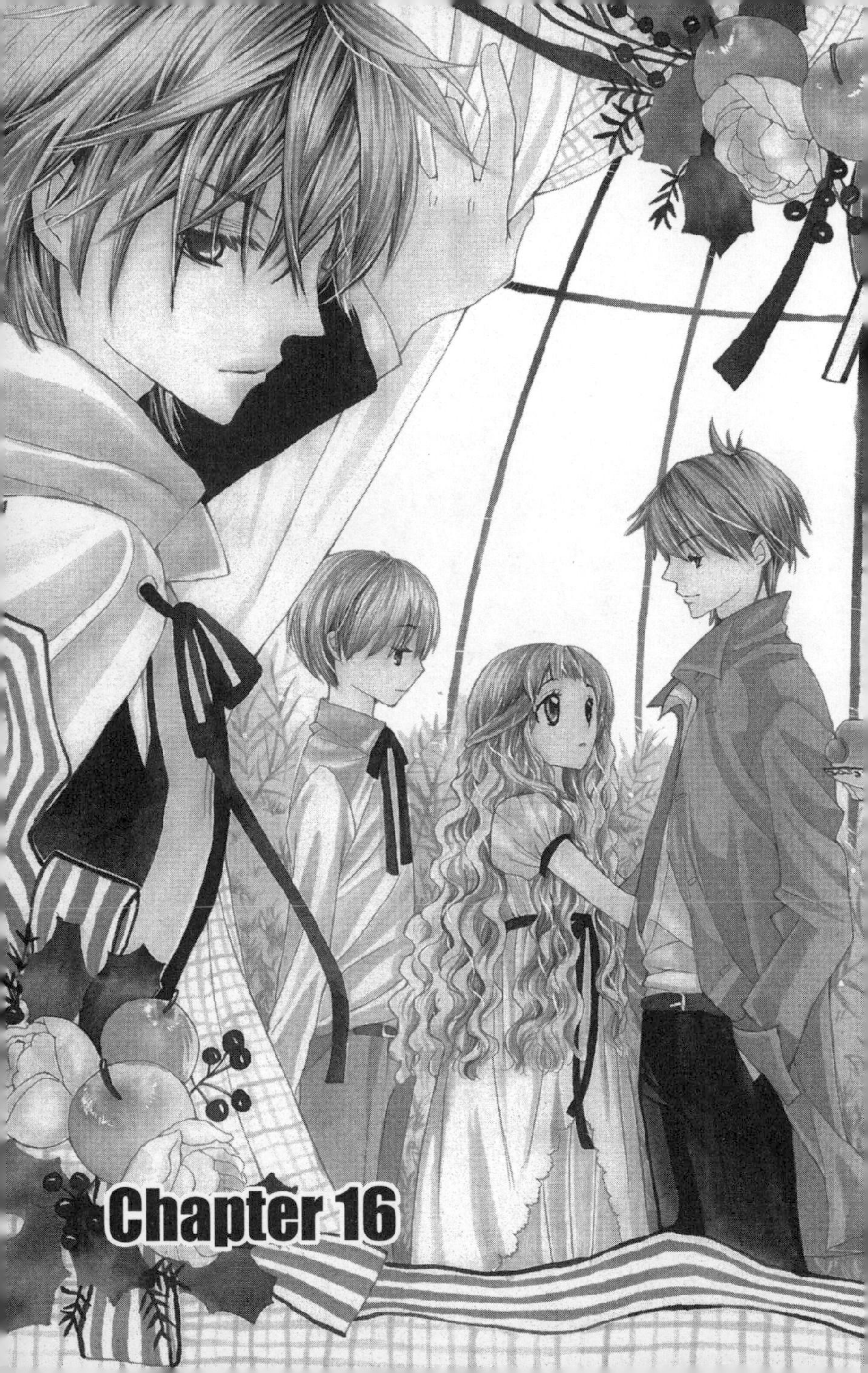
Chapter 16

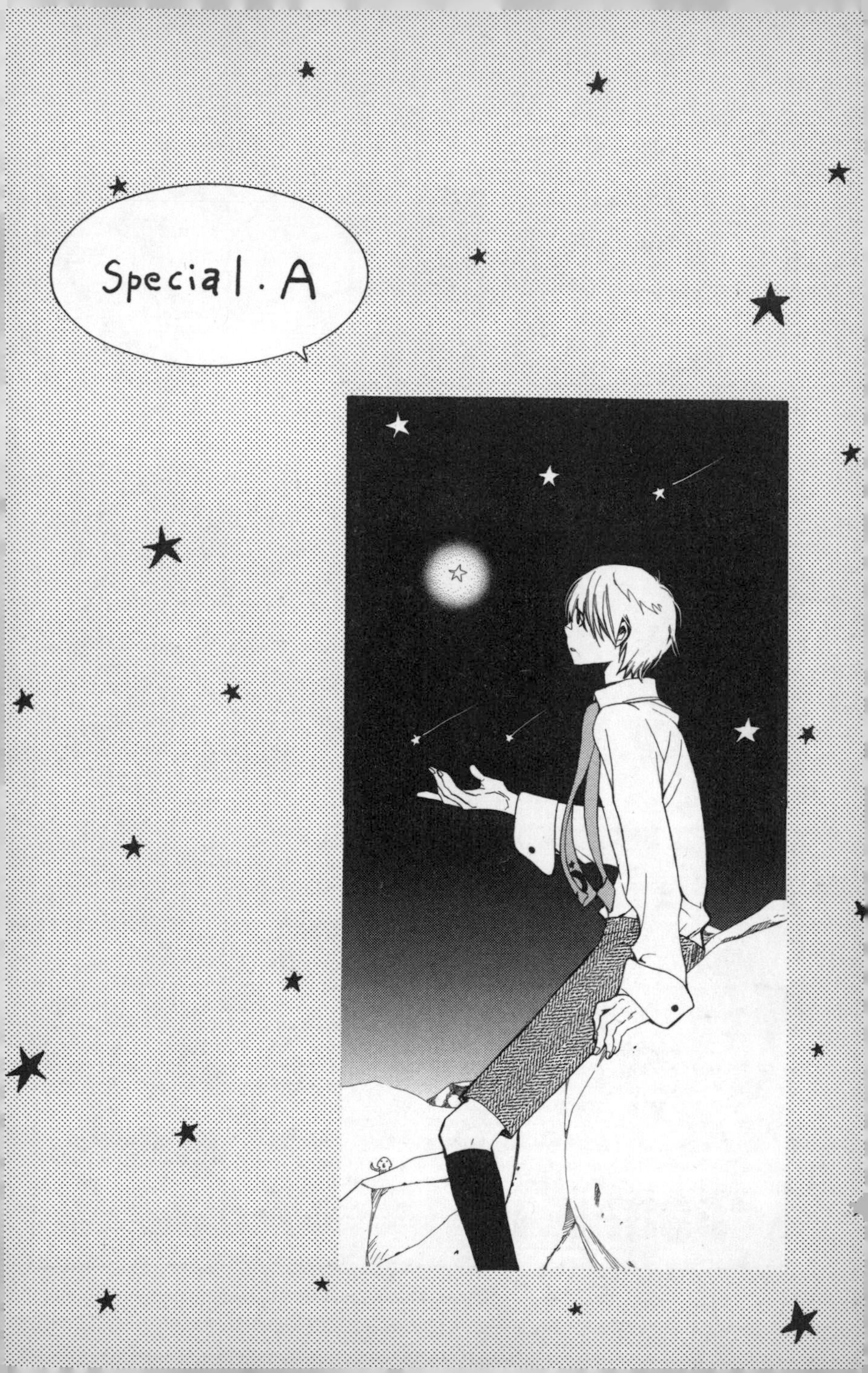
Special . A

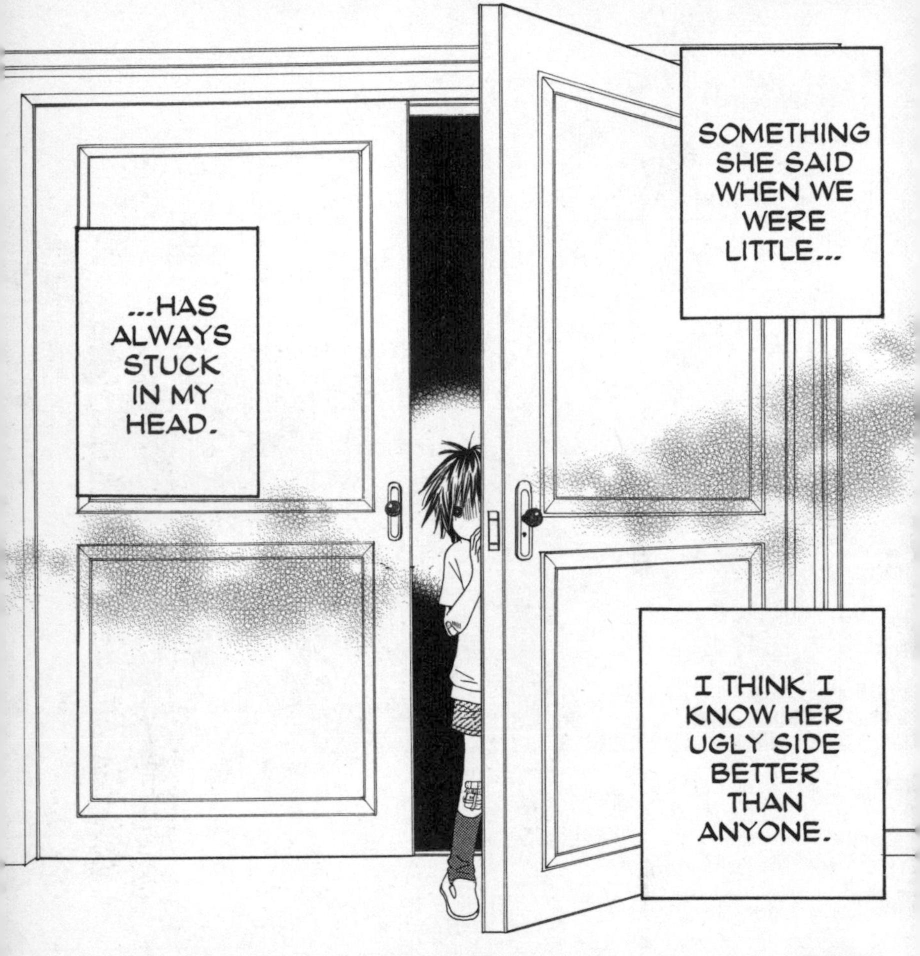
SOMETHING SHE SAID WHEN WE WERE LITTLE...
...HAS ALWAYS STUCK IN MY HEAD.
I THINK I KNOW HER UGLY SIDE BETTER THAN ANYONE.

•THIS AND THAT•

THANK YOU SO MUCH FOR READING SA! IN THIS VOLUME I GOT MY FIRST COVER FOR *HANA TO YUME* MAGAZINE AND MY FIRST COLOR TITLE PAGE, SO IT'S REALLY LIKE A DREAM COME TRUE! AND IT'S ALL THANKS TO YOU! THIS ONE'S COVER SHOWS RYU WITH JUN AND MEGUMI. WHO SHOULD I PUT ON THE NEXT VOLUME (I H-HOPE THERE IS ONE)? SHOULD I JUST KEEP MIXING IT UP? I WROTE A BONUS STORY FOR THIS VOLUME TOO! JOIN ME FOR THE NEXT ONE, IF YOU WILL. I CAN'T WAIT TO SEE YOU AGAIN!

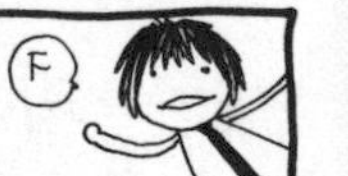
F

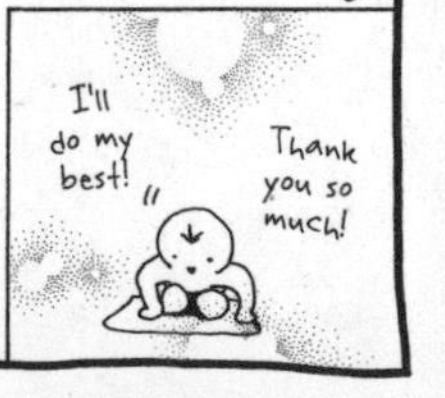
Thank you so much!
I'll do my best!

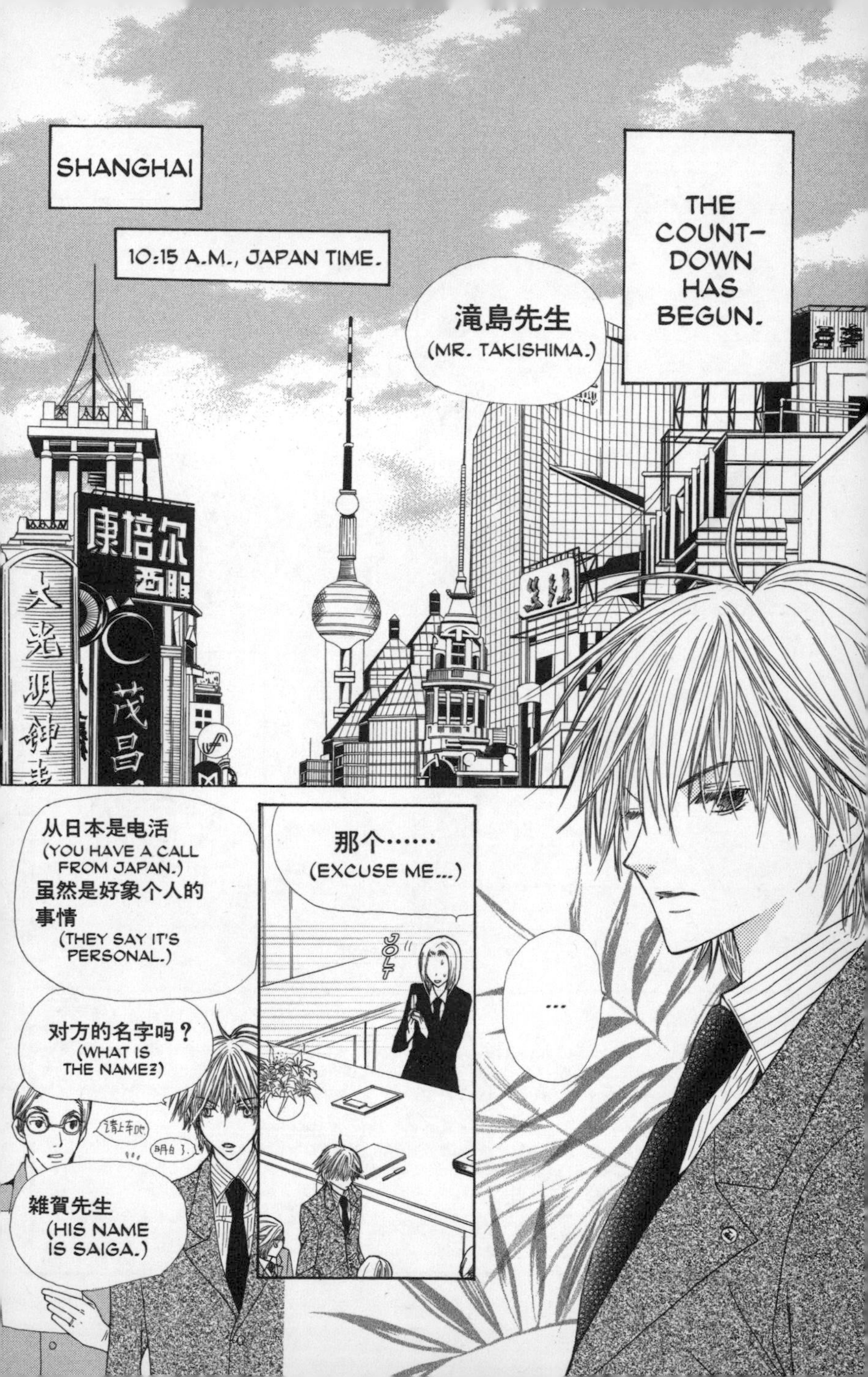
THE COUNT-DOWN HAS BEGUN.
SHANGHAI
10:15 A.M., JAPAN TIME.
康培尔 西服
滝島先生 (MR. TAKISHIMA.)
...
那个…… (EXCUSE ME...)
JOLT
从日本是电活 (YOU HAVE A CALL FROM JAPAN.) 虽然是好象个人的事情 (THEY SAY IT'S PERSONAL.)
对方的名字吗？ (WHAT IS THE NAME?)
雑賀先生 (HIS NAME IS SAIGA.)

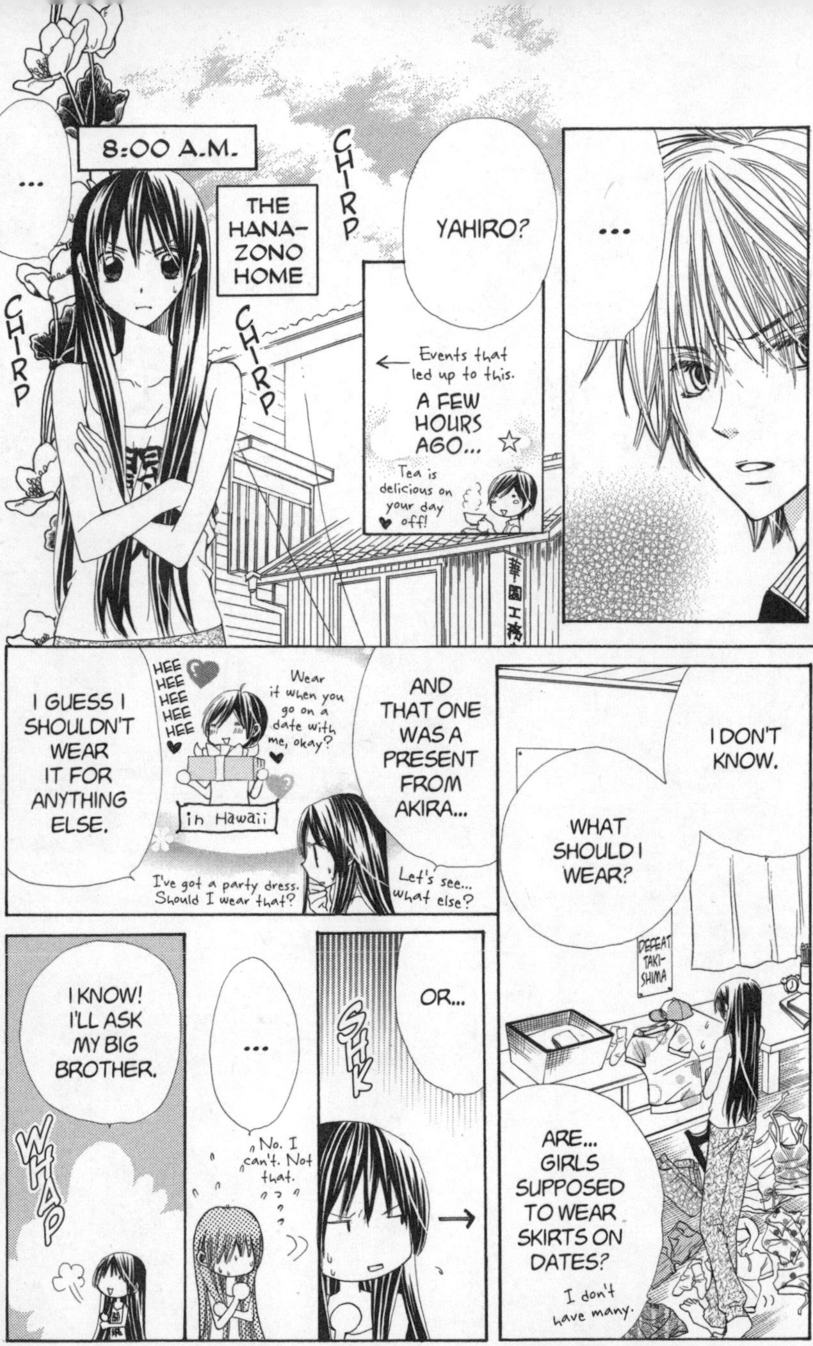
...
YAHIRO?
← Events that led up to this.
A FEW HOURS AGO... ☆
Tea is delicious on your day off! ♥
CHIRP
THE HANA-ZONO HOME
8:00 A.M.
...
CHIRP
CHIRP
I DON'T KNOW.
WHAT SHOULD I WEAR?
DEFEAT TAKI-SHIMA
ARE... GIRLS SUPPOSED TO WEAR SKIRTS ON DATES?
I don't have many.
AND THAT ONE WAS A PRESENT FROM AKIRA...
Let's see... what else?
I've got a party dress. Should I wear that?
Wear it when you go on a date with me, okay?
HEE HEE HEE HEE HEE
in Hawaii
I GUESS I SHOULDN'T WEAR IT FOR ANYTHING ELSE.
OR...
SHK
...
No. I can't. Not that.
I KNOW! I'LL ASK MY BIG BROTHER.
WHAP

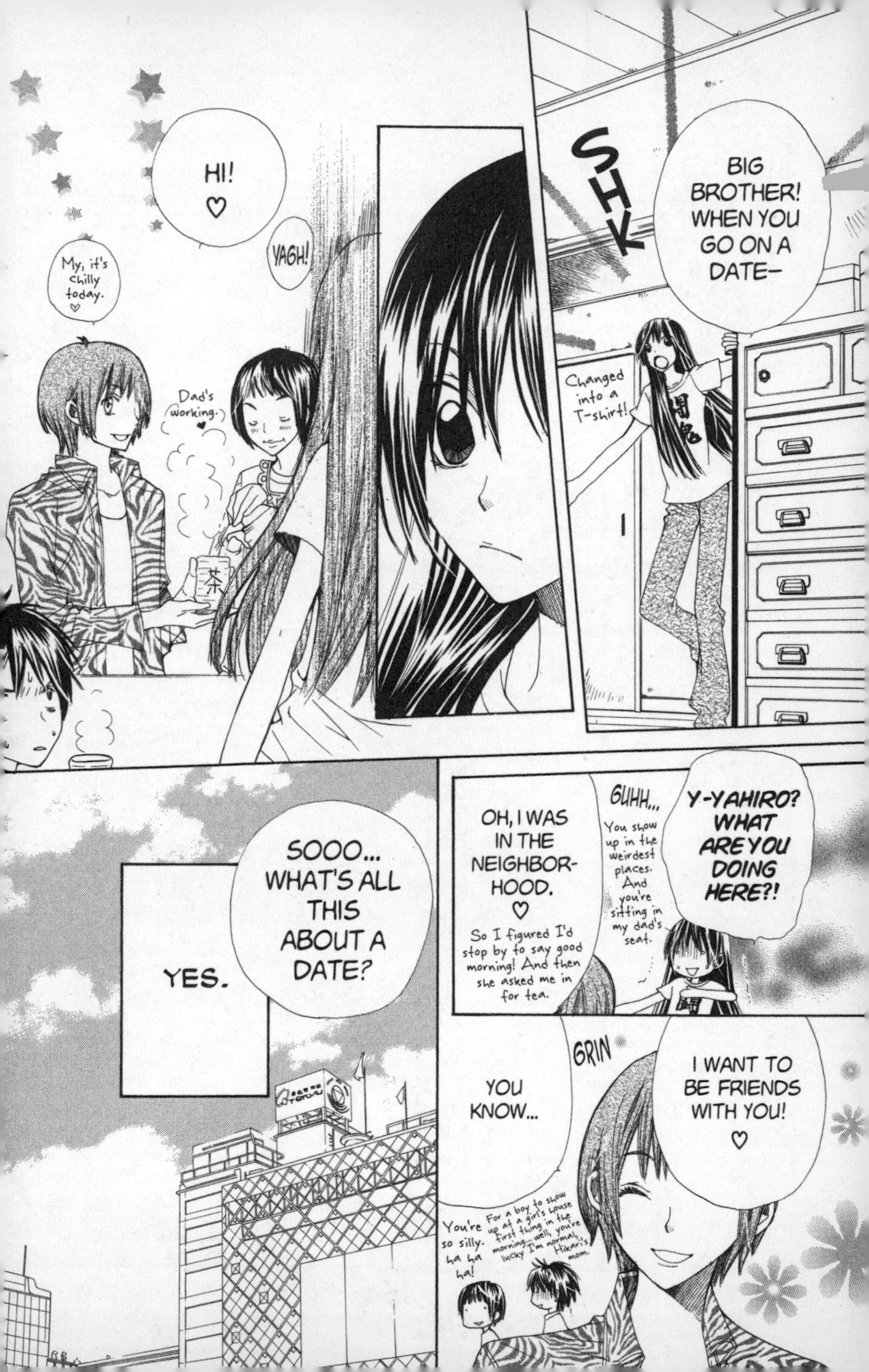
SHK
BIG BROTHER! WHEN YOU GO ON A DATE—
Changed into a T-shirt!
HI! ♡
YAGH!
My, it's chilly today. ♡
Dad's working. ♥
Y-YAHIRO? WHAT ARE YOU DOING HERE?!
GUHH...
You show up in the weirdest places. And you're sitting in my dad's seat.
OH, I WAS IN THE NEIGHBORHOOD. ♡
So I figured I'd stop by to say good morning! And then she asked me in for tea.
I WANT TO BE FRIENDS WITH YOU! ♡
GRIN
YOU KNOW...
For a boy to show up at a girl's house first thing in the morning... well, you're lucky I'm normal, Hikari's mom.
You're so silly. ha ha ha!
SOOO... WHAT'S ALL THIS ABOUT A DATE?
YES.

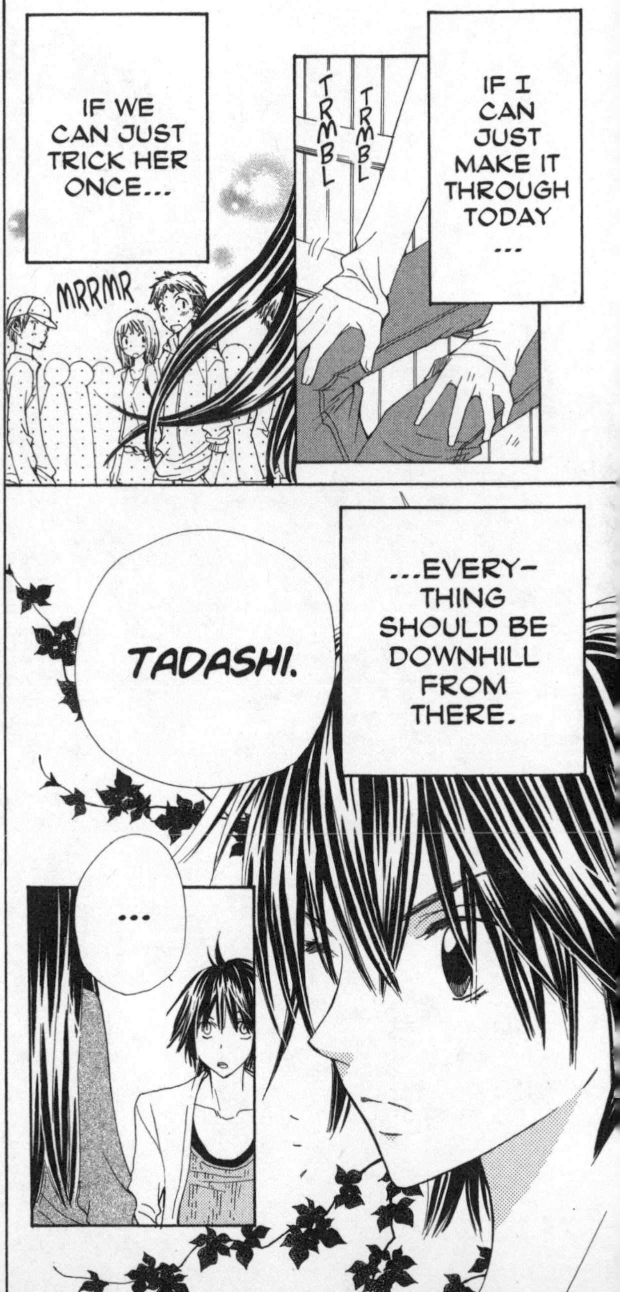
IF I CAN JUST MAKE IT THROUGH TODAY ...
TRMBL
TRMBL
IF WE CAN JUST TRICK HER ONCE...
MRRMR
...EVERY-THING SHOULD BE DOWNHILL FROM THERE.
TADASHI.
...

Last

• THIS AND THAT •

1/4

THIS IS MY LAST QUARTER PAGE IN THIS VOLUME. THANK YOU SO MUCH FOR READING THIS FAR! THANKS VERY MUCH TO EVERYBODY WHO HELPED! AND TO EVERYONE WHO SENT LETTERS AND ENTERED THEIR NAMES, THANK YOU VERY, VERY MUCH! I CAN'T EVEN EXPRESS HOW GRATEFUL I AM.

IF YOU ENJOYED THIS BOOK, EVEN JUST A LITTLE BIT, I'LL WORK HARD TO MAKE THE NEXT ONE EVEN BETTER! PLEASE FEEL FREE TO SEND ME YOUR REACTIONS, IF YOU'D LIKE.

• ADDRESS •

MAKI MINAMI
C/O SA EDITOR
P.O. BOX 77010
SAN FRANCISCO,
CA 94107

From the bottom of my heart...

And so...

+ + maki minami +

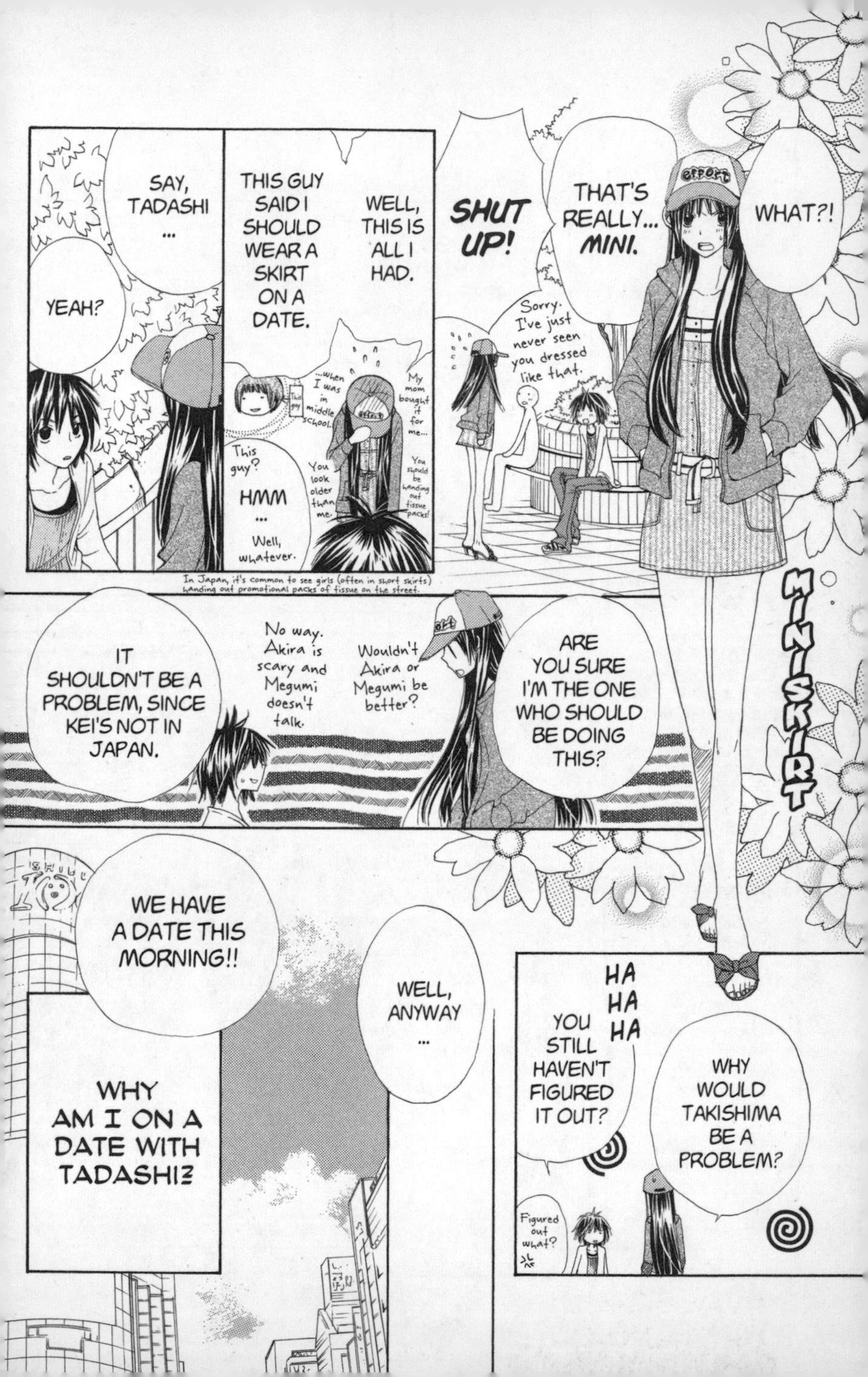
WHAT?!
THAT'S REALLY... MINI.
SHUT UP!
Sorry. I've just never seen you dressed like that.
MINISKIRT
WELL, THIS IS ALL I HAD.
THIS GUY SAID I SHOULD WEAR A SKIRT ON A DATE.
My mom bought it for me...
...when I was in middle school.
You should be handing out tissue packs!
You look older than me.
This guy
This guy?
HMM ...
Well, whatever.
SAY, TADASHI ...
YEAH?
ARE YOU SURE I'M THE ONE WHO SHOULD BE DOING THIS?
Wouldn't Akira or Megumi be better?
No way. Akira is scary and Megumi doesn't talk.
IT SHOULDN'T BE A PROBLEM, SINCE KEI'S NOT IN JAPAN.
WHY WOULD TAKISHIMA BE A PROBLEM?
HA HA HA
YOU STILL HAVEN'T FIGURED IT OUT?
Figured out what?
WELL, ANYWAY ...
WE HAVE A DATE THIS MORNING!!
WHY AM I ON A DATE WITH TADASHI!?
In Japan, it's common to see girls (often in short skirts) handing out promotional packs of tissue on the street.

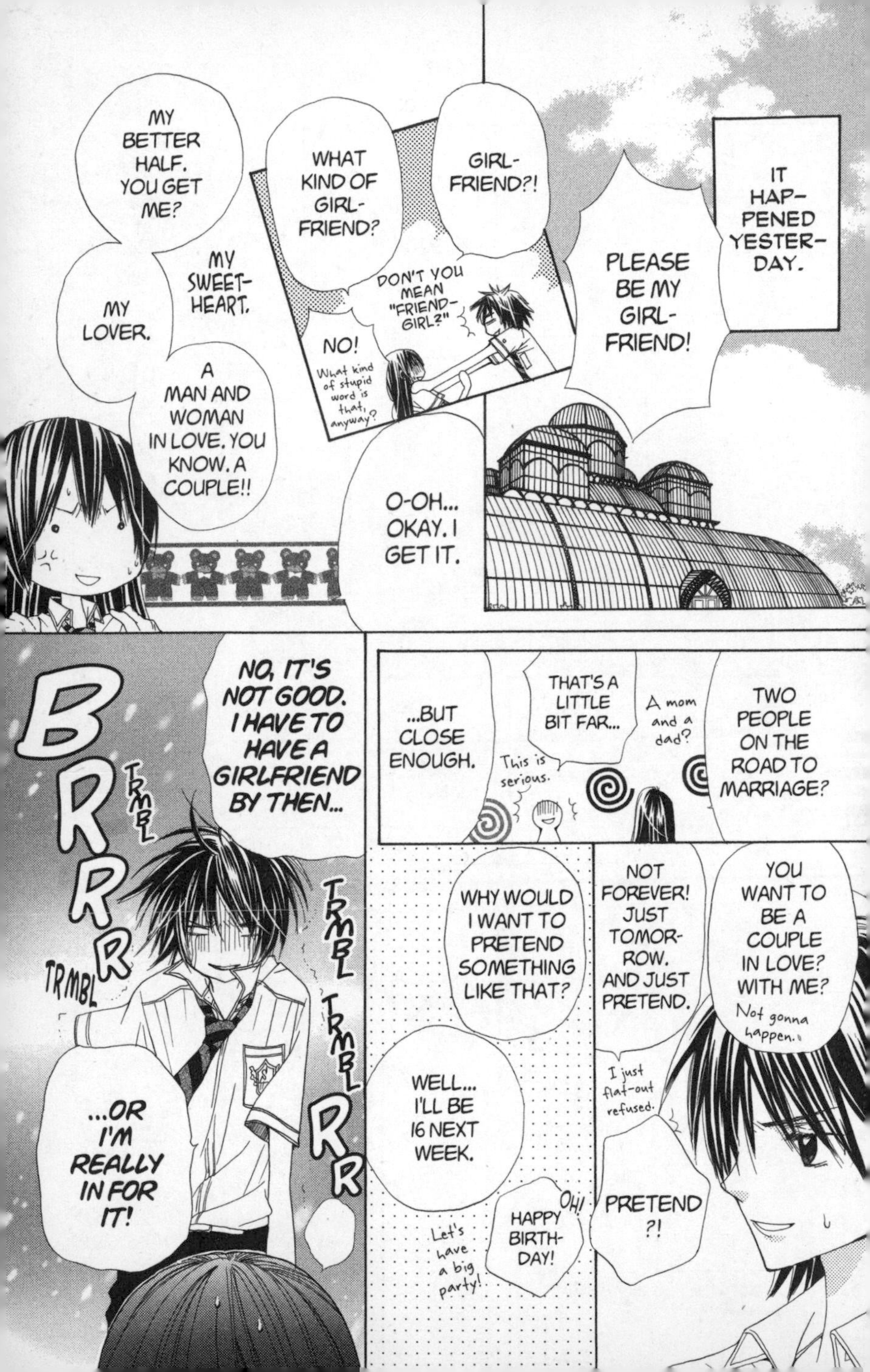
IT HAPPENED YESTERDAY.
PLEASE BE MY GIRLFRIEND!
GIRLFRIEND?!
WHAT KIND OF GIRLFRIEND?
DON'T YOU MEAN "FRIEND-GIRL?"
NO!
What kind of stupid word is that, anyway?
MY BETTER HALF. YOU GET ME?
MY SWEETHEART.
MY LOVER.
A MAN AND WOMAN IN LOVE. YOU KNOW. A COUPLE!!
O-OH... OKAY. I GET IT.
TWO PEOPLE ON THE ROAD TO MARRIAGE?
A mom and a dad?
THAT'S A LITTLE BIT FAR...
This is serious.
...BUT CLOSE ENOUGH.
YOU WANT TO BE A COUPLE IN LOVE? WITH ME?
Not gonna happen.
NOT FOREVER! JUST TOMORROW. AND JUST PRETEND.
I just flat-out refused.
PRETEND?!
WHY WOULD I WANT TO PRETEND SOMETHING LIKE THAT?
WELL... I'LL BE 16 NEXT WEEK.
OH!
HAPPY BIRTHDAY!
Let's have a big party!
NO, IT'S NOT GOOD. I HAVE TO HAVE A GIRLFRIEND BY THEN...
BRRRR
TRMBL
TRMBL
TRMBL
TRMBL
RR
...OR I'M REALLY IN FOR IT!

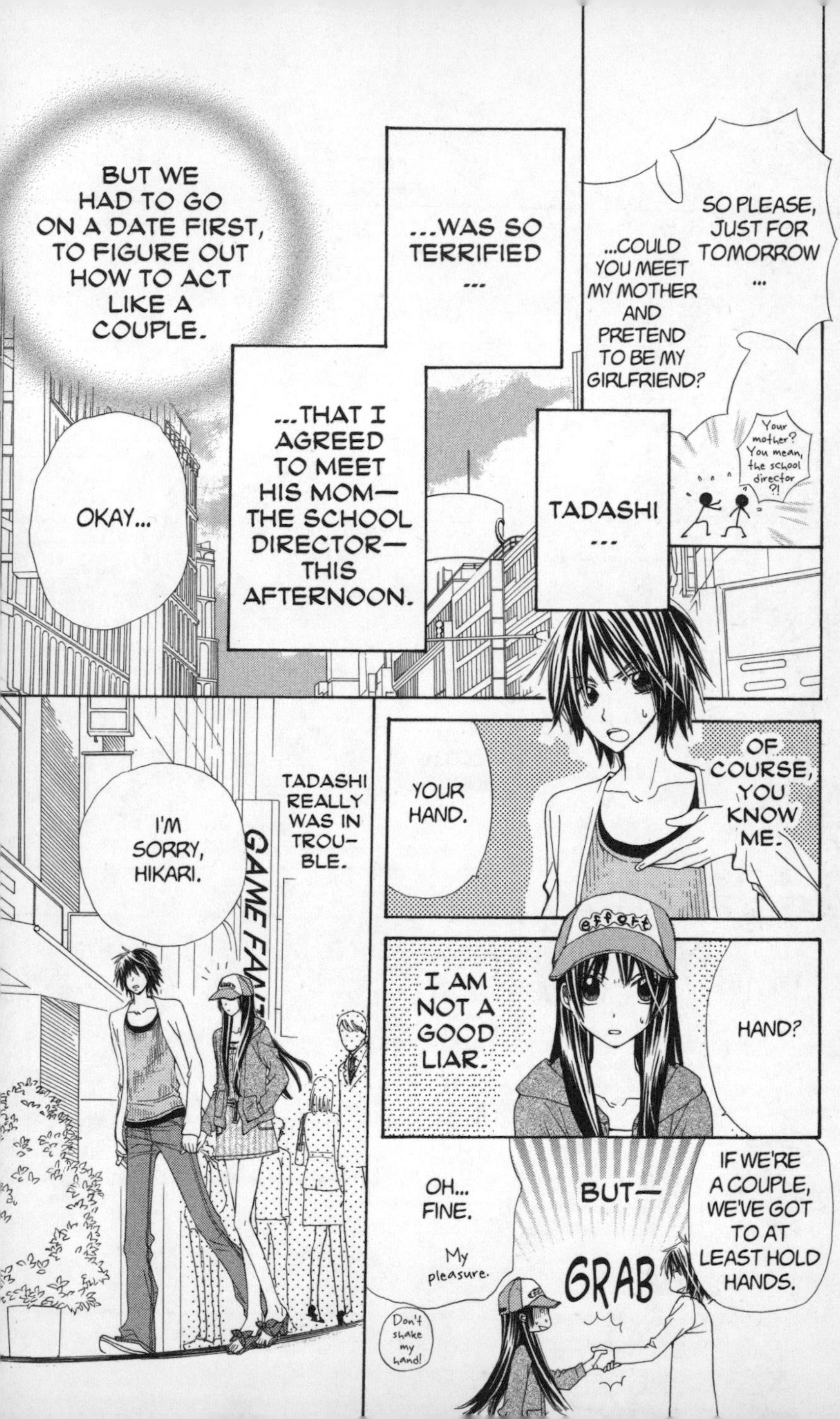
SO PLEASE, JUST FOR TOMORROW...
...COULD YOU MEET MY MOTHER AND PRETEND TO BE MY GIRLFRIEND?
Your mother? You mean, the school director?!
TADASHI...
...WAS SO TERRIFIED...
...THAT I AGREED TO MEET HIS MOM—THE SCHOOL DIRECTOR—THIS AFTERNOON.
BUT WE HAD TO GO ON A DATE FIRST, TO FIGURE OUT HOW TO ACT LIKE A COUPLE.
OKAY...
OF COURSE, YOU KNOW ME.
YOUR HAND.
HAND?
I AM NOT A GOOD LIAR.
IF WE'RE A COUPLE, WE'VE GOT TO AT LEAST HOLD HANDS.
BUT—
GRAB
OH... FINE.
My pleasure.
Don't shake my hand!
TADASHI REALLY WAS IN TROUBLE.
I'M SORRY, HIKARI.

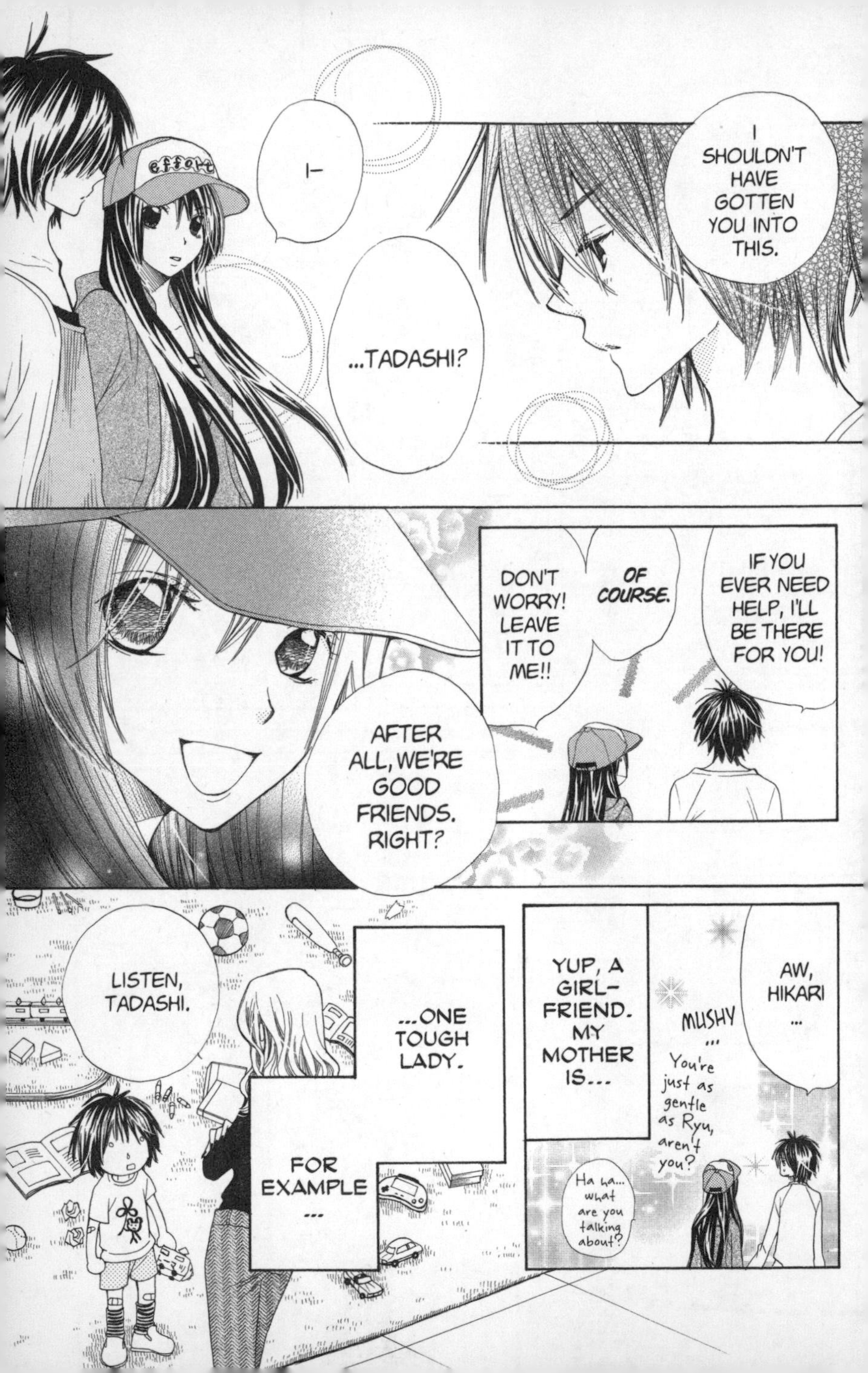
I SHOULDN'T HAVE GOTTEN YOU INTO THIS.
I–
...TADASHI?
IF YOU EVER NEED HELP, I'LL BE THERE FOR YOU!
OF COURSE.
DON'T WORRY! LEAVE IT TO ME!!
AFTER ALL, WE'RE GOOD FRIENDS. RIGHT?
AW, HIKARI ...
MUSHY ...
You're just as gentle as Ryu, aren't you?
Ha ha... what are you talking about?
YUP, A GIRL-FRIEND. MY MOTHER IS...
...ONE TOUGH LADY.
FOR EXAMPLE ...
LISTEN, TADASHI.

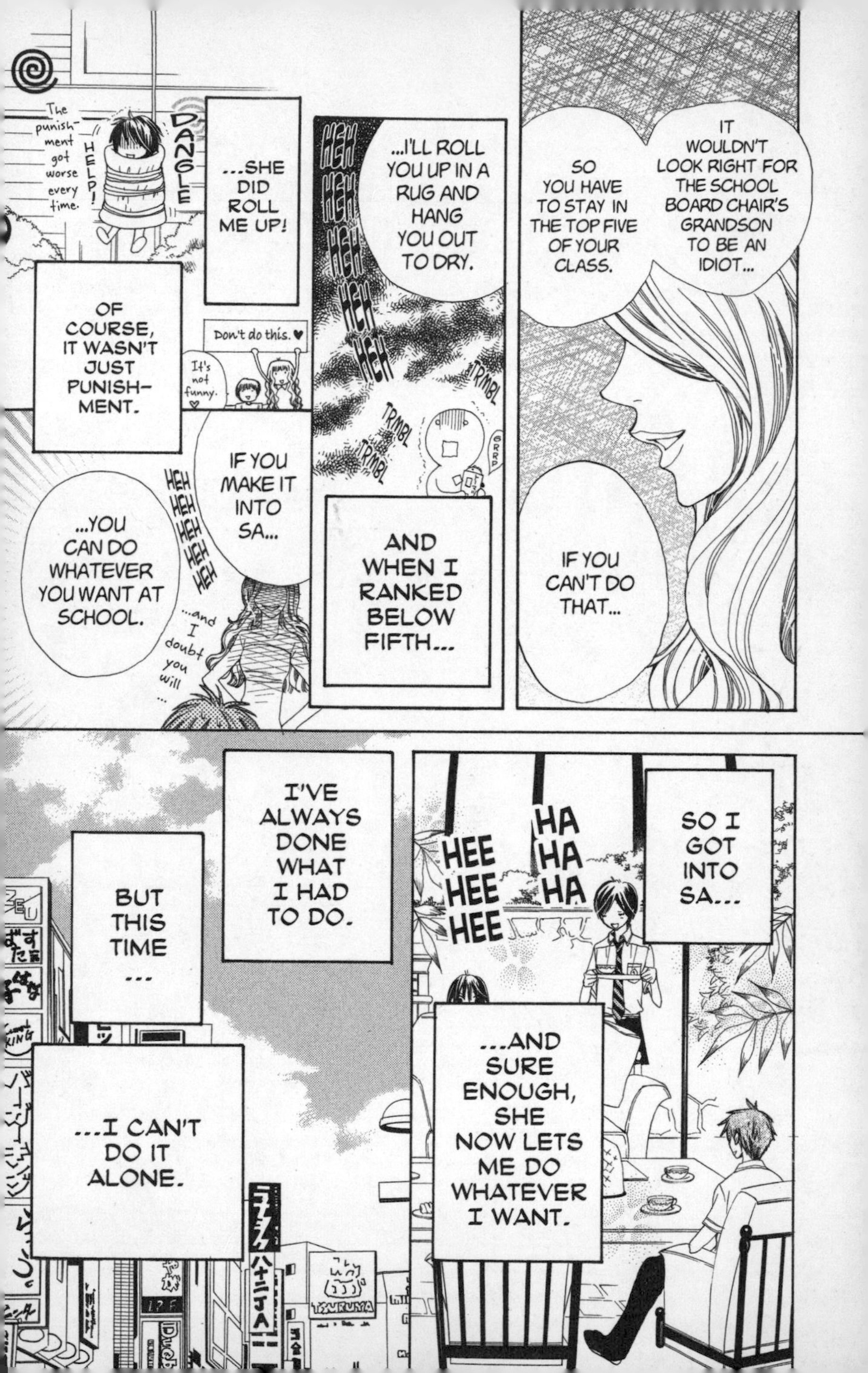
IT WOULDN'T LOOK RIGHT FOR THE SCHOOL BOARD CHAIR'S GRANDSON TO BE AN IDIOT...
SO YOU HAVE TO STAY IN THE TOP FIVE OF YOUR CLASS.
IF YOU CAN'T DO THAT...
...I'LL ROLL YOU UP IN A RUG AND HANG YOU OUT TO DRY.
HEH HEH HEH HEH HEH HEH HEH
TRMBL
TRMBL TRMBL
GRRP
AND WHEN I RANKED BELOW FIFTH...
...SHE DID ROLL ME UP!
DANGLE
HELP!
The punishment got worse every time.
Don't do this. ♥
It's not funny. ♥
OF COURSE, IT WASN'T JUST PUNISHMENT.
IF YOU MAKE IT INTO SA...
HEH HEH HEH HEH HEH
...YOU CAN DO WHATEVER YOU WANT AT SCHOOL.
...and I doubt you will...
SO I GOT INTO SA...
HA HA HA
HEE HEE HEE
...AND SURE ENOUGH, SHE NOW LETS ME DO WHATEVER I WANT.
I'VE ALWAYS DONE WHAT I HAD TO DO.
BUT THIS TIME...
...I CAN'T DO IT ALONE.
TSURUYA

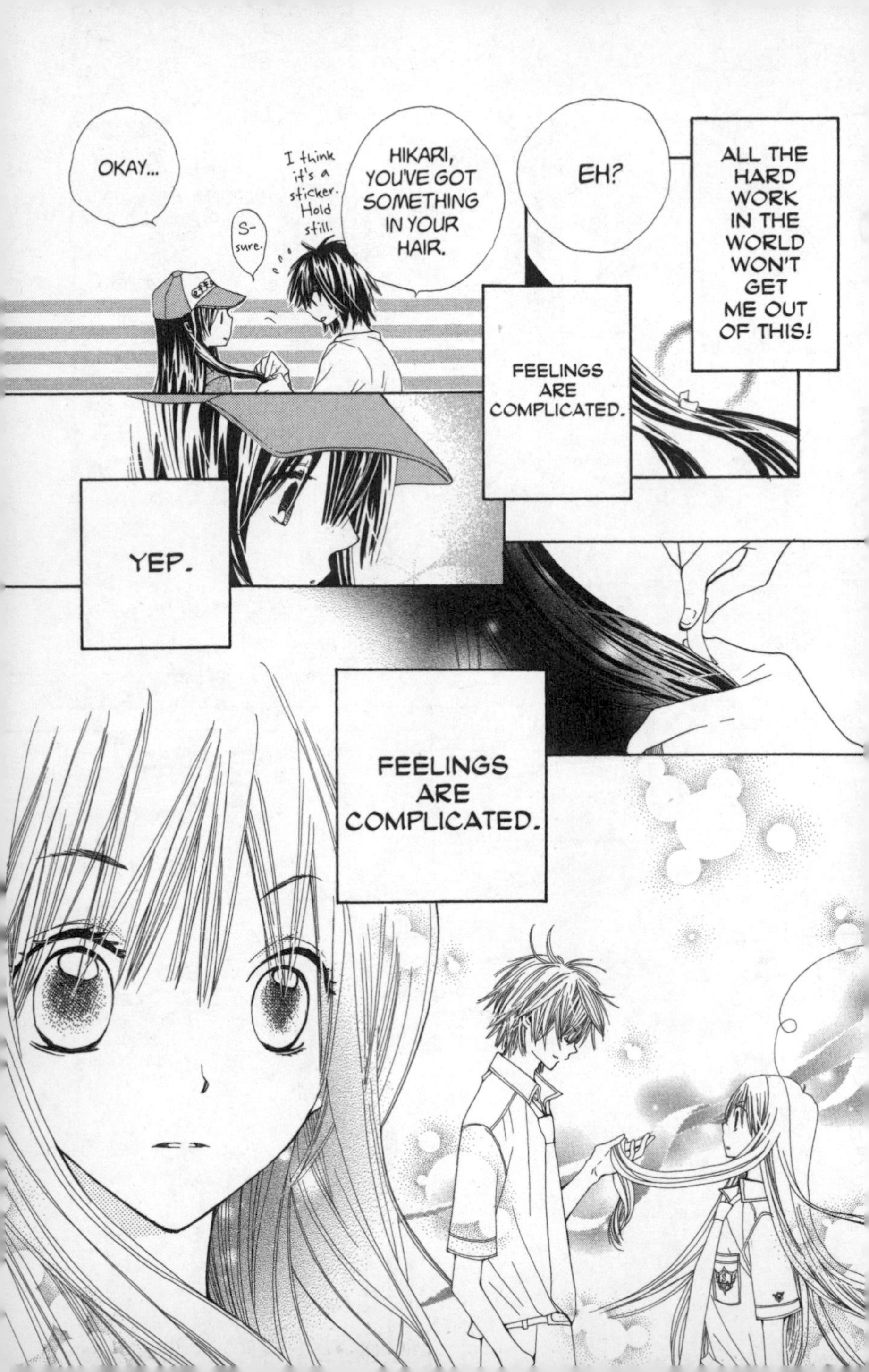
ALL THE HARD WORK IN THE WORLD WON'T GET ME OUT OF THIS!
EH?
FEELINGS ARE COMPLICATED.
HIKARI, YOU'VE GOT SOMETHING IN YOUR HAIR.
I think it's a sticker. Hold still.
S-sure.
OKAY...
YEP.
FEELINGS ARE COMPLICATED.

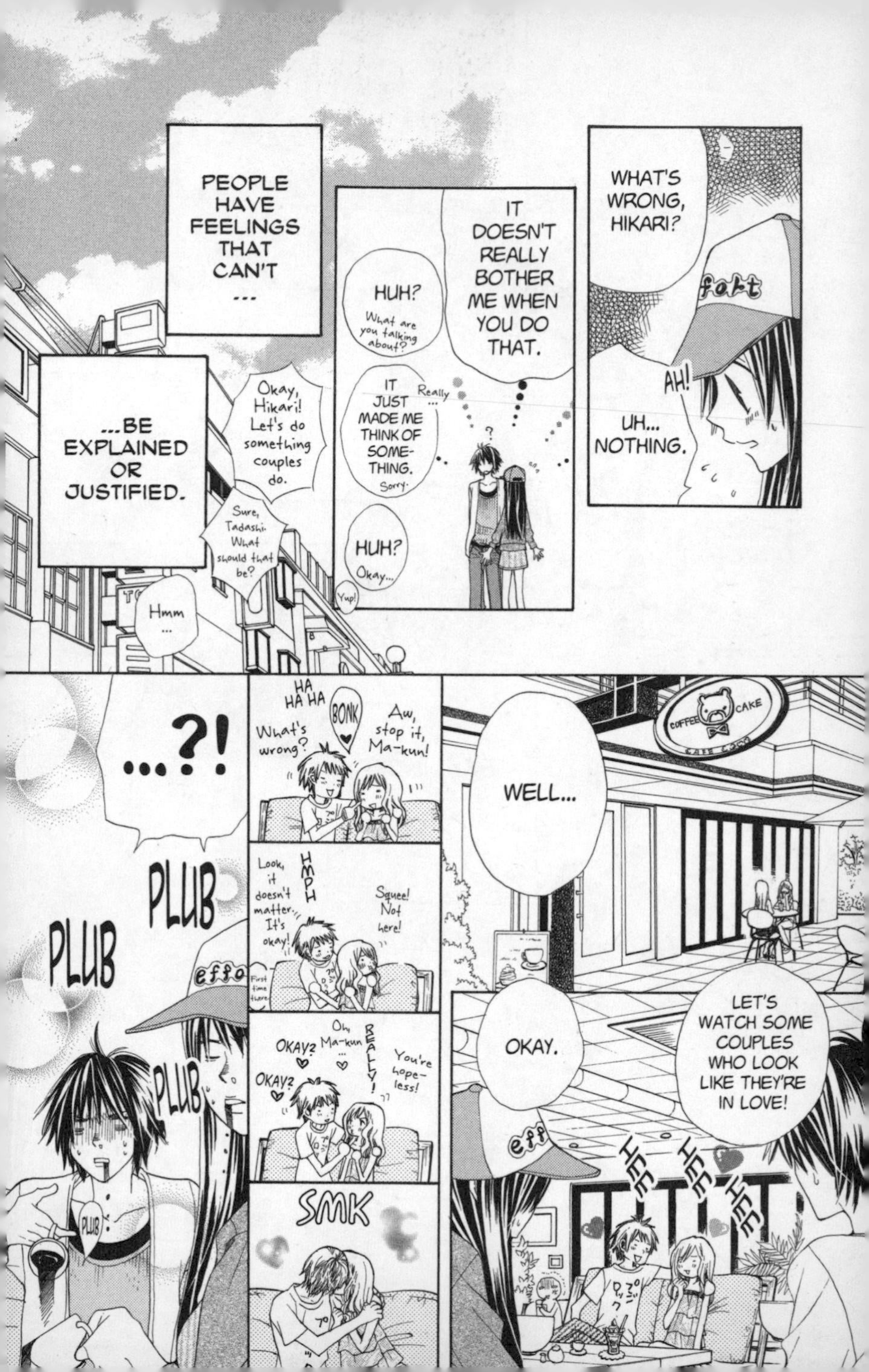
WHAT'S WRONG, HIKARI?
AH!
UH... NOTHING.
IT DOESN'T REALLY BOTHER ME WHEN YOU DO THAT.
HUH? What are you talking about?
Really...
IT JUST MADE ME THINK OF SOMETHING. Sorry.
HUH? Okay...
Yup!
PEOPLE HAVE FEELINGS THAT CAN'T ...
...BE EXPLAINED OR JUSTIFIED.
Okay, Hikari! Let's do something couples do.
Sure, Tadashi. What should that be?
Hmm...
COFFEE CAKE
WELL...
LET'S WATCH SOME COUPLES WHO LOOK LIKE THEY'RE IN LOVE!
OKAY.
HEE HEE HEE
Aw, stop it, Ma-kun!
BONK
HA HA HA
What's wrong?
Squee! Not here!
HMPH
Look, it doesn't matter. It's okay!
First time there.
You're hopeless!
REALLY!
Oh, Ma-kun...
OKAY?
OKAY?
SMK
...?!
PLUB
PLUB
PLUB
PLUB

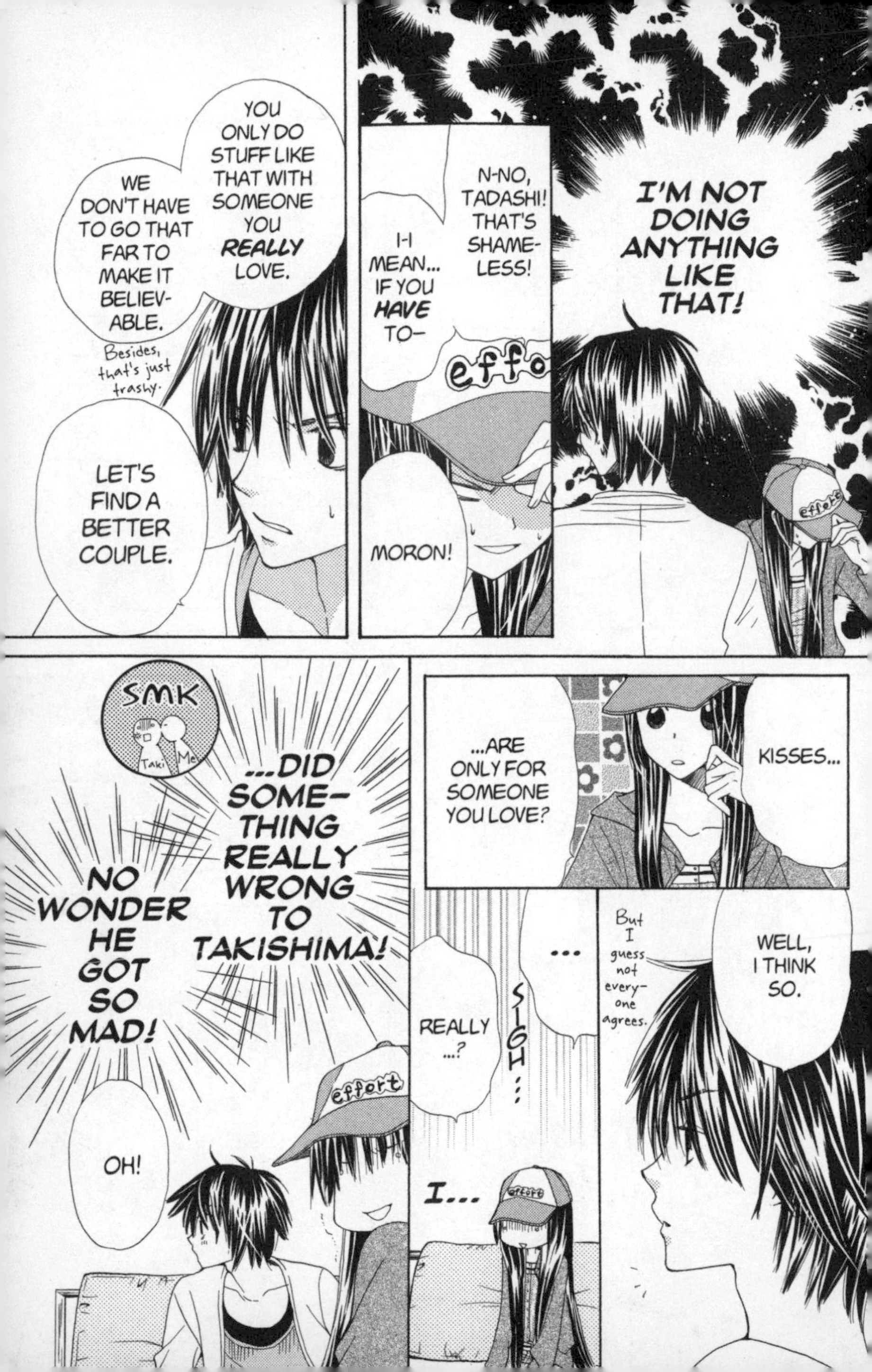
I'M NOT DOING ANYTHING LIKE THAT!
N-NO, TADASHI! THAT'S SHAME-LESS!
I-I MEAN... IF YOU HAVE TO—
MORON!
YOU ONLY DO STUFF LIKE THAT WITH SOMEONE YOU REALLY LOVE.
WE DON'T HAVE TO GO THAT FAR TO MAKE IT BELIEV-ABLE.
Besides, that's just trashy.
LET'S FIND A BETTER COUPLE.
KISSES...
...ARE ONLY FOR SOMEONE YOU LOVE?
WELL, I THINK SO.
But I guess not every-one agrees.
...
SIGH...
REALLY ...?
I...
...DID SOME-THING REALLY WRONG TO TAKISHIMA!
SMK
Taki
Me
NO WONDER HE GOT SO MAD!
OH!

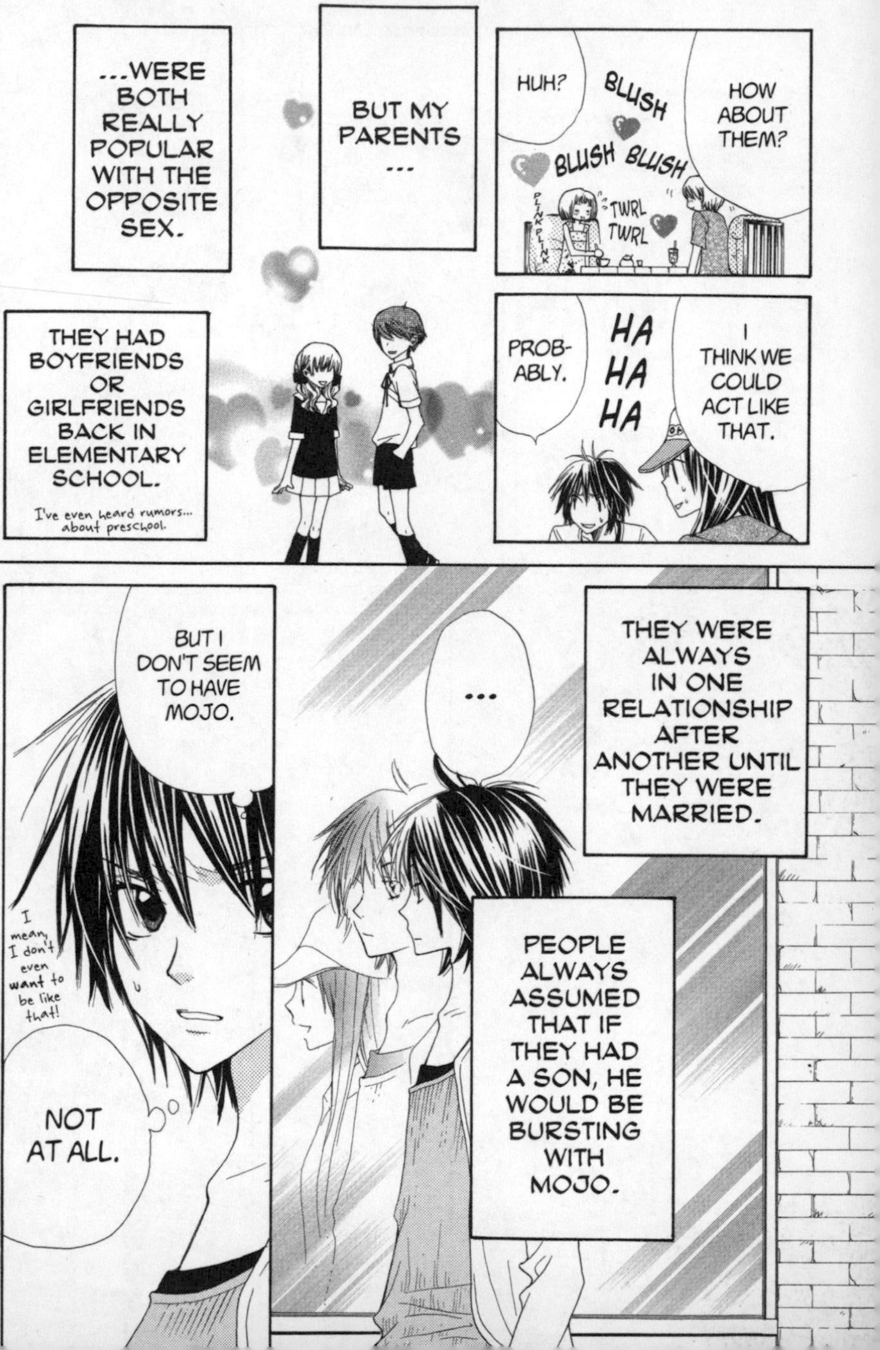
HOW ABOUT THEM?
BLUSH BLUSH
HUH?
BLUSH
TWRL TWRL
PLINK PLINK
BUT MY PARENTS ...
...WERE BOTH REALLY POPULAR WITH THE OPPOSITE SEX.
I THINK WE COULD ACT LIKE THAT.
HA HA HA
PROB-ABLY.
THEY HAD BOYFRIENDS OR GIRLFRIENDS BACK IN ELEMENTARY SCHOOL.
I've even heard rumors... about preschool.
THEY WERE ALWAYS IN ONE RELATIONSHIP AFTER ANOTHER UNTIL THEY WERE MARRIED.
...
BUT I DON'T SEEM TO HAVE MOJO.
PEOPLE ALWAYS ASSUMED THAT IF THEY HAD A SON, HE WOULD BE BURSTING WITH MOJO.
I mean, I don't even want to be like that!
NOT AT ALL.

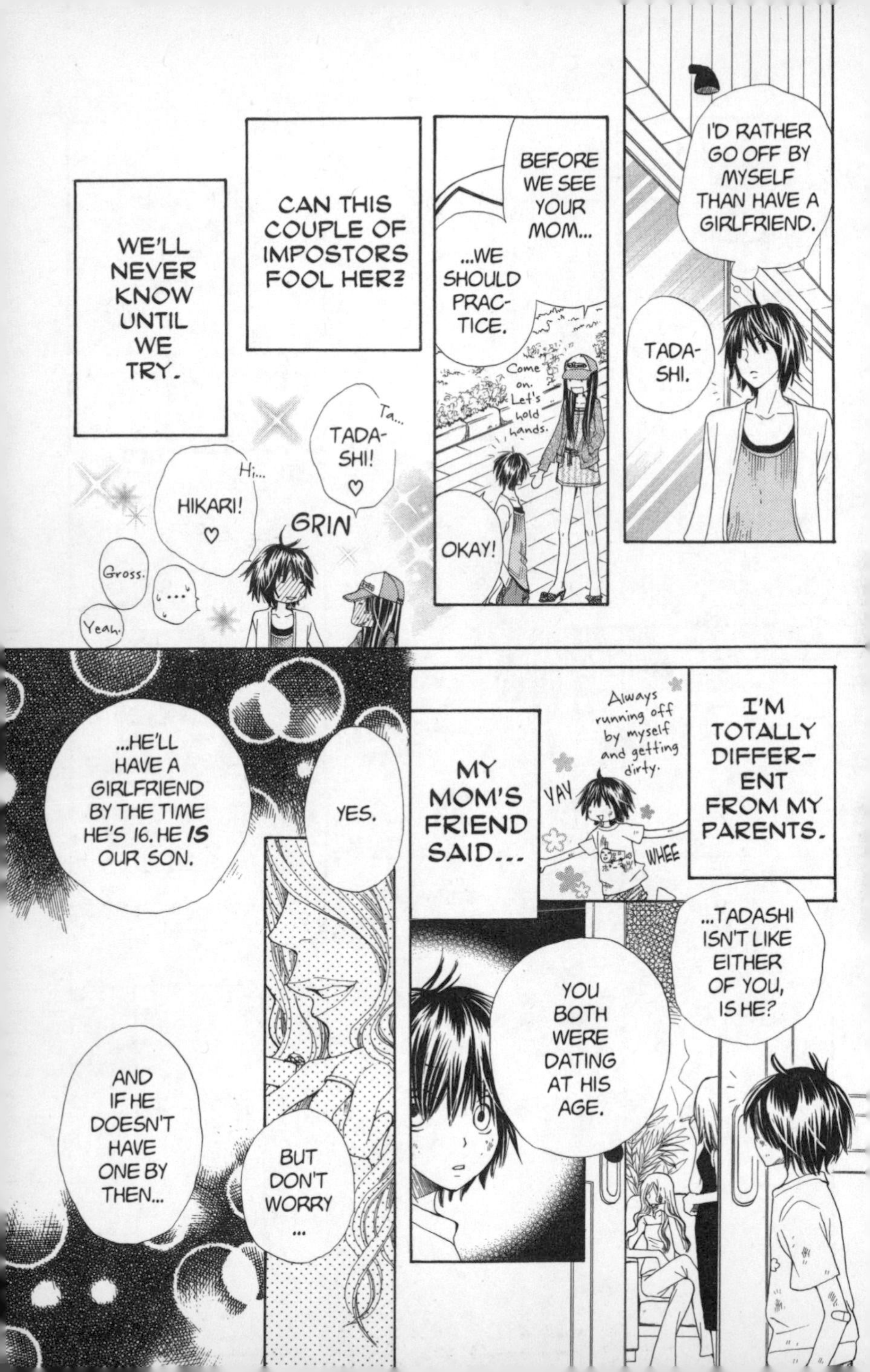
I'D RATHER GO OFF BY MYSELF THAN HAVE A GIRLFRIEND.
TADA-SHI.
BEFORE WE SEE YOUR MOM...
...WE SHOULD PRAC-TICE.
Come on. Let's hold hands.
OKAY!
CAN THIS COUPLE OF IMPOSTORS FOOL HER?
WE'LL NEVER KNOW UNTIL WE TRY.
Ta... TADA-SHI! ♡
GRIN
Hi... HIKARI! ♡
...
Gross.
Yeah.
I'M TOTALLY DIFFER-ENT FROM MY PARENTS.
Always running off by myself and getting dirty.
YAY
WHEE
MY MOM'S FRIEND SAID...
...TADASHI ISN'T LIKE EITHER OF YOU, IS HE?
YOU BOTH WERE DATING AT HIS AGE.
YES.
BUT DON'T WORRY ...
...HE'LL HAVE A GIRLFRIEND BY THE TIME HE'S 16. HE IS OUR SON.
AND IF HE DOESN'T HAVE ONE BY THEN...

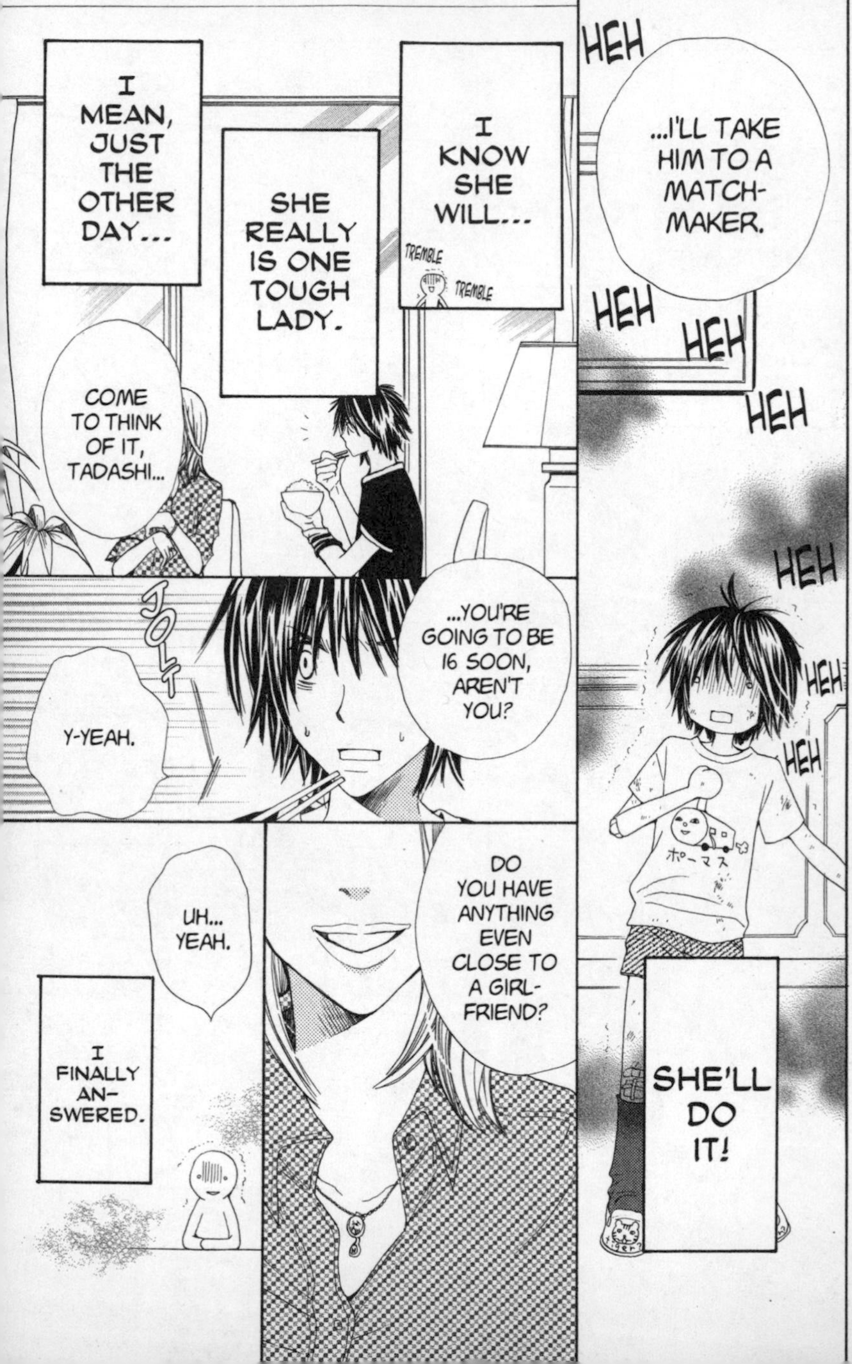
HEH
...I'LL TAKE HIM TO A MATCH-MAKER.
HEH
HEH
HEH
HEH
HEH
HEH
SHE'LL DO IT!
I KNOW SHE WILL...
TREMBLE TREMBLE
SHE REALLY IS ONE TOUGH LADY.
I MEAN, JUST THE OTHER DAY...
COME TO THINK OF IT, TADASHI...
...YOU'RE GOING TO BE 16 SOON, AREN'T YOU?
JOLT
Y-YEAH.
DO YOU HAVE ANYTHING EVEN CLOSE TO A GIRL-FRIEND?
UH... YEAH.
I FINALLY AN-SWERED.

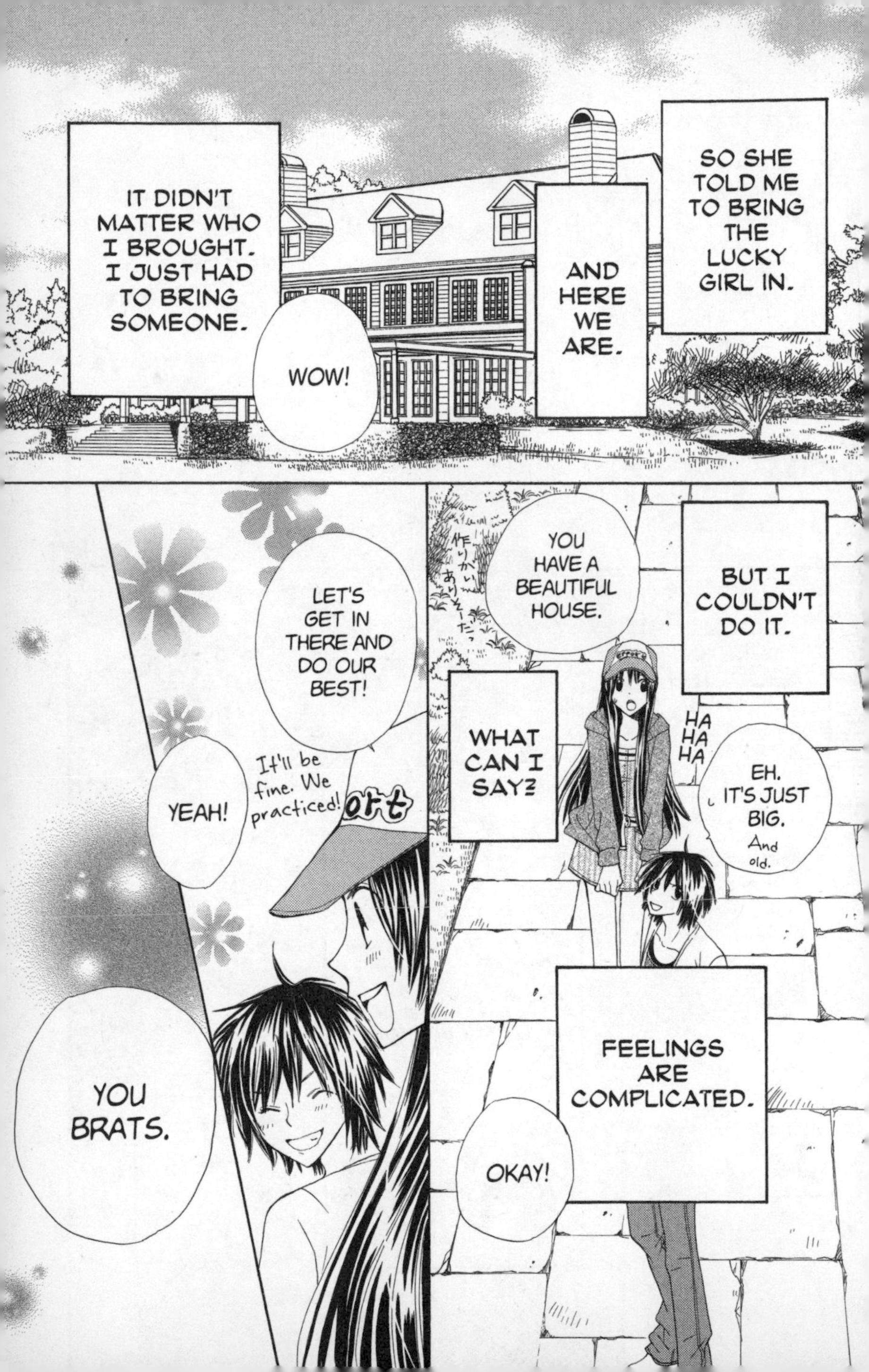
SO SHE TOLD ME TO BRING THE LUCKY GIRL IN.
AND HERE WE ARE.
WOW!
IT DIDN'T MATTER WHO I BROUGHT. I JUST HAD TO BRING SOMEONE.
BUT I COULDN'T DO IT.
YOU HAVE A BEAUTIFUL HOUSE.
HA HA HA
EH. IT'S JUST BIG.
And old.
WHAT CAN I SAY?
FEELINGS ARE COMPLICATED.
OKAY!
LET'S GET IN THERE AND DO OUR BEST!
It'll be fine. We practiced!
YEAH!
YOU BRATS.

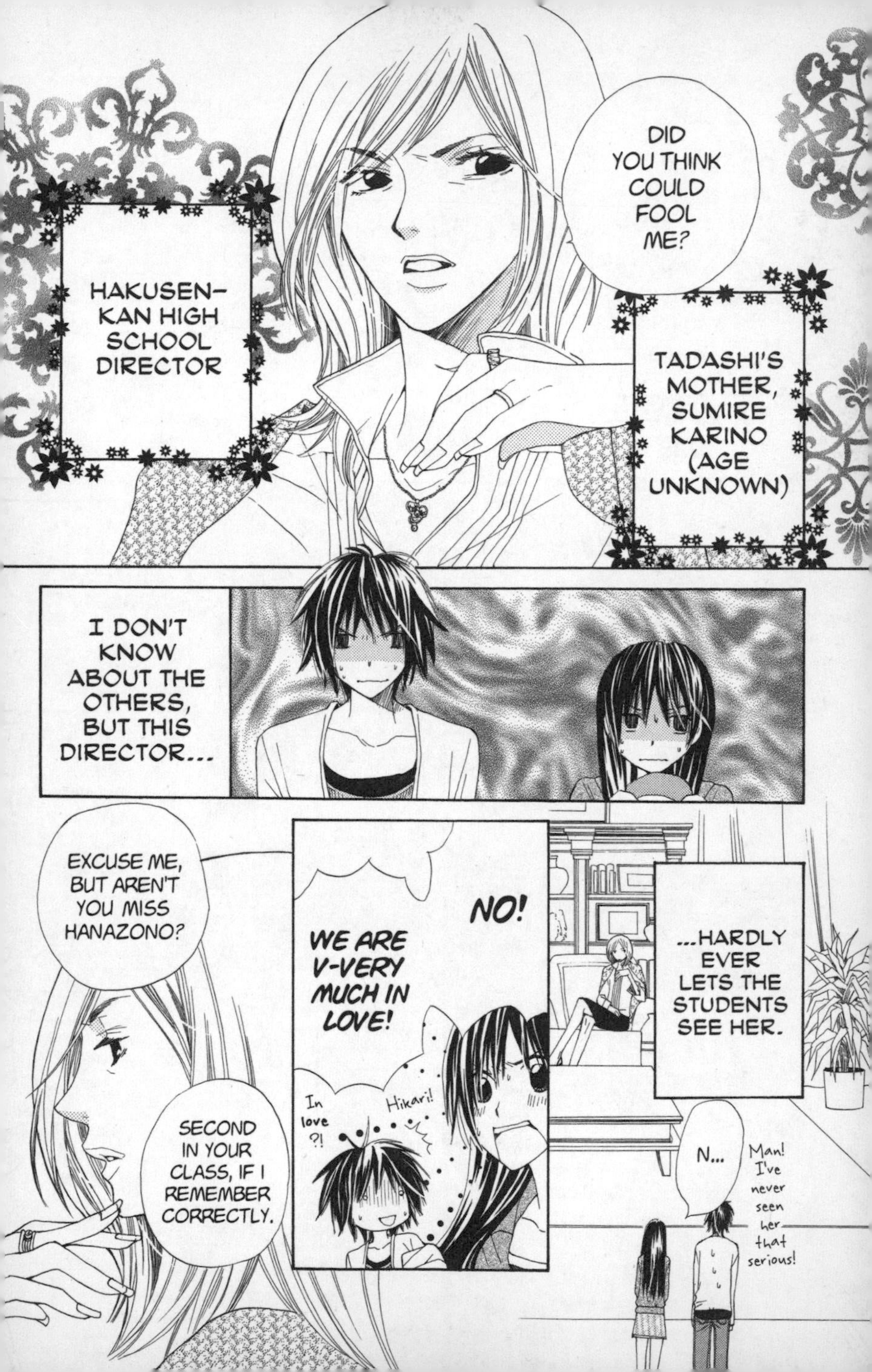
DID YOU THINK COULD FOOL ME?
TADASHI'S MOTHER, SUMIRE KARINO (AGE UNKNOWN)
HAKUSEN-KAN HIGH SCHOOL DIRECTOR
I DON'T KNOW ABOUT THE OTHERS, BUT THIS DIRECTOR...
...HARDLY EVER LETS THE STUDENTS SEE HER.
N...
Man! I've never seen her that serious!
NO!
WE ARE V-VERY MUCH IN LOVE!
Hikari!
In love ?!
EXCUSE ME, BUT AREN'T YOU MISS HANAZONO?
SECOND IN YOUR CLASS, IF I REMEMBER CORRECTLY.

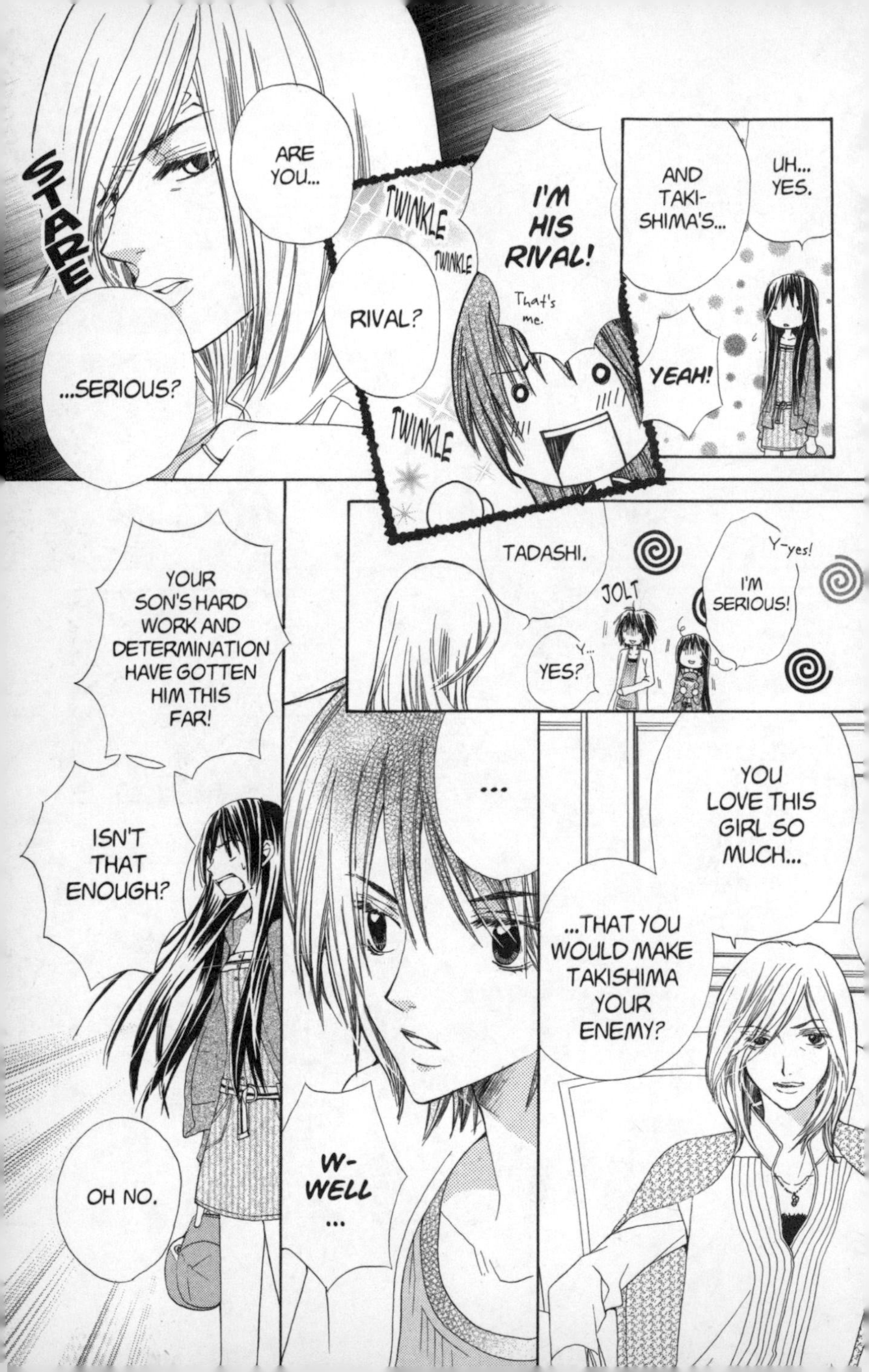

UH... YES.
AND TAKI-SHIMA'S...
YEAH!
I'M HIS RIVAL!
That's me.
TWINKLE
TWINKLE
TWINKLE
ARE YOU...
RIVAL?
STARE
...SERIOUS?
TADASHI.
JOLT
Y... YES?
Y-yes!
I'M SERIOUS!
YOU LOVE THIS GIRL SO MUCH...
...THAT YOU WOULD MAKE TAKISHIMA YOUR ENEMY?
...
W-WELL ...
YOUR SON'S HARD WORK AND DETERMINATION HAVE GOTTEN HIM THIS FAR!
ISN'T THAT ENOUGH?
OH NO.

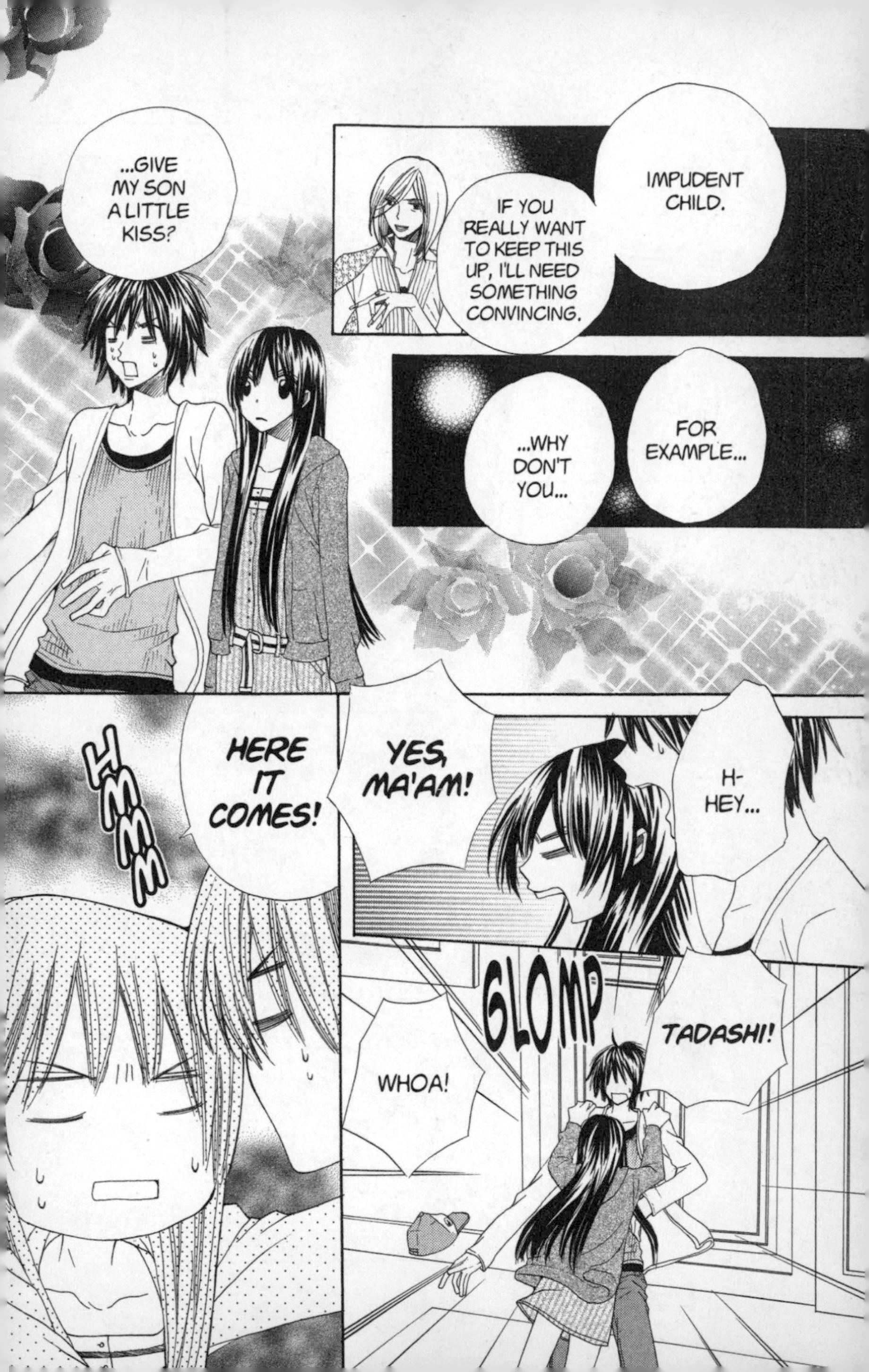
IMPUDENT CHILD.
IF YOU REALLY WANT TO KEEP THIS UP, I'LL NEED SOMETHING CONVINCING.
FOR EXAMPLE...
...WHY DON'T YOU...
...GIVE MY SON A LITTLE KISS?
H- HEY...
YES, MA'AM!
TADASHI!
GLOMP
WHOA!
HERE IT COMES!
HMMMM

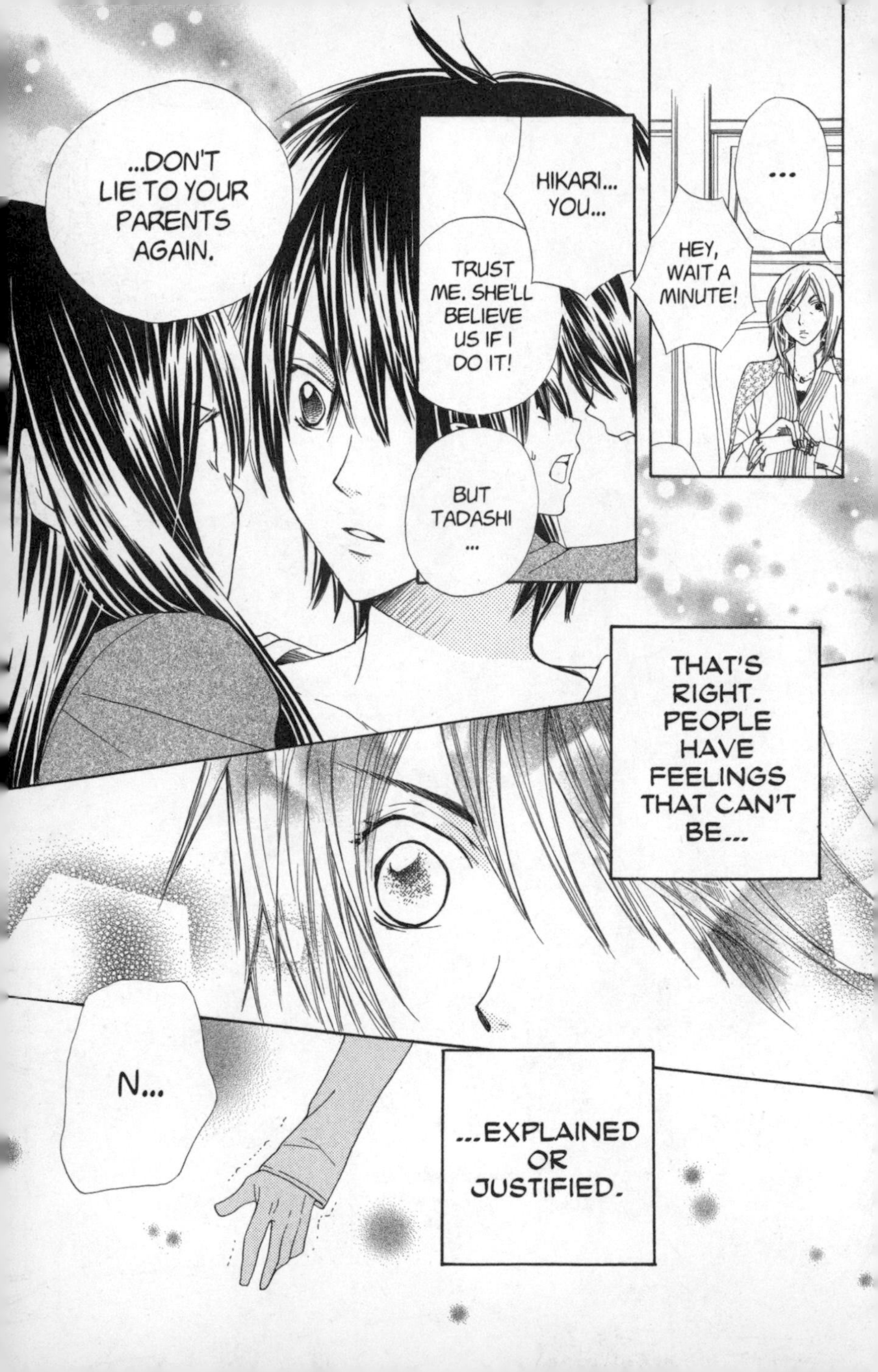
...
HEY, WAIT A MINUTE!
HIKARI... YOU...
TRUST ME. SHE'LL BELIEVE US IF I DO IT!
BUT TADASHI ...
...DON'T LIE TO YOUR PARENTS AGAIN.
THAT'S RIGHT. PEOPLE HAVE FEELINGS THAT CAN'T BE...
...EXPLAINED OR JUSTIFIED.
N...

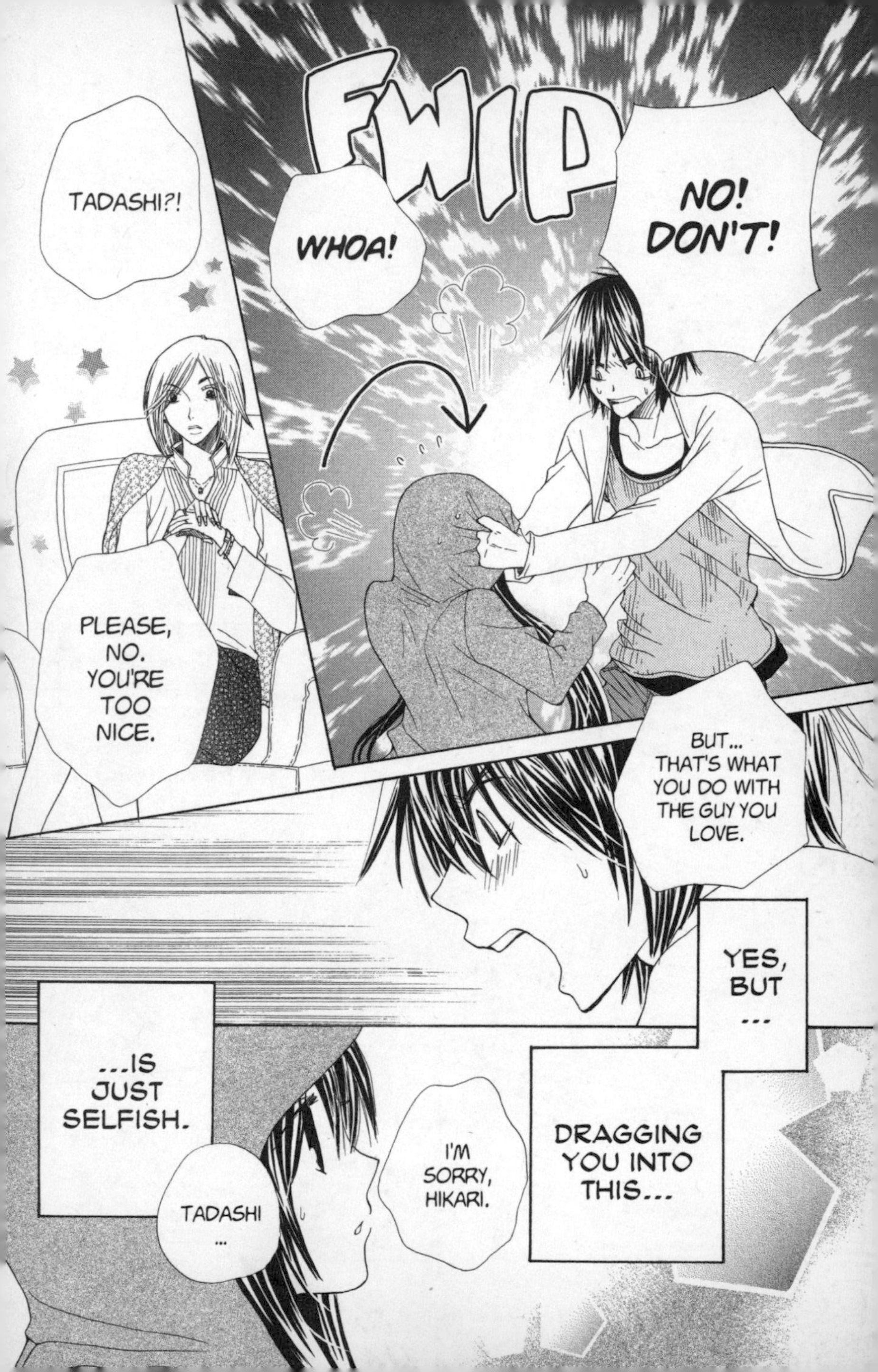
NO! DON'T!
FWIP
WHOA!
TADASHI?!
PLEASE, NO. YOU'RE TOO NICE.
BUT... THAT'S WHAT YOU DO WITH THE GUY YOU LOVE.
YES, BUT ...
DRAGGING YOU INTO THIS...
...IS JUST SELFISH.
I'M SORRY, HIKARI.
TADASHI ...

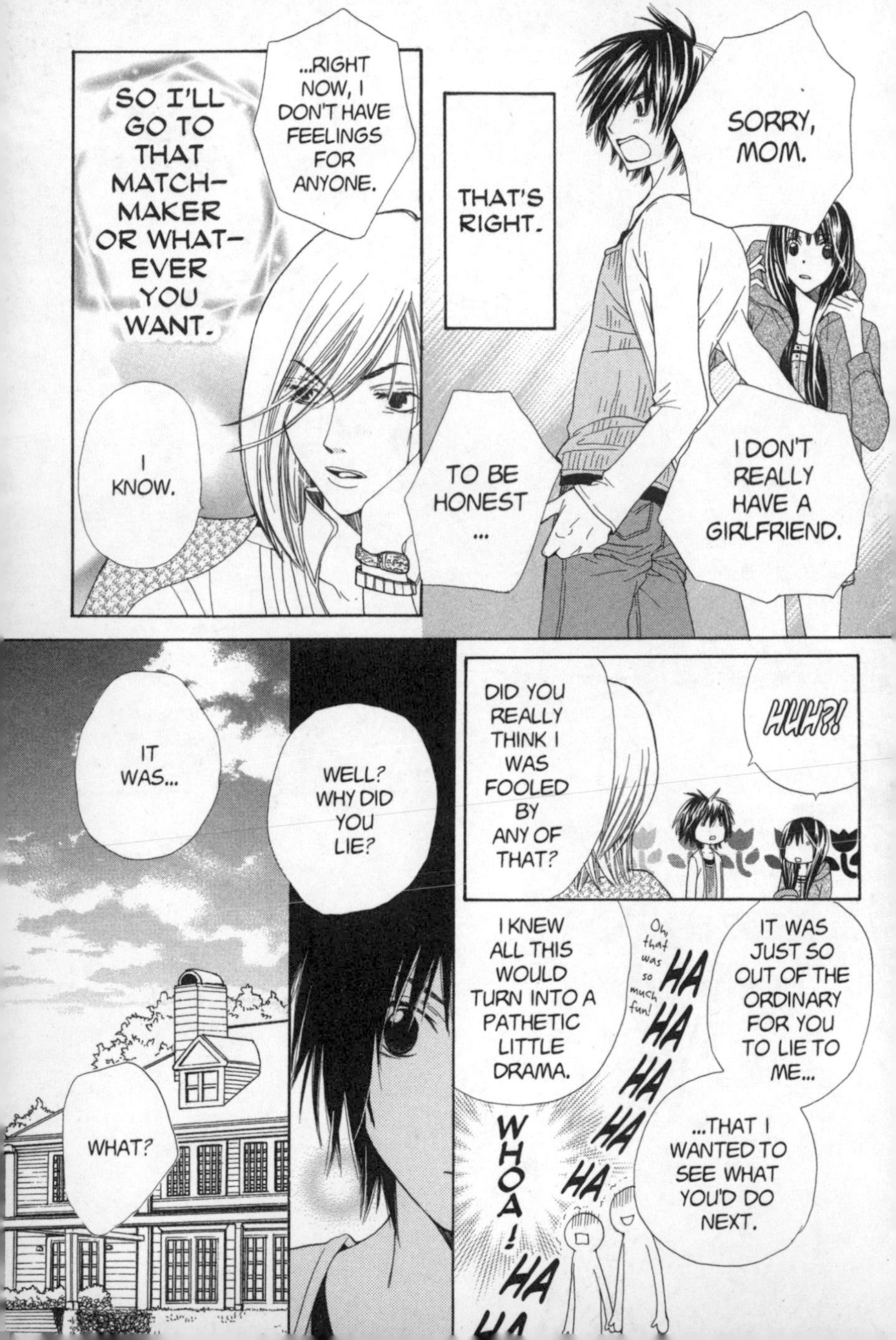
SORRY, MOM.
THAT'S RIGHT.
I DON'T REALLY HAVE A GIRLFRIEND.
TO BE HONEST...
...RIGHT NOW, I DON'T HAVE FEELINGS FOR ANYONE.
SO I'LL GO TO THAT MATCH-MAKER OR WHAT-EVER YOU WANT.
I KNOW.
HUH?!
DID YOU REALLY THINK I WAS FOOLED BY ANY OF THAT?
IT WAS JUST SO OUT OF THE ORDINARY FOR YOU TO LIE TO ME...
...THAT I WANTED TO SEE WHAT YOU'D DO NEXT.
I KNEW ALL THIS WOULD TURN INTO A PATHETIC LITTLE DRAMA.
Oh, that was so much fun!
HA HA HA HA HA HA HA
WHOA!
WELL? WHY DID YOU LIE?
IT WAS...
WHAT?

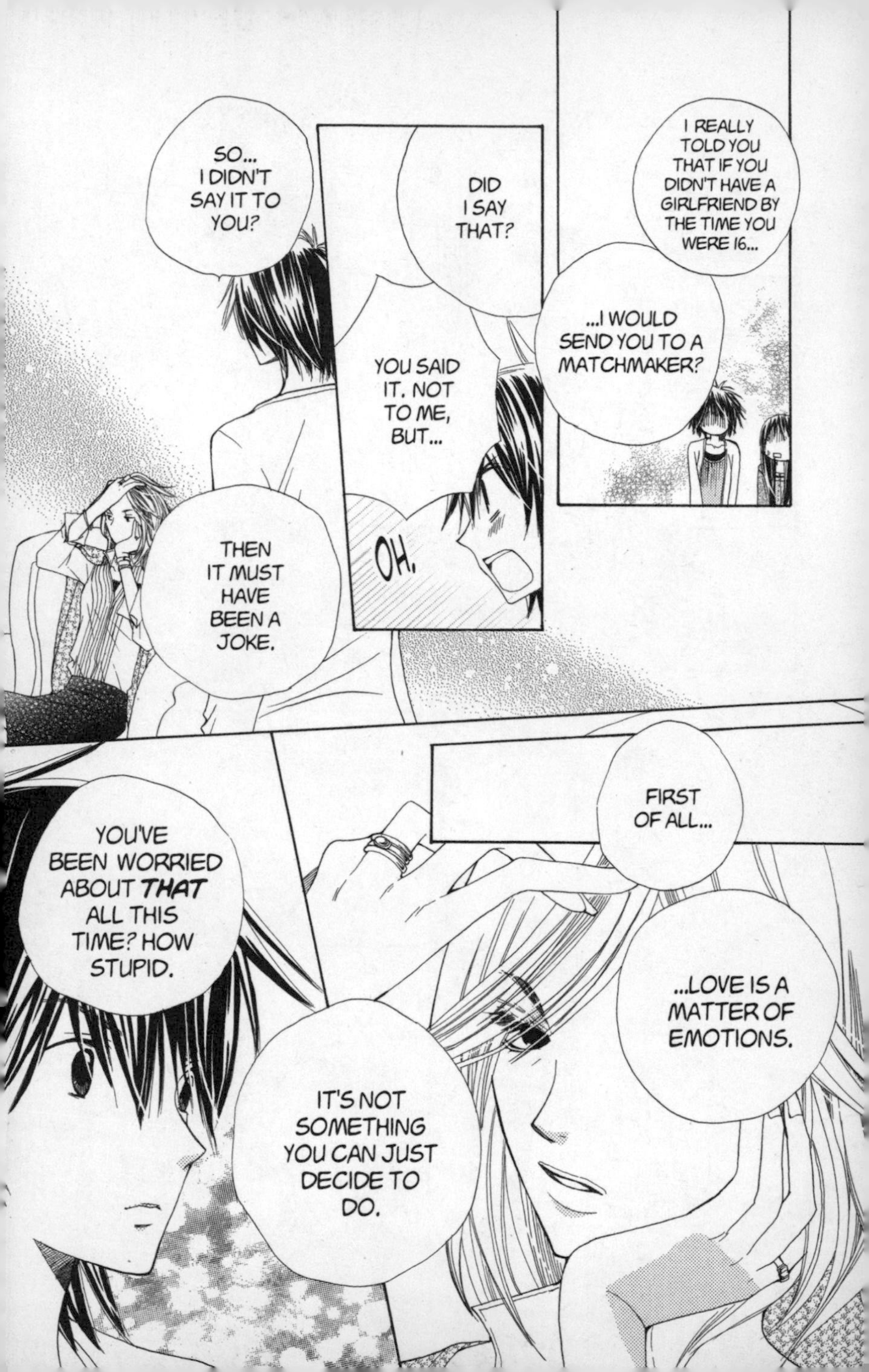
I REALLY TOLD YOU THAT IF YOU DIDN'T HAVE A GIRLFRIEND BY THE TIME YOU WERE 16...
...I WOULD SEND YOU TO A MATCHMAKER?
DID I SAY THAT?
YOU SAID IT. NOT TO ME, BUT...
OH.
SO... I DIDN'T SAY IT TO YOU?
THEN IT MUST HAVE BEEN A JOKE.
FIRST OF ALL...
...LOVE IS A MATTER OF EMOTIONS.
IT'S NOT SOMETHING YOU CAN JUST DECIDE TO DO.
YOU'VE BEEN WORRIED ABOUT ***THAT*** ALL THIS TIME? HOW STUPID.

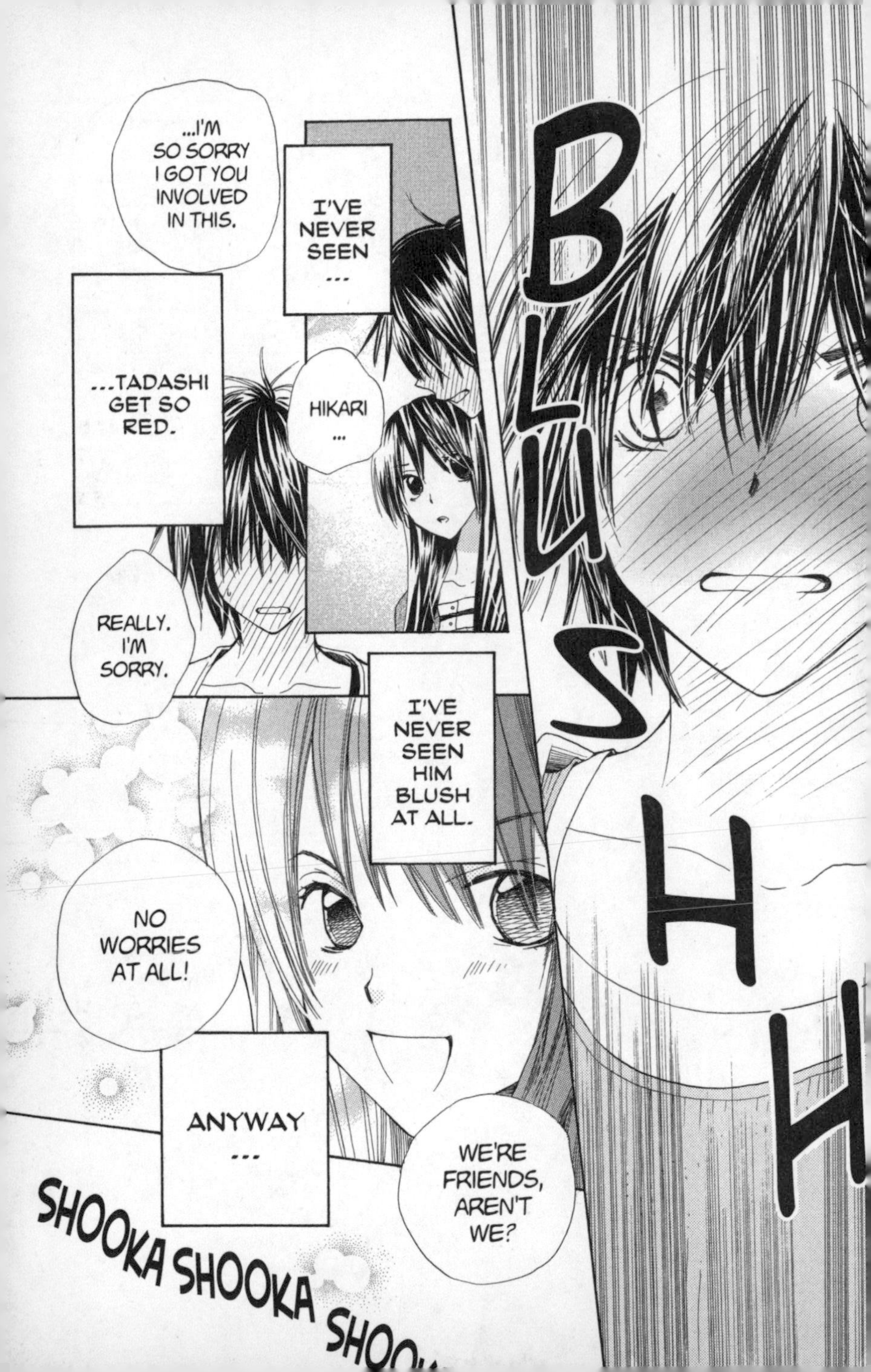
BLUSHHH
I'VE NEVER SEEN ...
...I'M SO SORRY I GOT YOU INVOLVED IN THIS.
HIKARI ...
...TADASHI GET SO RED.
REALLY. I'M SORRY.
I'VE NEVER SEEN HIM BLUSH AT ALL.
NO WORRIES AT ALL!
ANYWAY ...
WE'RE FRIENDS, AREN'T WE?
SHOOKA SHOOKA

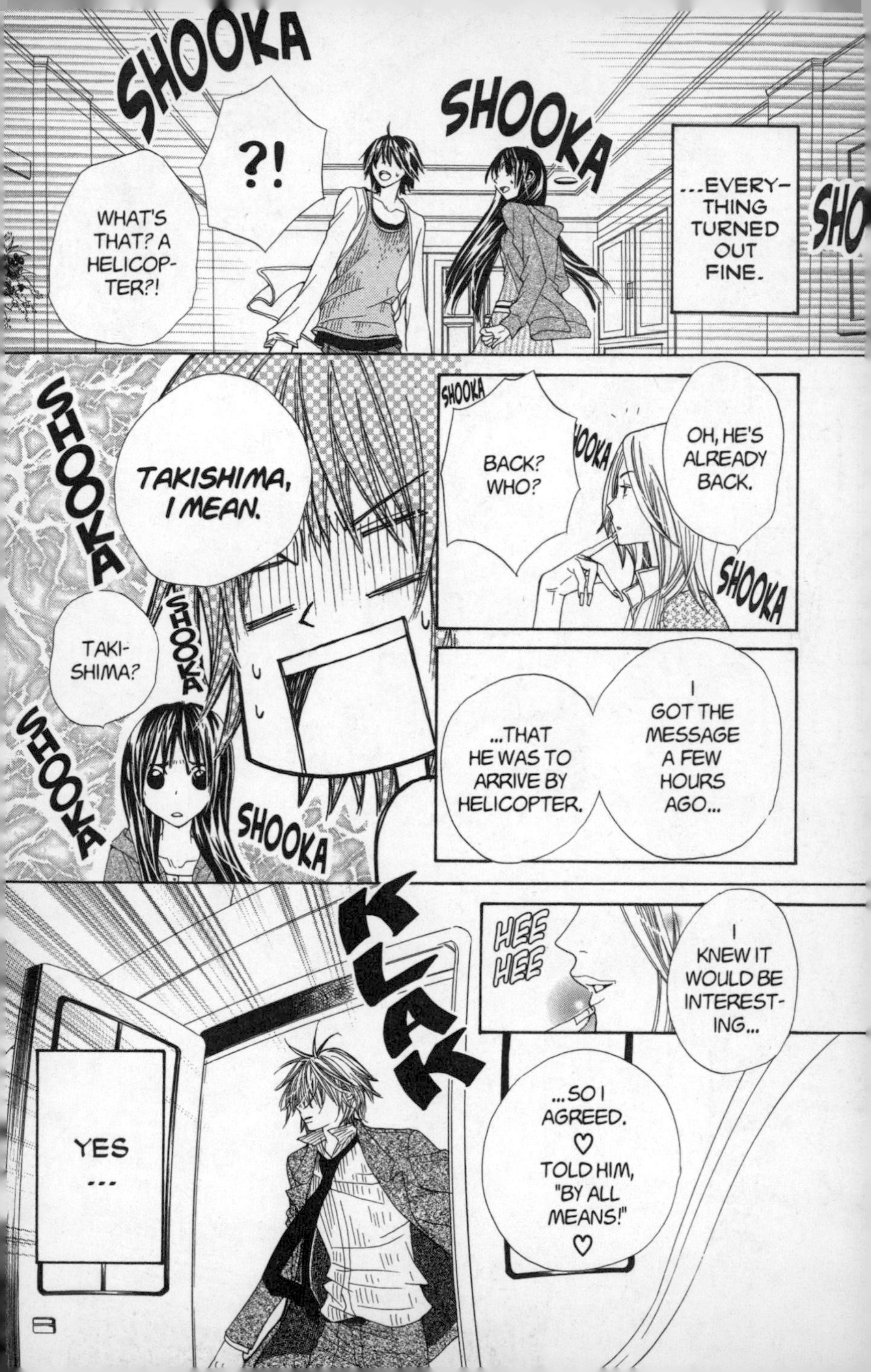
SHO
...EVERYTHING TURNED OUT FINE.
SHOOKA
?!
SHOOKA
WHAT'S THAT? A HELICOPTER?!
SHOOKA
OH, HE'S ALREADY BACK.
SHOOKA
BACK? WHO?
SHOOKA
SHOOKA
I GOT THE MESSAGE A FEW HOURS AGO...
...THAT HE WAS TO ARRIVE BY HELICOPTER.
TAKISHIMA, I MEAN.
SHOOKA
SHOOKA
TAKI-SHIMA?
SHOOKA
SHOOKA
I KNEW IT WOULD BE INTERESTING...
HEE HEE
...SO I AGREED. ♡ TOLD HIM, "BY ALL MEANS!" ♡
KLAK
YES ...

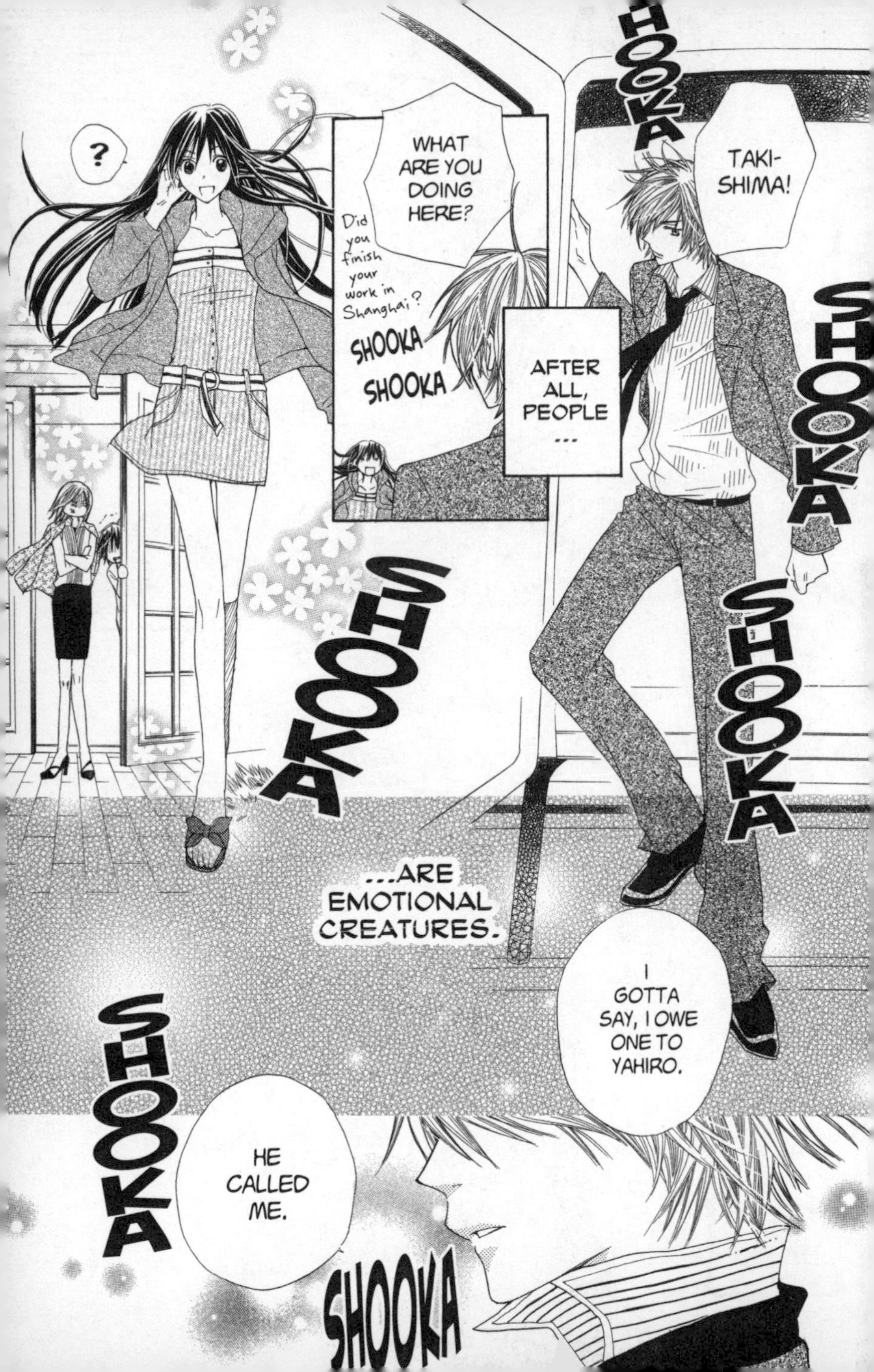
HOOKA
TAKI-SHIMA!
SHOOKA
WHAT ARE YOU DOING HERE?
Did you finish your work in Shanghai?
SHOOKA
SHOOKA
AFTER ALL, PEOPLE ...
?
SHOOKA
...ARE EMOTIONAL CREATURES.
SHOOKA
I GOTTA SAY, I OWE ONE TO YAHIRO.
HE CALLED ME.
SHOOKA
SHOOKA

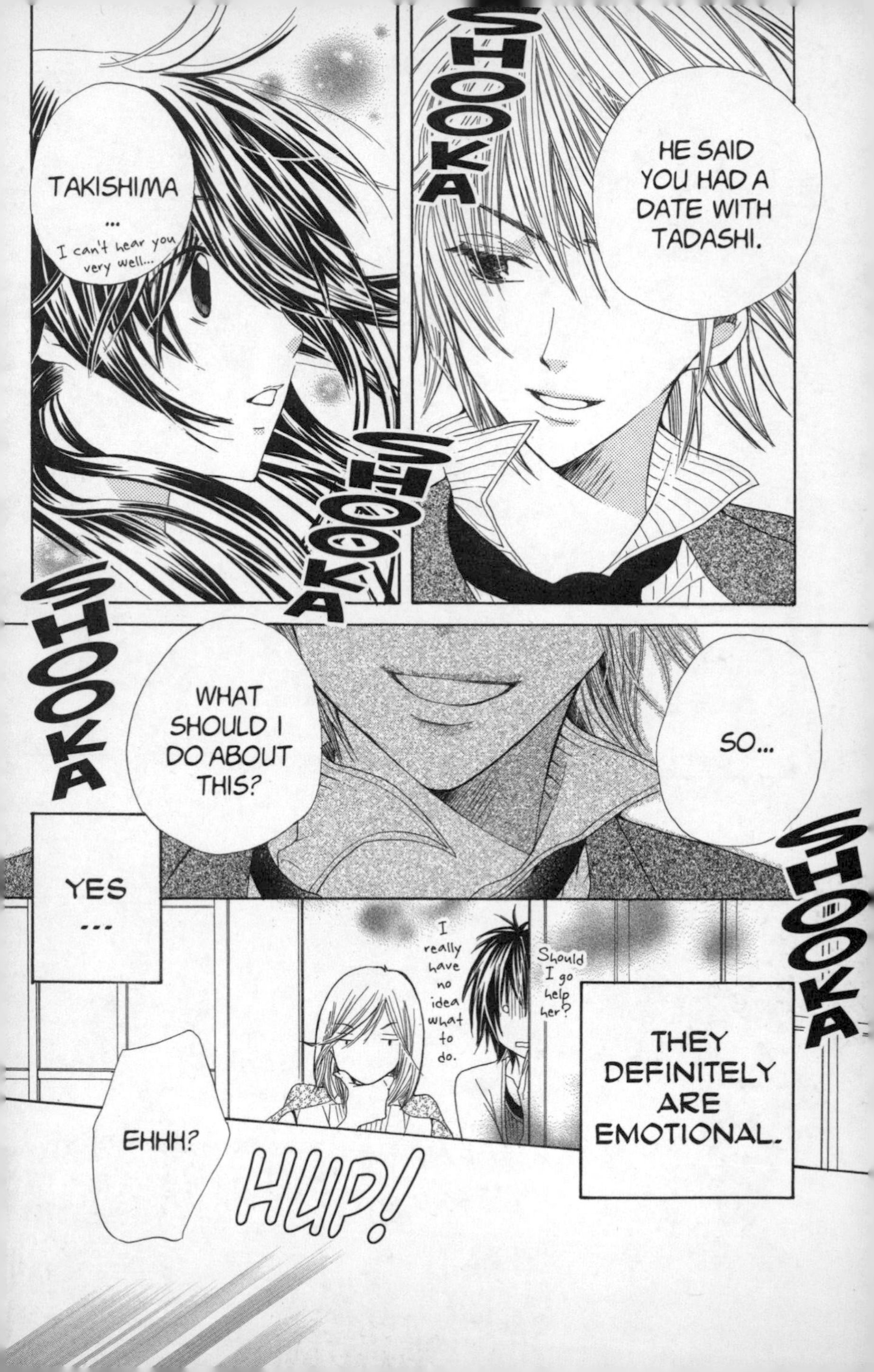
SHOOKA
HE SAID YOU HAD A DATE WITH TADASHI.
TAKISHIMA ... I can't hear you very well...
SHOOKA
SHOOKA
SO...
WHAT SHOULD I DO ABOUT THIS?
SHOOKA
SHOOKA
YES ...
THEY DEFINITELY ARE EMOTIONAL.
Should I go help her?
I really have no idea what to do.
EHHH?
HUP!

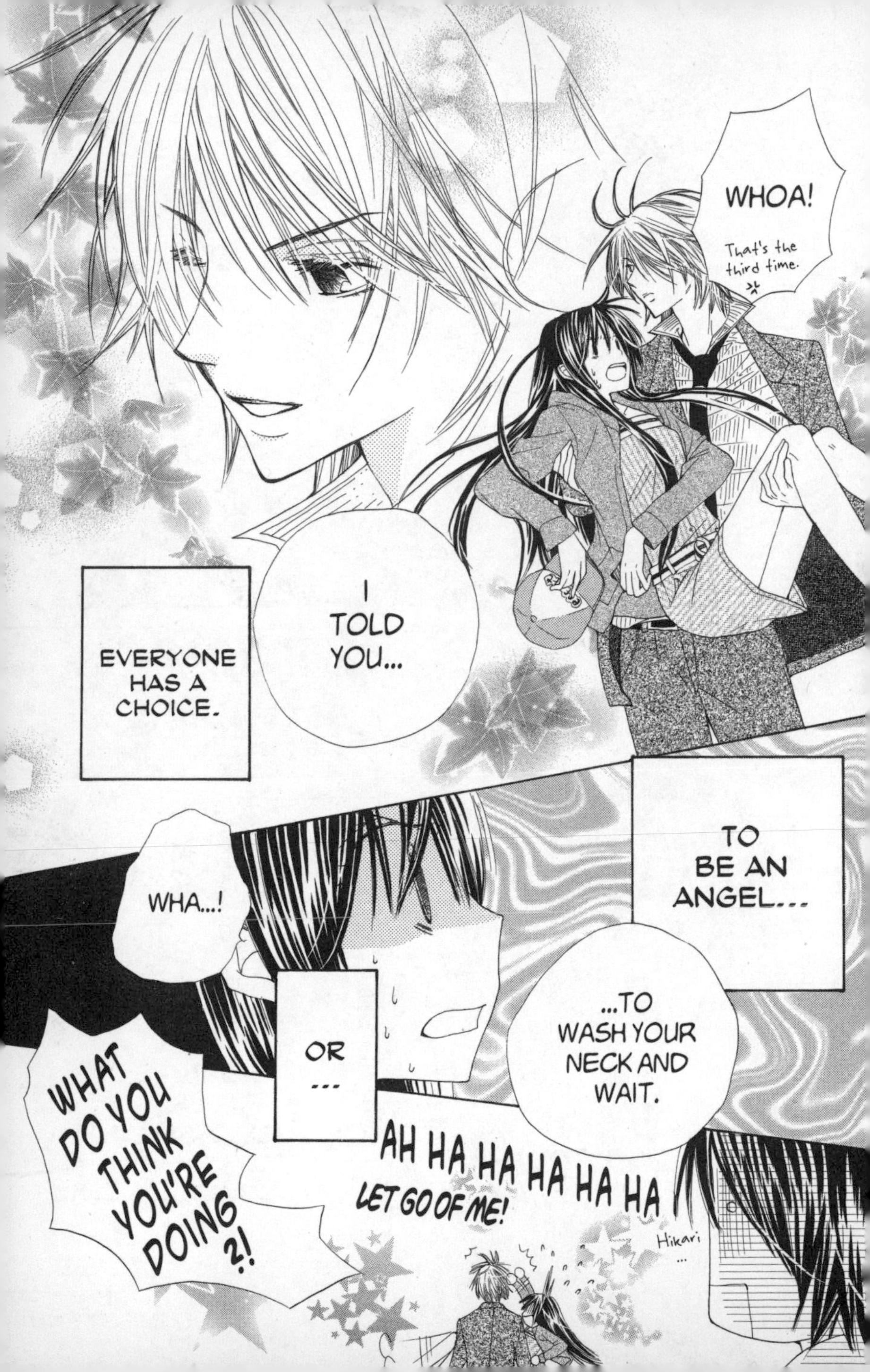
WHOA!
That's the third time.
I TOLD YOU...
EVERYONE HAS A CHOICE.
TO BE AN ANGEL...
...TO WASH YOUR NECK AND WAIT.
OR ...
WHA...!
WHAT DO YOU THINK YOU'RE DOING?!
Hikari ...
AH HA HA HA HA HA
LET GO OF ME!

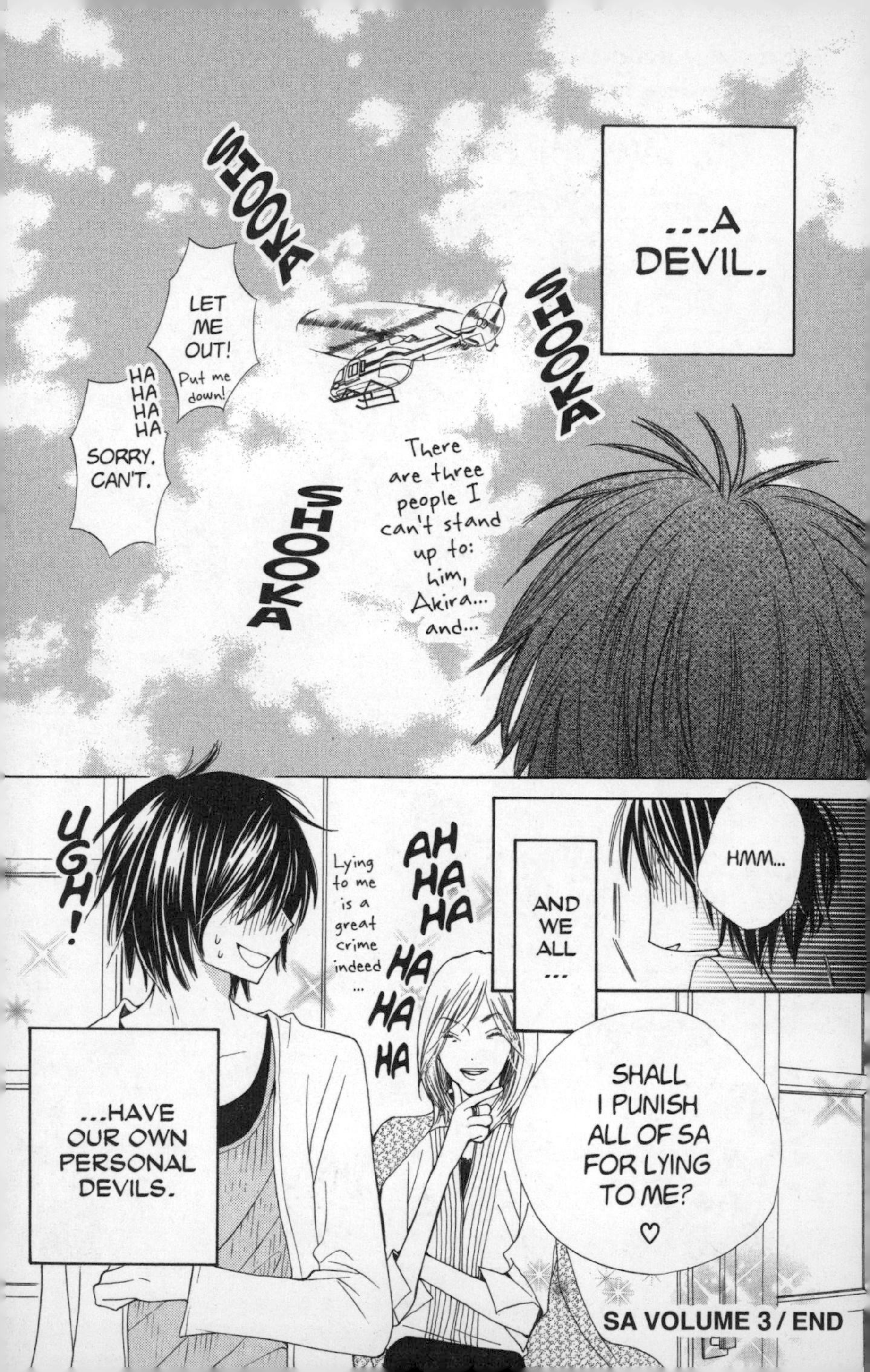
...A DEVIL.
SHOOKA
SHOOKA
LET ME OUT!
Put me down!
HA HA HA HA
SORRY. CAN'T.
There are three people I can't stand up to: him, Akira... and...
SHOOKA
HMM...
AND WE ALL ...
SHALL I PUNISH ALL OF SA FOR LYING TO ME? ♡
AH HA HA HA HA HA HA
Lying to me is a great crime indeed ...
UGH!
...HAVE OUR OWN PERSONAL DEVILS.
SA VOLUME 3 / END

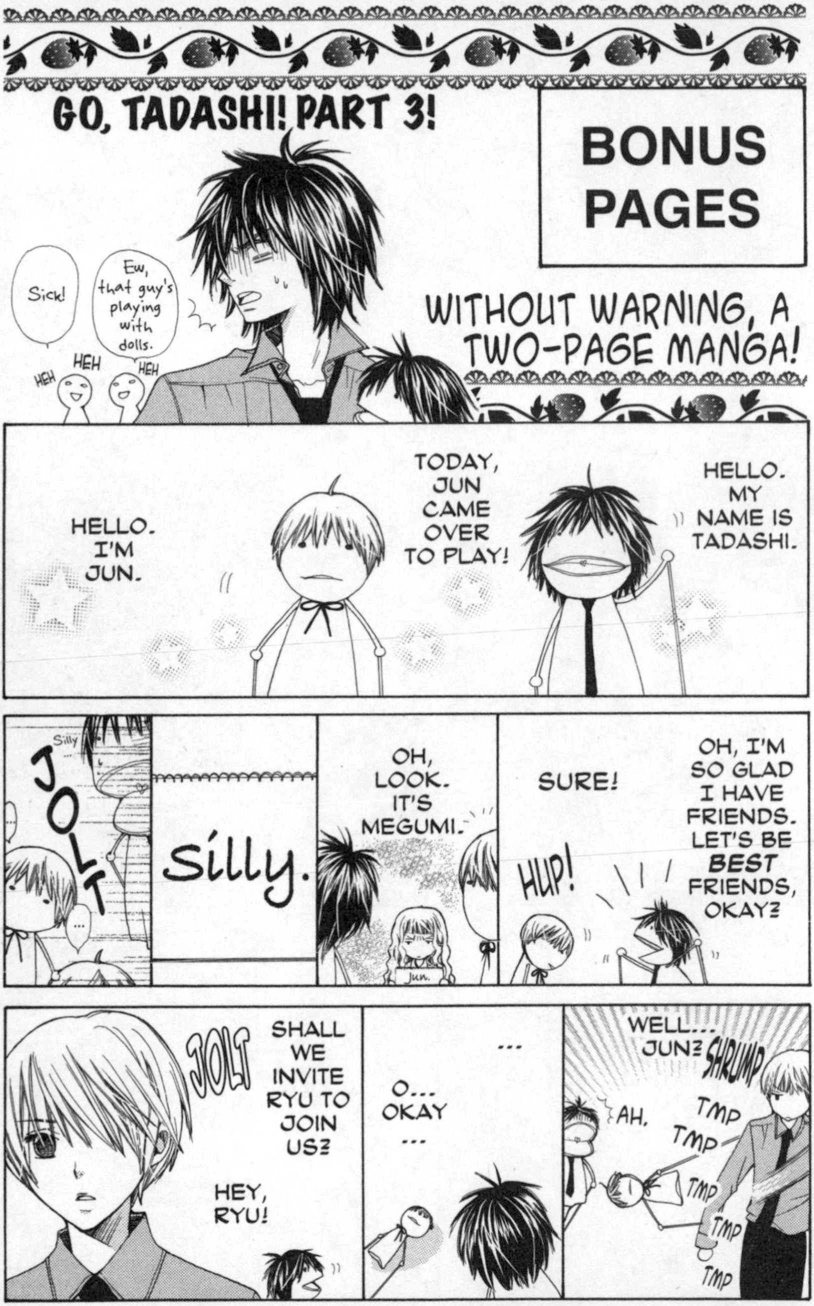
BONUS PAGES
WITHOUT WARNING, A TWO-PAGE MANGA!
GO, TADASHI! PART 3!
Ew, that guy's playing with dolls.
Sick!
HEH
HEH
HEH
HELLO. MY NAME IS TADASHI.
TODAY, JUN CAME OVER TO PLAY!
HELLO. I'M JUN.
OH, I'M SO GLAD I HAVE FRIENDS. LET'S BE BEST FRIENDS, OKAY?
SURE!
HUP!
OH, LOOK. IT'S MEGUMI.
Jun.
Silly.
Silly
JOLT
...
WELL... JUN?
SHRUMP
AH.
TMP
TMP
TMP
TMP
TMP
...
O... OKAY ...
SHALL WE INVITE RYU TO JOIN US?
JOLT
HEY, RYU!

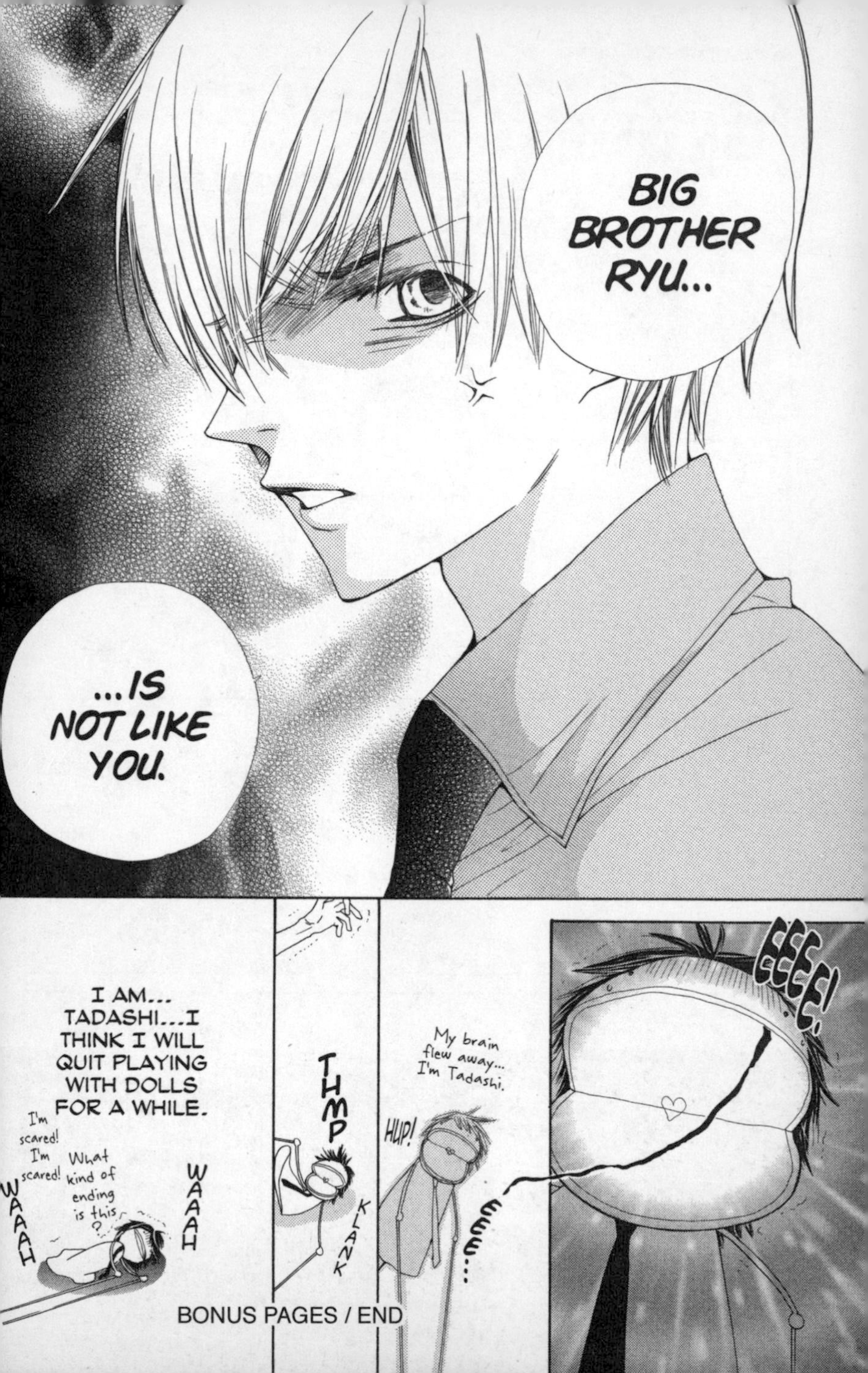
BIG BROTHER RYU...
...IS NOT LIKE YOU.
EEEE!
EEEE...
My brain flew away... I'm Tadashi.
HUP!
THMP
KLANK
I AM... TADASHI...I THINK I WILL QUIT PLAYING WITH DOLLS FOR A WHILE.
WAAAH
I'm scared! I'm scared!
What kind of ending is this?
WAAAH
BONUS PAGES / END

Maki Minami is from Saitama prefecture in Japan. She debuted in 2001 with *Kanata no Ao* (Faraway Blue). Her other works include *Kimi wa Girlfriend* (You're My Girlfriend), *Mainichi ga Takaramono* (Every Day Is a Treasure) and *Yuki Atataka* (Warm Winter). *S•A* is her current series in Japan's *Hana to Yume* magazine.

Shojo Beat

S•A

Vol. 3

The Shojo Beat Manga Edition

STORY & ART BY

MAKI MINAMI

English Adaptation/Amanda Hubbard
Translation/JN Productions
Touch-up Art & Lettering/Rina Mapa
Design/Izumi Hirayama
Editor/Carol Fox

VP, Production/Alvin Lu
VP, Publishing Licensing/Rika Inouye
VP, Sales & Product Marketing/Gonzalo Ferreyra
VP, Creative/Linda Espinosa
Publisher/Hyoe Narita

Printed in Canada

Published by VIZ Media, LLC
P.O. Box 77010
San Francisco, CA 94107

Shojo Beat Manga Edition
10 9 8 7 6 5 4 3 2
First printing, March 2008
Second printing, February 2009

viz media
www.viz.com

store.viz.com

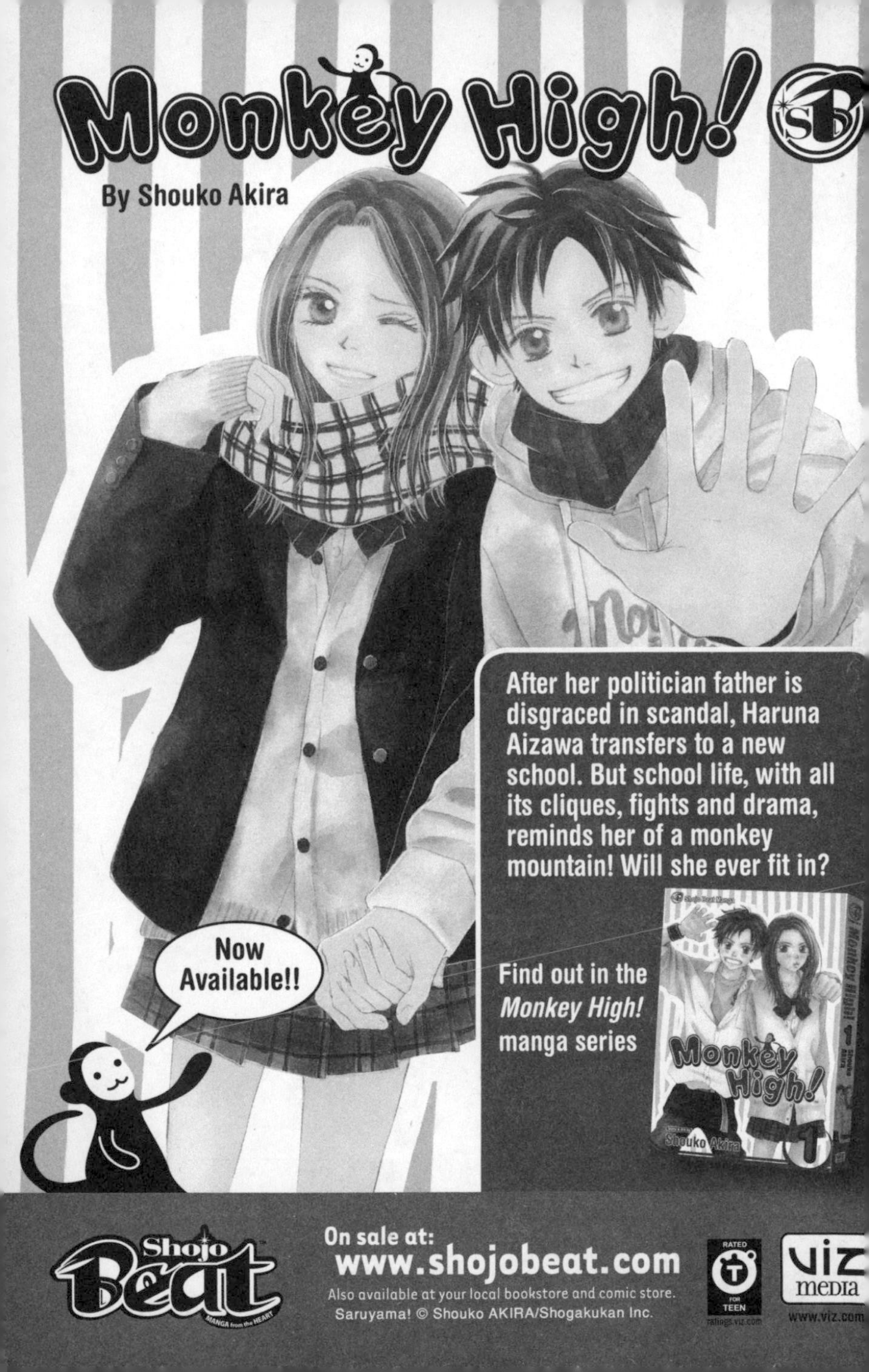
Monkey High!
SB
By Shouko Akira
After her politician father is disgraced in scandal, Haruna Aizawa transfers to a new school. But school life, with all its cliques, fights and drama, reminds her of a monkey mountain! Will she ever fit in?
Now Available!!
Find out in the *Monkey High!* manga series
Monkey High!
Shouko Akira
1
Shojo Beat
MANGA from the HEART
On sale at:
www.shojobeat.com
Also available at your local bookstore and comic store.
Saruyama! © Shouko AKIRA/Shogakukan Inc.
RATED
T
FOR TEEN
ratings.viz.com
VIZ media
www.viz.com

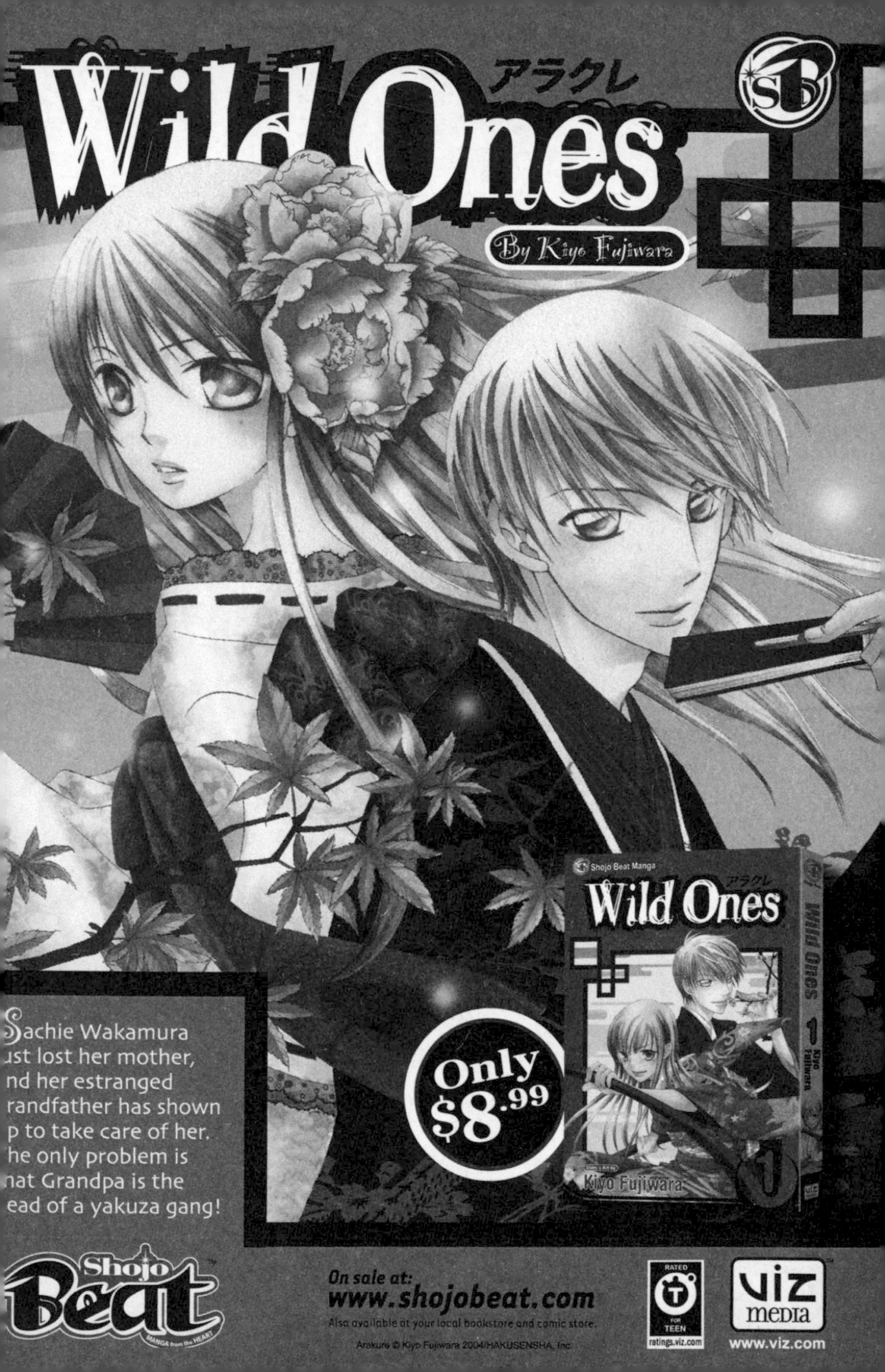

Wild Ones
アラクレ
SB
By Kiyo Fujiwara
Shojo Beat Manga
アラクレ
Wild Ones
Kiyo Fujiwara
1
Only
$8.99
Sachie Wakamura
ust lost her mother,
nd her estranged
randfather has shown
p to take care of her.
he only problem is
nat Grandpa is the
ead of a yakuza gang!
Shojo Beat
MANGA from the HEART
On sale at:
www.shojobeat.com
Also available at your local bookstore and comic store.
Arakure © Kiyo Fujiwara 2004/HAKUSENSHA, Inc.
RATED
T
FOR
TEEN
ratings.viz.com
VIZ media
www.viz.com

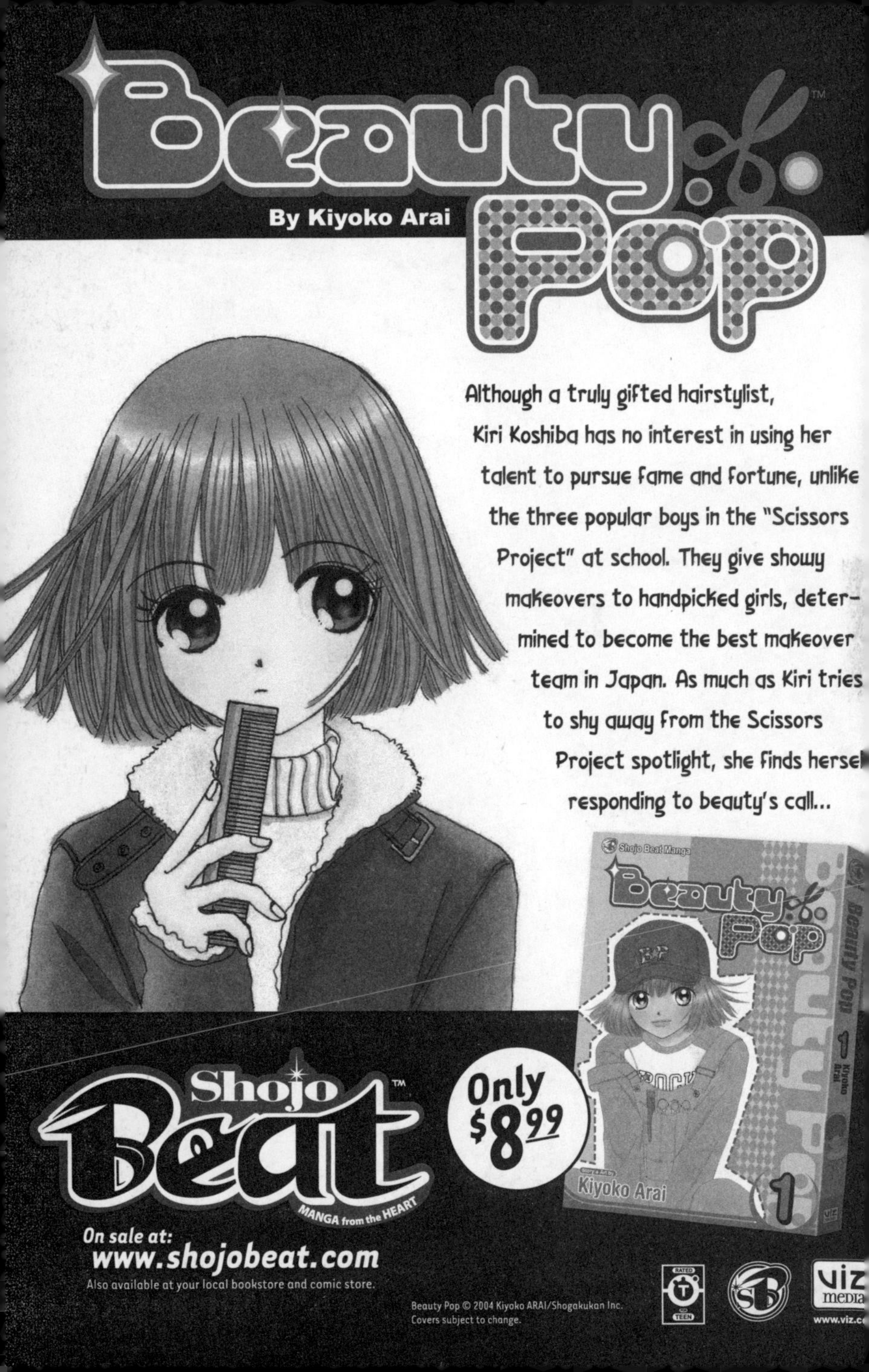
Beauty Pop™
By Kiyoko Arai
Although a truly gifted hairstylist, Kiri Koshiba has no interest in using her talent to pursue fame and fortune, unlike the three popular boys in the "Scissors Project" at school. They give showy makeovers to handpicked girls, determined to become the best makeover team in Japan. As much as Kiri tries to shy away from the Scissors Project spotlight, she finds hersel responding to beauty's call...
Shojo Beat Manga
Beauty Pop
1
Kiyoko Arai
Only $8.99
Shojo Beat™
MANGA from the HEART
On sale at:
www.shojobeat.com
Also available at your local bookstore and comic store.
Beauty Pop © 2004 Kiyoko ARAI/Shogakukan Inc.
Covers subject to change.
RATED T TEEN
viz media
www.viz.c

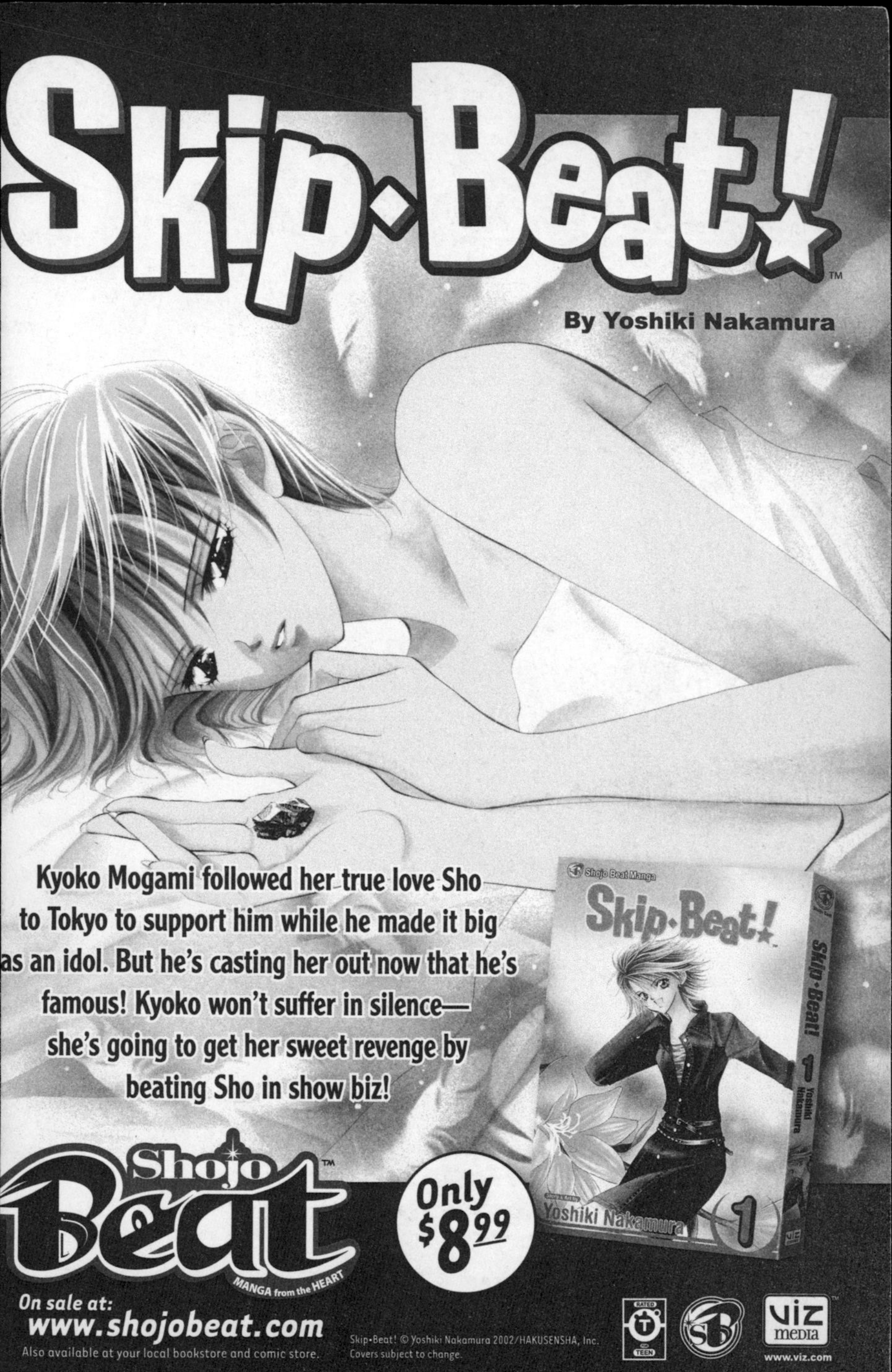
Skip·Beat!™
By Yoshiki Nakamura
Kyoko Mogami followed her true love Sho to Tokyo to support him while he made it big as an idol. But he's casting her out now that he's famous! Kyoko won't suffer in silence— she's going to get her sweet revenge by beating Sho in show biz!
Shojo Beat Manga
Skip·Beat!
Yoshiki Nakamura
1
Shojo Beat™
MANGA from the HEART
Only $8.99
On sale at:
www.shojobeat.com
Also available at your local bookstore and comic store.
Skip•Beat! © Yoshiki Nakamura 2002/HAKUSENSHA, Inc.
Covers subject to change.
RATED T TEEN
viz media
www.viz.com

Tell us what you think about Shojo Beat Manga!

Our survey is now available online. Go to:

shojobeat.com/mangasurvey

Help us make our product offerings better!